HELLBOY™

THE WILD HUNT

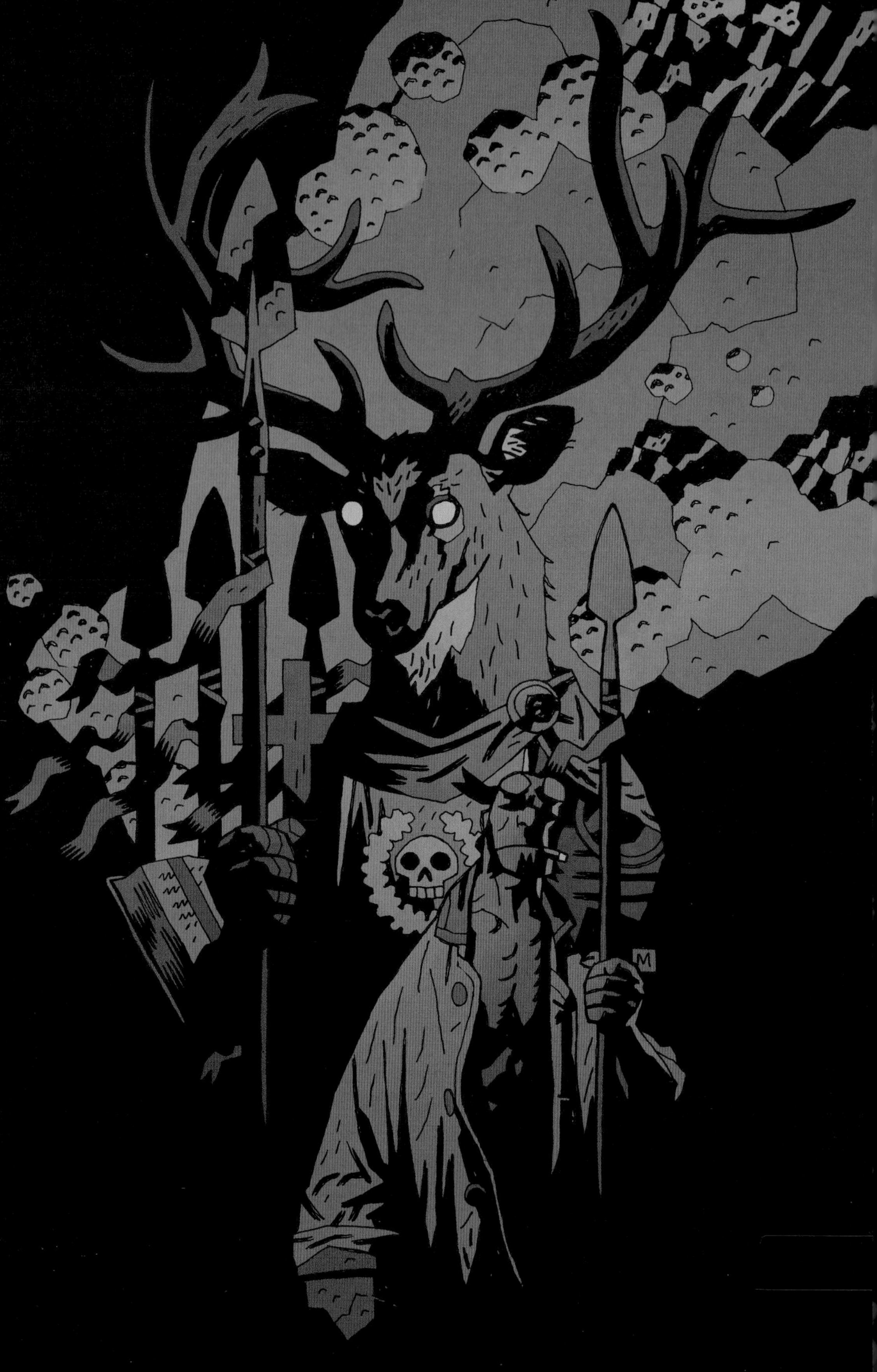

HELLBOY ™

THE WILD HUNT

Story by
MIKE MIGNOLA

Art by
DUNCAN FEGREDO

Colored by
DAVE STEWART

Lettered by
CLEM ROBINS

✠

Introduction by
MARK CHADBOURN

Edited by
SCOTT ALLIE

Hellboy logo designed by
KEVIN NOWLAN

Collection designed by
MIKE MIGNOLA & CARY GRAZZINI

Associate Editor
SAMANTHA ROBERTSON

Publisher
MIKE RICHARDSON

DARK HORSE BOOKS®

Published by
Dark Horse Books
A division of Dark Horse Comics, Inc.
10956 SE Main St.
Milwaukie, OR 97222

First Edition
March 2010
ISBN 978-1-59582-431-8

This volume collects *Hellboy: The Wild Hunt* #1–#8, published by Dark Horse Comics.

1 3 5 7 9 10 8 6 4 2

Printed by Midas Printing International, Ltd., Huizhou, China. 03/2010.

INTRODUCTION
by MARK CHADBOURN

The Wild Hunt has been with us for a long, long time.

When the Vikings crossed the seas in their dragon-ships, they brought with them tales of their god Woden hurtling across the sky on stormy winter nights with a pack of hounds baying at his horse's hooves. The unwary were torn away to a terrifying fate.

But the story was old even then.

In some versions, the hunters were the ancient Celtic gods, or the fairies those gods eventually became, or the dead, or, in Christian times, the Devil himself. One Hunt was led by Hereward the Wake, the great English hero who fought against the Norman invaders. In the seventeenth century, it was Sir Francis Drake, the sea captain and privateer who helped save England from the Spanish fleet, in a black coach with his dogs running alongside. In modern times, some say the Hunt was led by the Second World War leader Winston Churchill, in a black Spitfire warplane.

And this is something that Mike Mignola understands about mythology and folk tales—they're living, breathing stories that change over time to reflect the secret hopes and fears of the people.

In Hellboy he has created a hero to stand with the greatest of mythology. The roots of this character run back thousands of years, but he speaks with our voice. He's a twenty-first-century icon, slugging it out against the age-old fears that still…*still*…haunt us, even though we no longer believe in spectral hounds hunting for the unwitting traveler across the lonely moors and hilltops.

Too grand a claim for a comic-book guy?

Consider this: Hellboy straddles the world of humans and gods just like King Arthur, who was swept in from the Otherworld on the mystical ninth wave to look after us. Or Hercules, or the Irish hero Cuchulain. All of them born out of the supernatural yet undoubtedly and defiantly human. Like Arthur, Hellboy carries (or carried) a seemingly magical weapon—a frighteningly big gun.

And like all those heroes, Hellboy fights for *us* against *them*, the weird ones on the other side of the veil, his own.

You see, mythology is a map of our dark, unconscious mind and all the fears and dreams and screwy, twisted things that live there. It's always relevant. Those devils trying to seduce us with deals, those long-dead things that haunt us, those unbeatable, bone-crushing

giants of the id—they're never going to go away. You just need somebody you understand to get in there, and get down and dirty, and sort the bastards out so you can sleep peacefully.

This book you hold in your hands is about all of these things. It probes into traditions that have been around for thousands of years—old stories and deep-seated fears—but Mike makes them all seem fresh. Which is just how it should be with mythology.

Here you will find the old gods of the Celtic people and hints of the Arthurian legends they helped shape. You'll find the ancient race of giants that once stalked across Britain, which you can still see in the landscape, if you squint and look carefully (and which are celebrated in one of the finest buildings in London).

Old stories made new. But that's also the theme for Hellboy's own world. This book may well be one of the most important in Hellboy's history—it sends tendrils into the past, linking seemingly unrelated stories, perhaps ones you thought were totally standalone, and pulling them into a rich tapestry. Everything is connected, in a way you never imagined.

And to echo those mythological themes, *Hellboy: The Wild Hunt* points toward something huge…and I mean *huge*…in the future.

With a story of such epic scope, you need an artist who can capture the grandeur and the terror, the small, creepy interludes that are a signature of Hellboy's world, and those bone-smashing battles. Duncan Fegredo, for me, has become an essential *Hellboy* artist. His style is a nice fit with the one Mike established, but it has its own unmistakable flourishes. There are big moments here that I love—a battle on a crumbling bridge, which is a masterpiece of design and dynamism that throws you into the middle of the fight—and little moments that say so much, whether it's the unsettling angle of trees in a woodland glade or the body language of a seeming bad guy that reveals a deep well of emotion. I hope he hangs around Hellboy for a long, long time too.

The great thing is, we can all be a part of this new mythology as it unfolds. We can sit back and let it seep into our deep unconscious, where it speaks to us directly, in the same way that King Arthur spoke to our ancestors.

Hellboy's our guy, our mythological hero, and he's going to be around for as long as the Arthurs and the Robin Hoods, because he's cut from the same cloth. Trust me.

For my dad, with whom I enjoyed the comic thrills of musical, killer robots and a cute grocery-shopping/ spacefaring chick with a psychotic robo-dog.
Duncan Fegredo

CHAPTER ONE

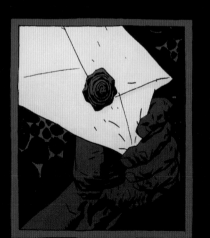

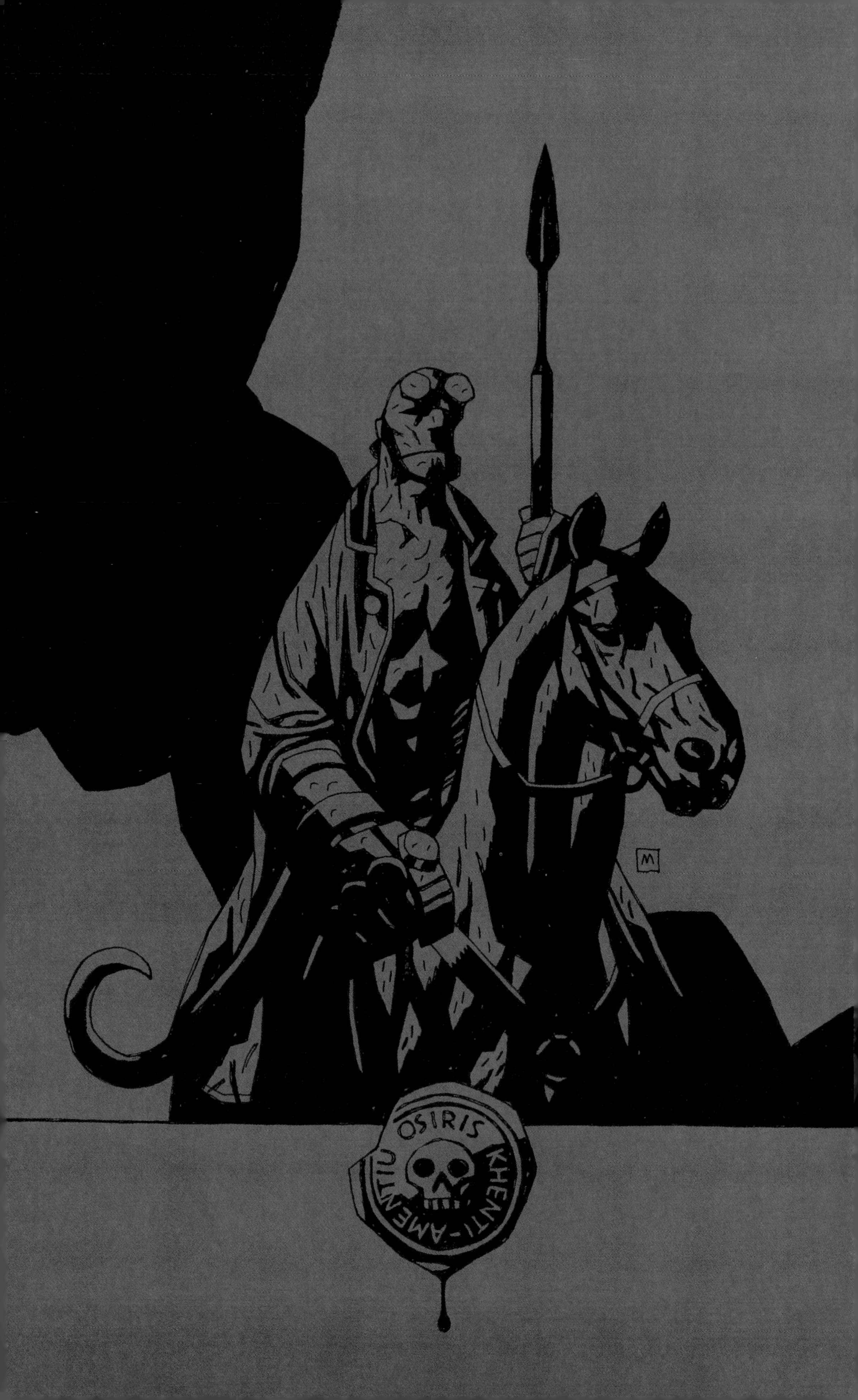

OSIRIS KHENTI-AMENTIU

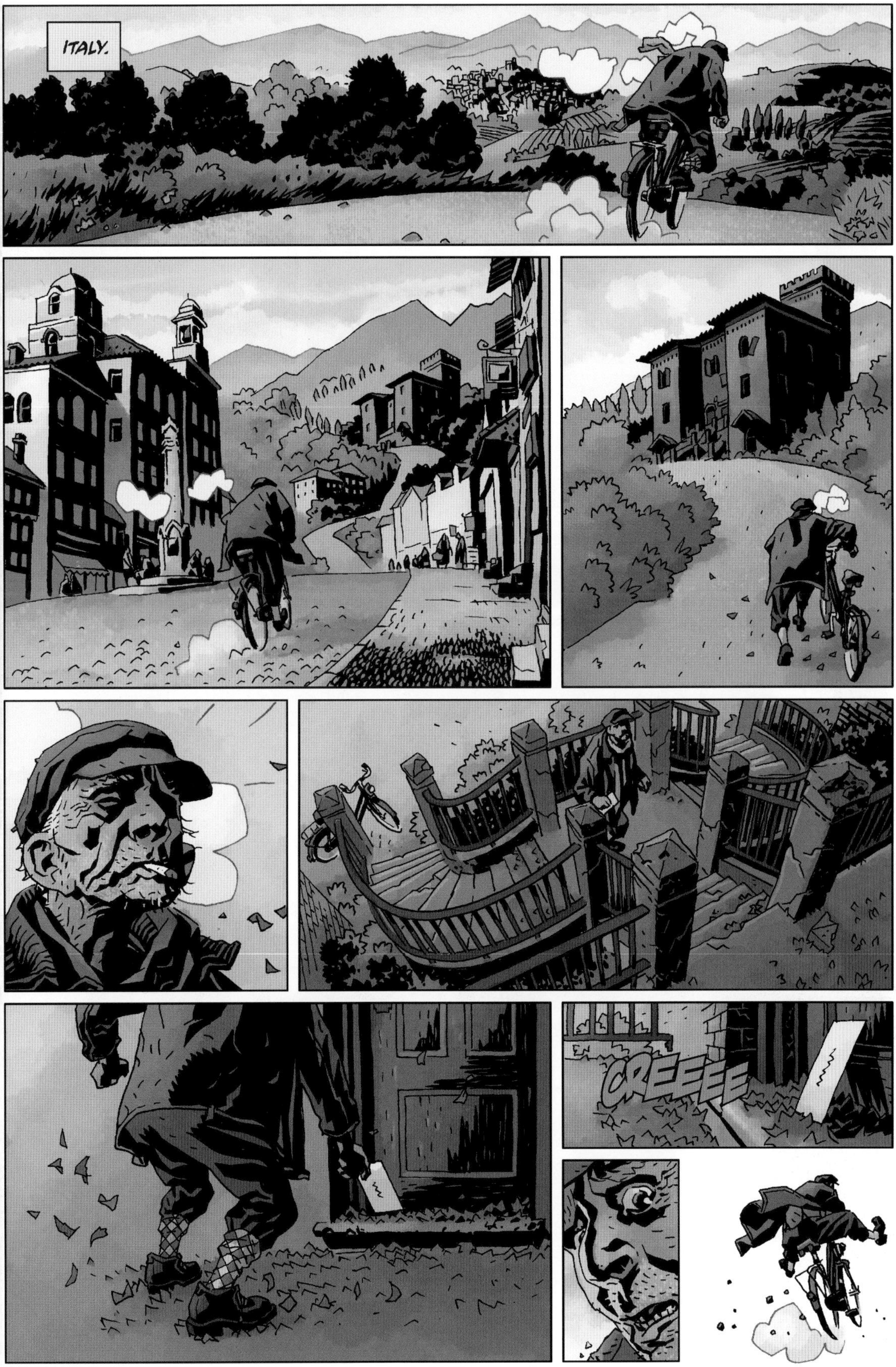
ITALY.
CREEEE

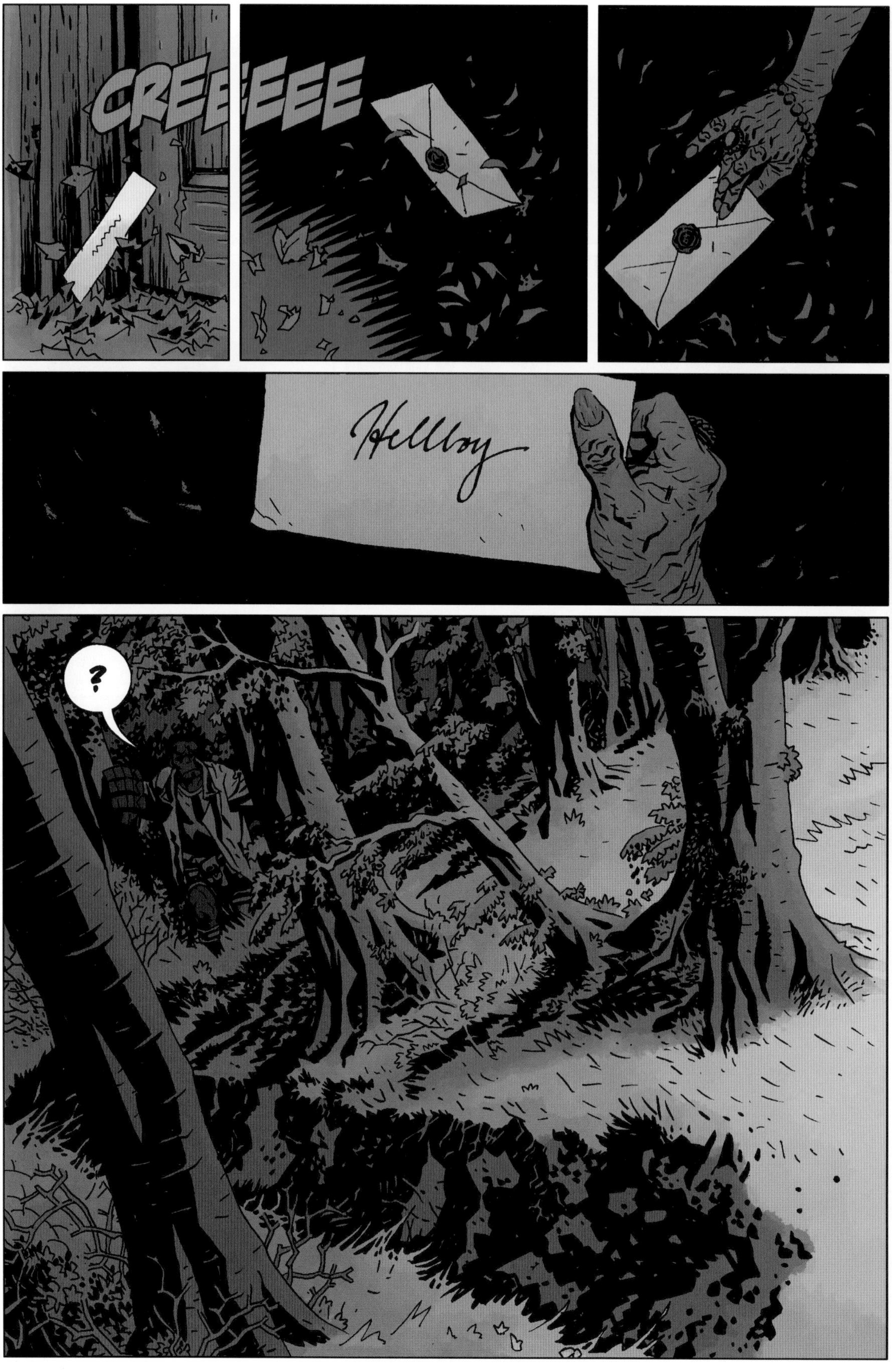
CREEEEEE
Hellboy
?

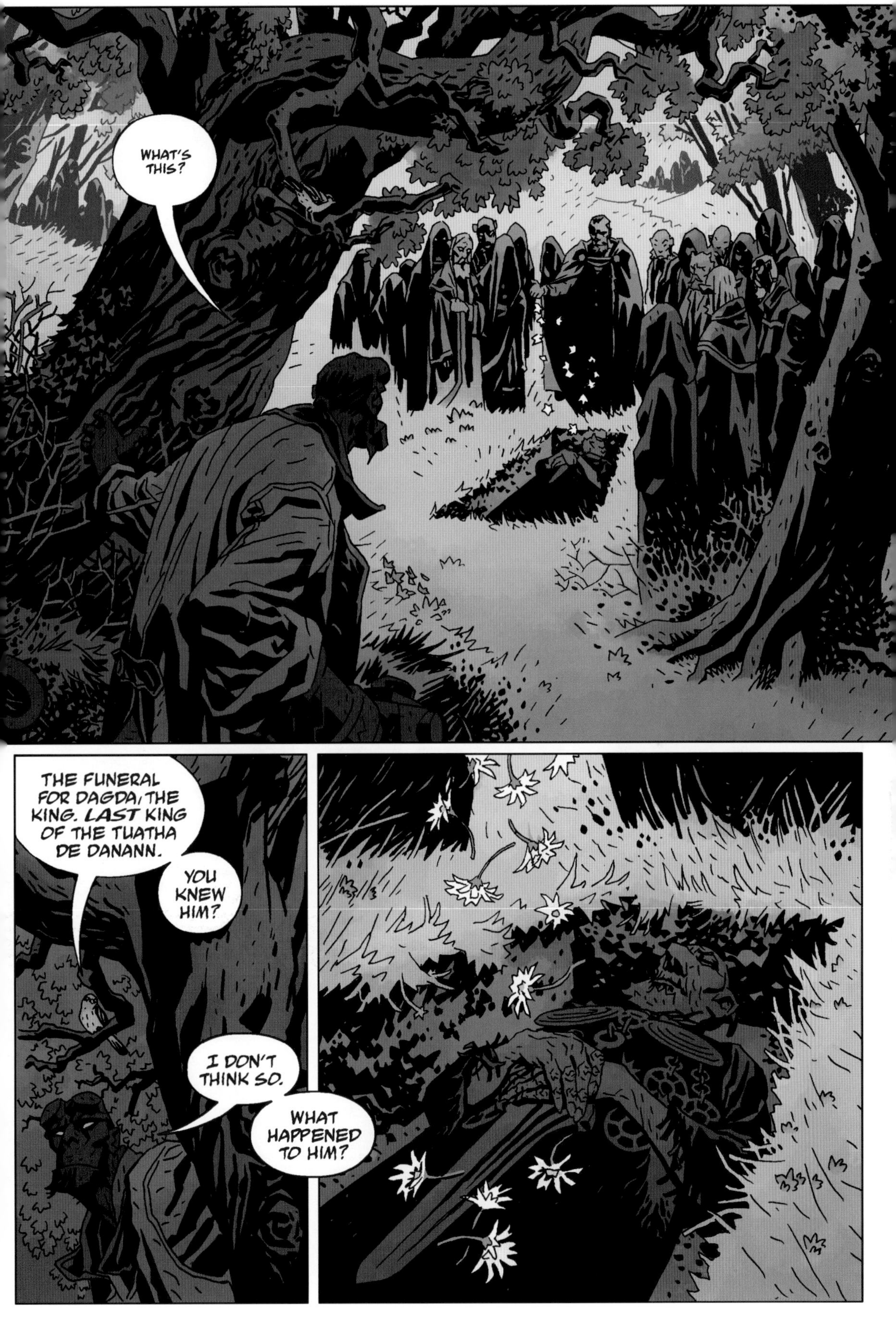
WHAT'S THIS?
THE FUNERAL FOR DAGDA, THE KING. *LAST* KING OF THE TUATHA DE DANANN.
YOU KNEW HIM?
I DON'T THINK SO.
WHAT HAPPENED TO HIM?

MURDER.

YOU SEE, THERE, STANDING AT THE HEAD OF HIS GRAVE?

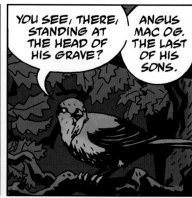

ANGUS MAC OG. THE LAST OF HIS SONS.

SEE? HE WILL NOT TAKE UP HIS FATHER'S SWORD.

HIS BROTHER AEDH WAS KILLED. LUG AND OGME WENT DOWN INTO THE SHADOWS UNDER THE WORLD AGES AGO. SOON HE'LL FOLLOW, AND WITH HIM THE LAST OF HIS PEOPLE.

NONE OF THAT RACE WILL REMAIN TO FIGHT FOR THIS WORLD.

IT'S COMING. I SMELL THE SMOKE.

WHAT?

WHAT'S COMING?

WAR.

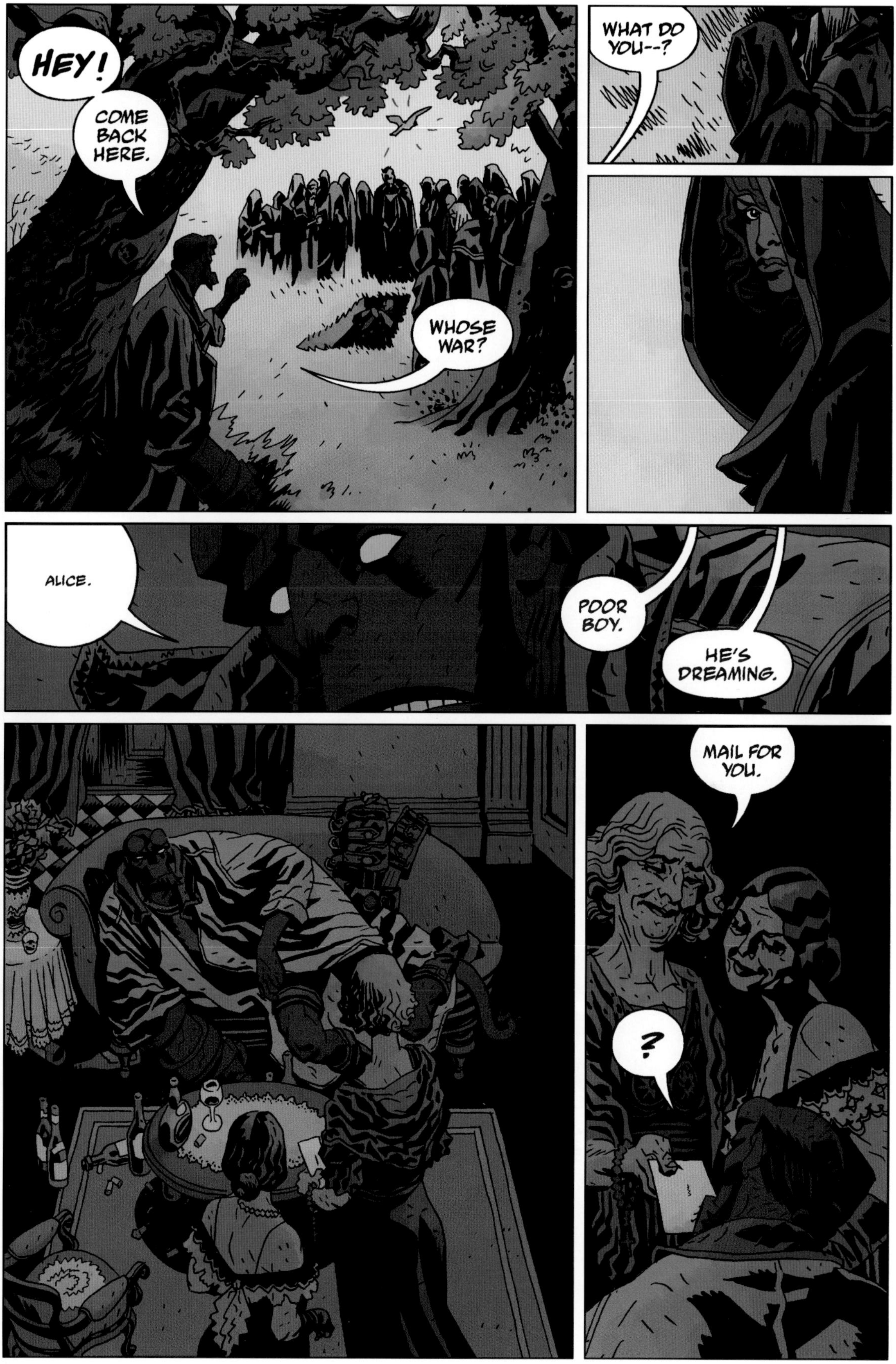
HEY!
COME BACK HERE.
WHOSE WAR?
WHAT DO YOU--?
ALICE.
POOR BOY.
HE'S DREAMING.
MAIL FOR YOU.
?

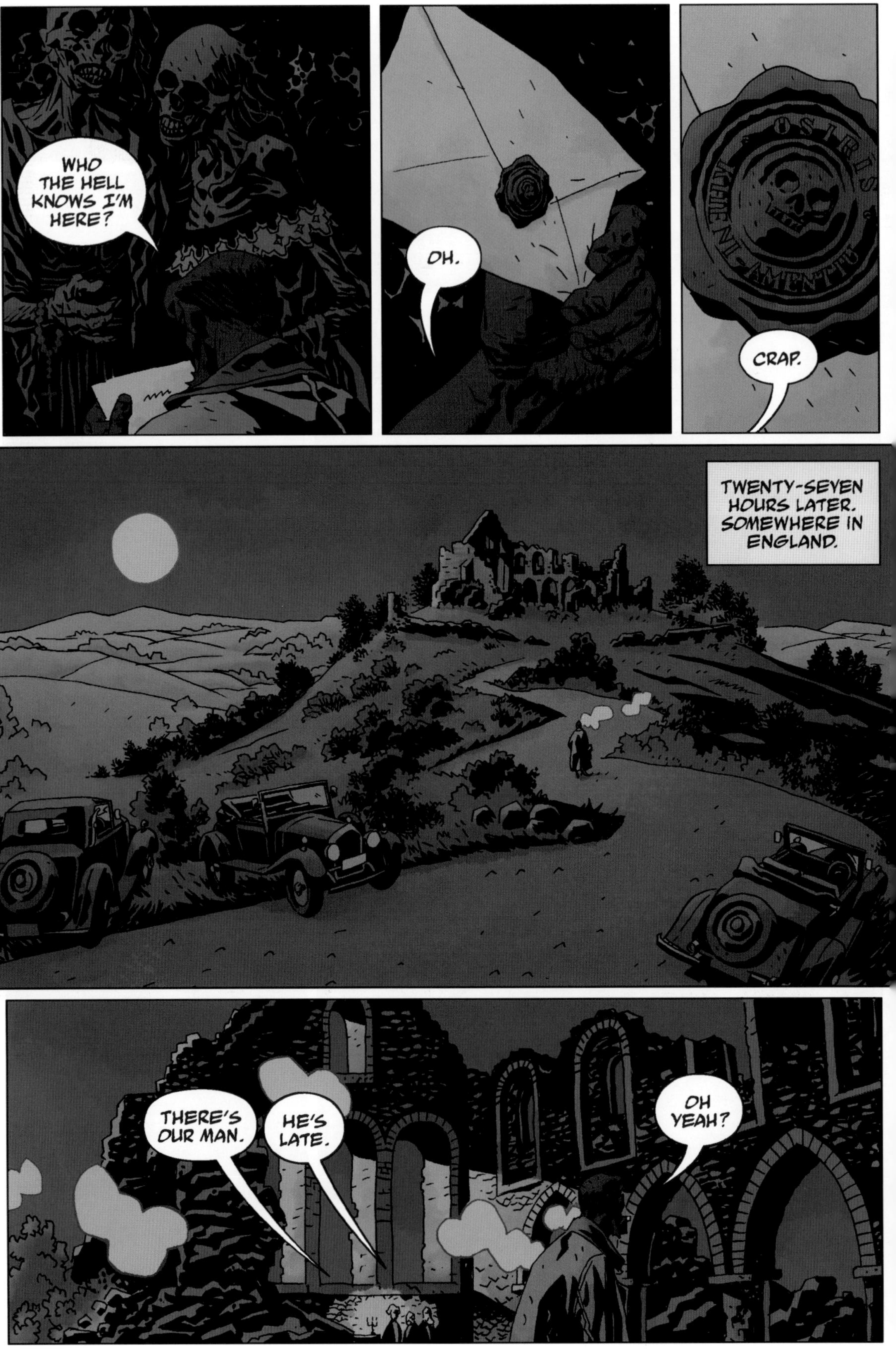
WHO THE HELL KNOWS I'M HERE?
OH.
OSIRIS
KHENTI-AMENTIU
CRAP.
TWENTY-SEVEN HOURS LATER. SOMEWHERE IN ENGLAND.
THERE'S OUR MAN.
HE'S LATE.
OH YEAH?

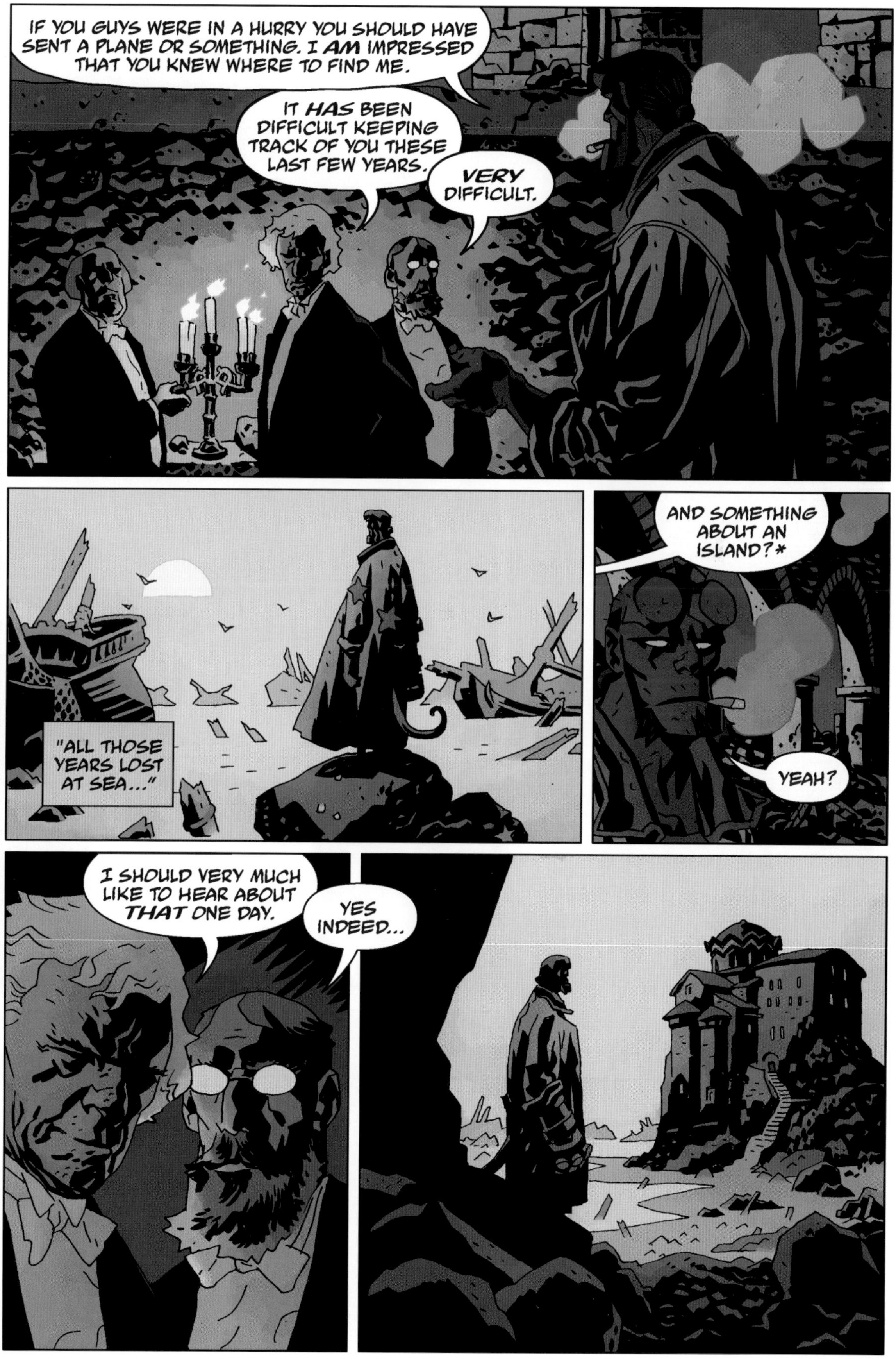
IF YOU GUYS WERE IN A HURRY YOU SHOULD HAVE SENT A PLANE OR SOMETHING. I AM IMPRESSED THAT YOU KNEW WHERE TO FIND ME.
IT HAS BEEN DIFFICULT KEEPING TRACK OF YOU THESE LAST FEW YEARS.
VERY DIFFICULT.
"ALL THOSE YEARS LOST AT SEA..."
AND SOMETHING ABOUT AN ISLAND?*
YEAH?
I SHOULD VERY MUCH LIKE TO HEAR ABOUT THAT ONE DAY.
YES INDEED...

*HELLBOY: STRANGE PLACES

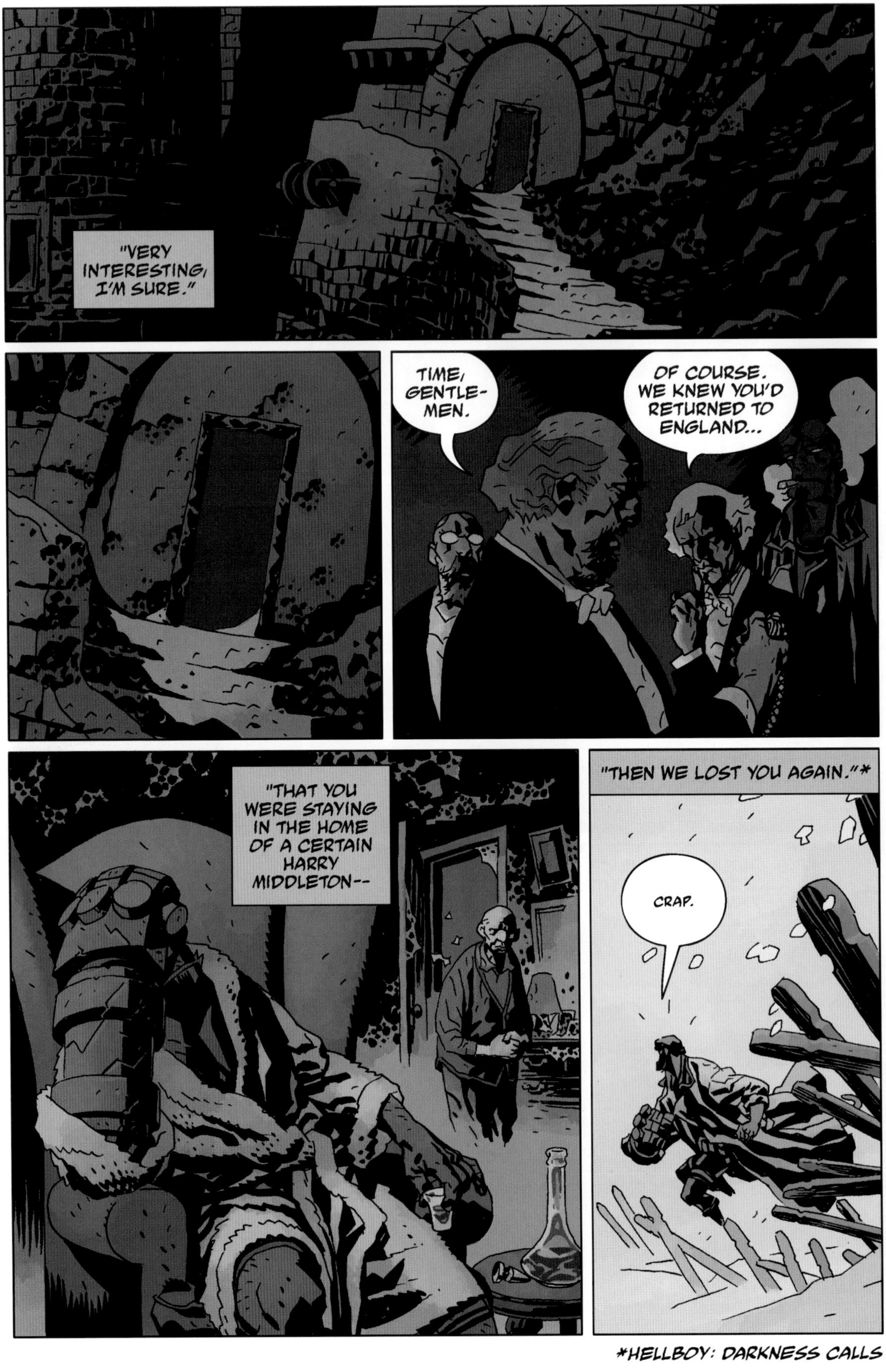
"VERY INTERESTING, I'M SURE."
TIME, GENTLE-MEN.
OF COURSE. WE KNEW YOU'D RETURNED TO ENGLAND...
"THAT YOU WERE STAYING IN THE HOME OF A CERTAIN HARRY MIDDLETON--
"THEN WE LOST YOU AGAIN."*
CRAP.

*HELLBOY: DARKNESS CALLS

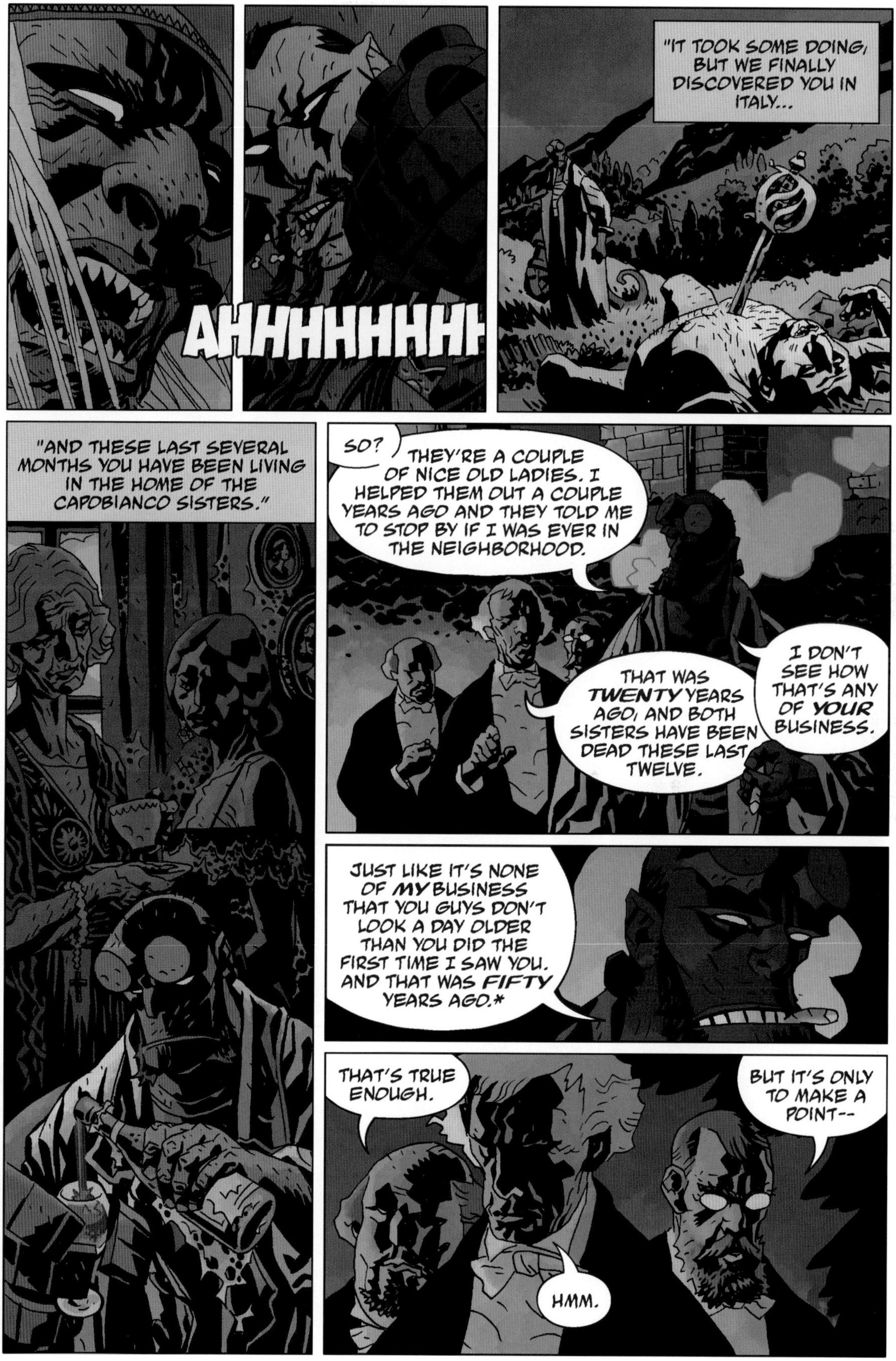
AHHHHHHHH
"IT TOOK SOME DOING, BUT WE FINALLY DISCOVERED YOU IN ITALY...
"AND THESE LAST SEVERAL MONTHS YOU HAVE BEEN LIVING IN THE HOME OF THE CAPOBIANCO SISTERS."
SO?
THEY'RE A COUPLE OF NICE OLD LADIES. I HELPED THEM OUT A COUPLE YEARS AGO AND THEY TOLD ME TO STOP BY IF I WAS EVER IN THE NEIGHBORHOOD.
THAT WAS TWENTY YEARS AGO, AND BOTH SISTERS HAVE BEEN DEAD THESE LAST TWELVE.
I DON'T SEE HOW THAT'S ANY OF YOUR BUSINESS.
JUST LIKE IT'S NONE OF MY BUSINESS THAT YOU GUYS DON'T LOOK A DAY OLDER THAN YOU DID THE FIRST TIME I SAW YOU. AND THAT WAS FIFTY YEARS AGO.*
THAT'S TRUE ENOUGH.
BUT IT'S ONLY TO MAKE A POINT--
HMM.

*HELLBOY: THE NATURE OF THE BEAST

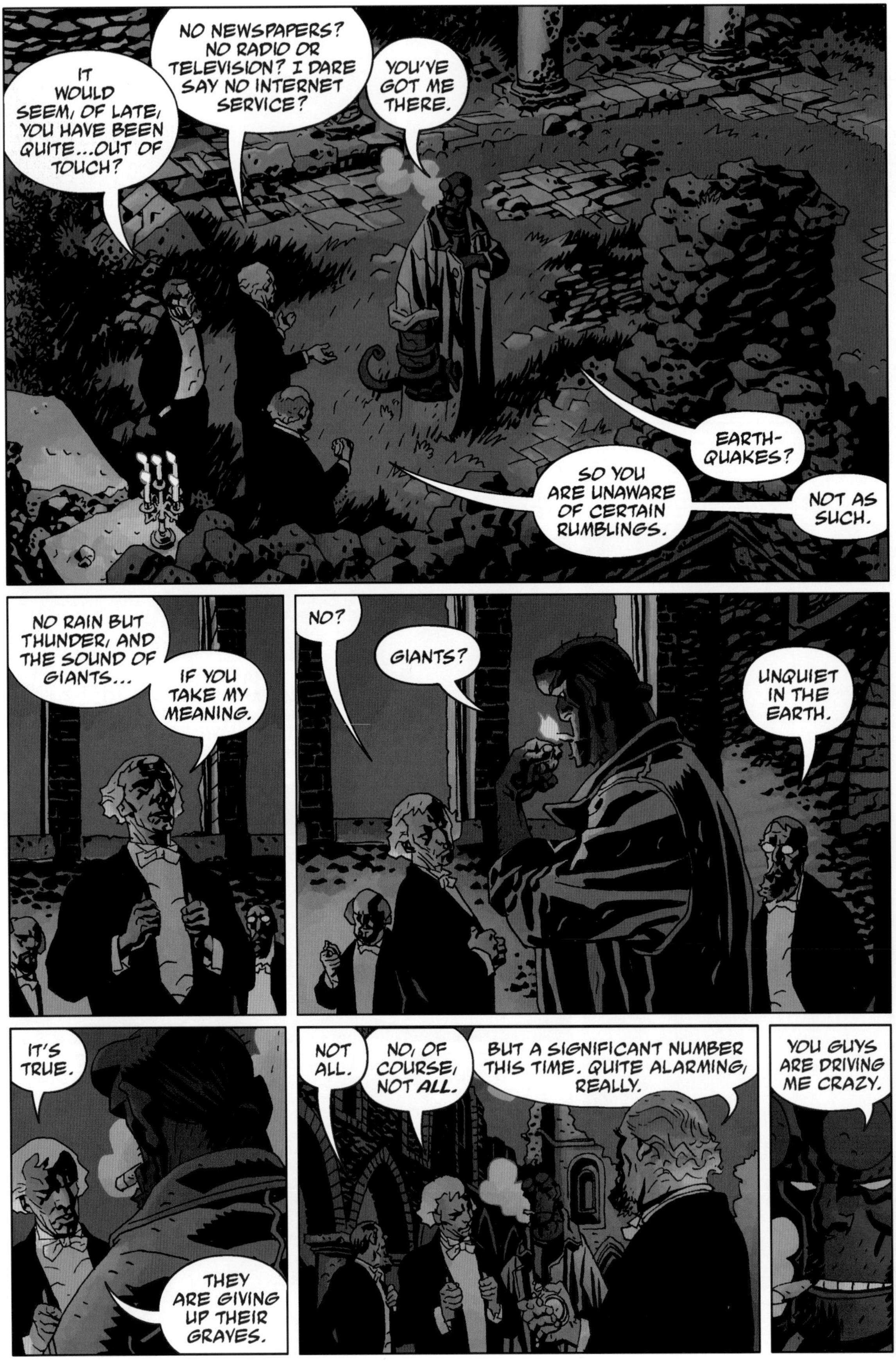
IT WOULD SEEM, OF LATE, YOU HAVE BEEN QUITE...OUT OF TOUCH?
NO NEWSPAPERS? NO RADIO OR TELEVISION? I DARE SAY NO INTERNET SERVICE?
YOU'VE GOT ME THERE.
EARTH-QUAKES?
SO YOU ARE UNAWARE OF CERTAIN RUMBLINGS.
NOT AS SUCH.
NO RAIN BUT THUNDER, AND THE SOUND OF GIANTS...
IF YOU TAKE MY MEANING.
NO?
GIANTS?
UNQUIET IN THE EARTH.
IT'S TRUE.
THEY ARE GIVING UP THEIR GRAVES.
NOT ALL.
NO, OF COURSE, NOT ALL.
BUT A SIGNIFICANT NUMBER THIS TIME. QUITE ALARMING, REALLY.
YOU GUYS ARE DRIVING ME CRAZY.

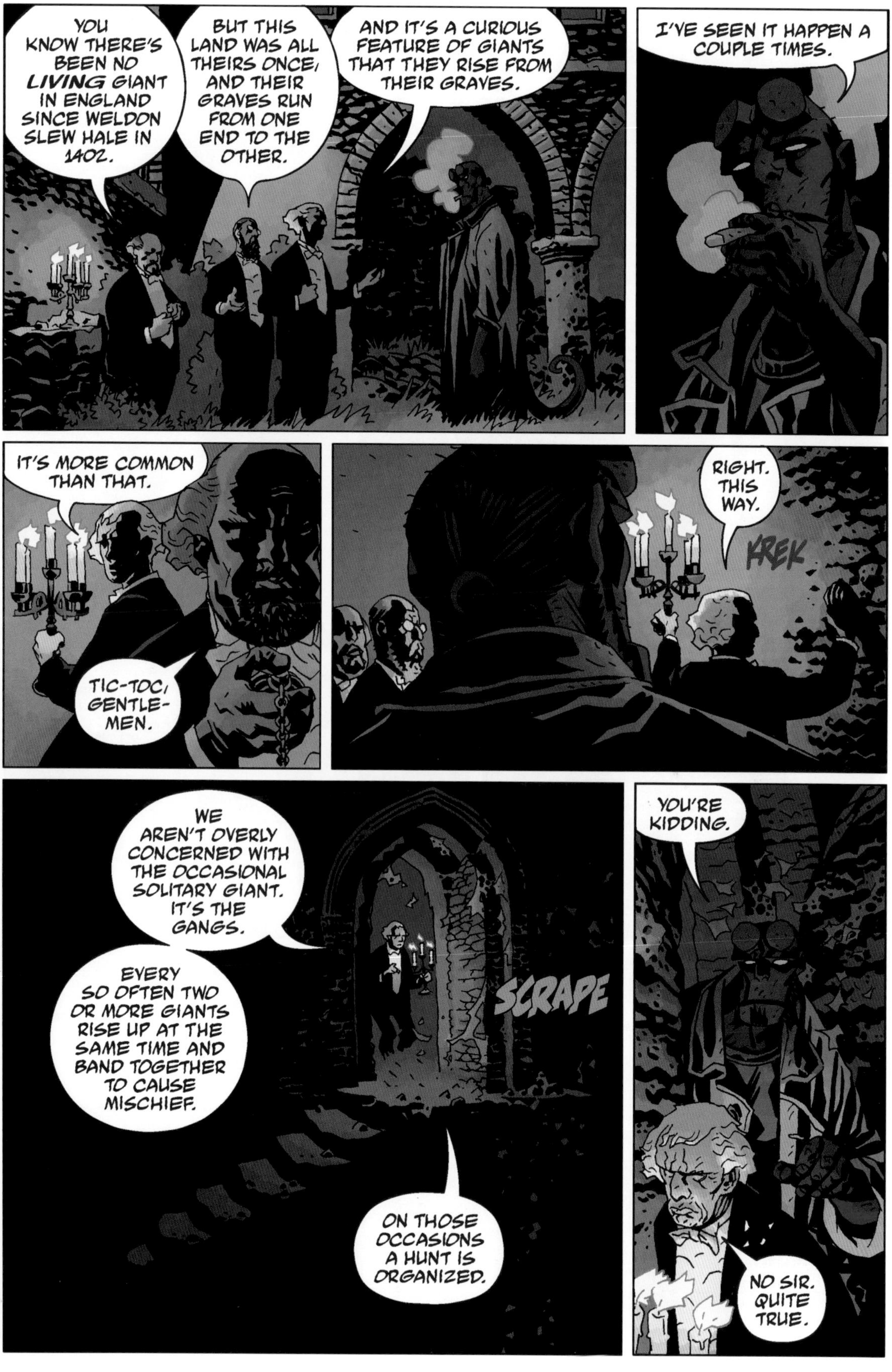
YOU KNOW THERE'S BEEN NO LIVING GIANT IN ENGLAND SINCE WELDON SLEW HALE IN 1402.
BUT THIS LAND WAS ALL THEIRS ONCE, AND THEIR GRAVES RUN FROM ONE END TO THE OTHER.
AND IT'S A CURIOUS FEATURE OF GIANTS THAT THEY RISE FROM THEIR GRAVES.
I'VE SEEN IT HAPPEN A COUPLE TIMES.
IT'S MORE COMMON THAN THAT.
TIC-TOC, GENTLE-MEN.
RIGHT. THIS WAY.
KREK
WE AREN'T OVERLY CONCERNED WITH THE OCCASIONAL SOLITARY GIANT. IT'S THE GANGS.
EVERY SO OFTEN TWO OR MORE GIANTS RISE UP AT THE SAME TIME AND BAND TOGETHER TO CAUSE MISCHIEF.
SCRAPE
ON THOSE OCCASIONS A HUNT IS ORGANIZED.
YOU'RE KIDDING.
NO SIR. QUITE TRUE.

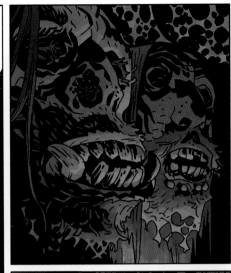

VERY HUSH-HUSH, OF COURSE. THE **WILD HUNT.** ESTABLISHED, WE BELIEVE, IN 1259.

HOLY CRAP.

USUALLY IT'S NO MORE THAN THREE GIANTS TOGETHER AT A TIME. NOT **TOO** MUCH TROUBLE.

SIR BENWICK TOOK **FOUR** AT DURHAM HILL.

THAT MUST'VE BEEN SOMETHING.

YES, WELL, I'M AFRAID IT'S ANOTHER MATTER ALTOGETHER THIS TIME.

IT APPEARS A GANG OF SIX ARE OUT ONLY A FEW MILES FROM HERE. **AND** SEVERAL MORE UP NORTH.

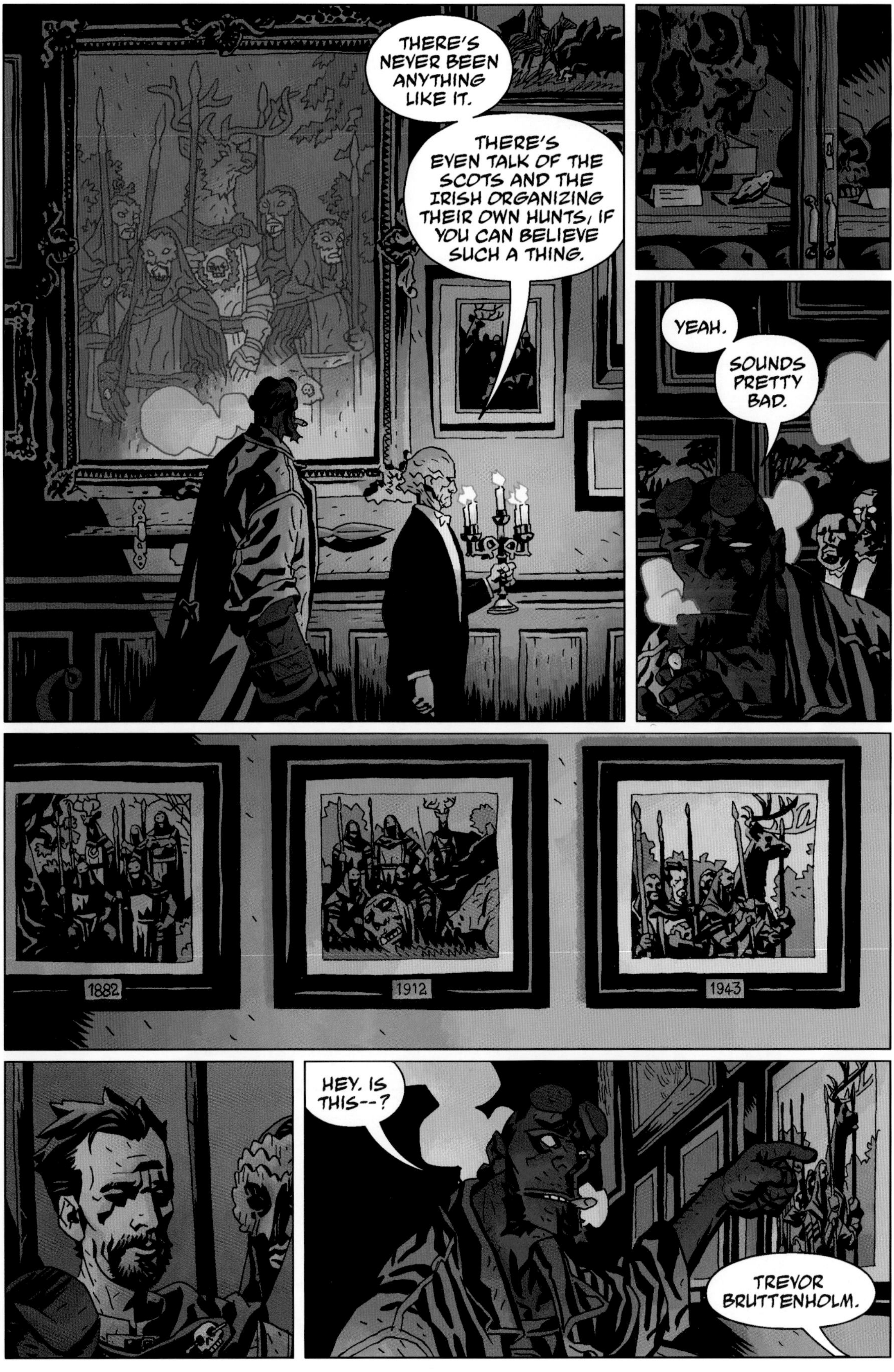
THERE'S NEVER BEEN ANYTHING LIKE IT.
THERE'S EVEN TALK OF THE SCOTS AND THE IRISH ORGANIZING THEIR OWN HUNTS, IF YOU CAN BELIEVE SUCH A THING.
YEAH.
SOUNDS PRETTY BAD.
1882
1912
1943
HEY. IS THIS--?
TREVOR BRUTTENHOLM.

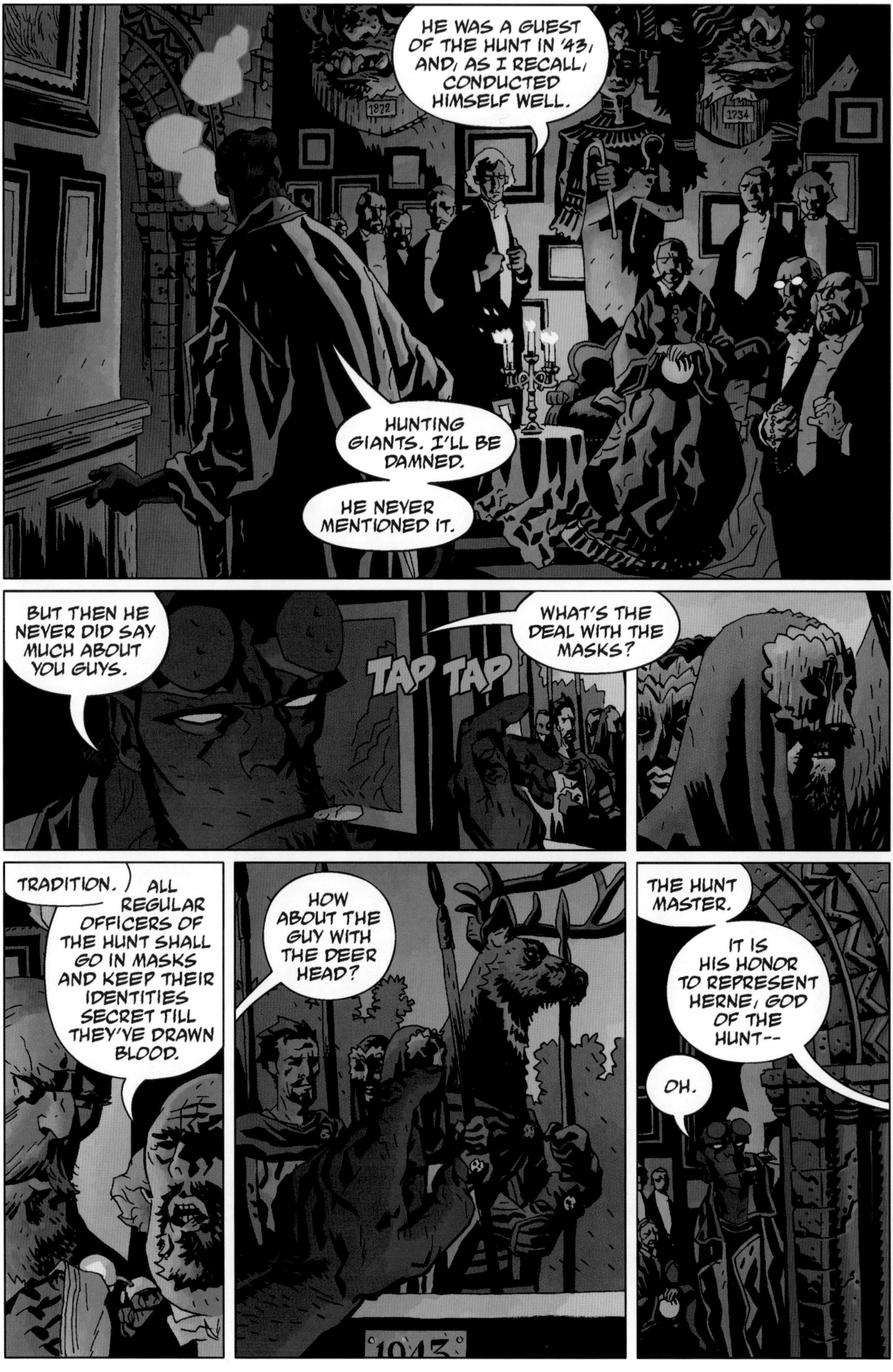

HE WAS A GUEST OF THE HUNT IN '43, AND, AS I RECALL, CONDUCTED HIMSELF WELL.
1872
1734
HUNTING GIANTS. I'LL BE DAMNED.
HE NEVER MENTIONED IT.
BUT THEN HE NEVER DID SAY MUCH ABOUT YOU GUYS.
TAP TAP
WHAT'S THE DEAL WITH THE MASKS?
TRADITION.
ALL REGULAR OFFICERS OF THE HUNT SHALL GO IN MASKS AND KEEP THEIR IDENTITIES SECRET TILL THEY'VE DRAWN BLOOD.
HOW ABOUT THE GUY WITH THE DEER HEAD?
1943
THE HUNT MASTER.
IT IS HIS HONOR TO REPRESENT HERNE, GOD OF THE HUNT--
OH.

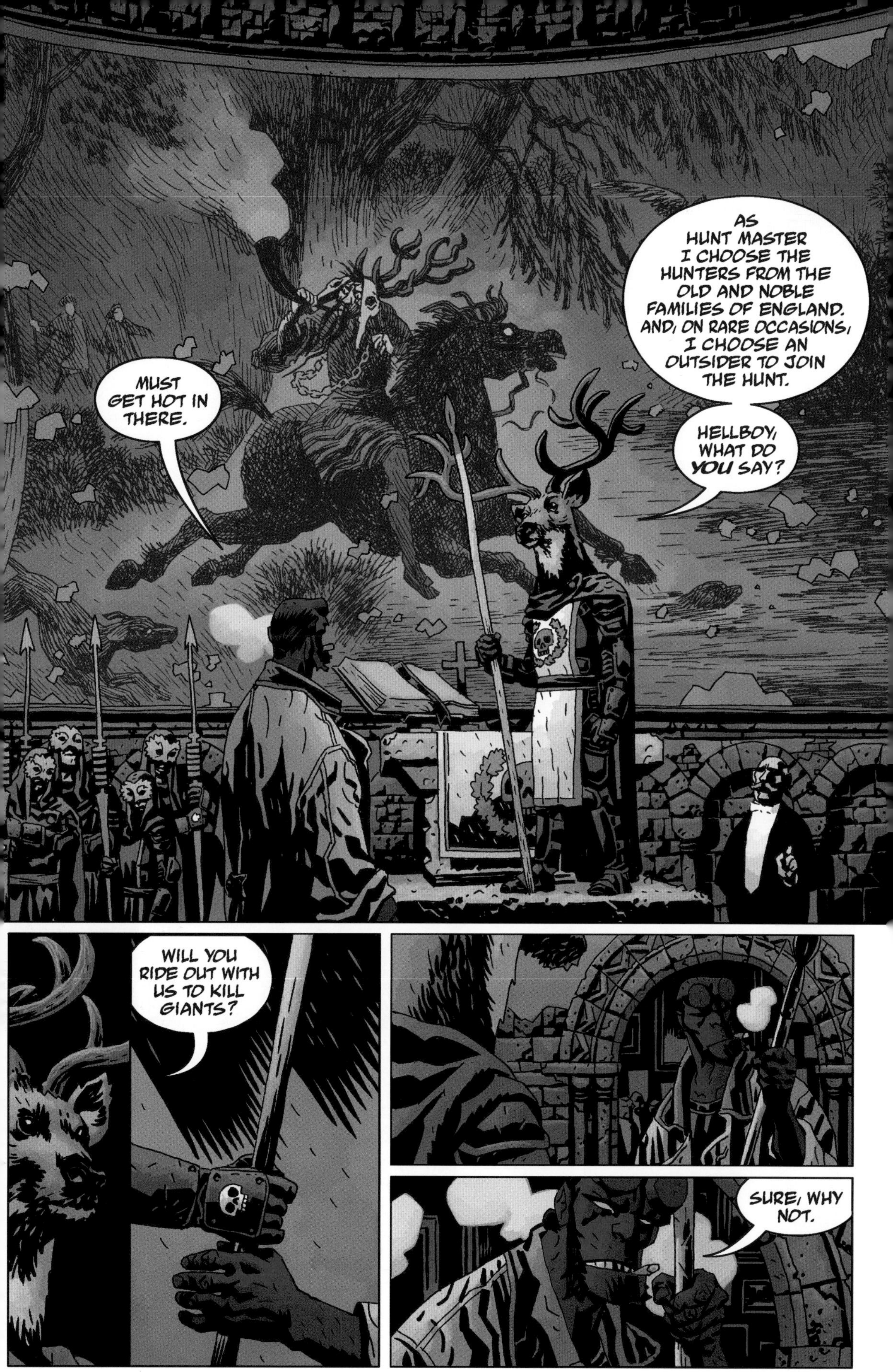
MUST GET HOT IN THERE.
AS HUNT MASTER I CHOOSE THE HUNTERS FROM THE OLD AND NOBLE FAMILIES OF ENGLAND. AND, ON RARE OCCASIONS, I CHOOSE AN OUTSIDER TO JOIN THE HUNT.
HELLBOY, WHAT DO *YOU* SAY?
WILL YOU RIDE OUT WITH US TO KILL GIANTS?
SURE, WHY NOT.

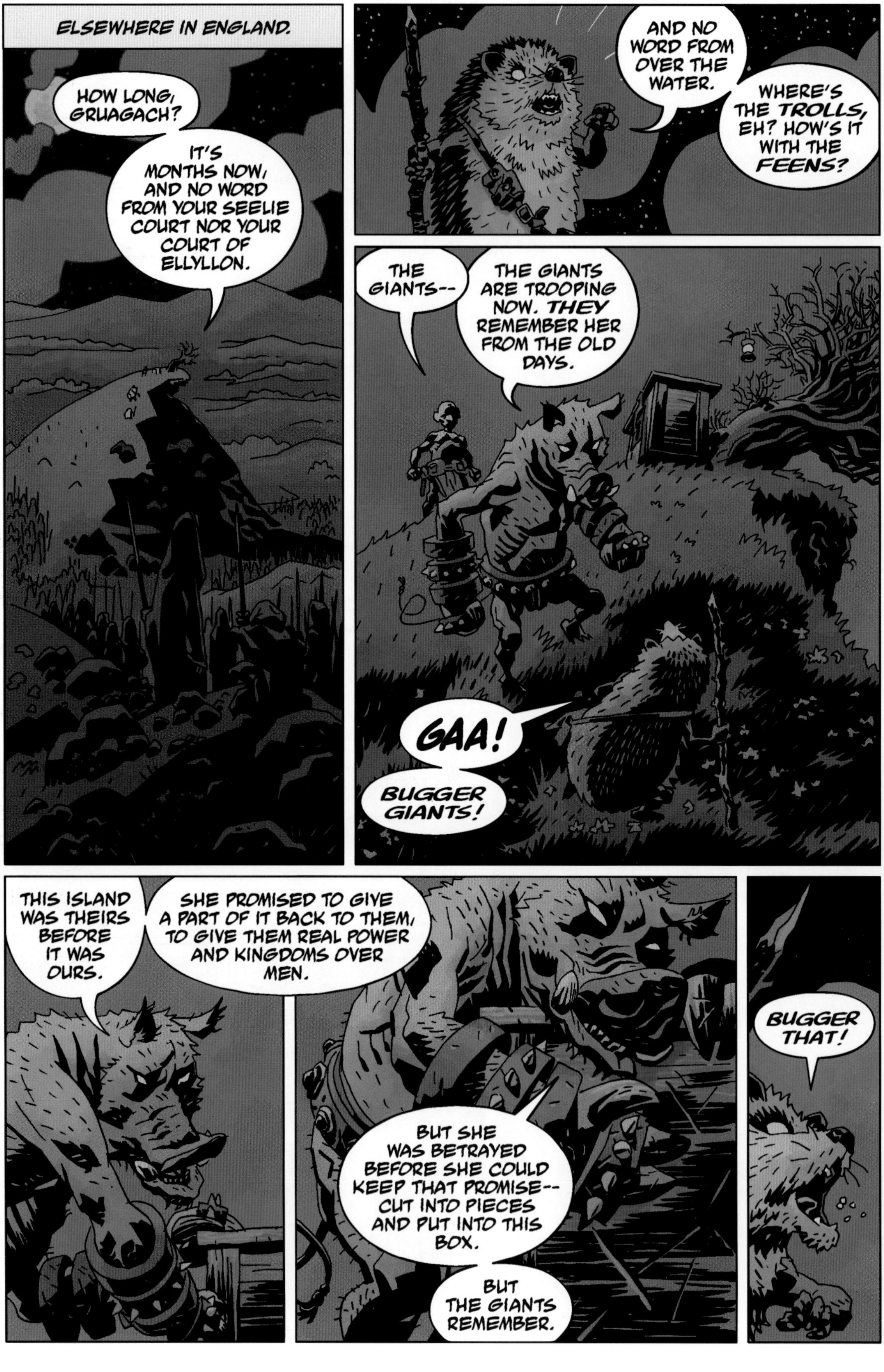
ELSEWHERE IN ENGLAND.
HOW LONG, GRUAGACH?
IT'S MONTHS NOW, AND NO WORD FROM YOUR SEELIE COURT NOR YOUR COURT OF ELLYLLON.
AND NO WORD FROM OVER THE WATER.
WHERE'S THE TROLLS, EH? HOW'S IT WITH THE FEENS?
THE GIANTS--
THE GIANTS ARE TROOPING NOW. THEY REMEMBER HER FROM THE OLD DAYS.
GAA!
BUGGER GIANTS!
THIS ISLAND WAS THEIRS BEFORE IT WAS OURS.
SHE PROMISED TO GIVE A PART OF IT BACK TO THEM, TO GIVE THEM REAL POWER AND KINGDOMS OVER MEN.
BUT SHE WAS BETRAYED BEFORE SHE COULD KEEP THAT PROMISE-- CUT INTO PIECES AND PUT INTO THIS BOX.
BUT THE GIANTS REMEMBER.
BUGGER THAT!

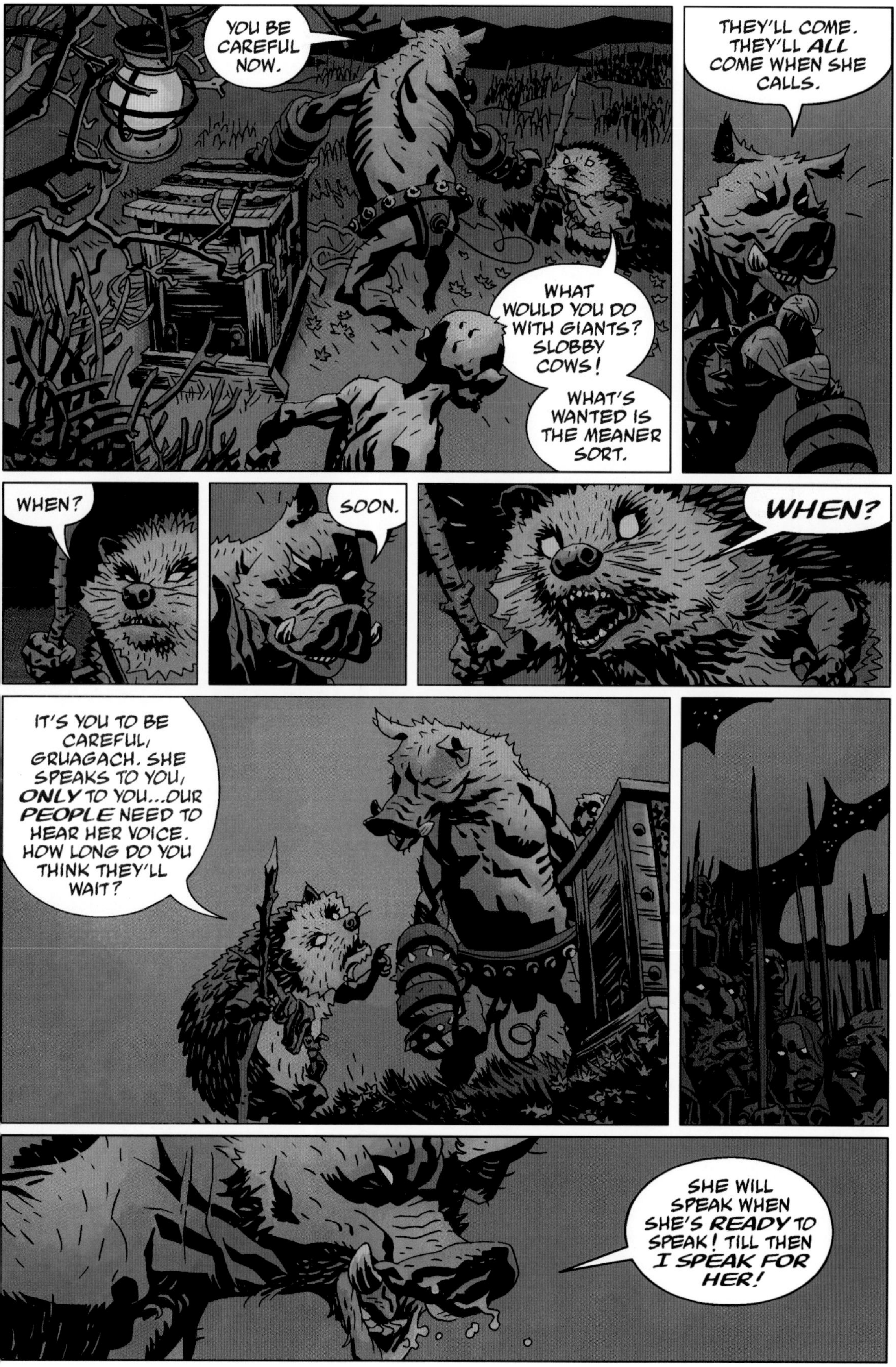
YOU BE CAREFUL NOW.
WHAT WOULD YOU DO WITH GIANTS? SLOBBY COWS!
WHAT'S WANTED IS THE MEANER SORT.
THEY'LL COME. THEY'LL *ALL* COME WHEN SHE CALLS.
WHEN?
SOON.
WHEN?
IT'S YOU TO BE CAREFUL, GRUAGACH. SHE SPEAKS TO YOU, *ONLY* TO YOU...OUR *PEOPLE* NEED TO HEAR HER VOICE. HOW LONG DO YOU THINK THEY'LL WAIT?
SHE WILL SPEAK WHEN SHE'S *READY* TO SPEAK! TILL THEN *I SPEAK FOR HER!*

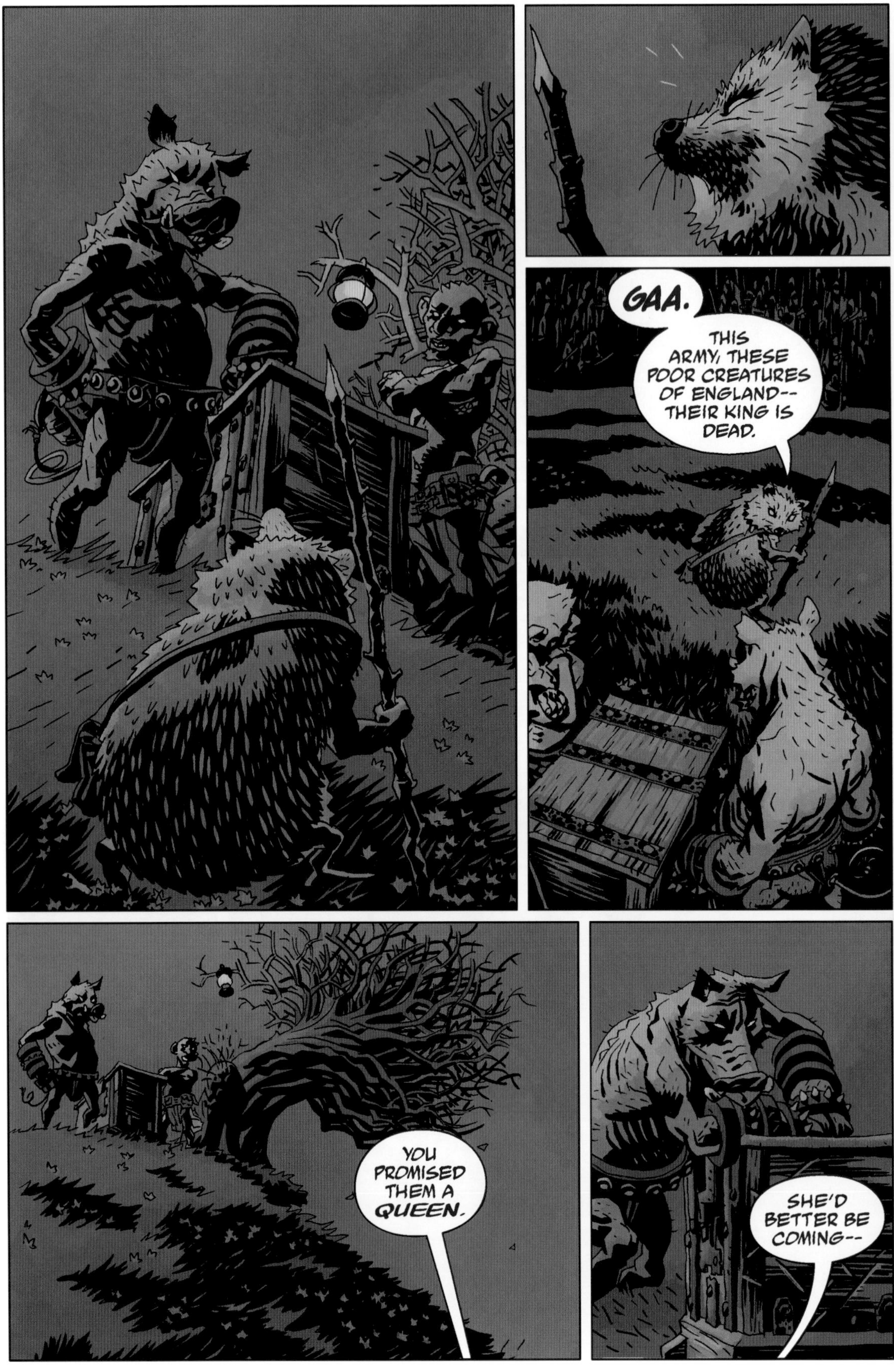
GAA.
THIS ARMY, THESE POOR CREATURES OF ENGLAND-- THEIR KING IS DEAD.
YOU PROMISED THEM A QUEEN.
SHE'D BETTER BE COMING--

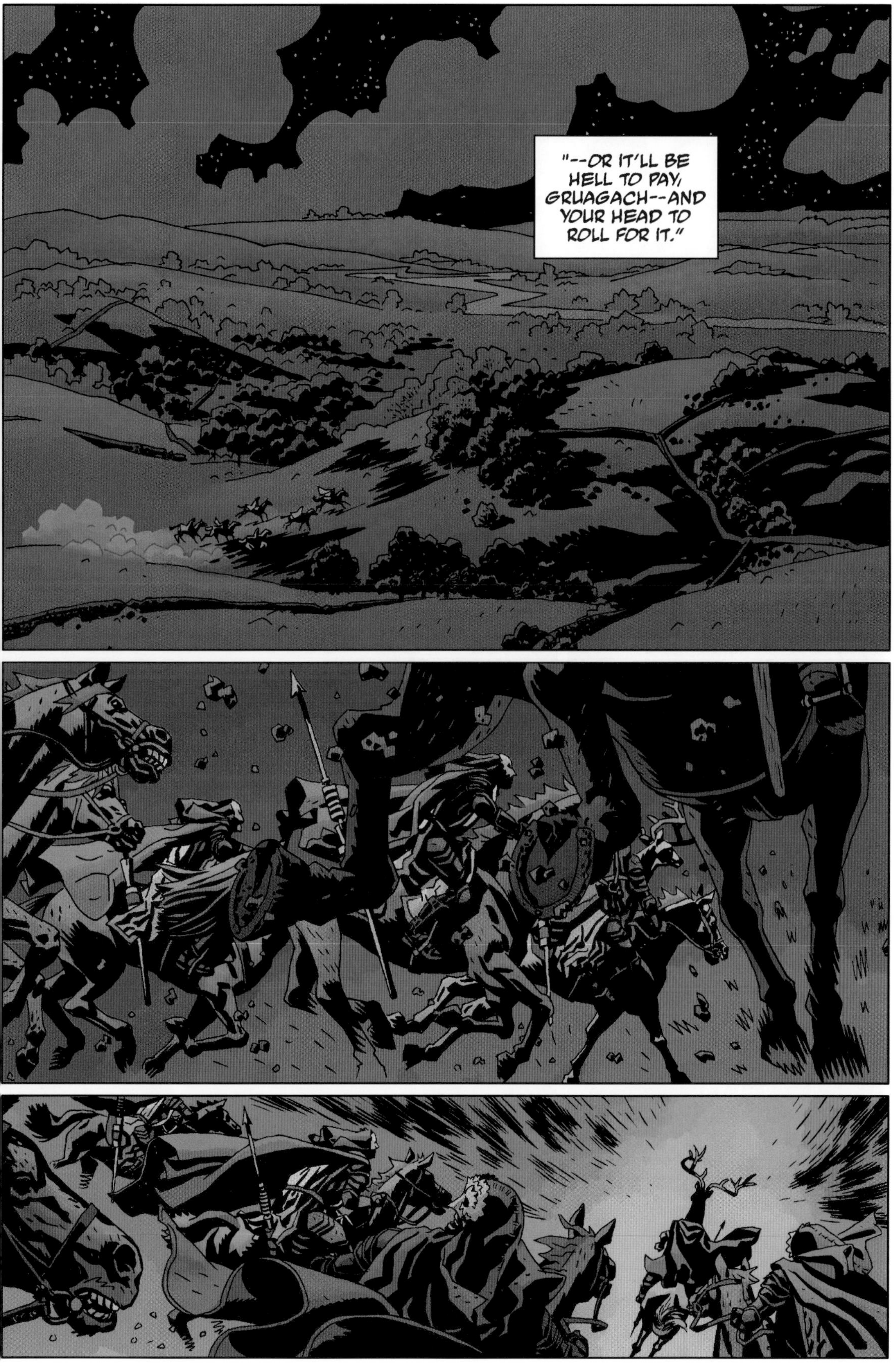
"--OR IT'LL BE HELL TO PAY, GRUAGACH--AND YOUR HEAD TO ROLL FOR IT."

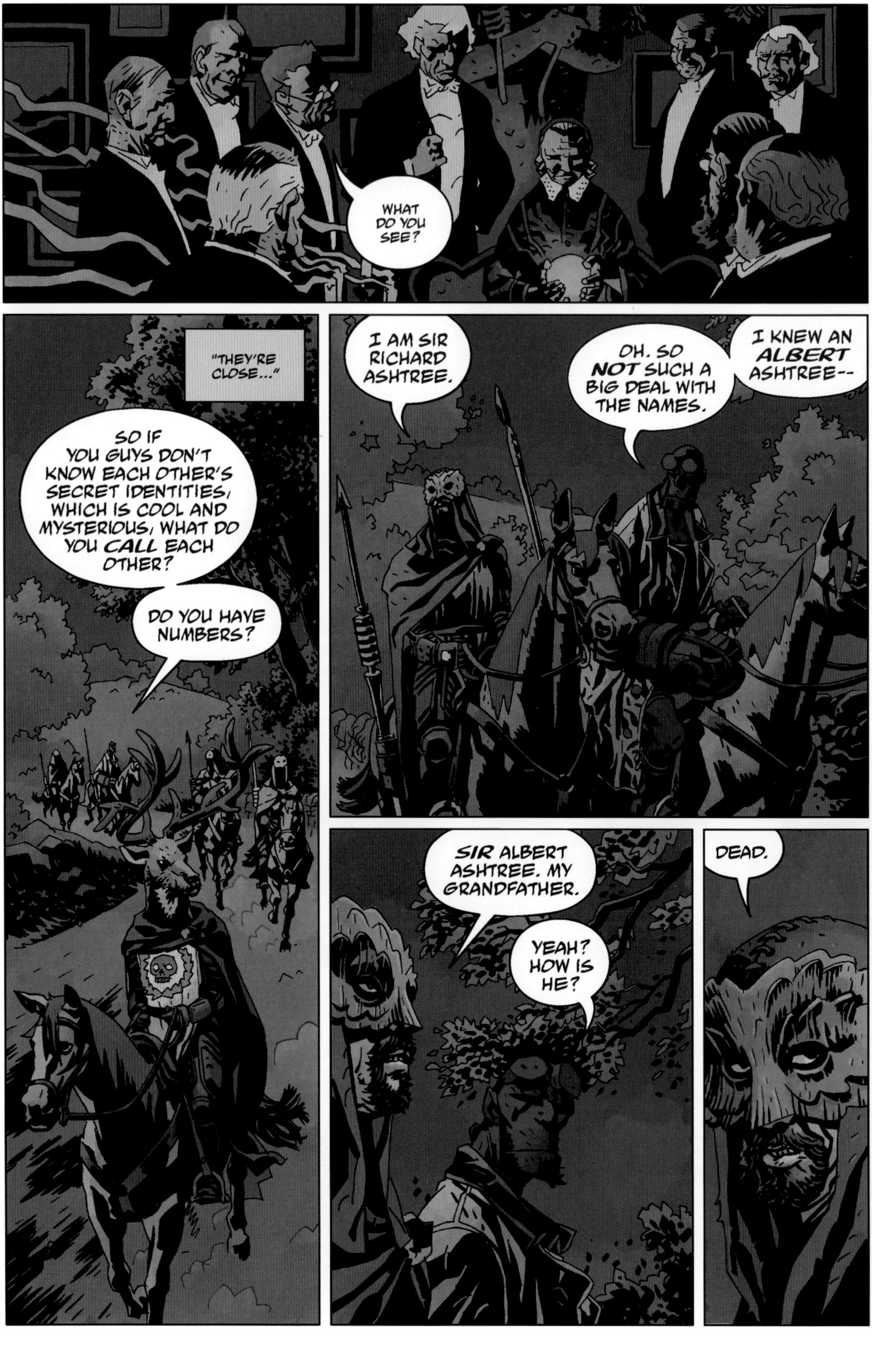
WHAT DO YOU SEE?
"THEY'RE CLOSE..."
SO IF YOU GUYS DON'T KNOW EACH OTHER'S SECRET IDENTITIES, WHICH IS COOL AND MYSTERIOUS, WHAT DO YOU CALL EACH OTHER?
DO YOU HAVE NUMBERS?
I AM SIR RICHARD ASHTREE.
OH. SO NOT SUCH A BIG DEAL WITH THE NAMES.
I KNEW AN ALBERT ASHTREE--
SIR ALBERT ASHTREE. MY GRANDFATHER.
YEAH? HOW IS HE?
DEAD.

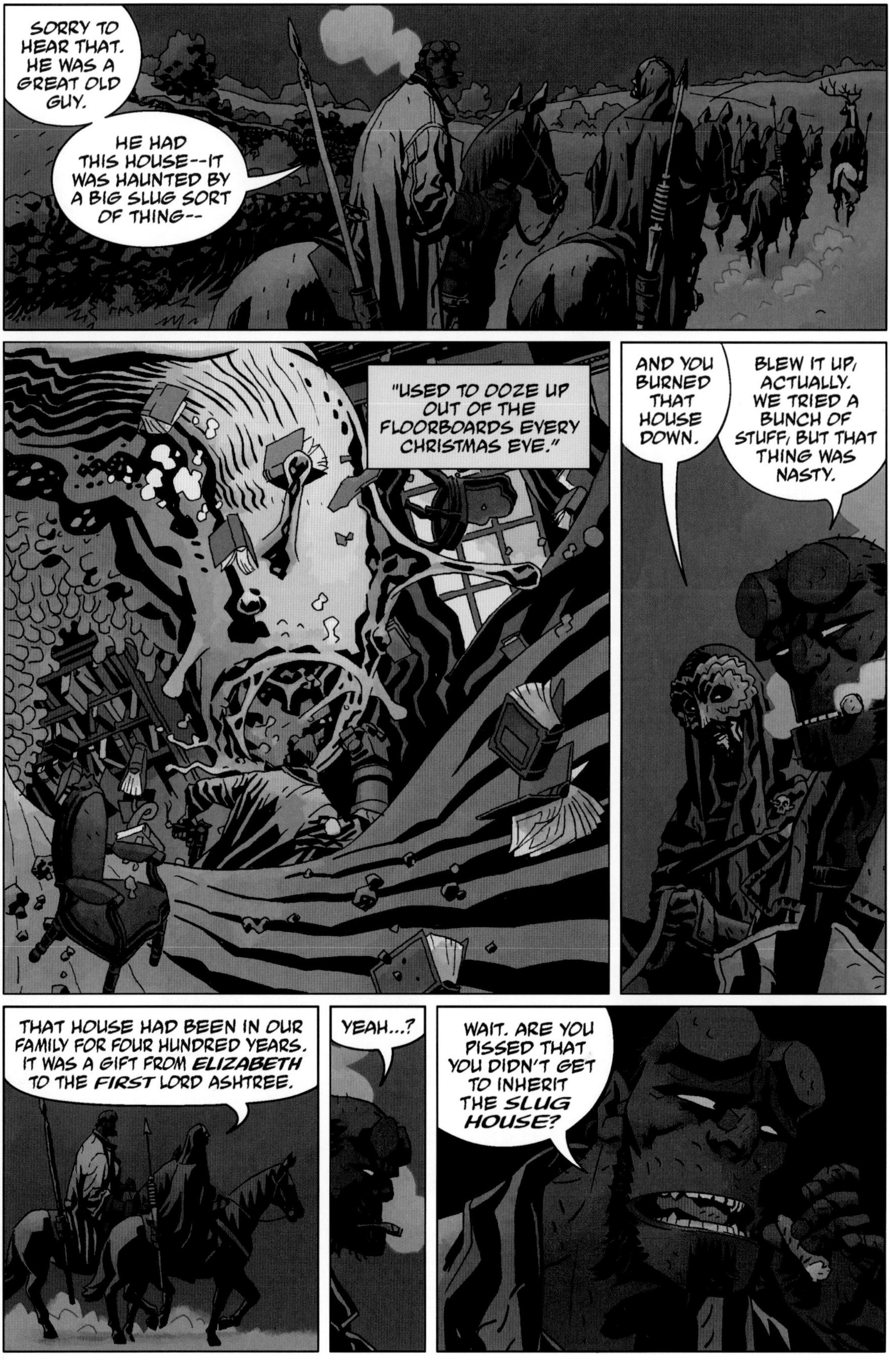
SORRY TO HEAR THAT. HE WAS A GREAT OLD GUY.
HE HAD THIS HOUSE--IT WAS HAUNTED BY A BIG SLUG SORT OF THING--
"USED TO OOZE UP OUT OF THE FLOORBOARDS EVERY CHRISTMAS EVE."
AND YOU BURNED THAT HOUSE DOWN.
BLEW IT UP, ACTUALLY. WE TRIED A BUNCH OF STUFF, BUT THAT THING WAS NASTY.
THAT HOUSE HAD BEEN IN OUR FAMILY FOR FOUR HUNDRED YEARS. IT WAS A GIFT FROM *ELIZABETH* TO THE *FIRST* LORD ASHTREE.
YEAH...?
WAIT. ARE YOU PISSED THAT YOU DIDN'T GET TO INHERIT THE *SLUG HOUSE*?

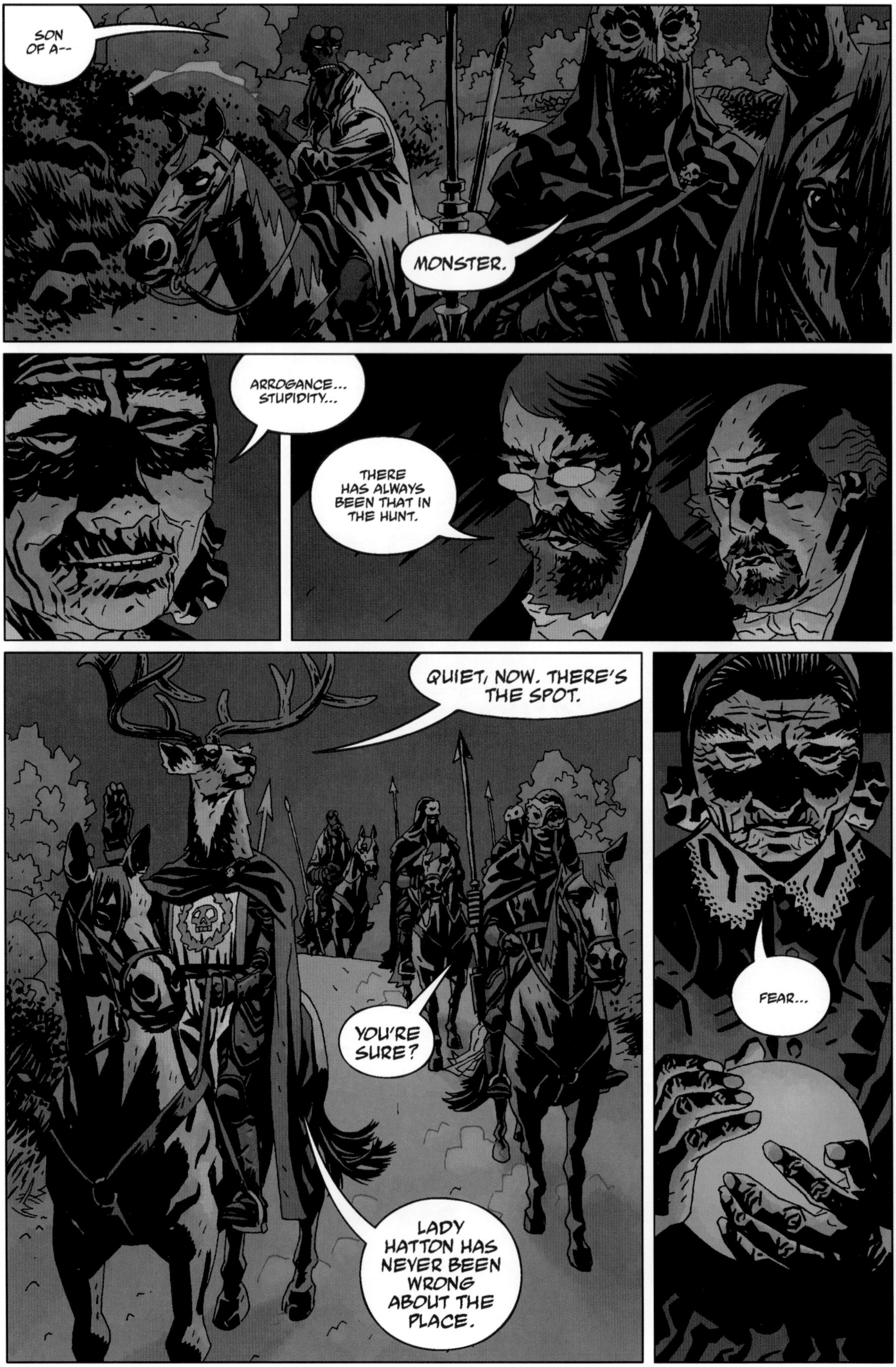
SON OF A--
MONSTER.
ARROGANCE... STUPIDITY...
THERE HAS ALWAYS BEEN THAT IN THE HUNT.
QUIET, NOW. THERE'S THE SPOT.
YOU'RE SURE?
LADY HATTON HAS NEVER BEEN WRONG ABOUT THE PLACE.
FEAR...

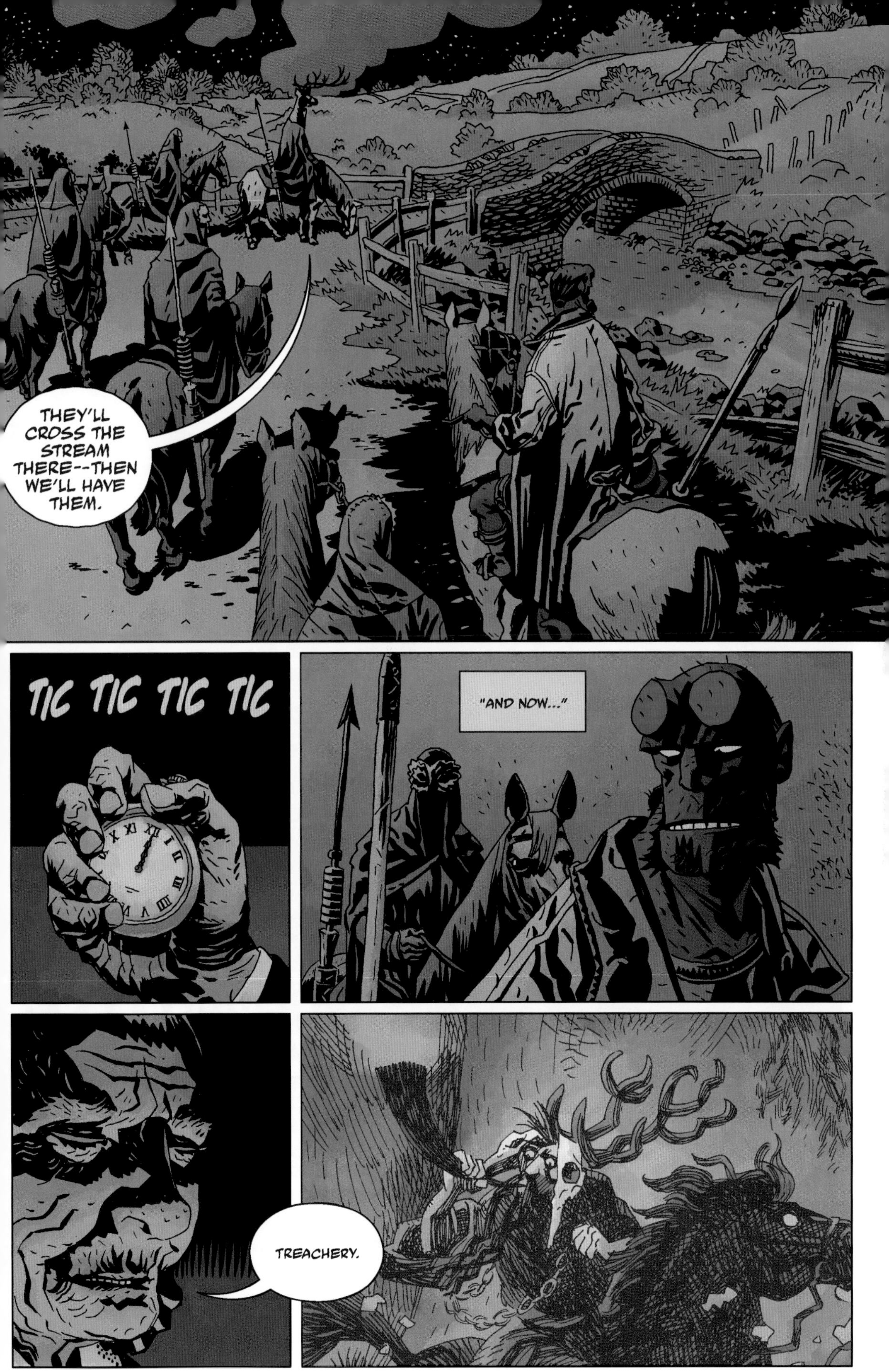
THEY'LL CROSS THE STREAM THERE--THEN WE'LL HAVE THEM.
TIC TIC TIC TIC
"AND NOW..."
TREACHERY.

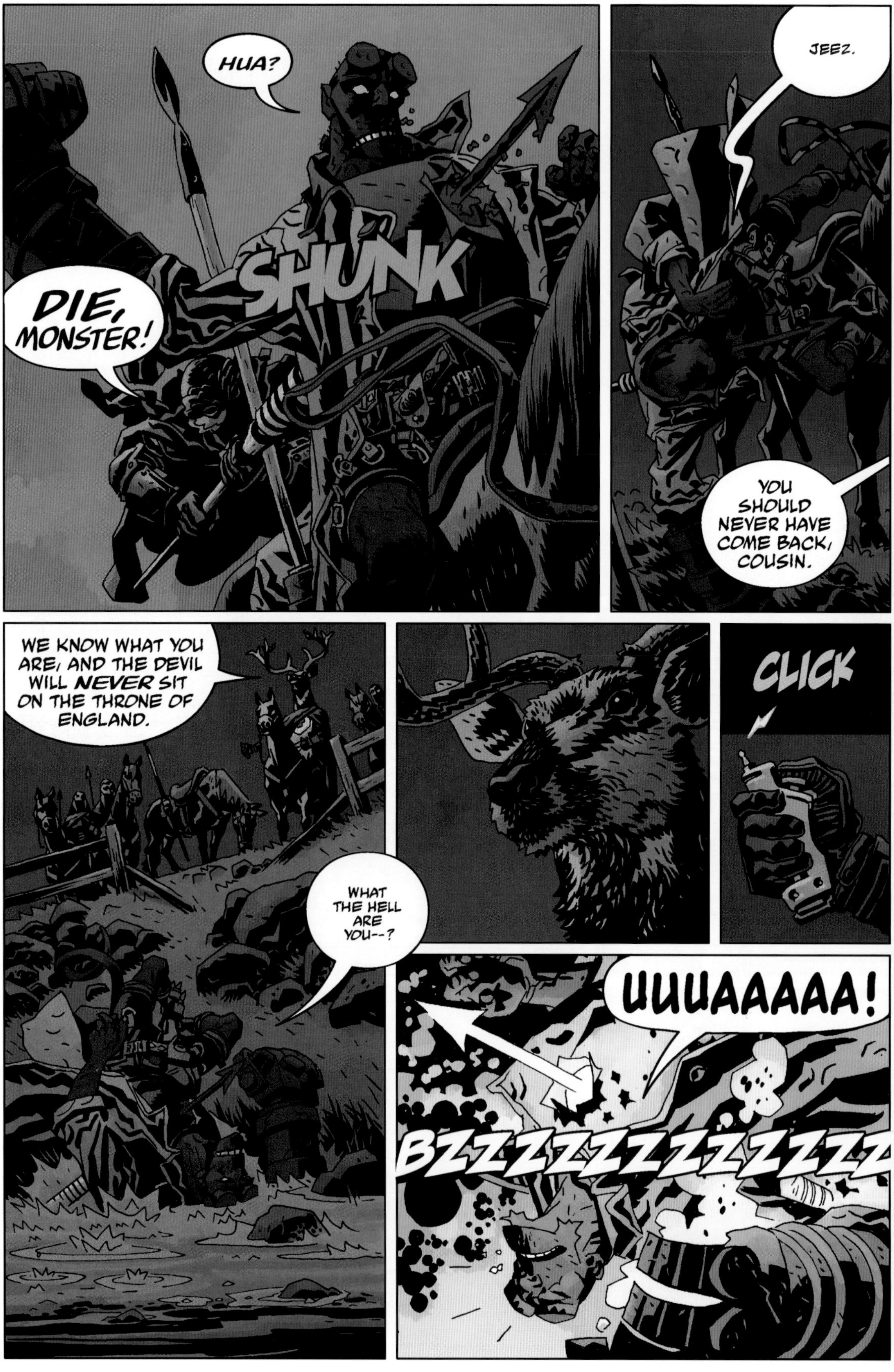
HUA?
SHUNK
DIE, MONSTER!
JEEZ.
YOU SHOULD NEVER HAVE COME BACK, COUSIN.
WE KNOW WHAT YOU ARE, AND THE DEVIL WILL NEVER SIT ON THE THRONE OF ENGLAND.
WHAT THE HELL ARE YOU--?
CLICK
UUUAAAAA!
BZZZZZZZZZZZZZ

Chapter Two

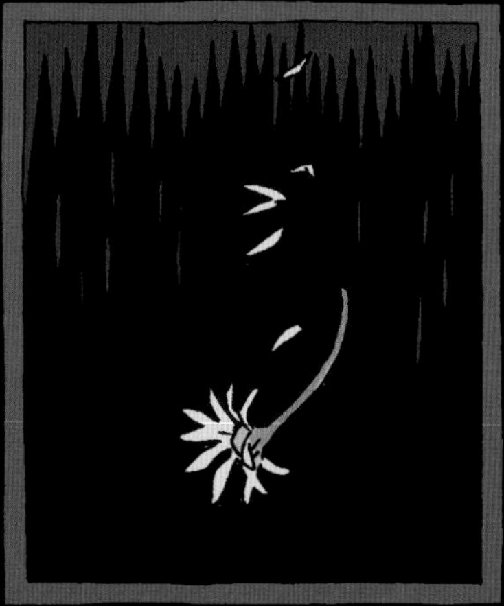

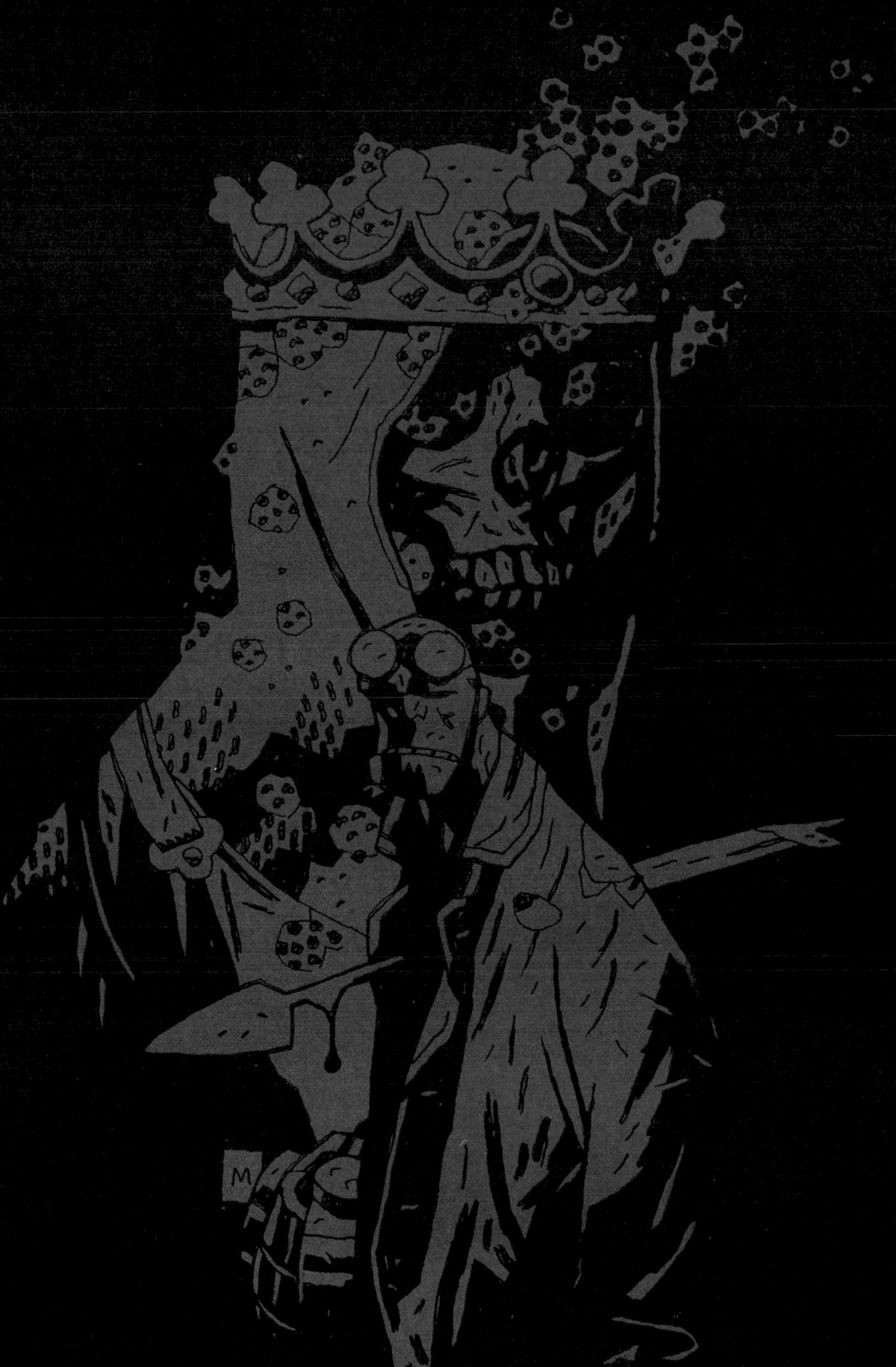

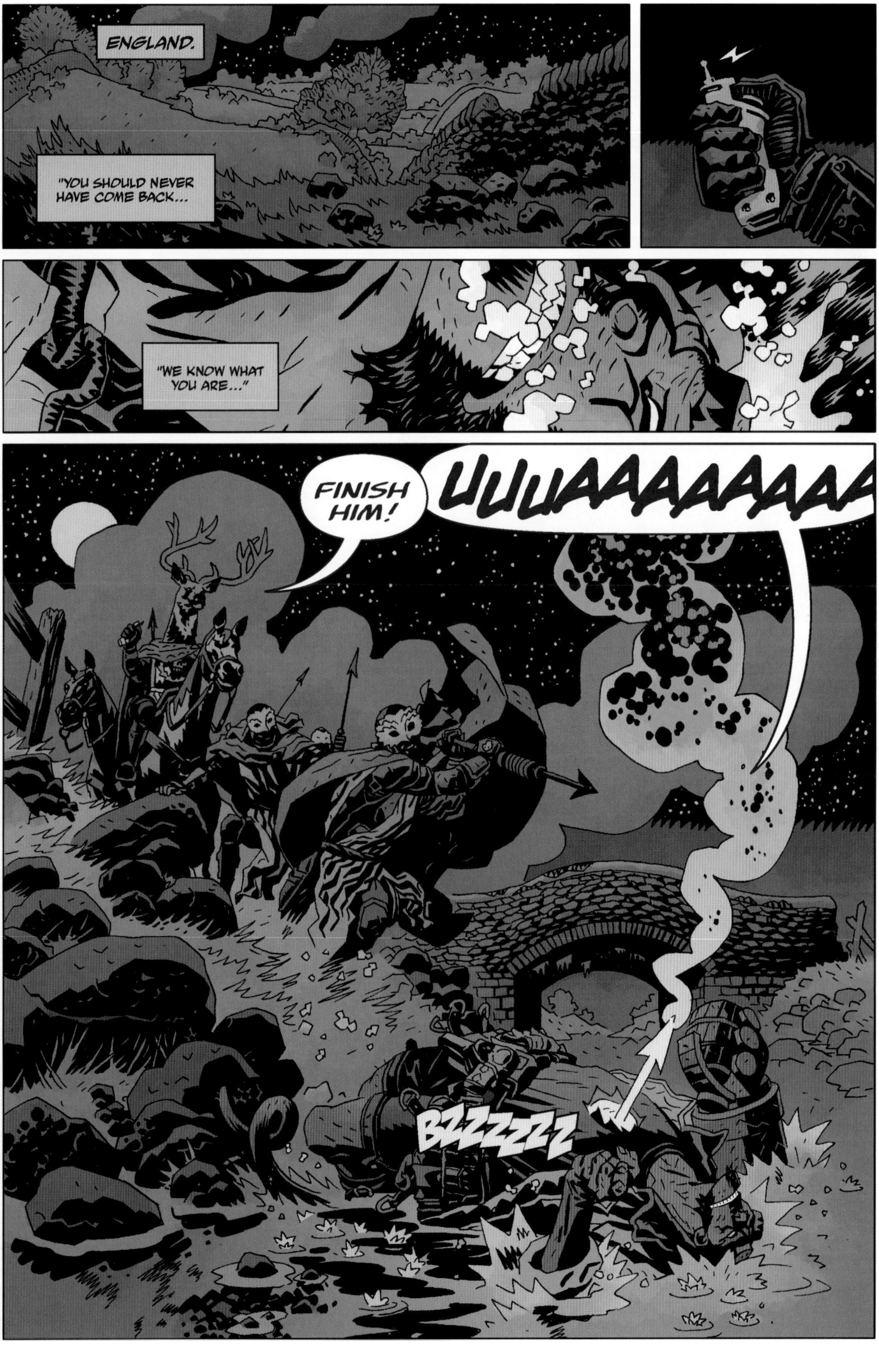
ENGLAND.
"YOU SHOULD NEVER HAVE COME BACK...
"WE KNOW WHAT YOU ARE..."
FINISH HIM!
UUUAAAAAAAAA
BZZZZZZ

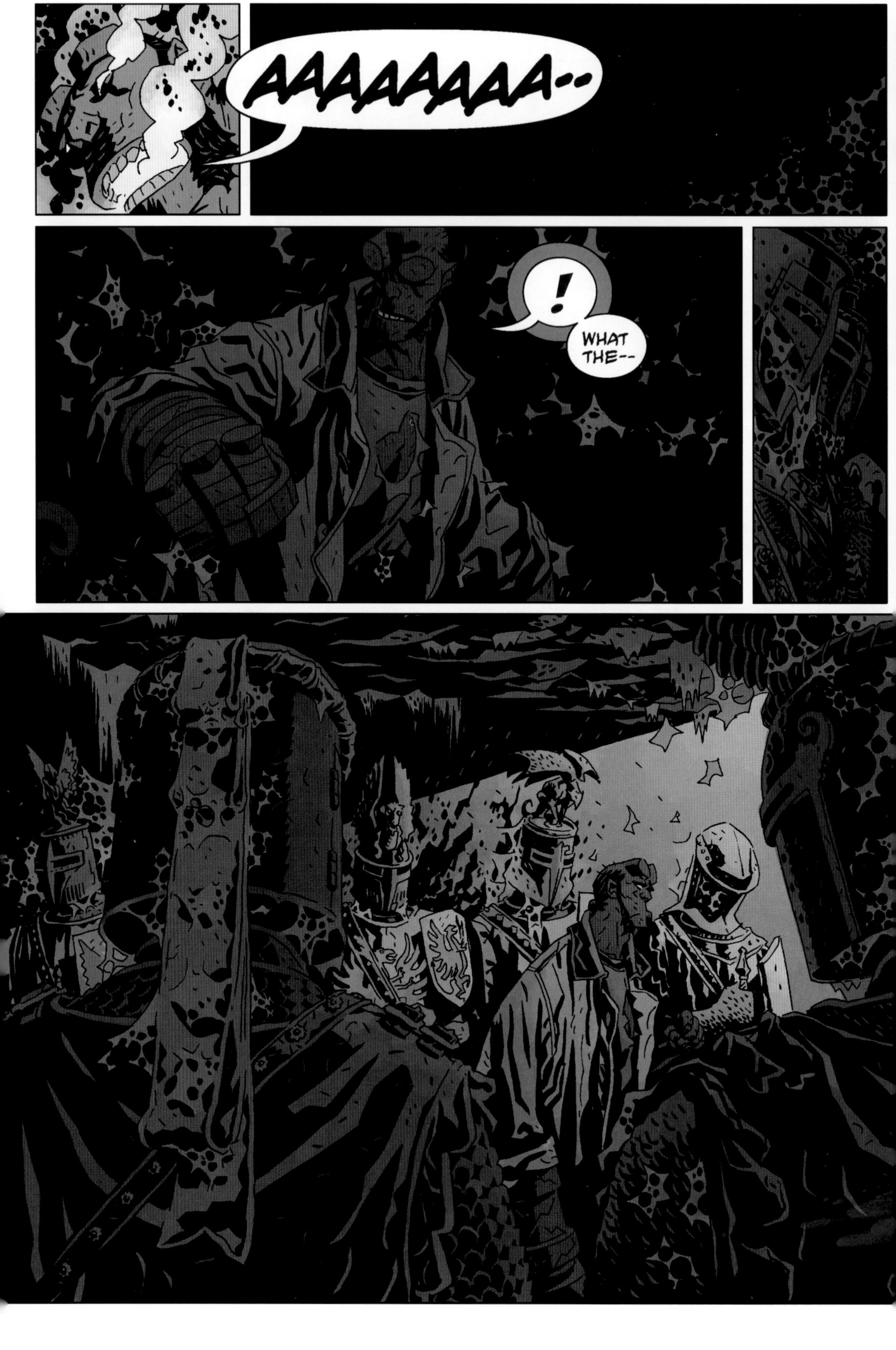
AAAAAAAA--
!
WHAT THE--

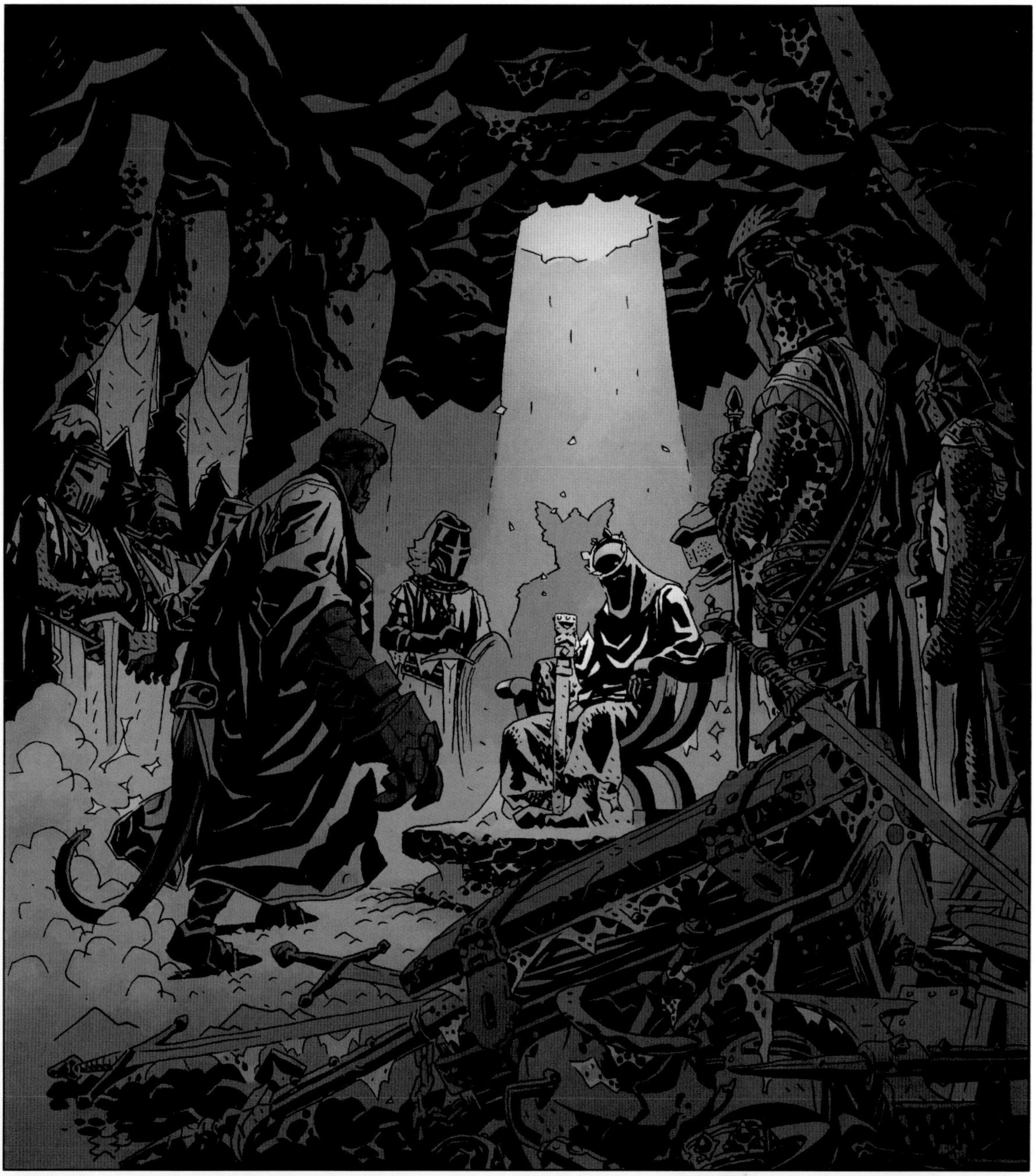

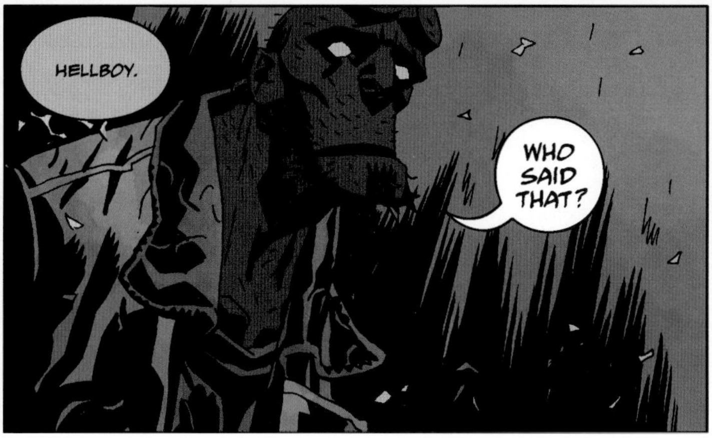
HELLBOY.
WHO SAID THAT?

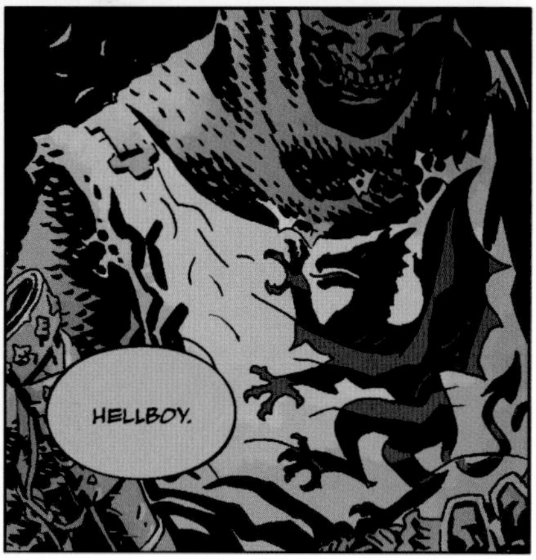
HELLBOY.

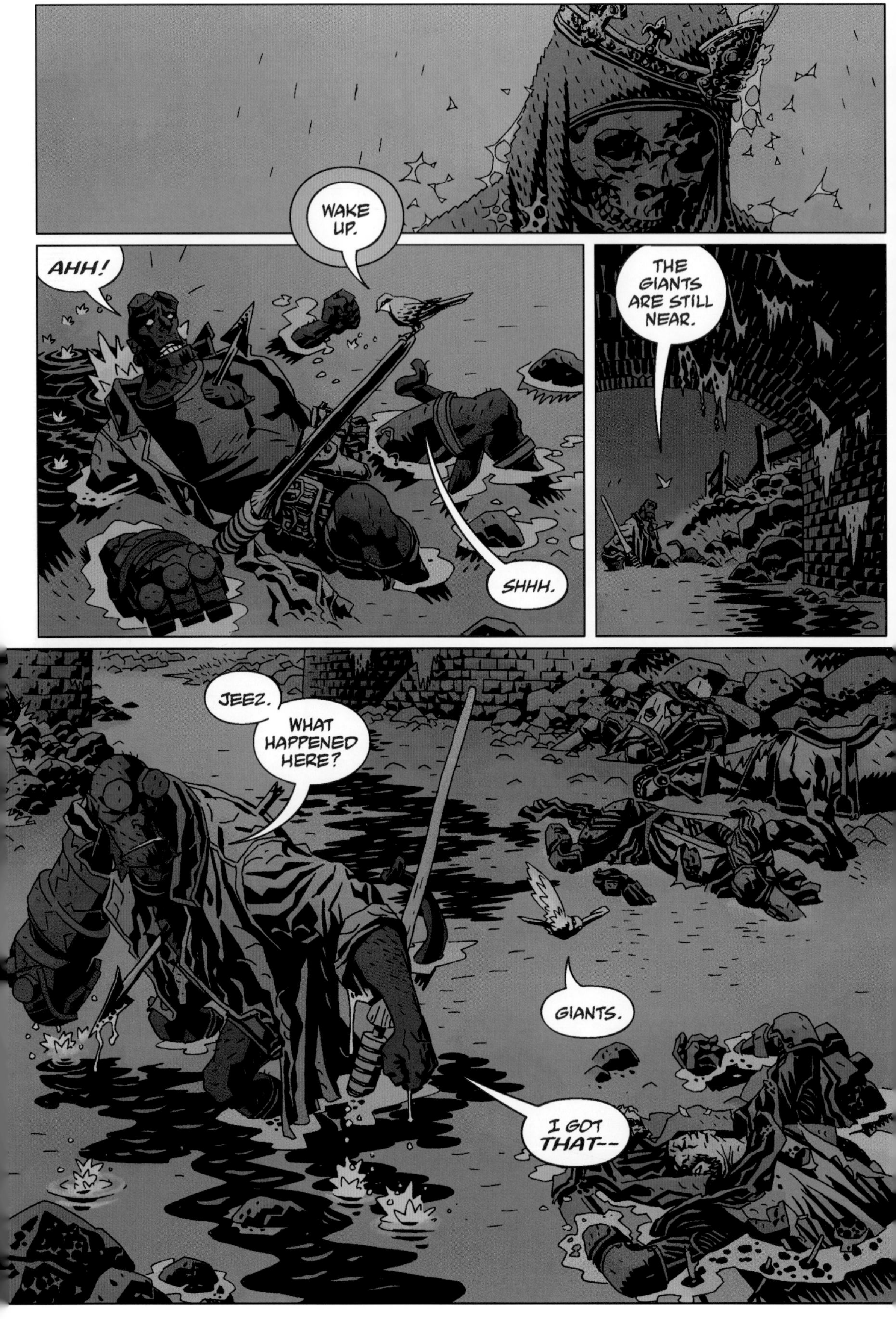
WAKE UP.
AHH!
SHHH.
THE GIANTS ARE STILL NEAR.
JEEZ.
WHAT HAPPENED HERE?
GIANTS.
I GOT THAT--

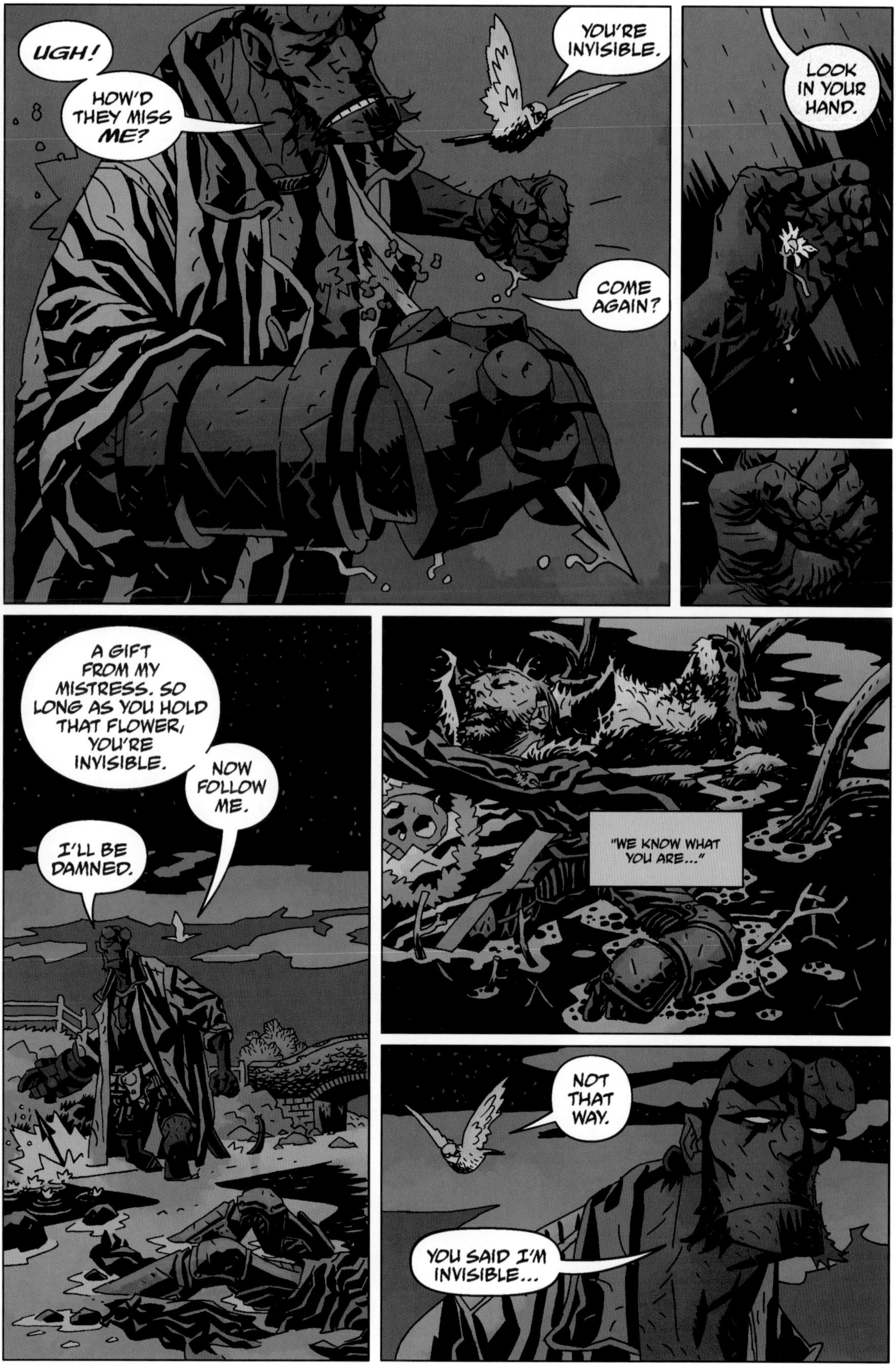
UGH!
HOW'D THEY MISS ME?
YOU'RE INVISIBLE.
COME AGAIN?
LOOK IN YOUR HAND.
A GIFT FROM MY MISTRESS. SO LONG AS YOU HOLD THAT FLOWER, YOU'RE INVISIBLE.
NOW FOLLOW ME.
I'LL BE DAMNED.
"WE KNOW WHAT YOU ARE..."
NOT THAT WAY.
YOU SAID I'M INVISIBLE...

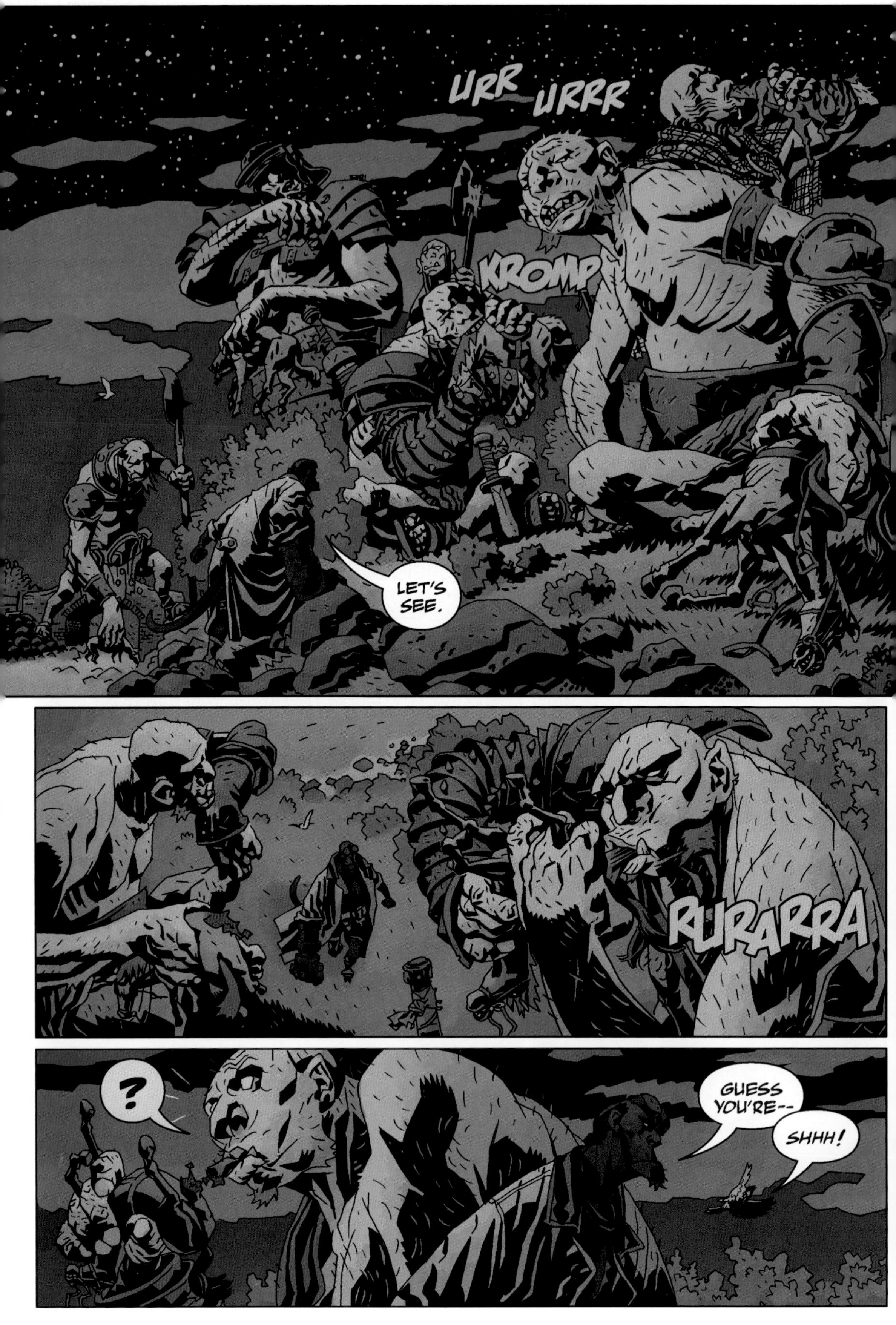
URR URRR
KROMP
LET'S SEE.
RURARRA
?
GUESS YOU'RE--
SHHH!

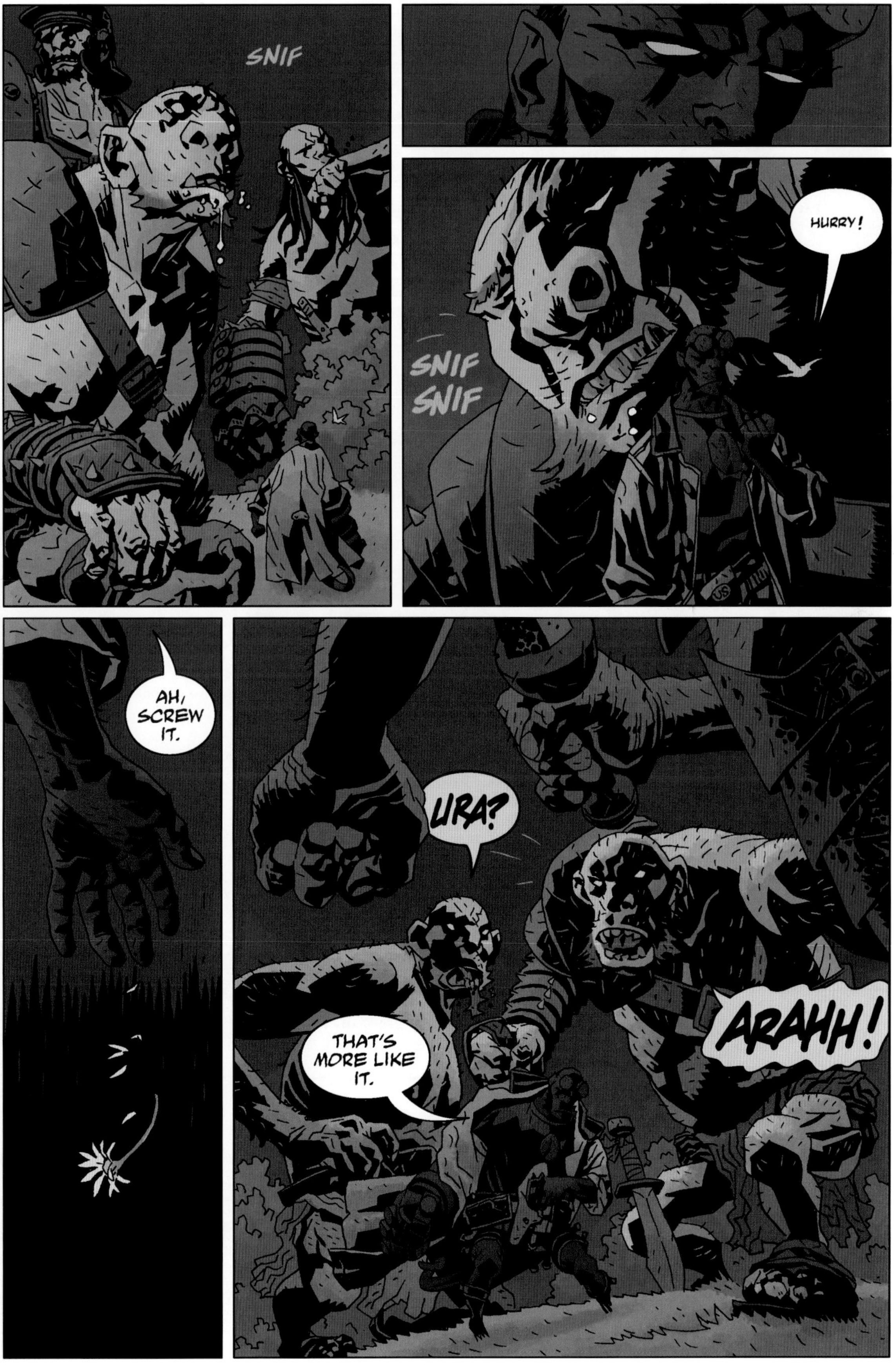
SNIF
SNIF
SNIF
HURRY!
AH, SCREW IT.
URA?
ARAHH!
THAT'S MORE LIKE IT.

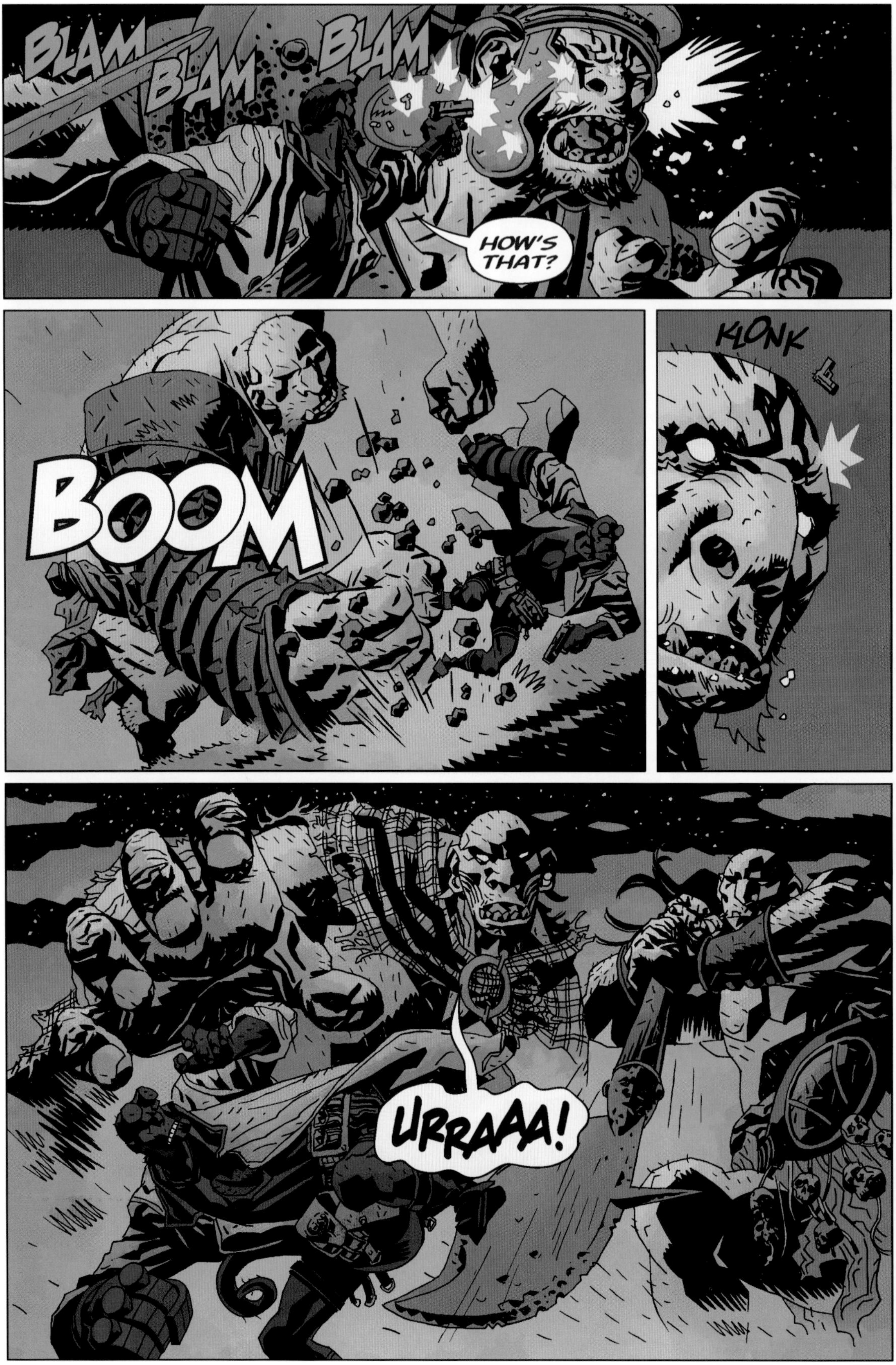
BLAM
BLAM
BLAM
HOW'S THAT?
BOOM
KLONK
URRAAA!

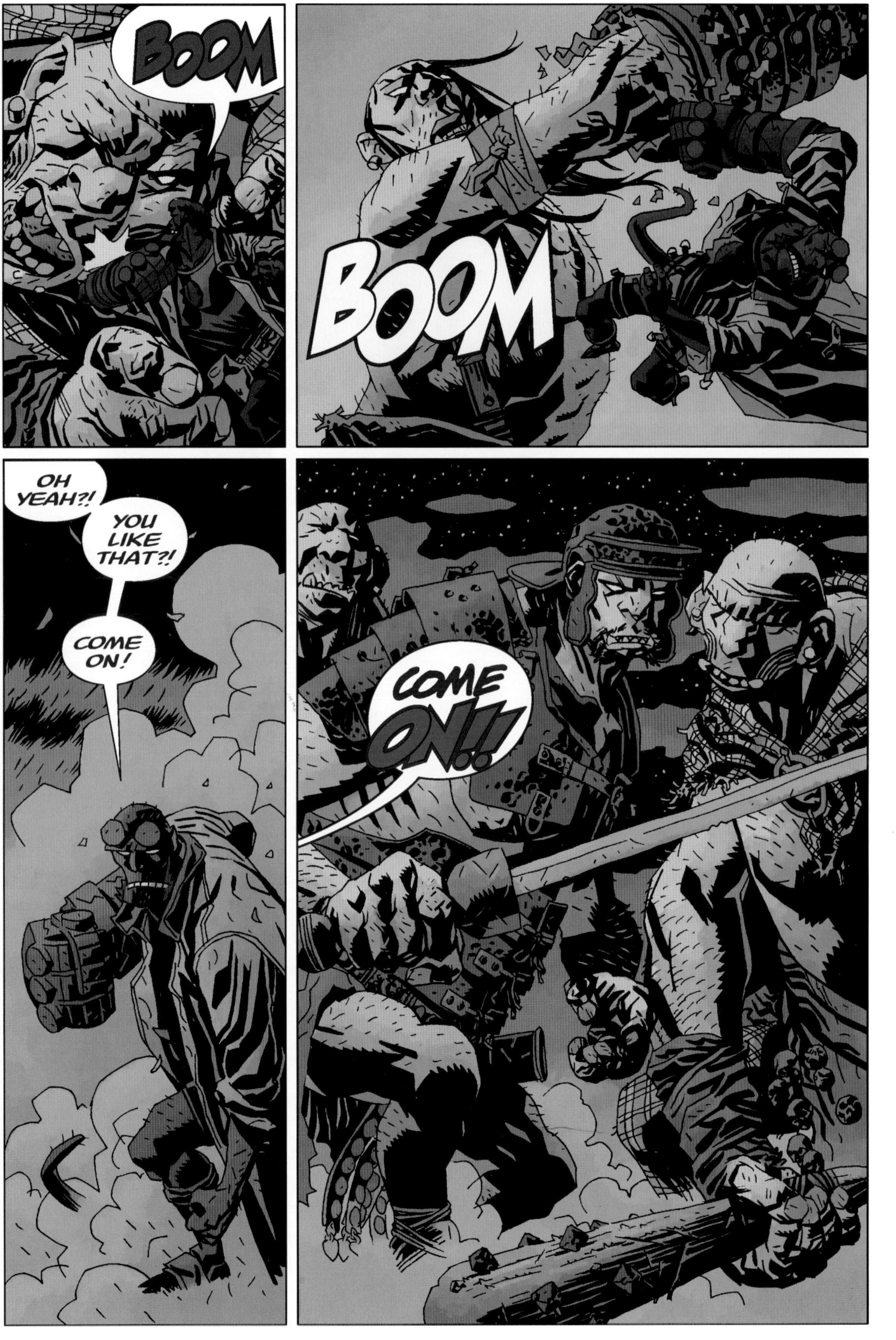
BOOM
BOOM
OH YEAH?!
YOU LIKE THAT?!
COME ON!
COME ON!!

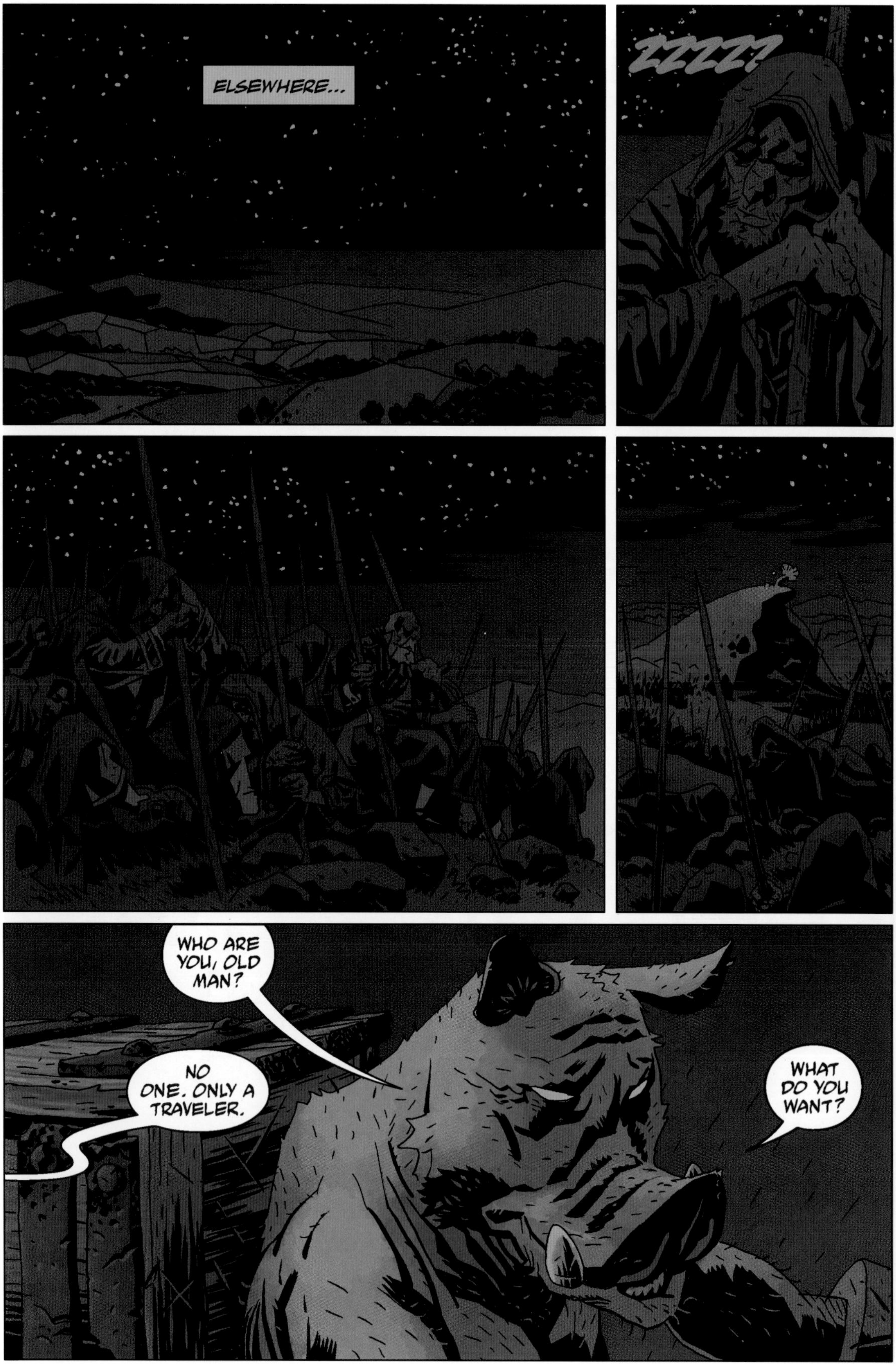
ELSEWHERE...
ZZZZZ?
WHO ARE YOU, OLD MAN?
NO ONE. ONLY A TRAVELER.
WHAT DO YOU WANT?

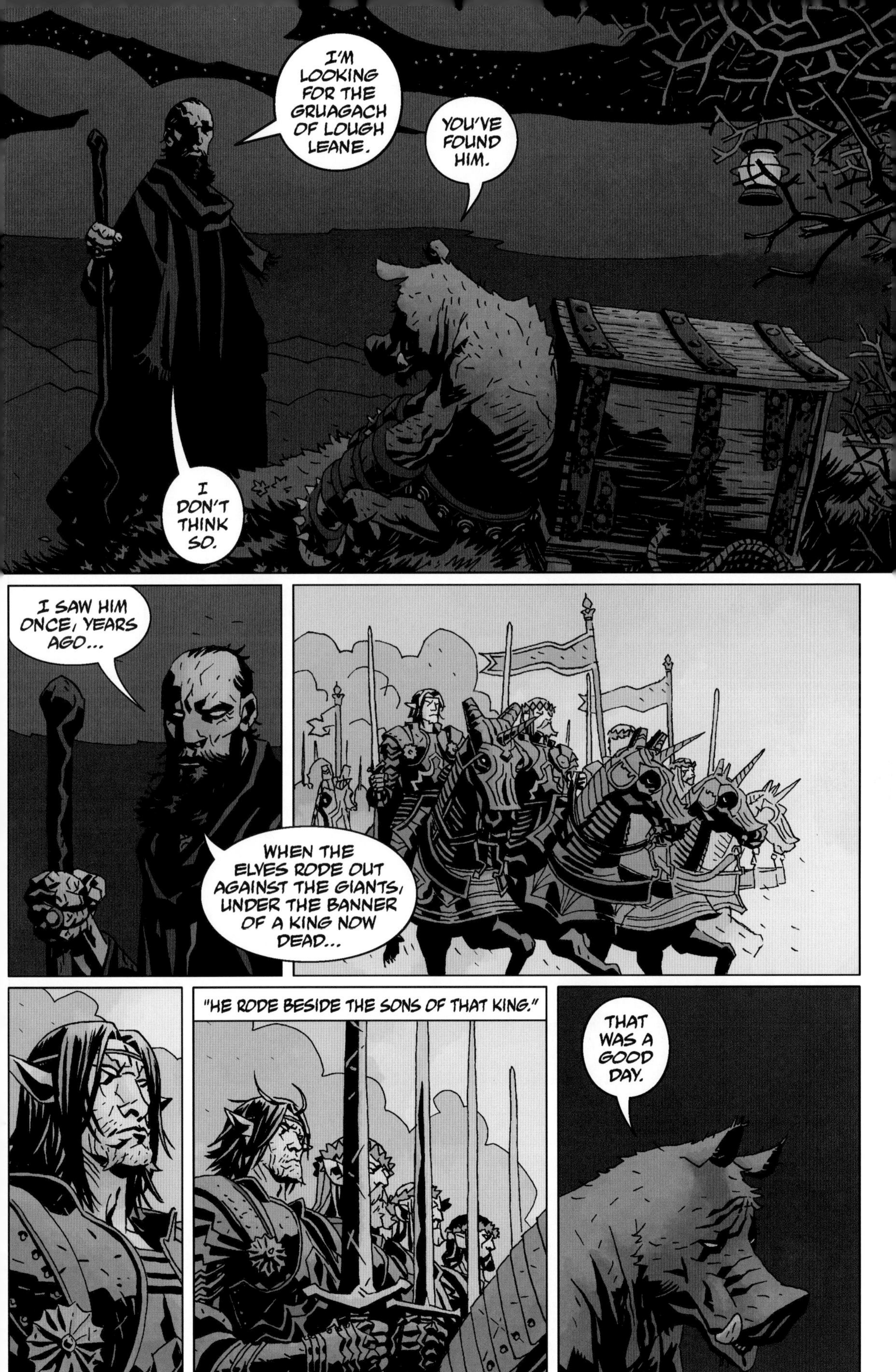
I'M LOOKING FOR THE GRUAGACH OF LOUGH LEANE.
YOU'VE FOUND HIM.
I DON'T THINK SO.
I SAW HIM ONCE, YEARS AGO...
WHEN THE ELVES RODE OUT AGAINST THE GIANTS, UNDER THE BANNER OF A KING NOW DEAD...
"HE RODE BESIDE THE SONS OF THAT KING."
THAT WAS A GOOD DAY.

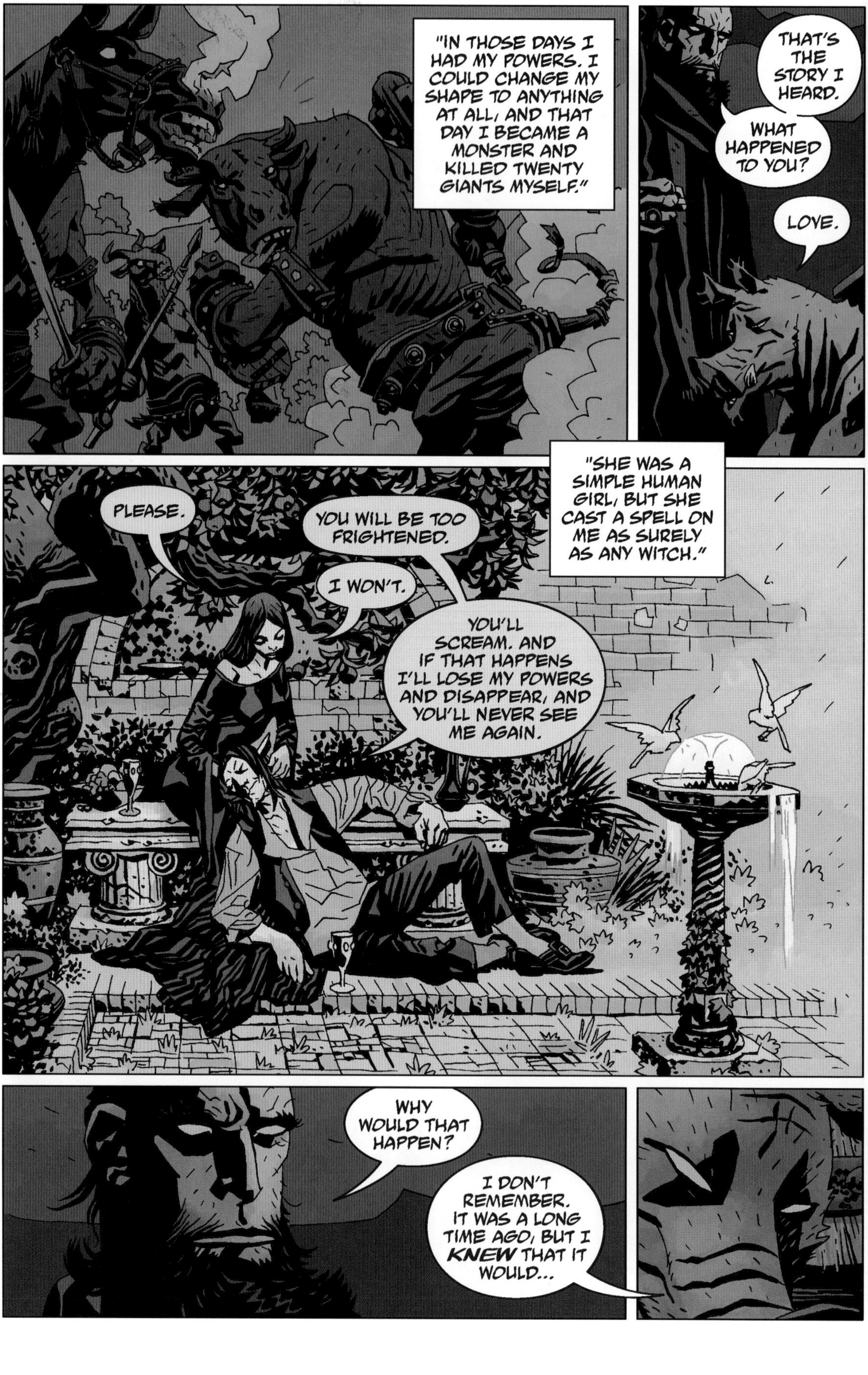
"IN THOSE DAYS I HAD MY POWERS. I COULD CHANGE MY SHAPE TO ANYTHING AT ALL, AND THAT DAY I BECAME A MONSTER AND KILLED TWENTY GIANTS MYSELF."
THAT'S THE STORY I HEARD.
WHAT HAPPENED TO YOU?
LOVE.
"SHE WAS A SIMPLE HUMAN GIRL, BUT SHE CAST A SPELL ON ME AS SURELY AS ANY WITCH."
PLEASE.
YOU WILL BE TOO FRIGHTENED.
I WON'T.
YOU'LL SCREAM. AND IF THAT HAPPENS I'LL LOSE MY POWERS AND DISAPPEAR, AND YOU'LL NEVER SEE ME AGAIN.
WHY WOULD THAT HAPPEN?
I DON'T REMEMBER. IT WAS A LONG TIME AGO, BUT I KNEW THAT IT WOULD...

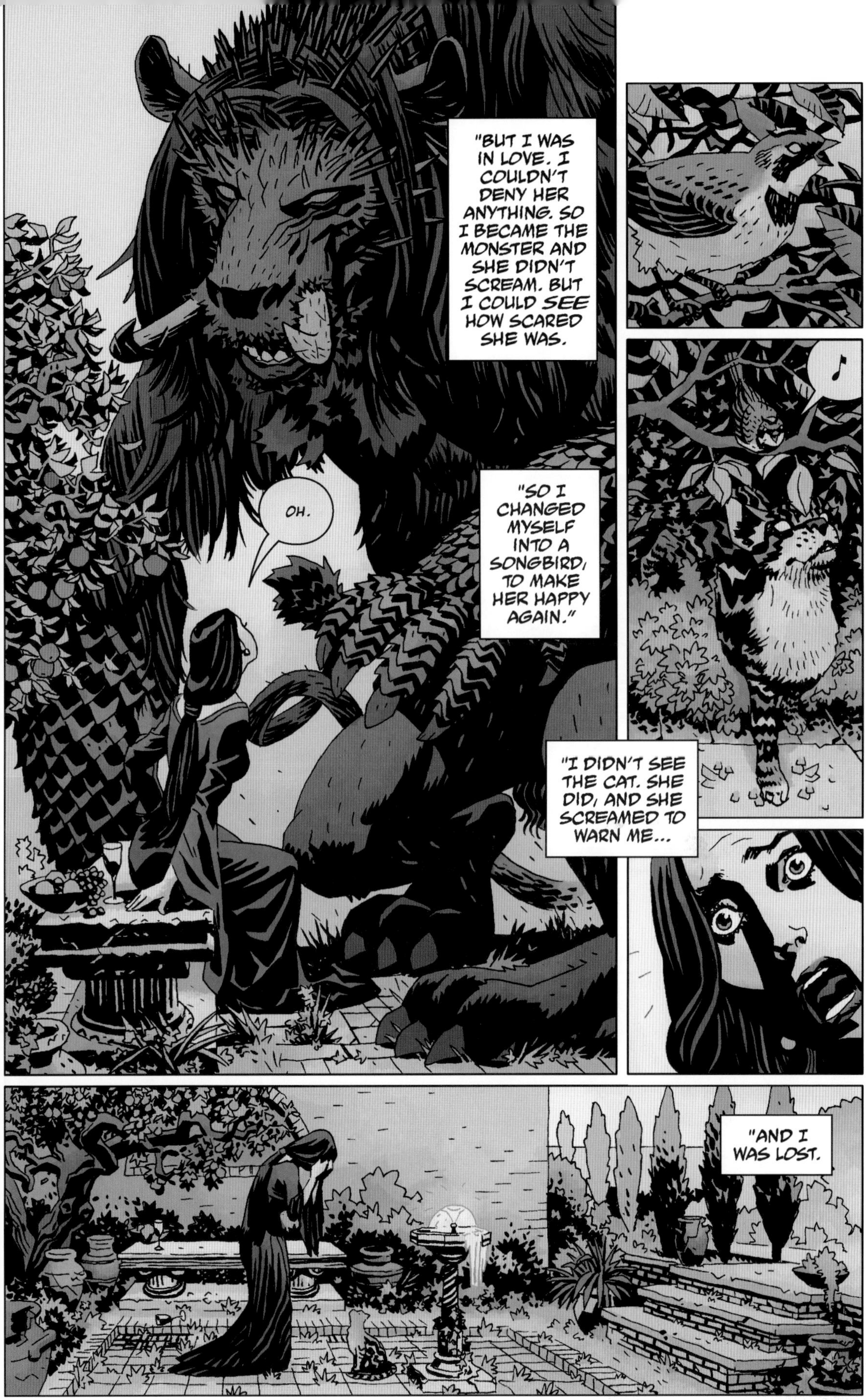
"BUT I WAS IN LOVE. I COULDN'T DENY HER ANYTHING. SO I BECAME THE MONSTER AND SHE DIDN'T SCREAM. BUT I COULD SEE HOW SCARED SHE WAS.
OH.
"SO I CHANGED MYSELF INTO A SONGBIRD, TO MAKE HER HAPPY AGAIN."
♪
"I DIDN'T SEE THE CAT. SHE DID, AND SHE SCREAMED TO WARN ME...
"AND I WAS LOST.

"I WANDERED ALONE IN THE DARK FOR A LONG, LONG TIME...

"...TILL I NEARLY FORGOT MYSELF. THEN I STUMBLED BACK INTO THE WORLD...

"AND WITH THE LAST SCRAP OF MY POWER I TOOK THE SHAPE OF A HUMAN BABY SO A REAL ONE COULD BE STOLEN.

"I DON'T REMEMBER WHY.

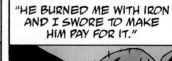

"BUT IT WASN'T FOR LONG...

"I WAS FOUND OUT BY THE CREATURE HELL-BOY. YOU'VE HEARD OF HIM?"

WHERE'S THAT BABY?

SQUEEE

"I HAVE."

"HE BURNED ME WITH IRON AND I SWORE TO MAKE HIM PAY FOR IT."

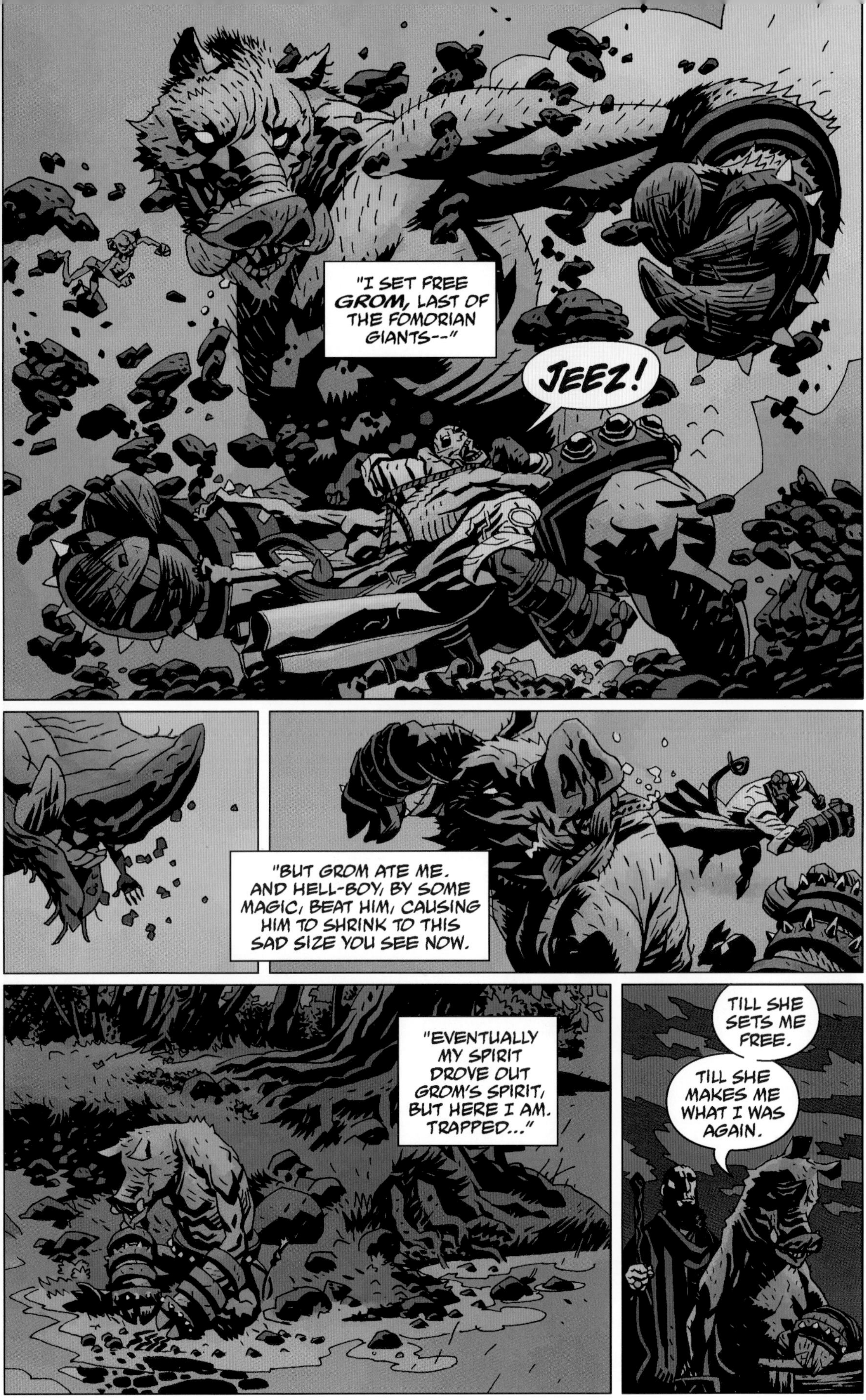
"I SET FREE GROM, LAST OF THE FOMORIAN GIANTS--"
JEEZ!
"BUT GROM ATE ME. AND HELL-BOY, BY SOME MAGIC, BEAT HIM, CAUSING HIM TO SHRINK TO THIS SAD SIZE YOU SEE NOW.
"EVENTUALLY MY SPIRIT DROVE OUT GROM'S SPIRIT, BUT HERE I AM. TRAPPED..."
TILL SHE SETS ME FREE.
TILL SHE MAKES ME WHAT I WAS AGAIN.

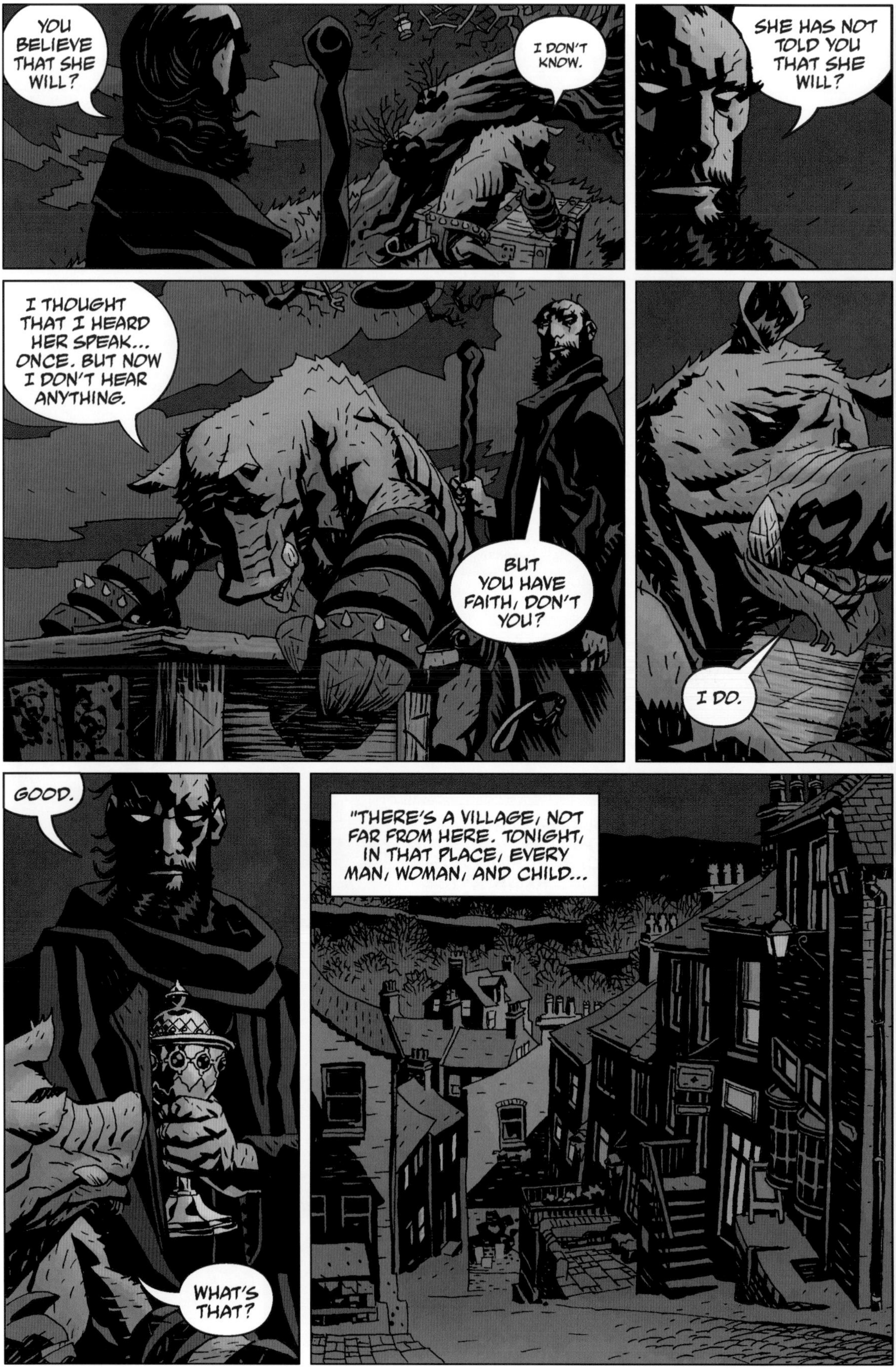
YOU BELIEVE THAT SHE WILL?
I DON'T KNOW.
SHE HAS NOT TOLD YOU THAT SHE WILL?
I THOUGHT THAT I HEARD HER SPEAK... ONCE. BUT NOW I DON'T HEAR ANYTHING.
BUT YOU HAVE FAITH, DON'T YOU?
I DO.
GOOD.
WHAT'S THAT?
"THERE'S A VILLAGE, NOT FAR FROM HERE. TONIGHT, IN THAT PLACE, EVERY MAN, WOMAN, AND CHILD...

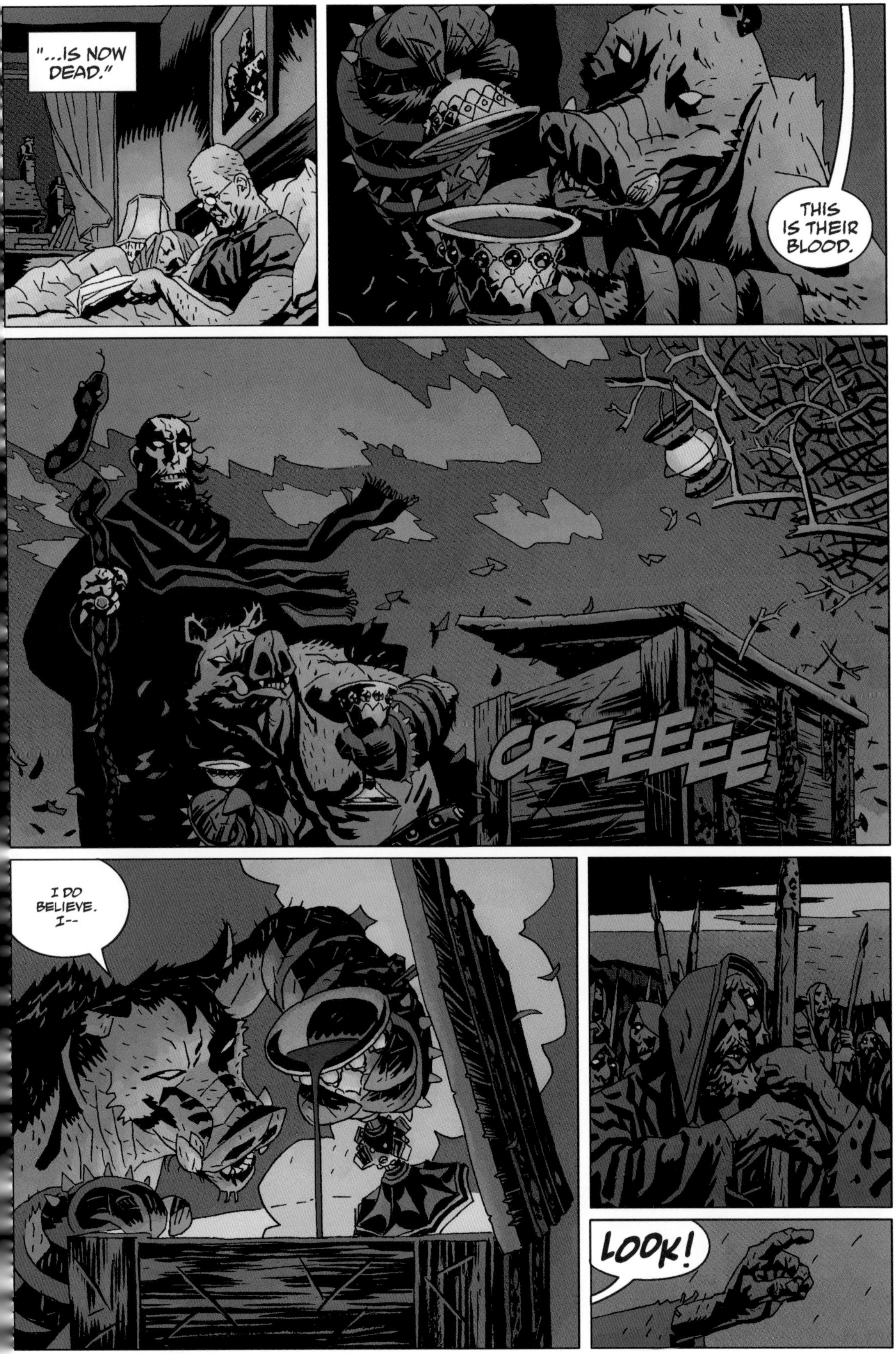
"...IS NOW DEAD."
THIS IS THEIR BLOOD.
CREEEEE
I DO BELIEVE. I--
LOOK!

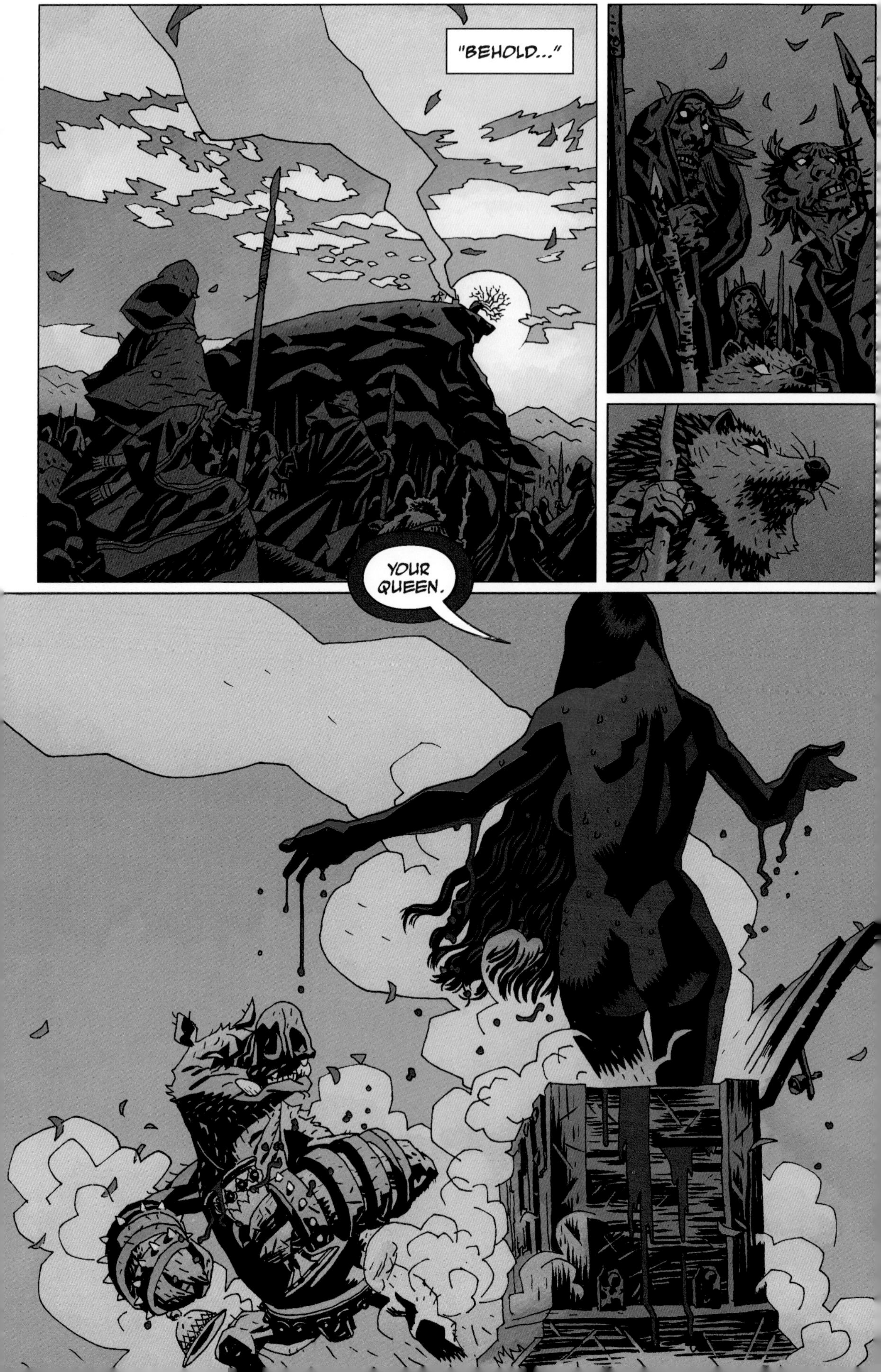
"BEHOLD..."
YOUR QUEEN.

CHAPTER THREE

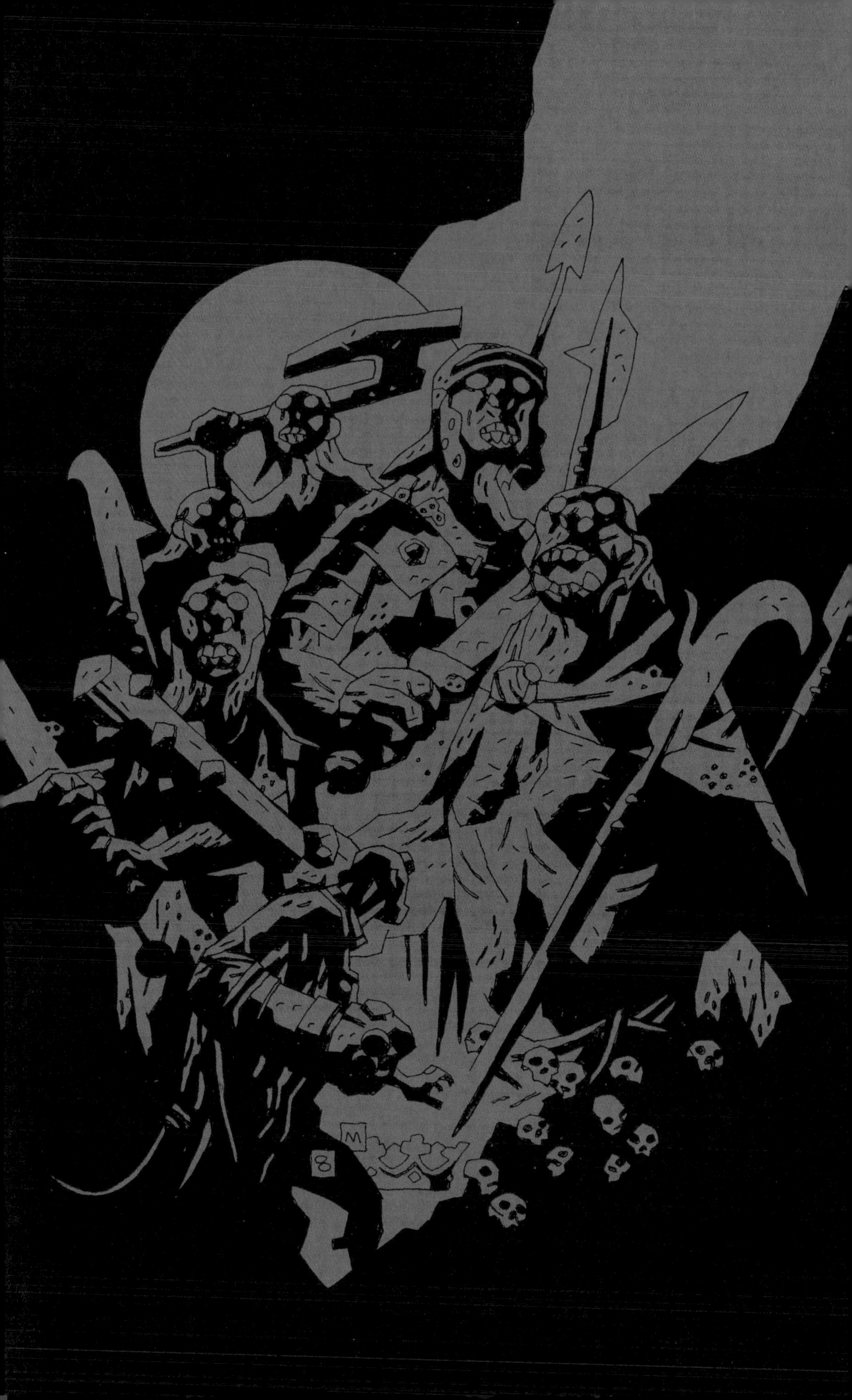

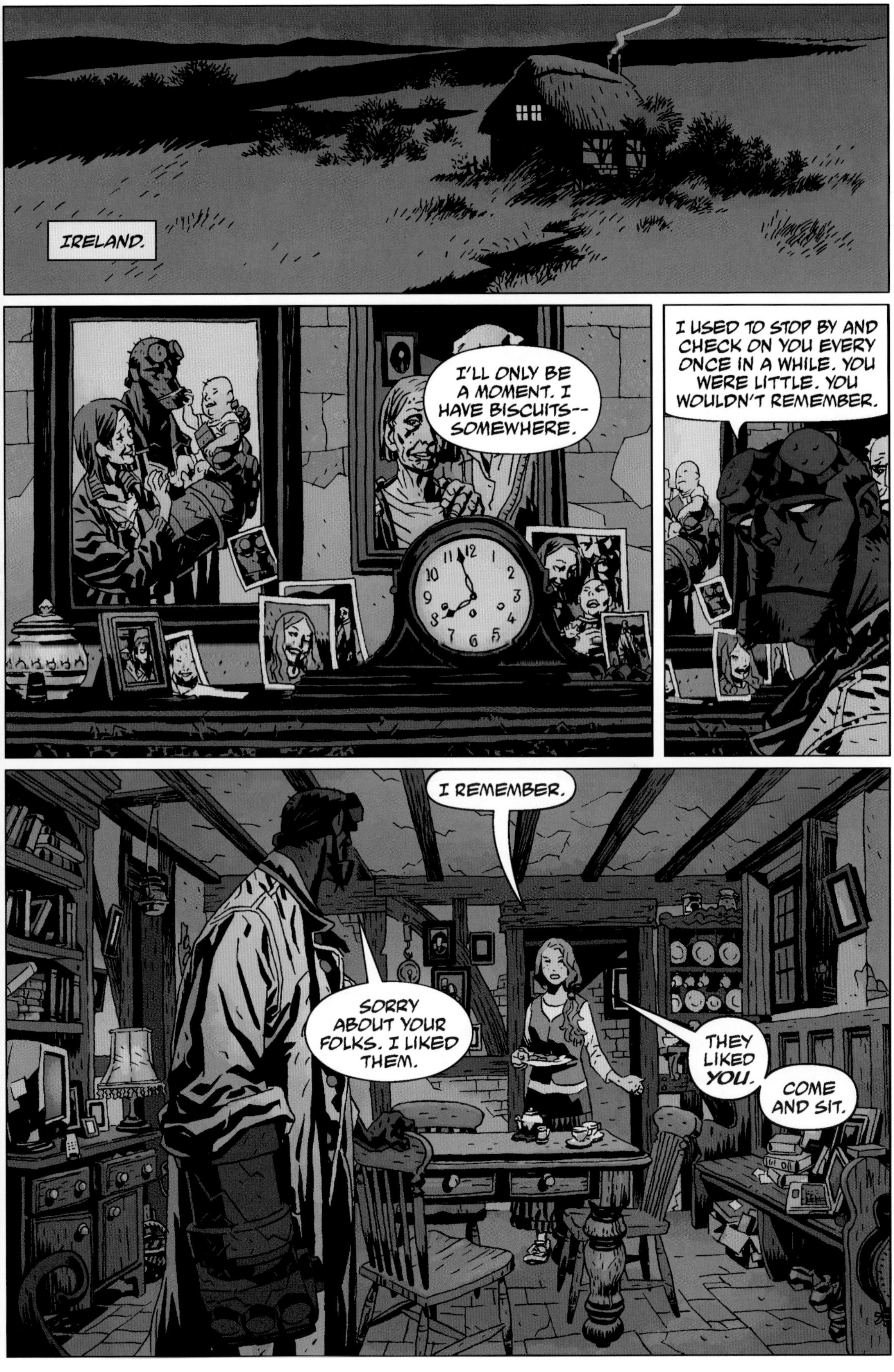
IRELAND.
I'LL ONLY BE A MOMENT. I HAVE BISCUITS-- SOMEWHERE.
I USED TO STOP BY AND CHECK ON YOU EVERY ONCE IN A WHILE. YOU WERE LITTLE. YOU WOULDN'T REMEMBER.
I REMEMBER.
SORRY ABOUT YOUR FOLKS. I LIKED THEM.
THEY LIKED *YOU*.
COME AND SIT.

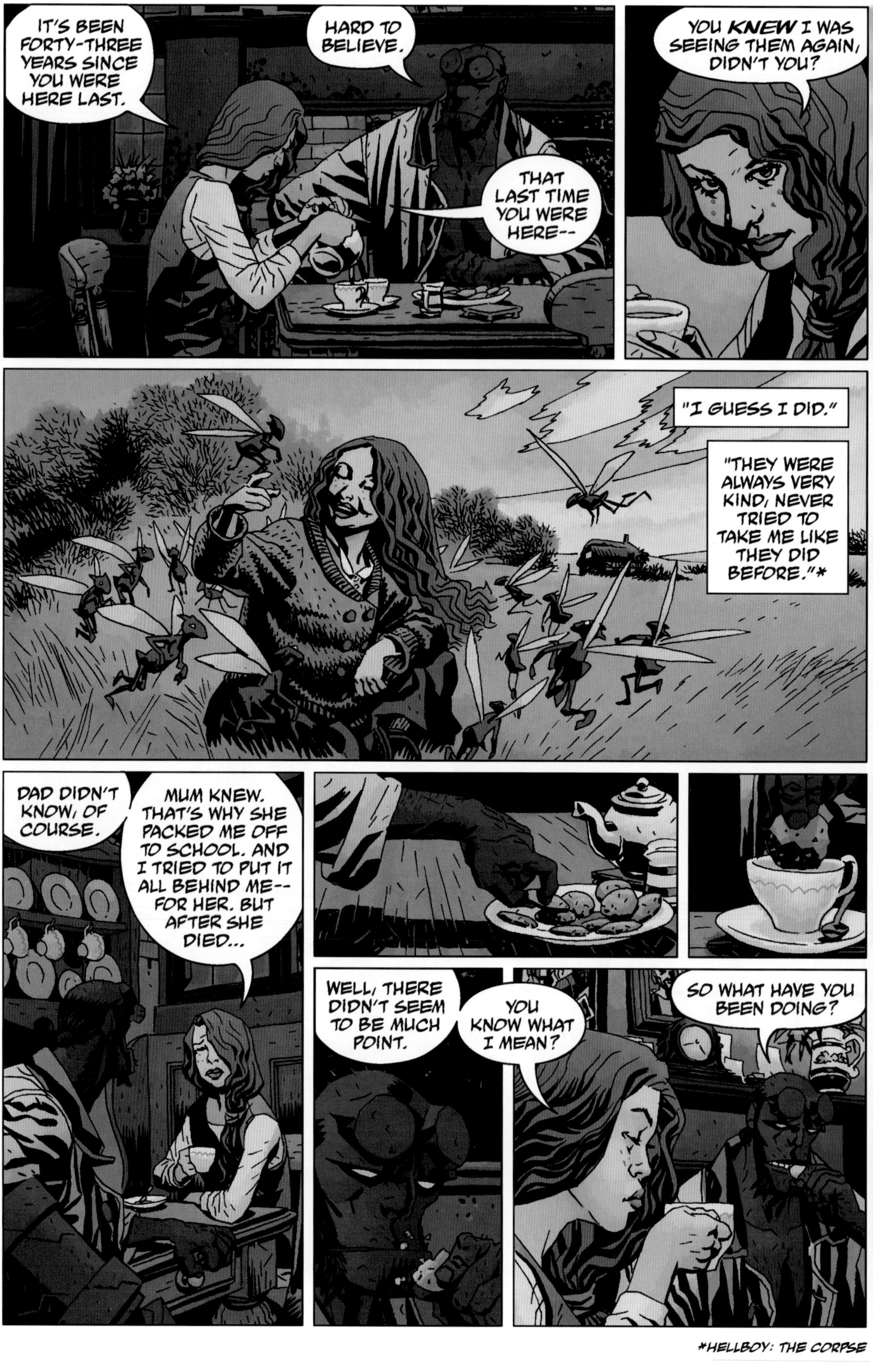
IT'S BEEN FORTY-THREE YEARS SINCE YOU WERE HERE LAST.
HARD TO BELIEVE.
THAT LAST TIME YOU WERE HERE--
YOU KNEW I WAS SEEING THEM AGAIN, DIDN'T YOU?
"I GUESS I DID."
"THEY WERE ALWAYS VERY KIND, NEVER TRIED TO TAKE ME LIKE THEY DID BEFORE."*
DAD DIDN'T KNOW, OF COURSE.
MUM KNEW. THAT'S WHY SHE PACKED ME OFF TO SCHOOL. AND I TRIED TO PUT IT ALL BEHIND ME-- FOR HER. BUT AFTER SHE DIED...
WELL, THERE DIDN'T SEEM TO BE MUCH POINT.
YOU KNOW WHAT I MEAN?
SO WHAT HAVE YOU BEEN DOING?

*HELLBOY: THE CORPSE

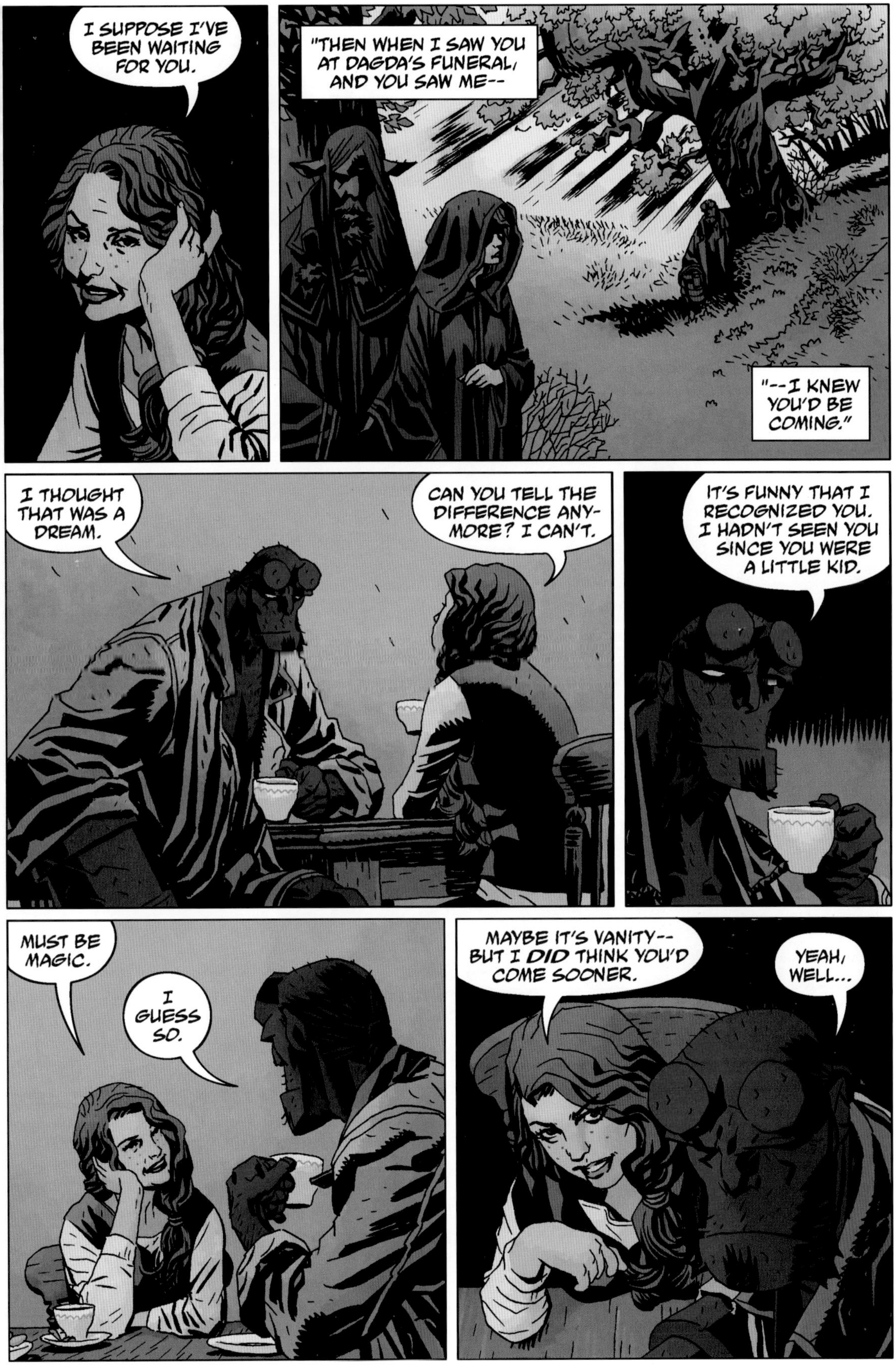
I SUPPOSE I'VE BEEN WAITING FOR YOU.
"THEN WHEN I SAW YOU AT DAGDA'S FUNERAL, AND YOU SAW ME--
"--I KNEW YOU'D BE COMING."
I THOUGHT THAT WAS A DREAM.
CAN YOU TELL THE DIFFERENCE ANY-MORE? I CAN'T.
IT'S FUNNY THAT I RECOGNIZED YOU. I HADN'T SEEN YOU SINCE YOU WERE A LITTLE KID.
MUST BE MAGIC.
I GUESS SO.
MAYBE IT'S VANITY-- BUT I ***DID*** THINK YOU'D COME SOONER.
YEAH, WELL...

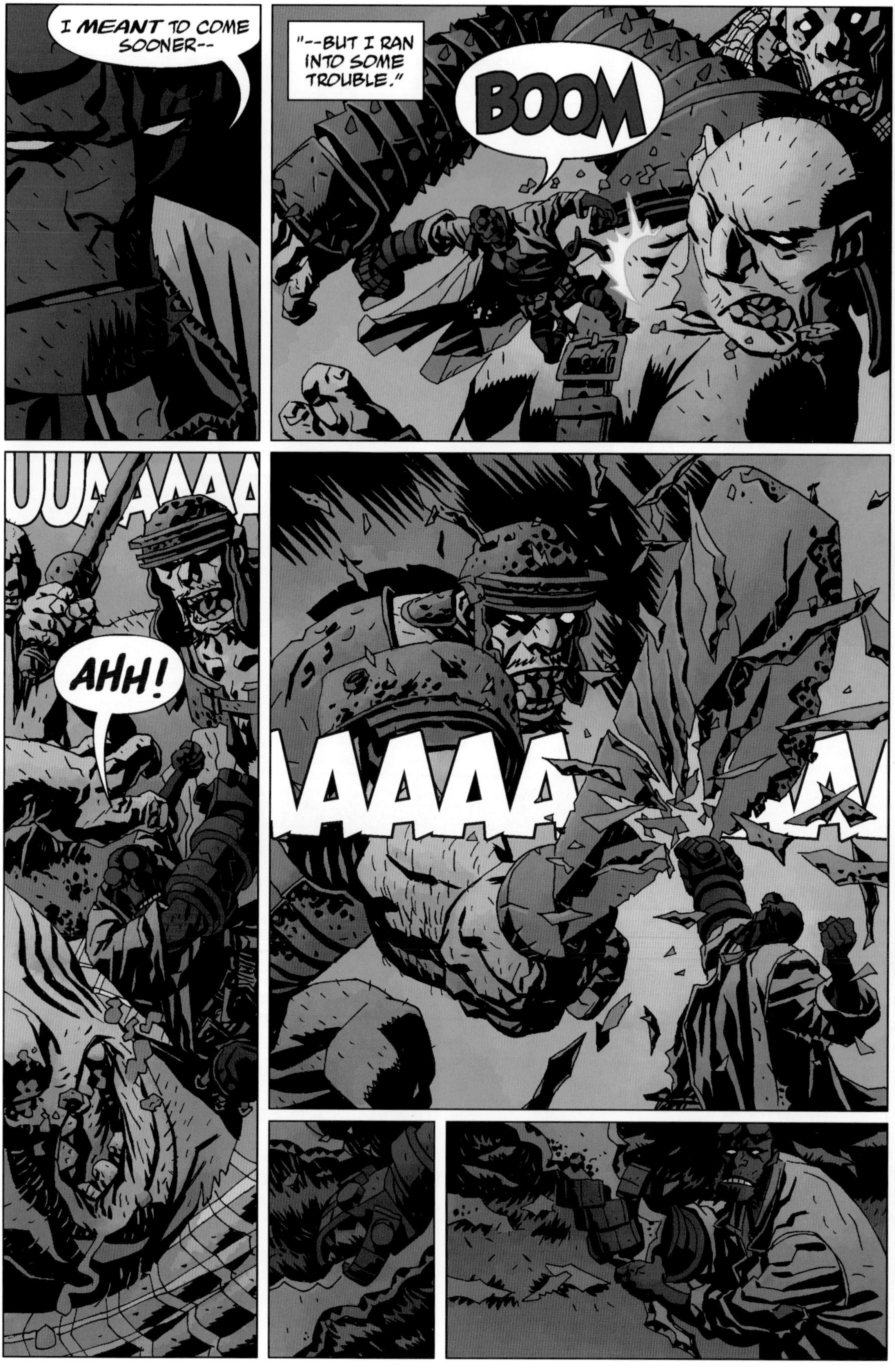
I MEANT TO COME SOONER--
"--BUT I RAN INTO SOME TROUBLE."
BOOM
UUAAAAA
AHH!
AAAAAAA

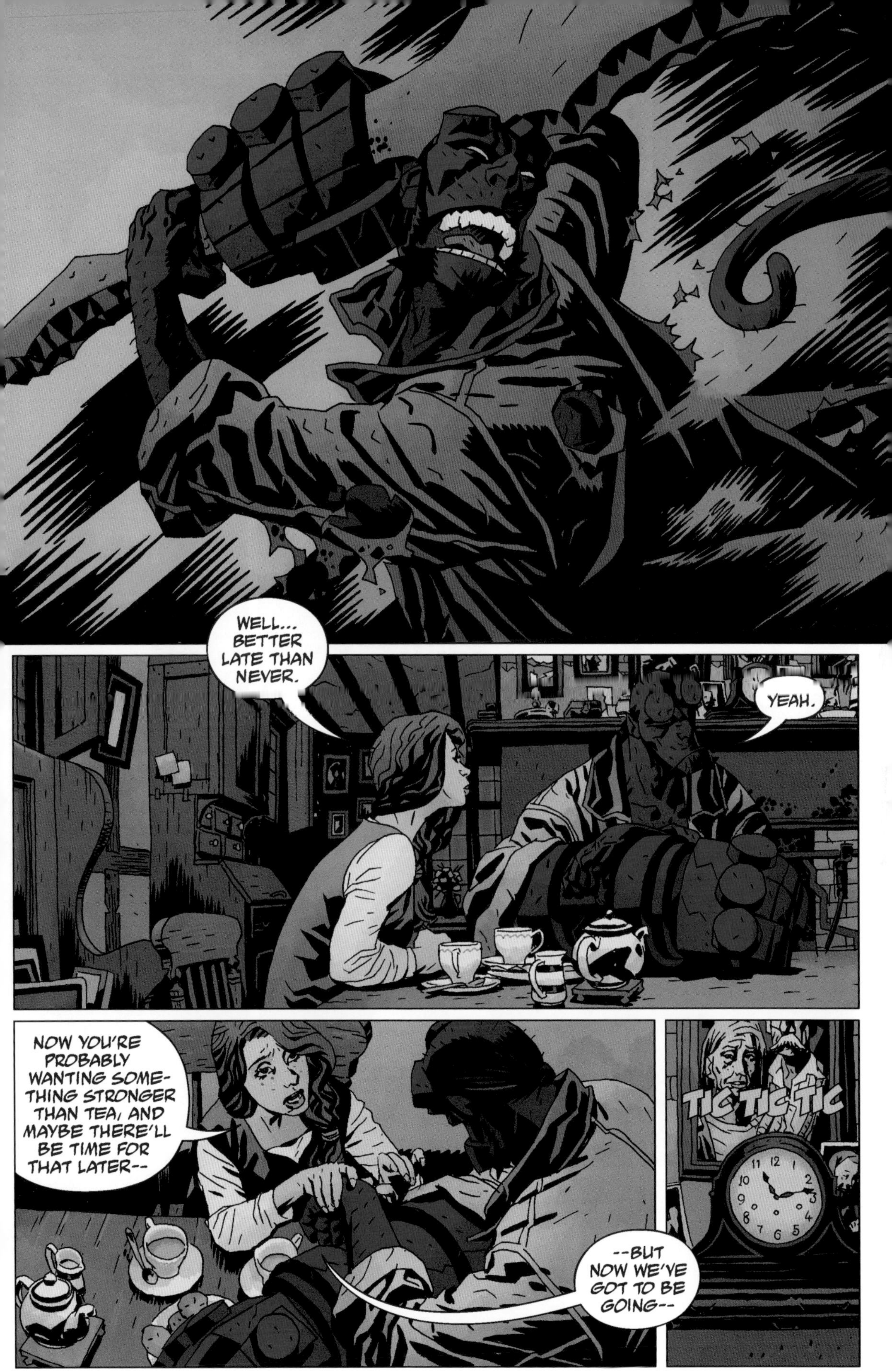
WELL... BETTER LATE THAN NEVER.
YEAH.
NOW YOU'RE PROBABLY WANTING SOME-THING STRONGER THAN TEA, AND MAYBE THERE'LL BE TIME FOR THAT LATER--
--BUT NOW WE'VE GOT TO BE GOING--
TIC TIC TIC

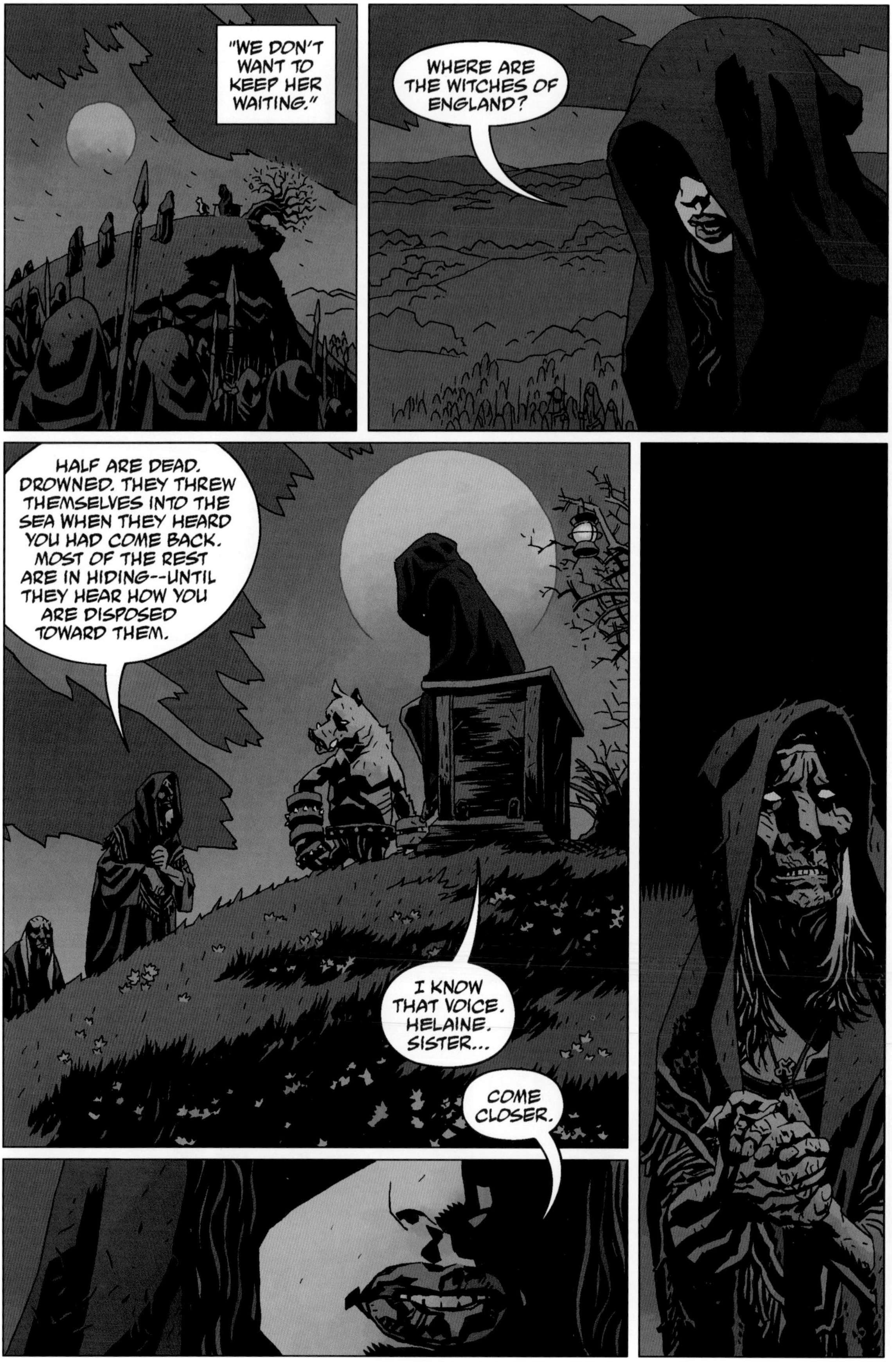
"WE DON'T WANT TO KEEP HER WAITING."
WHERE ARE THE WITCHES OF ENGLAND?
HALF ARE DEAD. DROWNED. THEY THREW THEMSELVES INTO THE SEA WHEN THEY HEARD YOU HAD COME BACK. MOST OF THE REST ARE IN HIDING--UNTIL THEY HEAR HOW YOU ARE DISPOSED TOWARD THEM.
I KNOW THAT VOICE. HELAINE. SISTER...
COME CLOSER.

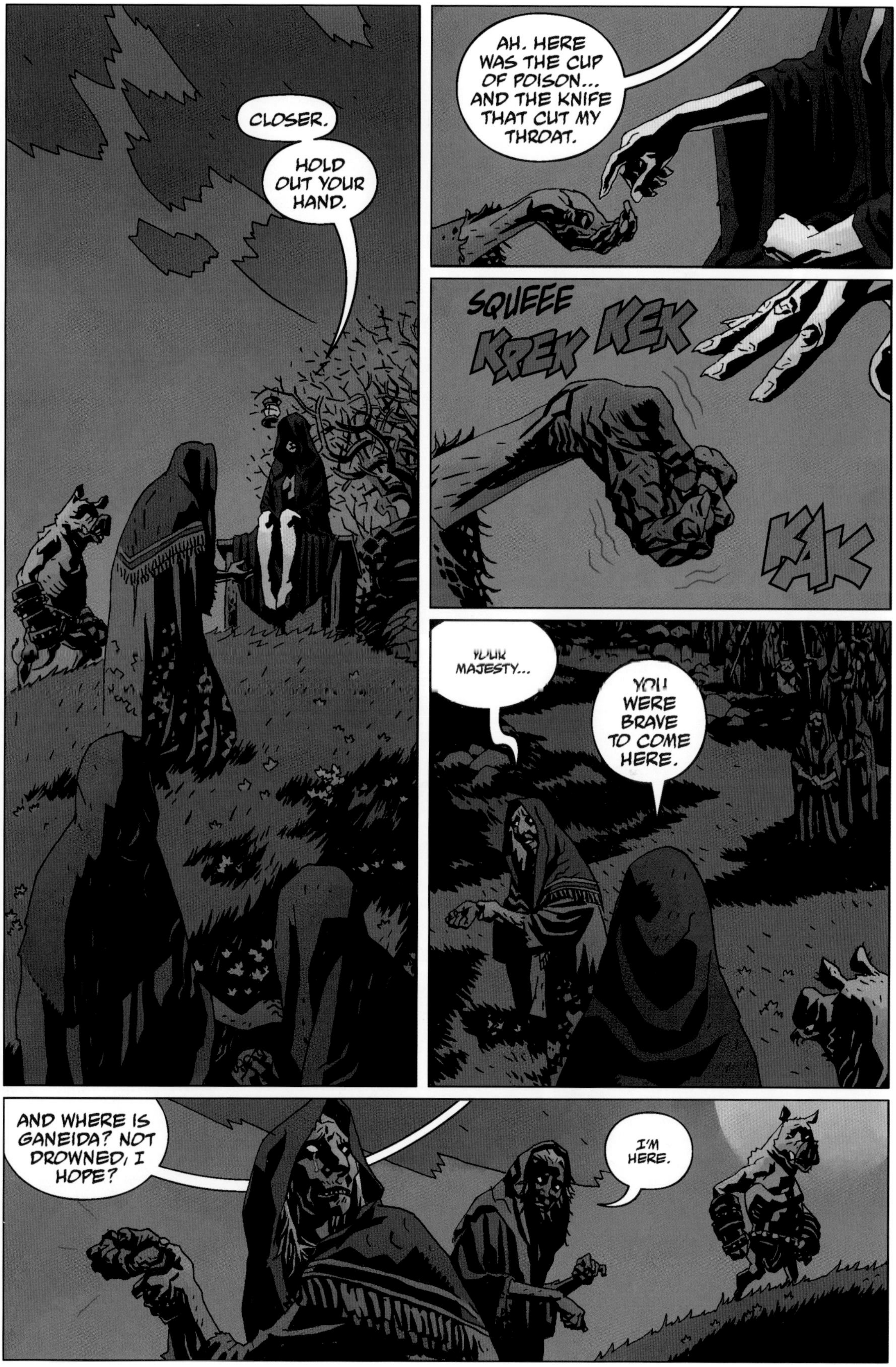
CLOSER.
HOLD OUT YOUR HAND.
AH. HERE WAS THE CUP OF POISON... AND THE KNIFE THAT CUT MY THROAT.
SQUEEE
KREK KEK
KAK
YOUR MAJESTY...
YOU WERE BRAVE TO COME HERE.
AND WHERE IS GANEIDA? NOT DROWNED, I HOPE?
I'M HERE.

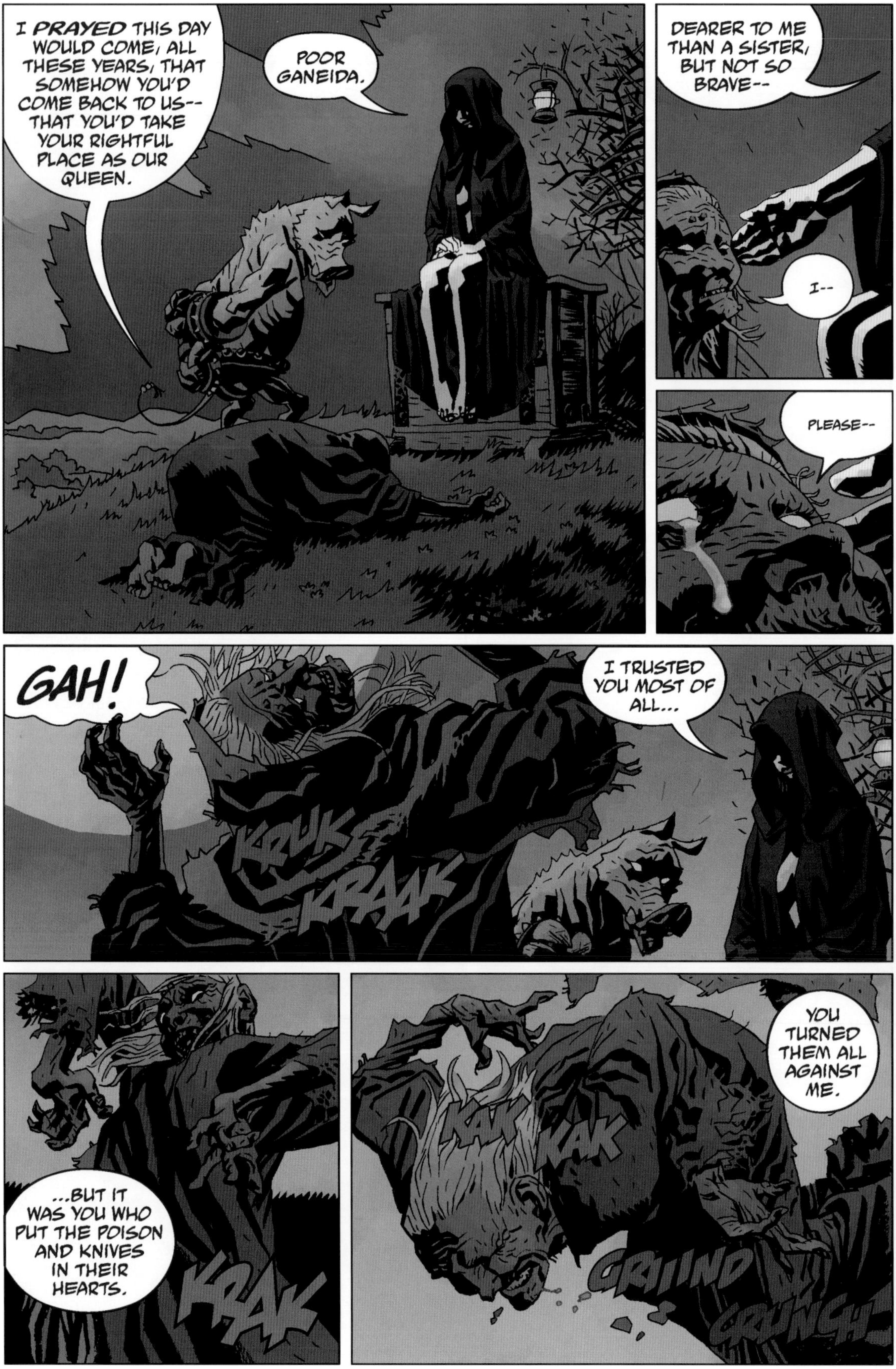

I PRAYED THIS DAY WOULD COME, ALL THESE YEARS, THAT SOMEHOW YOU'D COME BACK TO US--THAT YOU'D TAKE YOUR RIGHTFUL PLACE AS OUR QUEEN.
POOR GANEIDA.
DEARER TO ME THAN A SISTER, BUT NOT SO BRAVE--
I--
PLEASE--
GAH!
I TRUSTED YOU MOST OF ALL...
KRUK
KRAAK
...BUT IT WAS YOU WHO PUT THE POISON AND KNIVES IN THEIR HEARTS.
KRAK
YOU TURNED THEM ALL AGAINST ME.
KAK KAK
GRIIND
CRUNCH

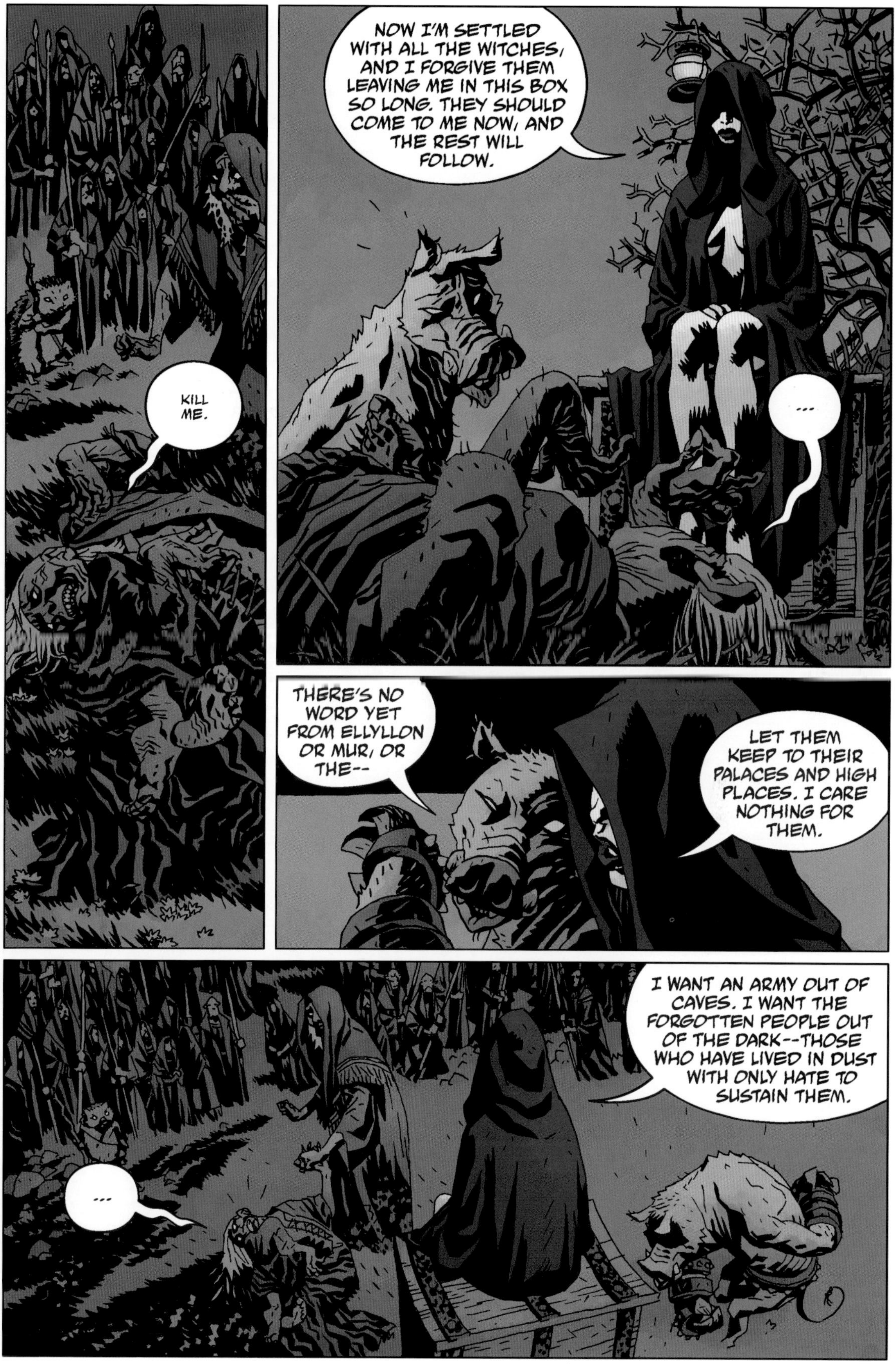
NOW I'M SETTLED WITH ALL THE WITCHES, AND I FORGIVE THEM LEAVING ME IN THIS BOX SO LONG. THEY SHOULD COME TO ME NOW, AND THE REST WILL FOLLOW.
KILL ME.
...
THERE'S NO WORD YET FROM ELLYLLON OR MUR, OR THE--
LET THEM KEEP TO THEIR PALACES AND HIGH PLACES. I CARE NOTHING FOR THEM.
I WANT AN ARMY OUT OF CAVES. I WANT THE FORGOTTEN PEOPLE OUT OF THE DARK--THOSE WHO HAVE LIVED IN DUST WITH ONLY HATE TO SUSTAIN THEM.
...

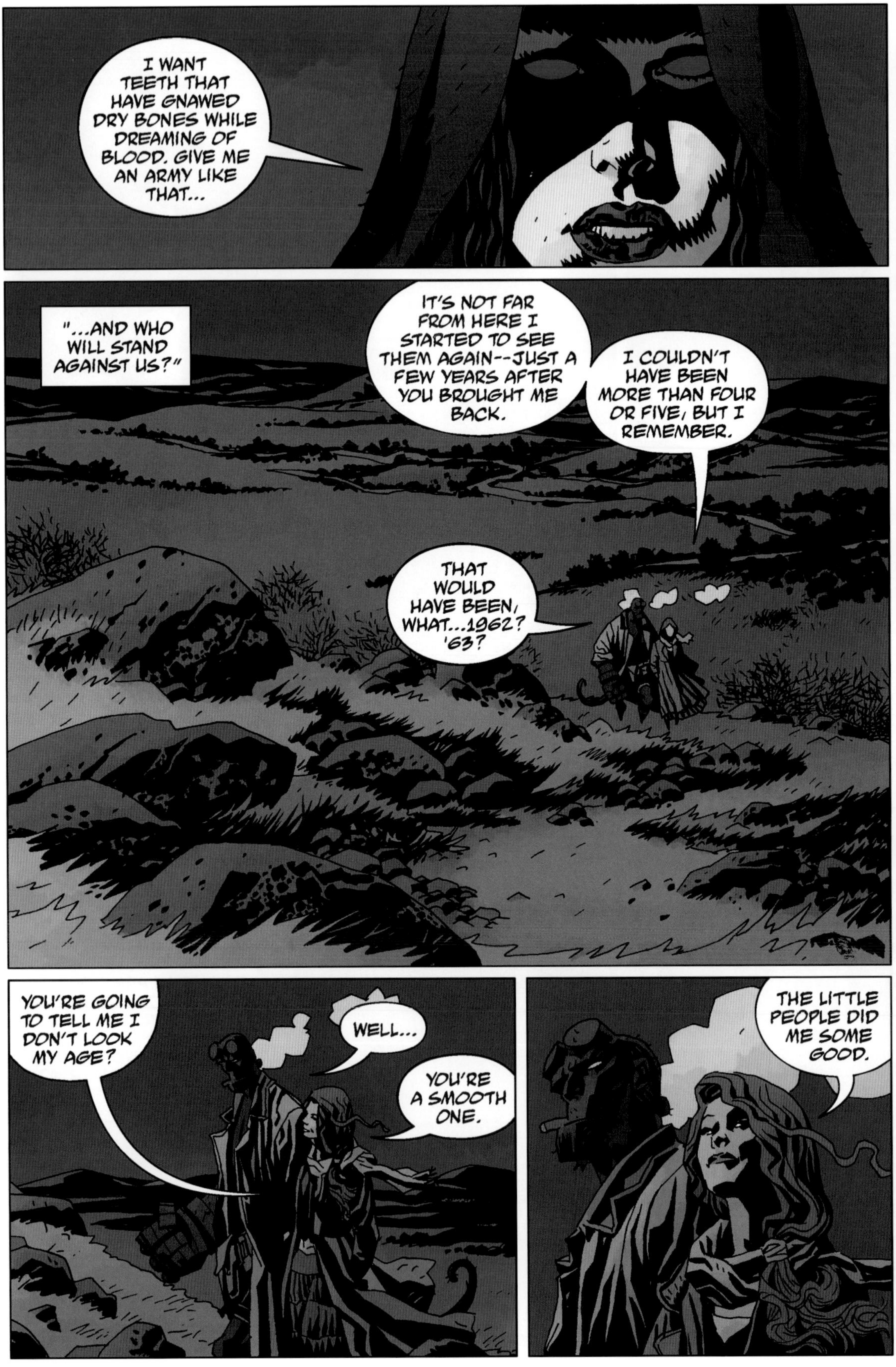

I WANT TEETH THAT HAVE GNAWED DRY BONES WHILE DREAMING OF BLOOD. GIVE ME AN ARMY LIKE THAT...
"...AND WHO WILL STAND AGAINST US?"
IT'S NOT FAR FROM HERE I STARTED TO SEE THEM AGAIN--JUST A FEW YEARS AFTER YOU BROUGHT ME BACK.
I COULDN'T HAVE BEEN MORE THAN FOUR OR FIVE, BUT I REMEMBER.
THAT WOULD HAVE BEEN, WHAT...1962? '63?
YOU'RE GOING TO TELL ME I DON'T LOOK MY AGE?
WELL...
YOU'RE A SMOOTH ONE.
THE LITTLE PEOPLE DID ME SOME GOOD.

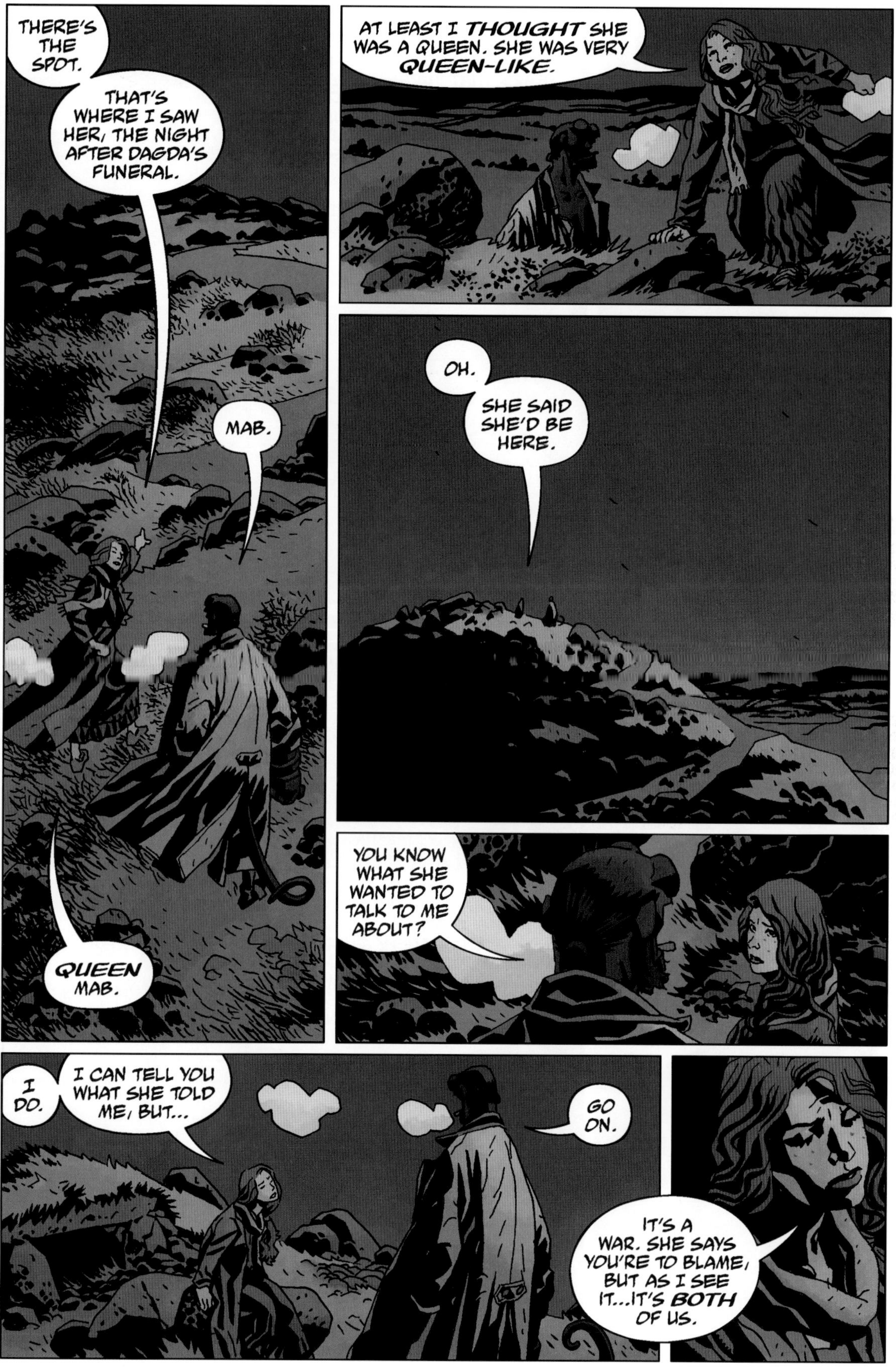
THERE'S THE SPOT.
THAT'S WHERE I SAW HER, THE NIGHT AFTER DAGDA'S FUNERAL.
MAB.
QUEEN MAB.
AT LEAST I THOUGHT SHE WAS A QUEEN. SHE WAS VERY QUEEN-LIKE.
OH.
SHE SAID SHE'D BE HERE.
YOU KNOW WHAT SHE WANTED TO TALK TO ME ABOUT?
I DO.
I CAN TELL YOU WHAT SHE TOLD ME, BUT...
GO ON.
IT'S A WAR. SHE SAYS YOU'RE TO BLAME, BUT AS I SEE IT...IT'S BOTH OF US.

WHAT DO YOU MEAN?

SHE SAID IT WAS FROM YOUR HANDLING OF THAT CHANGELING LEFT IN MY PLACE--

"HE SWORE HE'D GET EVEN WITH YOU. OVER THE YEARS THAT TURNED INTO A HATE FOR ALL MANKIND, AND A DREAM TO HAVE HIS PEOPLE TAKE THE WORLD BACK. THEN THERE WAS SOMETHING ABOUT HECATE, THE FIRST QUEEN OF WITCHES, AND YOU DESTROYING HER, AND HER BEING BORN AGAIN, THEN LOCKED AWAY SOMEWHERE--"

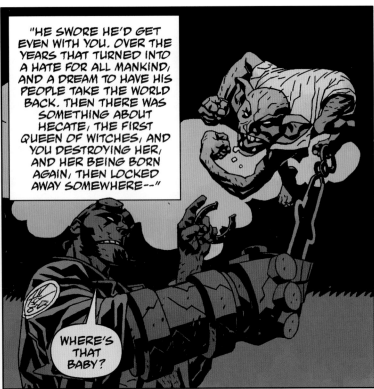

WHERE'S THAT BABY?

I COULDN'T REALLY FOLLOW THAT LAST BIT, BUT SHE SAID YOU'D KNOW...AND HOW IT WAS ALL YOUR DOING.

YEAH.

AND SHE SAID, WITH HECATE LOCKED AWAY, THE WITCHES ASKED YOU TO BE THEIR KING.

I THINK IT'S GOOD YOU TURNED THAT DOWN.

ME TOO.

WELL, I GUESS THAT CHANGELING WENT TO THOSE WITCHES AND SOLD THEM ON AN IDEA FOR A NEW QUEEN--SOMEONE A HUNDRED TIMES MORE HORRIBLE THAN THEIR FIRST. SOMEONE WHO'S GOING TO STIR UP THE WORST OF THE OLD CREATURES AND BAND THEM TOGETHER.

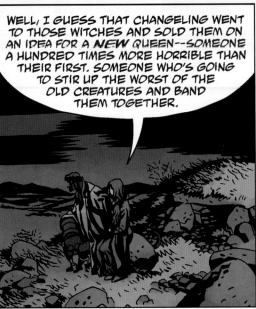

ALL BECAUSE OF ME.

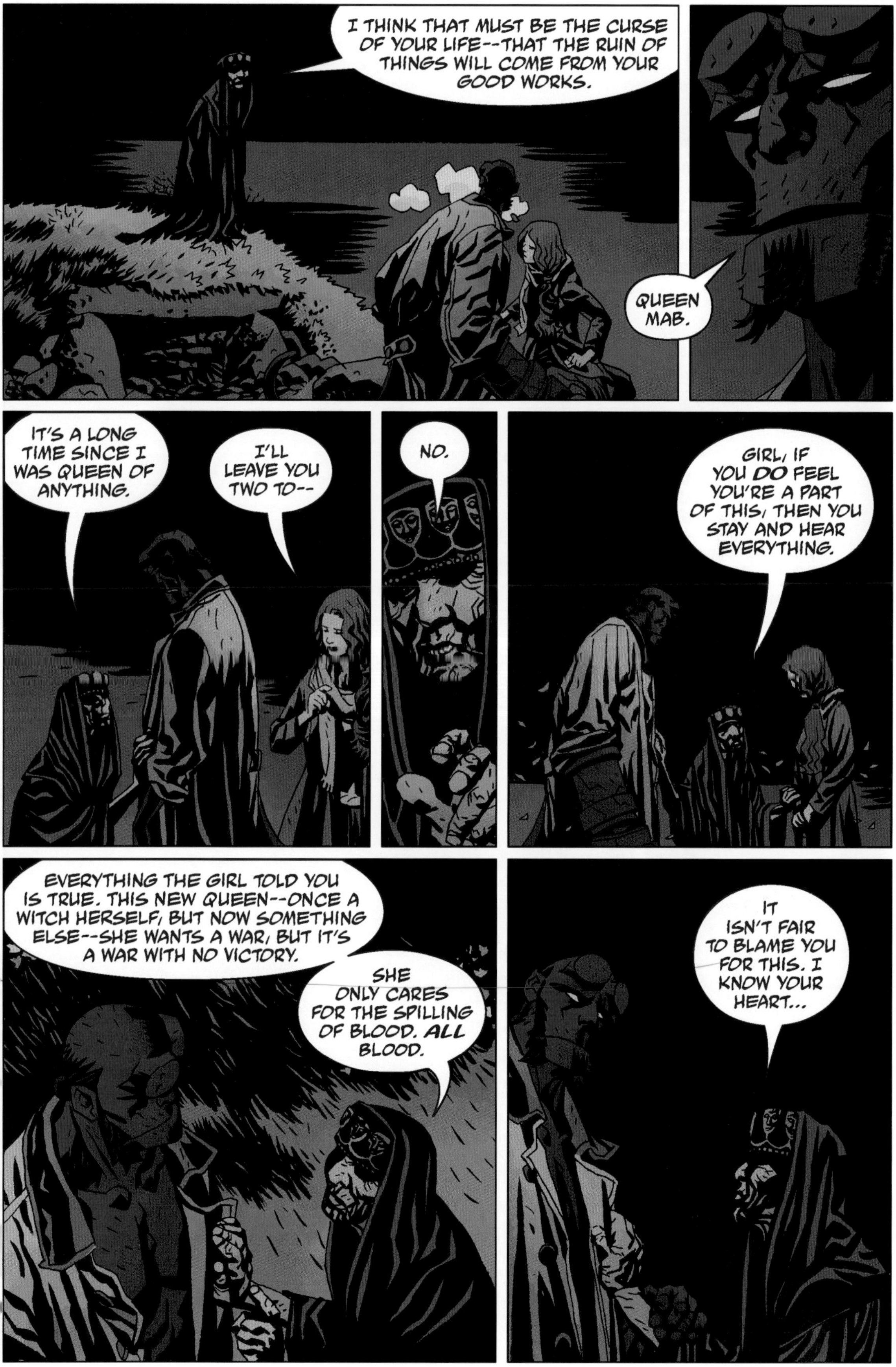
I THINK THAT MUST BE THE CURSE OF YOUR LIFE--THAT THE RUIN OF THINGS WILL COME FROM YOUR GOOD WORKS.
QUEEN MAB.
IT'S A LONG TIME SINCE I WAS QUEEN OF ANYTHING.
I'LL LEAVE YOU TWO TO--
NO.
GIRL, IF YOU DO FEEL YOU'RE A PART OF THIS, THEN YOU STAY AND HEAR EVERYTHING.
EVERYTHING THE GIRL TOLD YOU IS TRUE. THIS NEW QUEEN--ONCE A WITCH HERSELF, BUT NOW SOMETHING ELSE--SHE WANTS A WAR, BUT IT'S A WAR WITH NO VICTORY.
SHE ONLY CARES FOR THE SPILLING OF BLOOD. ALL BLOOD.
IT ISN'T FAIR TO BLAME YOU FOR THIS. I KNOW YOUR HEART...

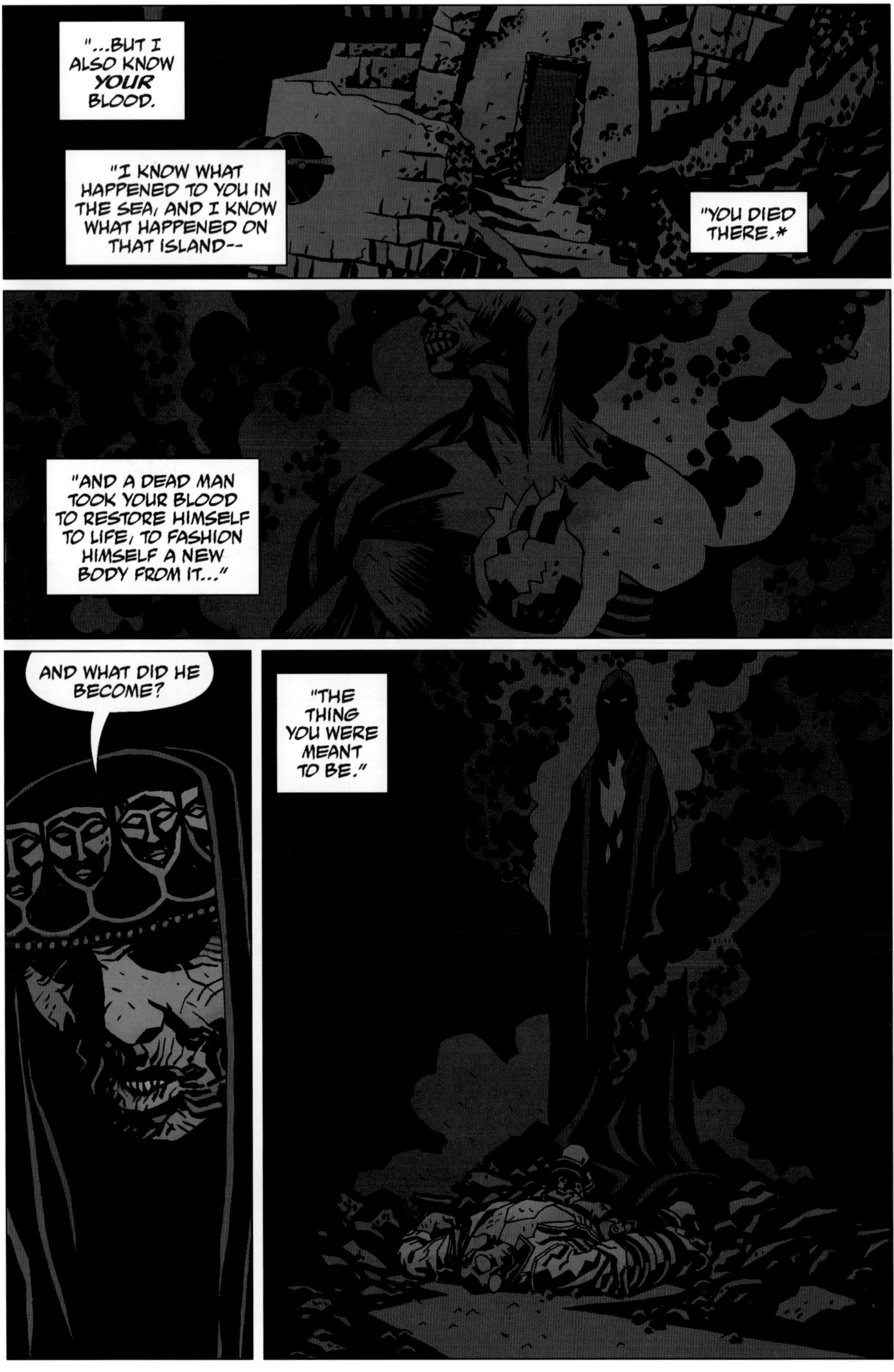
"...BUT I ALSO KNOW YOUR BLOOD.
"I KNOW WHAT HAPPENED TO YOU IN THE SEA, AND I KNOW WHAT HAPPENED ON THAT ISLAND--
"YOU DIED THERE.*
"AND A DEAD MAN TOOK YOUR BLOOD TO RESTORE HIMSELF TO LIFE, TO FASHION HIMSELF A NEW BODY FROM IT..."
AND WHAT DID HE BECOME?
"THE THING YOU WERE MEANT TO BE."

*HELLBOY: STRANGE PLACES

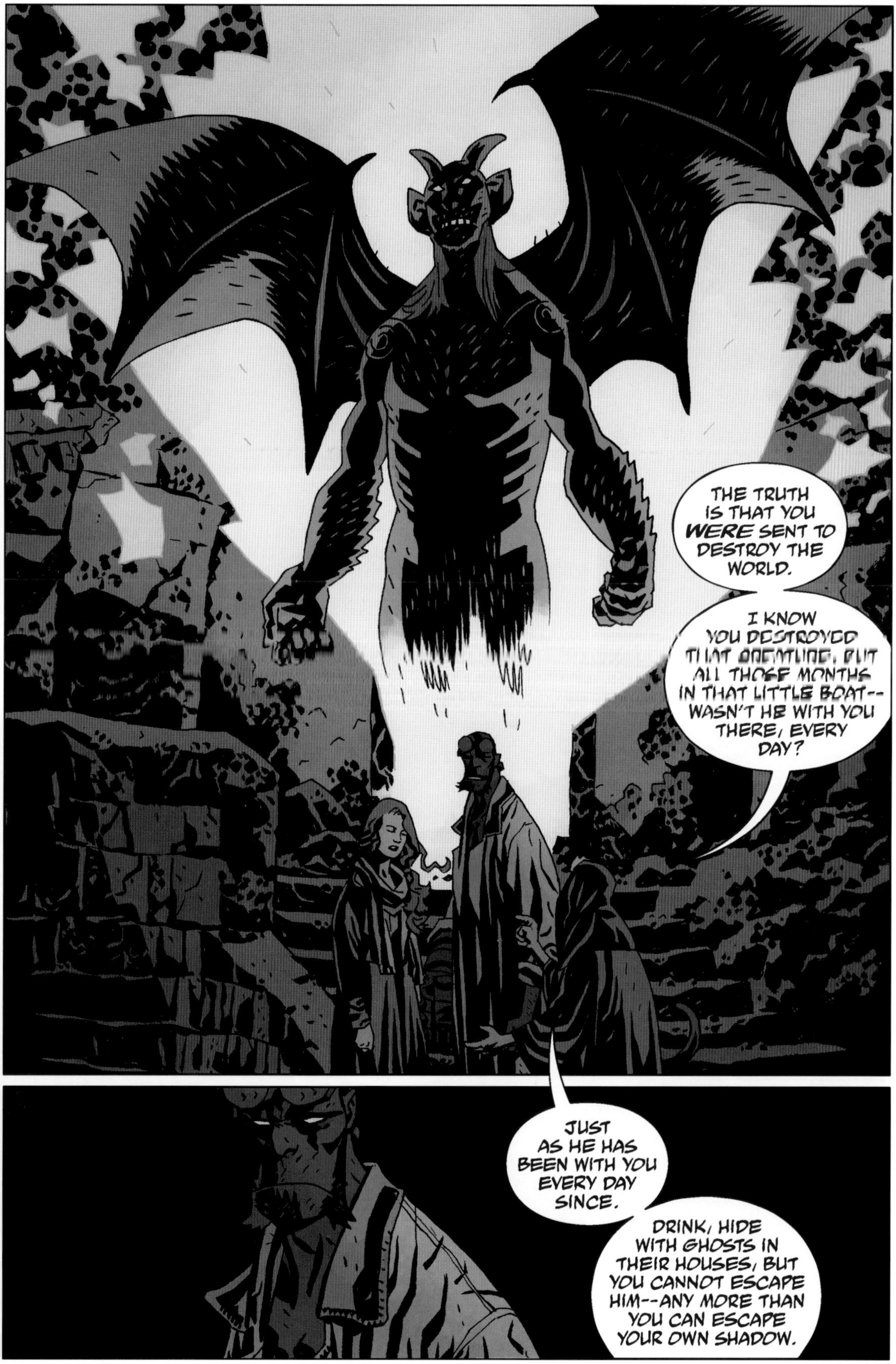
THE TRUTH IS THAT YOU WERE SENT TO DESTROY THE WORLD.
I KNOW YOU DESTROYED THAT CREATURE, BUT ALL THOSE MONTHS IN THAT LITTLE BOAT-- WASN'T HE WITH YOU THERE, EVERY DAY?
JUST AS HE HAS BEEN WITH YOU EVERY DAY SINCE.
DRINK, HIDE WITH GHOSTS IN THEIR HOUSES, BUT YOU CANNOT ESCAPE HIM--ANY MORE THAN YOU CAN ESCAPE YOUR OWN SHADOW.

THIS THING IS PART OF YOU, MAYBE THE BIGGEST PART, AND CONTINUE AS YOU HAVE BEEN, AND IT WILL CONSUME YOU.

THE TRUTH IS THAT IT'S ALREADY BEGUN--

"--HASN'T IT?"

WHAT DO YOU MEAN?

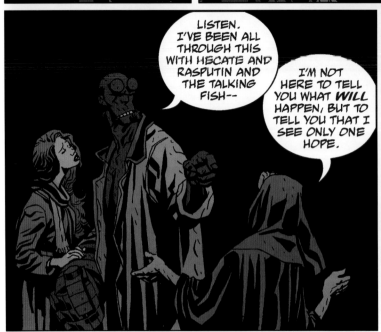

LISTEN. I'VE BEEN ALL THROUGH THIS WITH HECATE AND RASPUTIN AND THE TALKING FISH--

I'M NOT HERE TO TELL YOU WHAT *WILL* HAPPEN, BUT TO TELL YOU THAT I SEE ONLY ONE HOPE.

ONE CHANCE FOR YOU TO ESCAPE YOUR FATE.

YOU ARE YOUR FATHER'S SON, BUT YOU ALSO HAD A MOTHER...

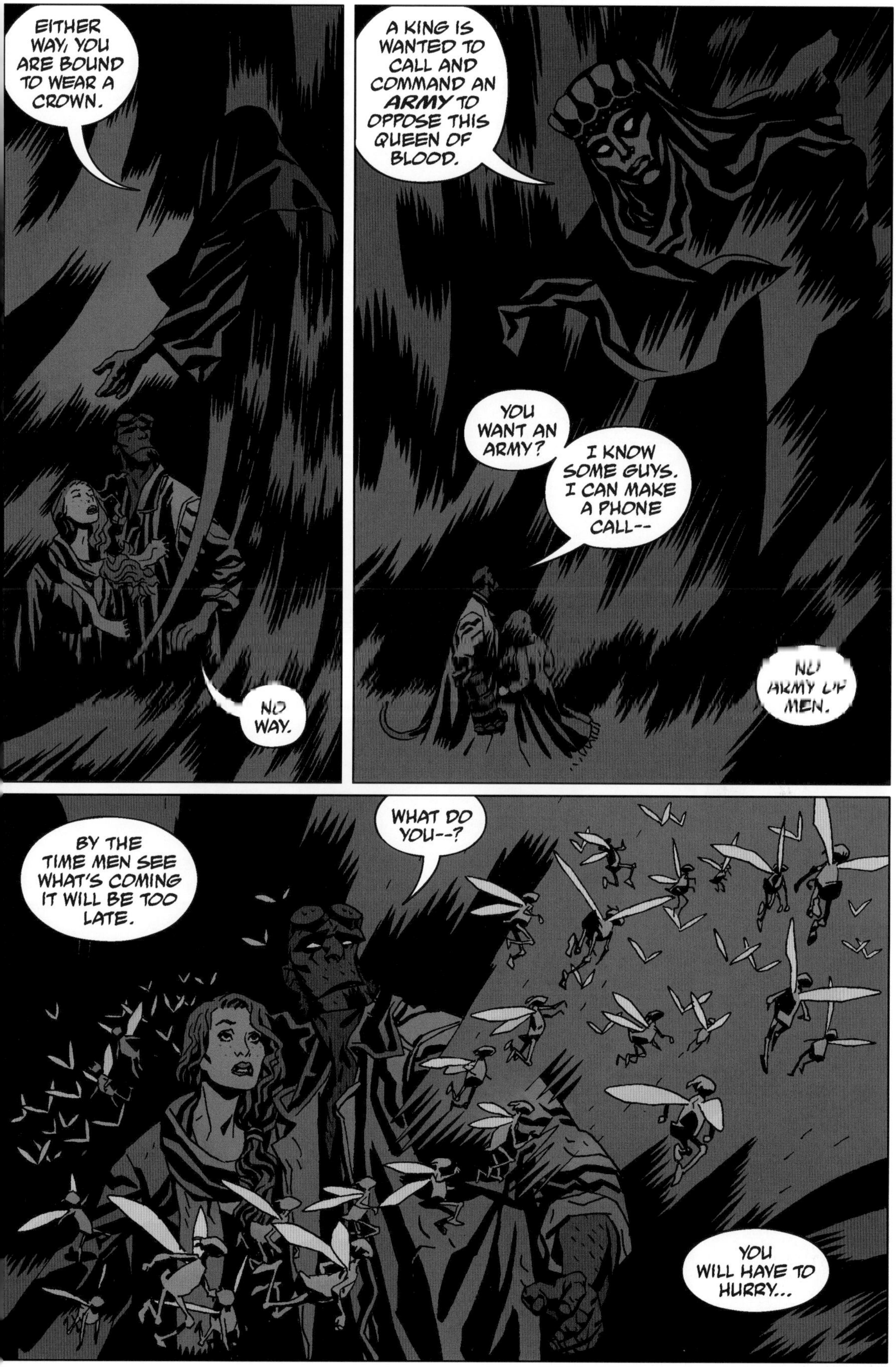
EITHER WAY, YOU ARE BOUND TO WEAR A CROWN.
NO WAY.
A KING IS WANTED TO CALL AND COMMAND AN ARMY TO OPPOSE THIS QUEEN OF BLOOD.
YOU WANT AN ARMY?
I KNOW SOME GUYS. I CAN MAKE A PHONE CALL--
NO ARMY OF MEN.
BY THE TIME MEN SEE WHAT'S COMING IT WILL BE TOO LATE.
WHAT DO YOU--?
YOU WILL HAVE TO HURRY...

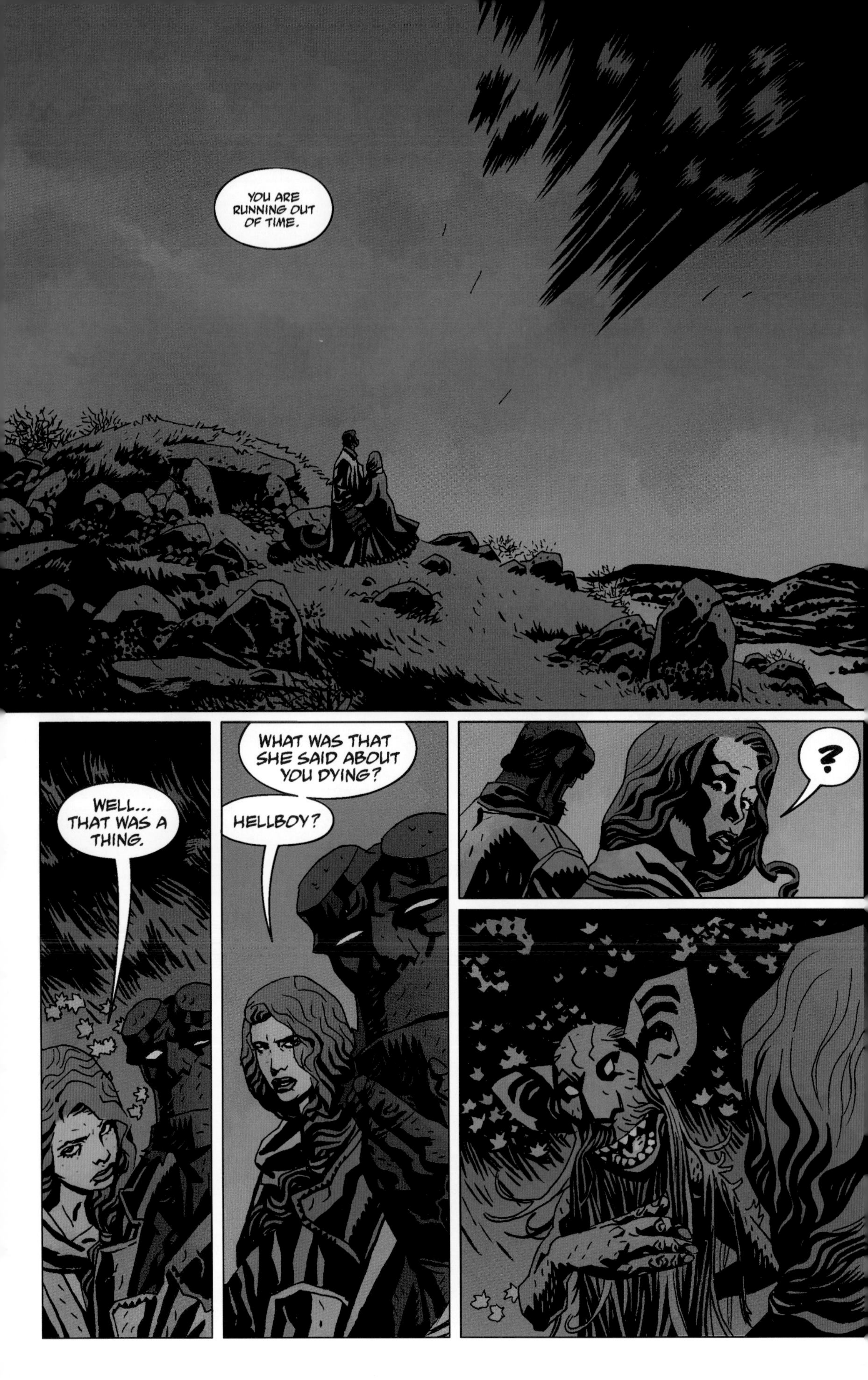
YOU ARE RUNNING OUT OF TIME.
WELL... THAT WAS A THING.
WHAT WAS THAT SHE SAID ABOUT YOU DYING?
HELLBOY?
?

CHAPTER FOUR

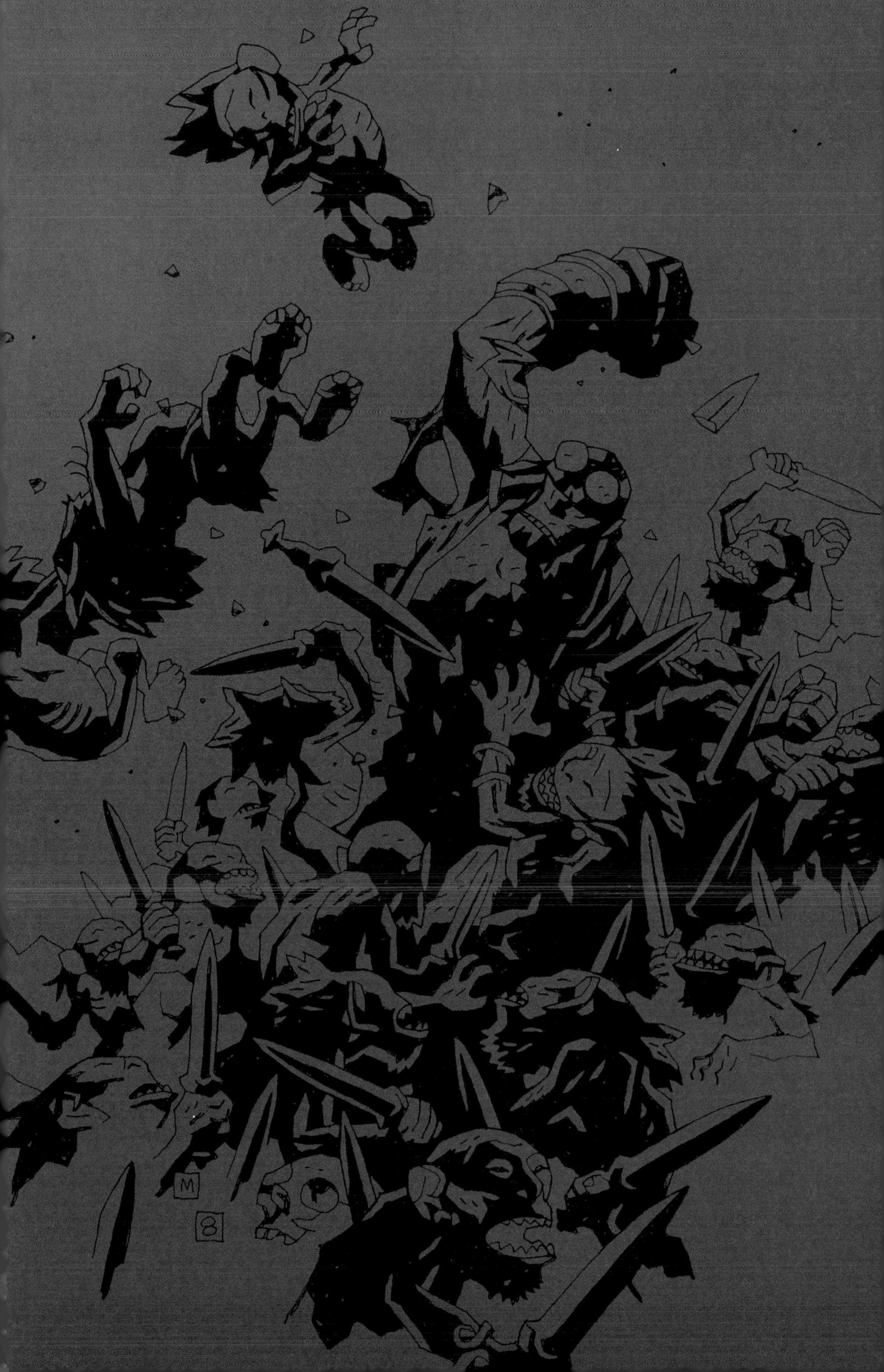

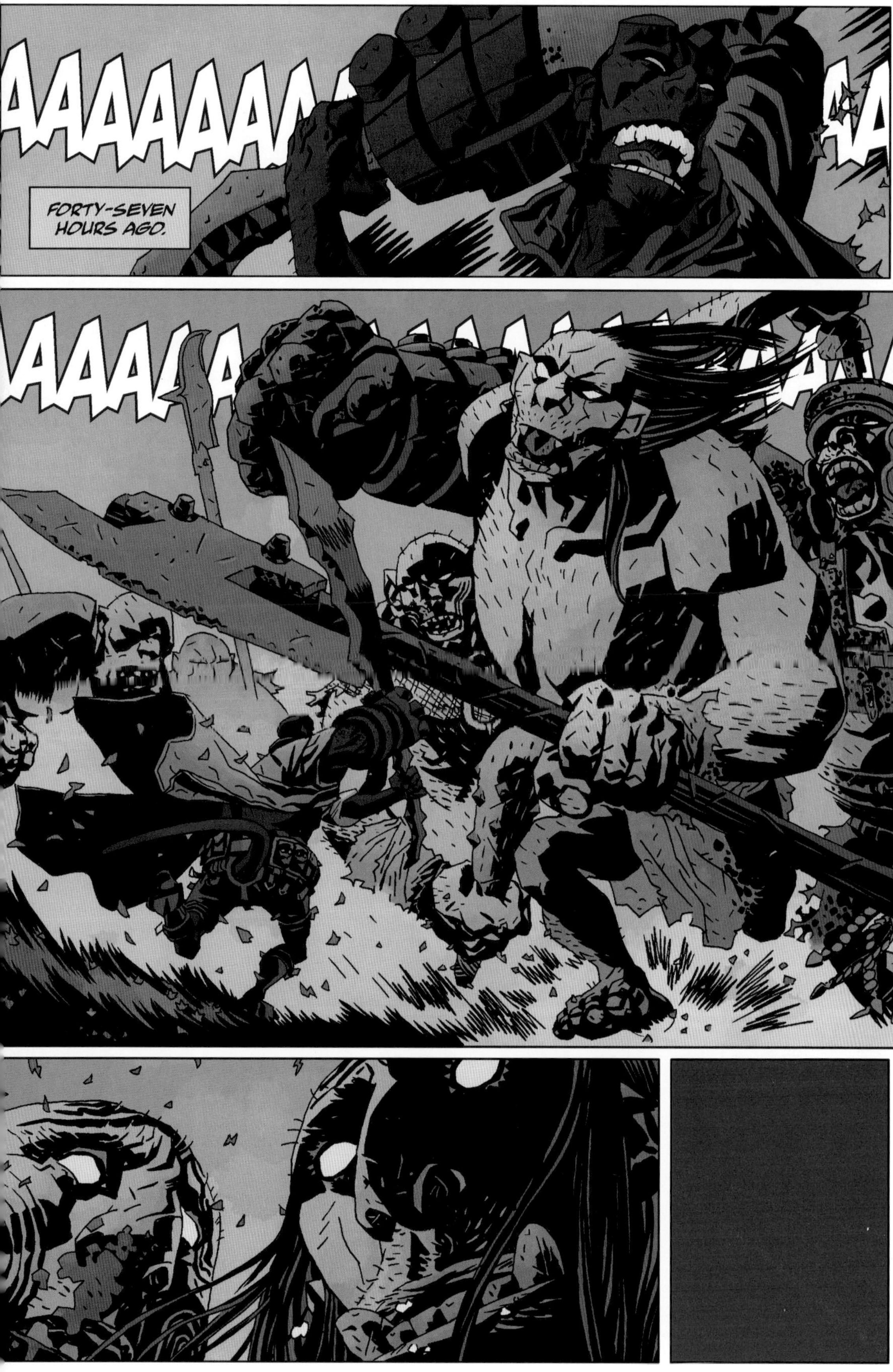
AAAAAAAA
FORTY-SEVEN HOURS AGO.
AAAAAAAAA

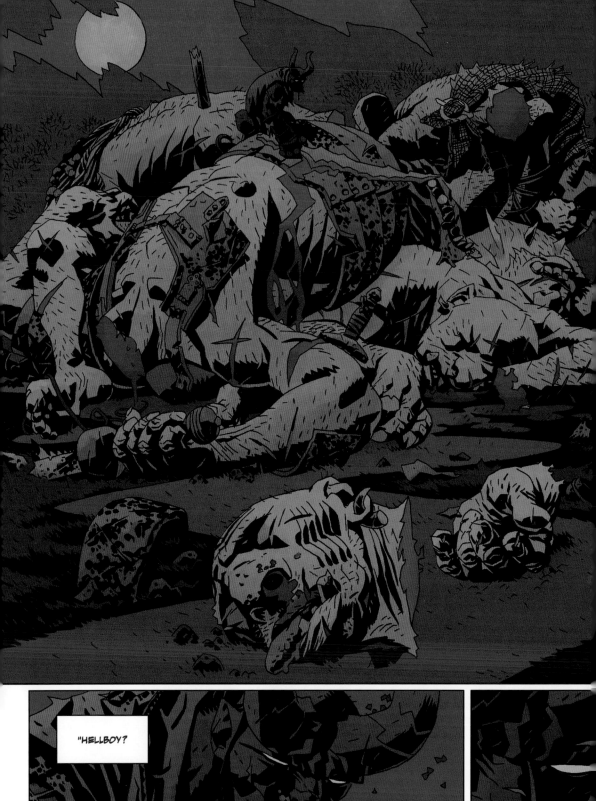

"HELLBOY?

"HEY--"

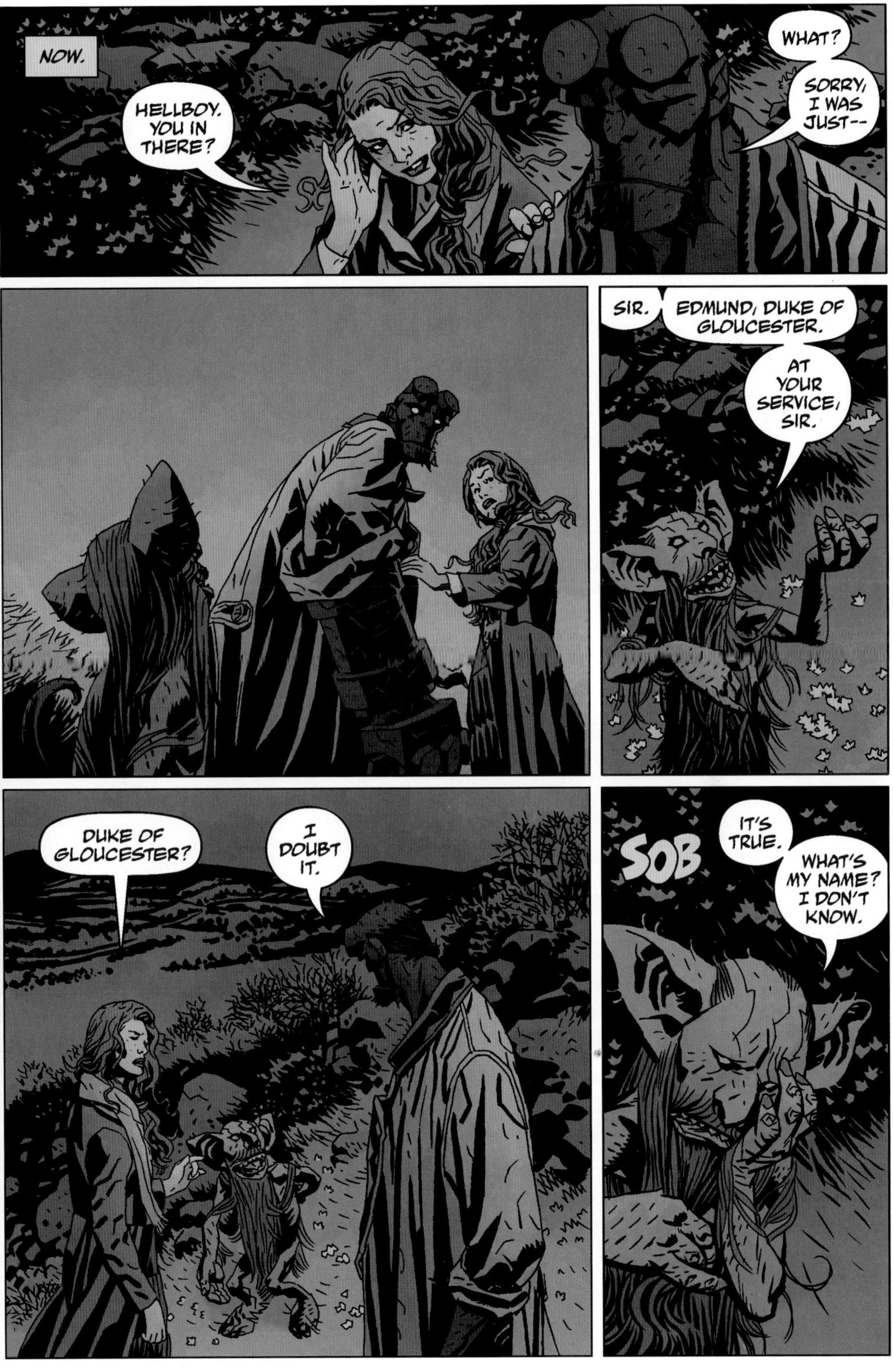
NOW.
HELLBOY. YOU IN THERE?
WHAT?
SORRY, I WAS JUST--
SIR.
EDMUND, DUKE OF GLOUCESTER.
AT YOUR SERVICE, SIR.
DUKE OF GLOUCESTER?
I DOUBT IT.
SOB
IT'S TRUE.
WHAT'S MY NAME? I DON'T KNOW.

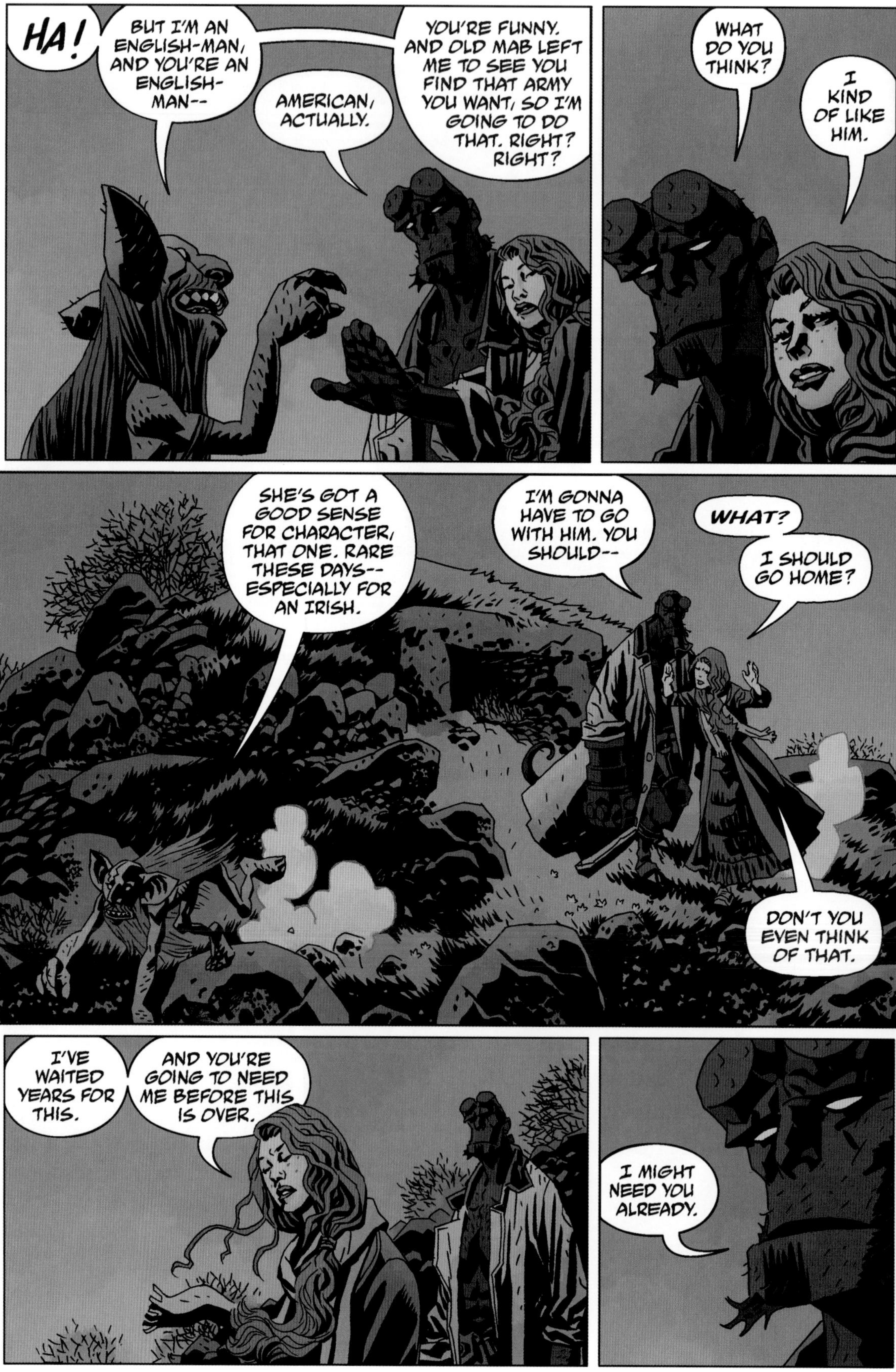
HA!
BUT I'M AN ENGLISH-MAN, AND YOU'RE AN ENGLISH-MAN--
AMERICAN, ACTUALLY.
YOU'RE FUNNY. AND OLD MAB LEFT ME TO SEE YOU FIND THAT ARMY YOU WANT, SO I'M GOING TO DO THAT. RIGHT? RIGHT?
WHAT DO YOU THINK?
I KIND OF LIKE HIM.
SHE'S GOT A GOOD SENSE FOR CHARACTER, THAT ONE. RARE THESE DAYS--ESPECIALLY FOR AN IRISH.
I'M GONNA HAVE TO GO WITH HIM. YOU SHOULD--
WHAT?
I SHOULD GO HOME?
DON'T YOU EVEN THINK OF THAT.
I'VE WAITED YEARS FOR THIS.
AND YOU'RE GOING TO NEED ME BEFORE THIS IS OVER.
I MIGHT NEED YOU ALREADY.

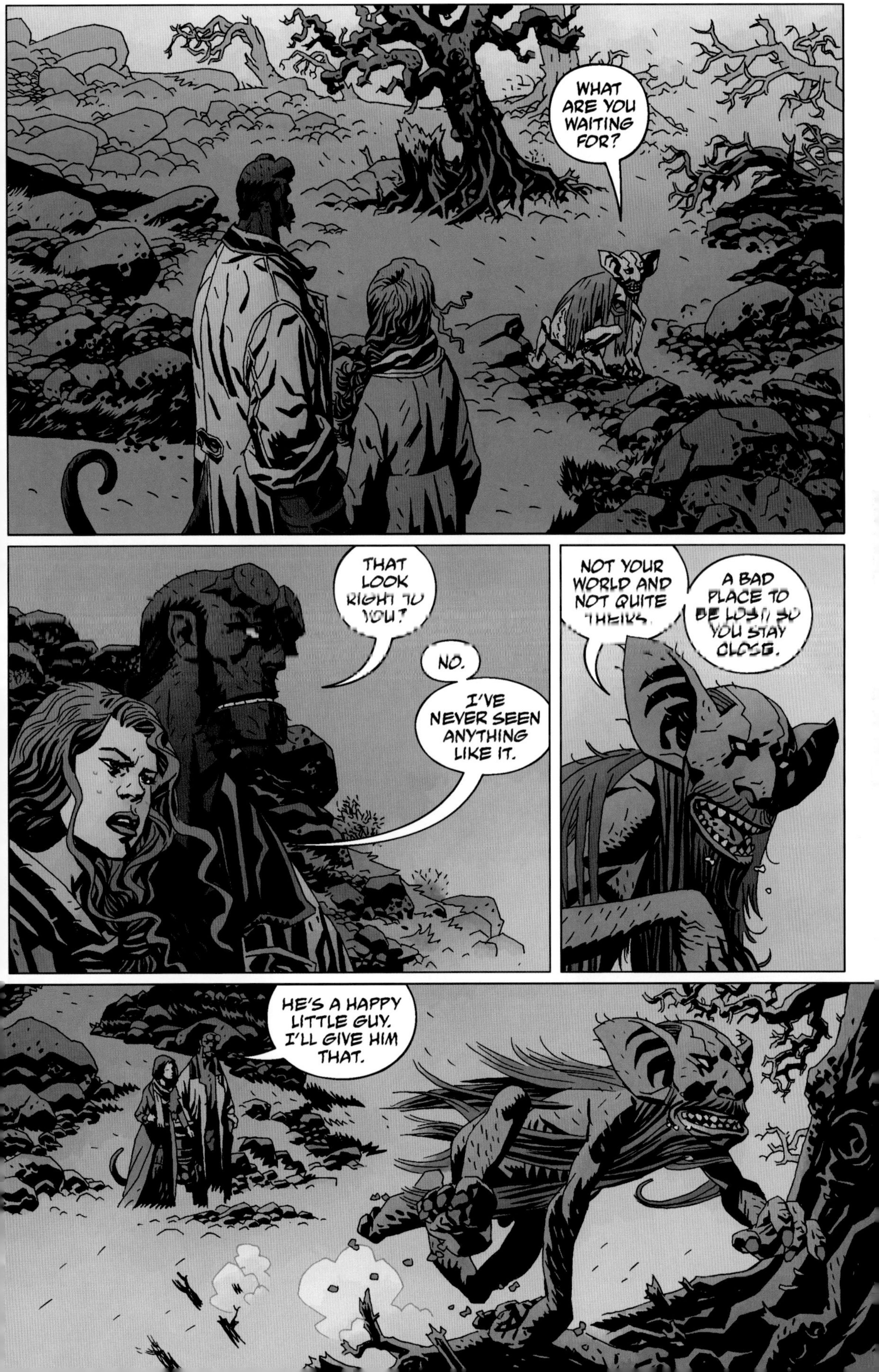
WHAT ARE YOU WAITING FOR?
THAT LOOK RIGHT TO YOU?
NO.
I'VE NEVER SEEN ANYTHING LIKE IT.
NOT YOUR WORLD AND NOT QUITE THEIRS.
A BAD PLACE TO BE LOST, SO YOU STAY CLOSE.
HE'S A HAPPY LITTLE GUY. I'LL GIVE HIM THAT.

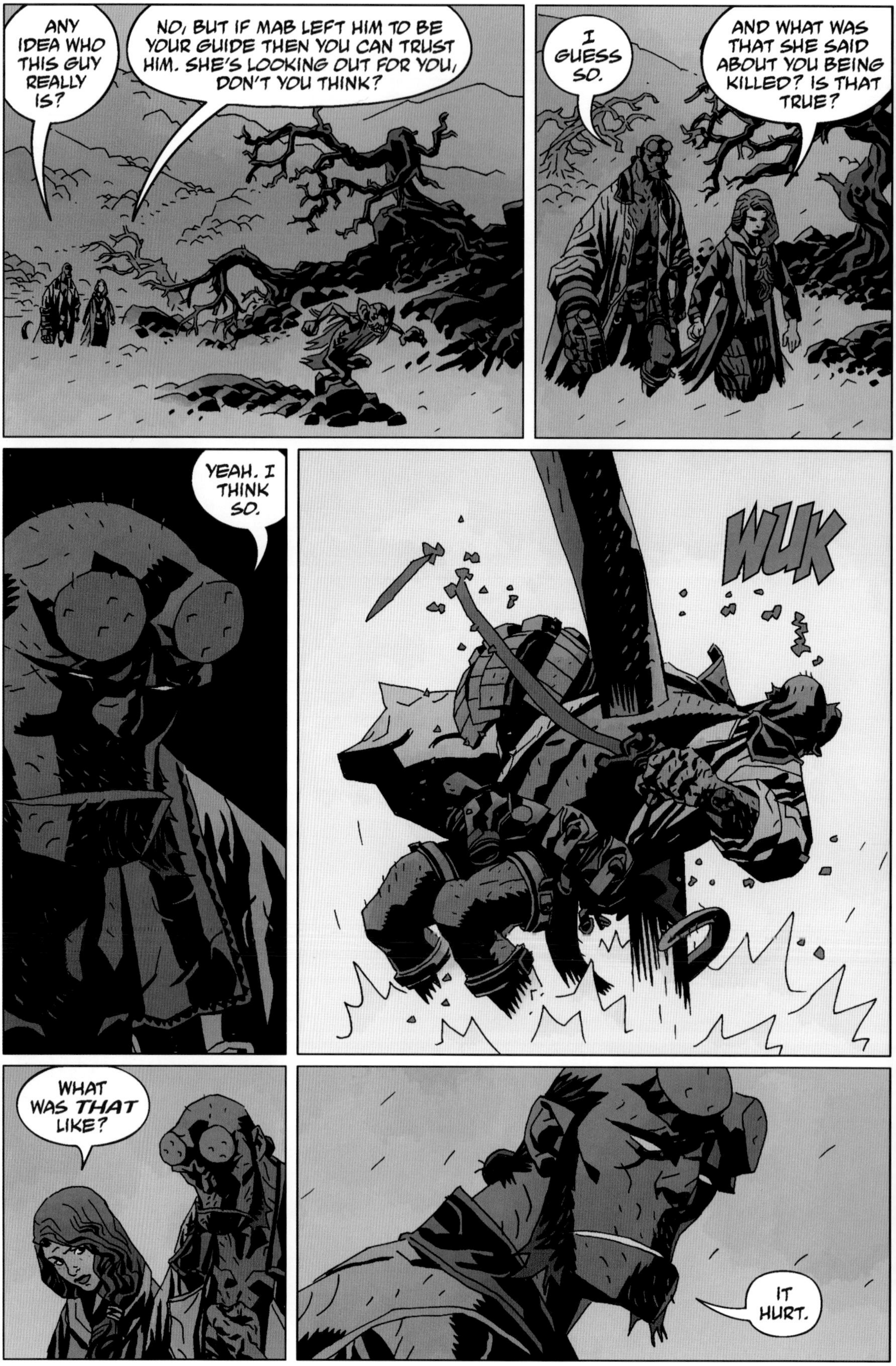
ANY IDEA WHO THIS GUY REALLY IS?
NO, BUT IF MAB LEFT HIM TO BE YOUR GUIDE THEN YOU CAN TRUST HIM. SHE'S LOOKING OUT FOR YOU, DON'T YOU THINK?
I GUESS SO.
AND WHAT WAS THAT SHE SAID ABOUT YOU BEING KILLED? IS THAT TRUE?
YEAH. I THINK SO.
WUK
WHAT WAS *THAT* LIKE?
IT HURT.

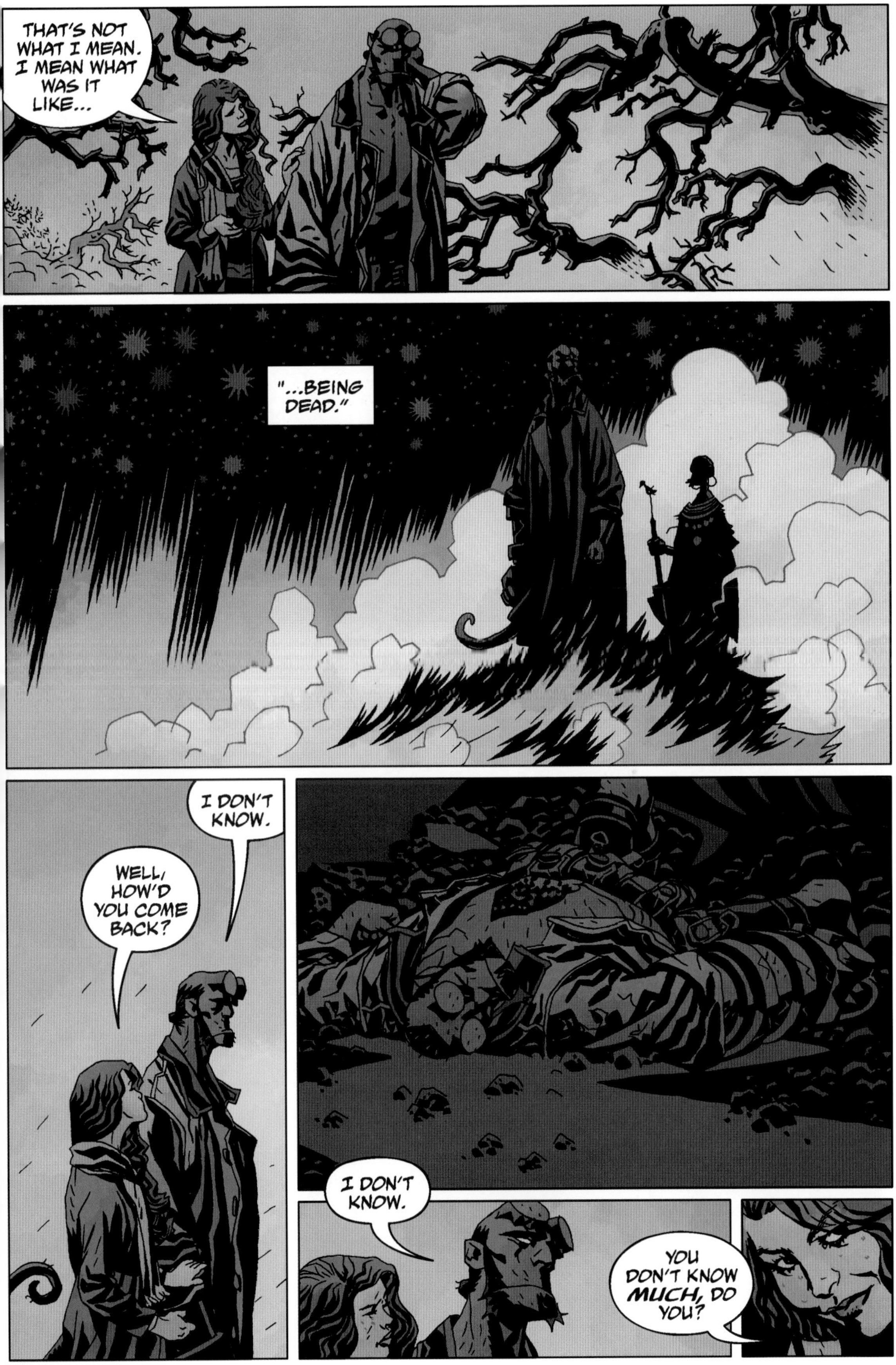
THAT'S NOT WHAT I MEAN. I MEAN WHAT WAS IT LIKE...
"...BEING DEAD."
I DON'T KNOW.
WELL, HOW'D YOU COME BACK?
I DON'T KNOW.
YOU DON'T KNOW MUCH, DO YOU?

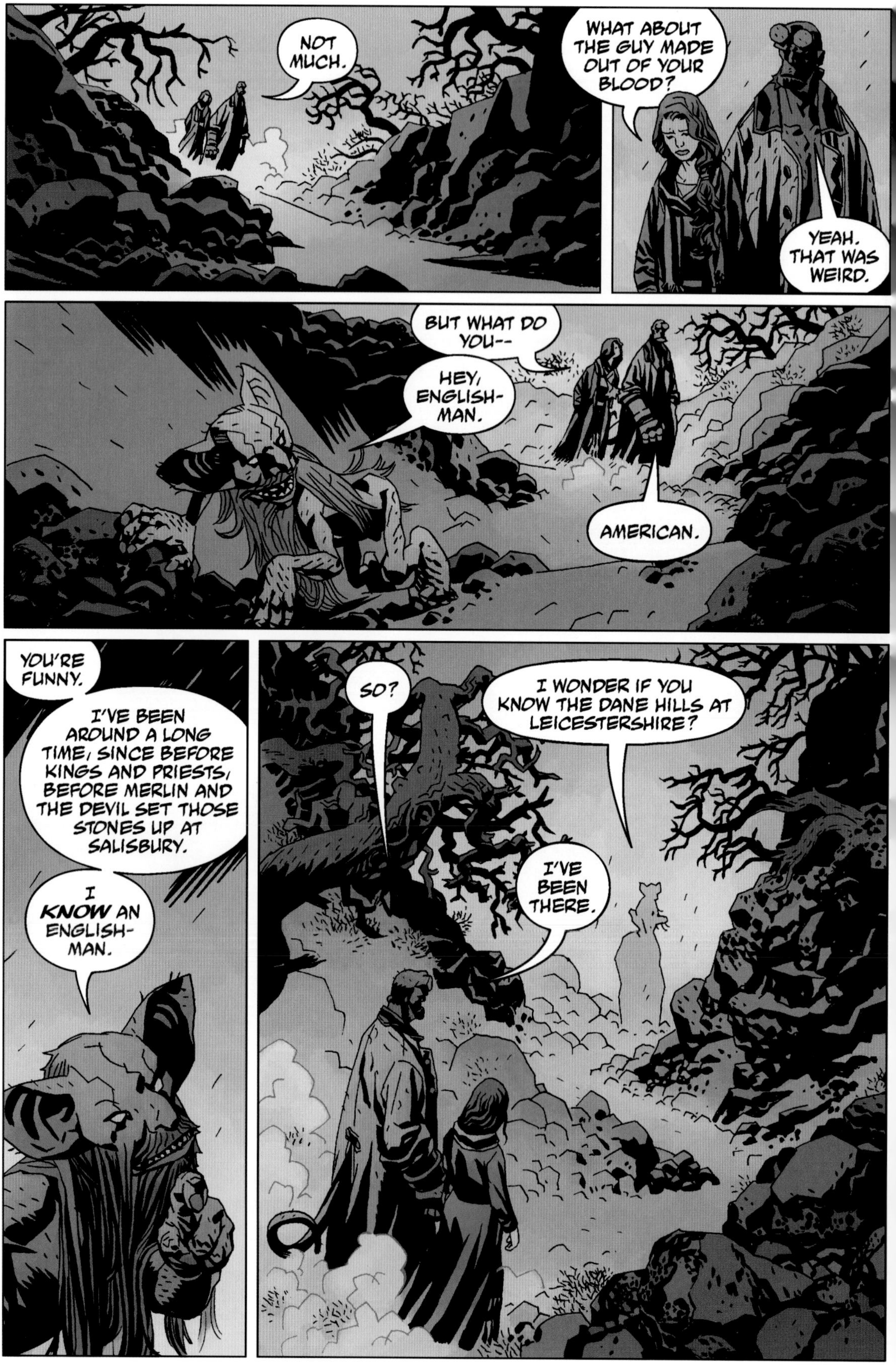
NOT MUCH.
WHAT ABOUT THE GUY MADE OUT OF YOUR BLOOD?
YEAH. THAT WAS WEIRD.
BUT WHAT DO YOU--
HEY, ENGLISH-MAN.
AMERICAN.
YOU'RE FUNNY.
I'VE BEEN AROUND A LONG TIME, SINCE BEFORE KINGS AND PRIESTS, BEFORE MERLIN AND THE DEVIL SET THOSE STONES UP AT SALISBURY.
I *KNOW* AN ENGLISH-MAN.
SO?
I WONDER IF YOU KNOW THE DANE HILLS AT LEICESTERSHIRE?
I'VE BEEN THERE.

WHEN I WAS THERE LAST THERE WAS AN OAK TREE, AND A GODDESS LIVED UNDER IT. AND PEOPLE USED TO HANG GIFTS FOR HER IN THAT TREE...

"I WONDER, IS IT STILL THERE?"

I THINK I KNOW THE TREE.

IT'S IN FRONT OF A CAVE. A CANNIBAL HAG USED TO LIVE IN THAT CAVE, AND EVERY ONCE IN A WHILE SHE'D GRAB LITTLE KIDS, EAT THEM, AND HANG THEIR SKINS IN THAT TREE.

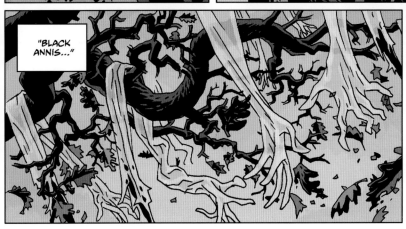

"BLACK ANNIS..."

DOES SHE STILL LIVE?

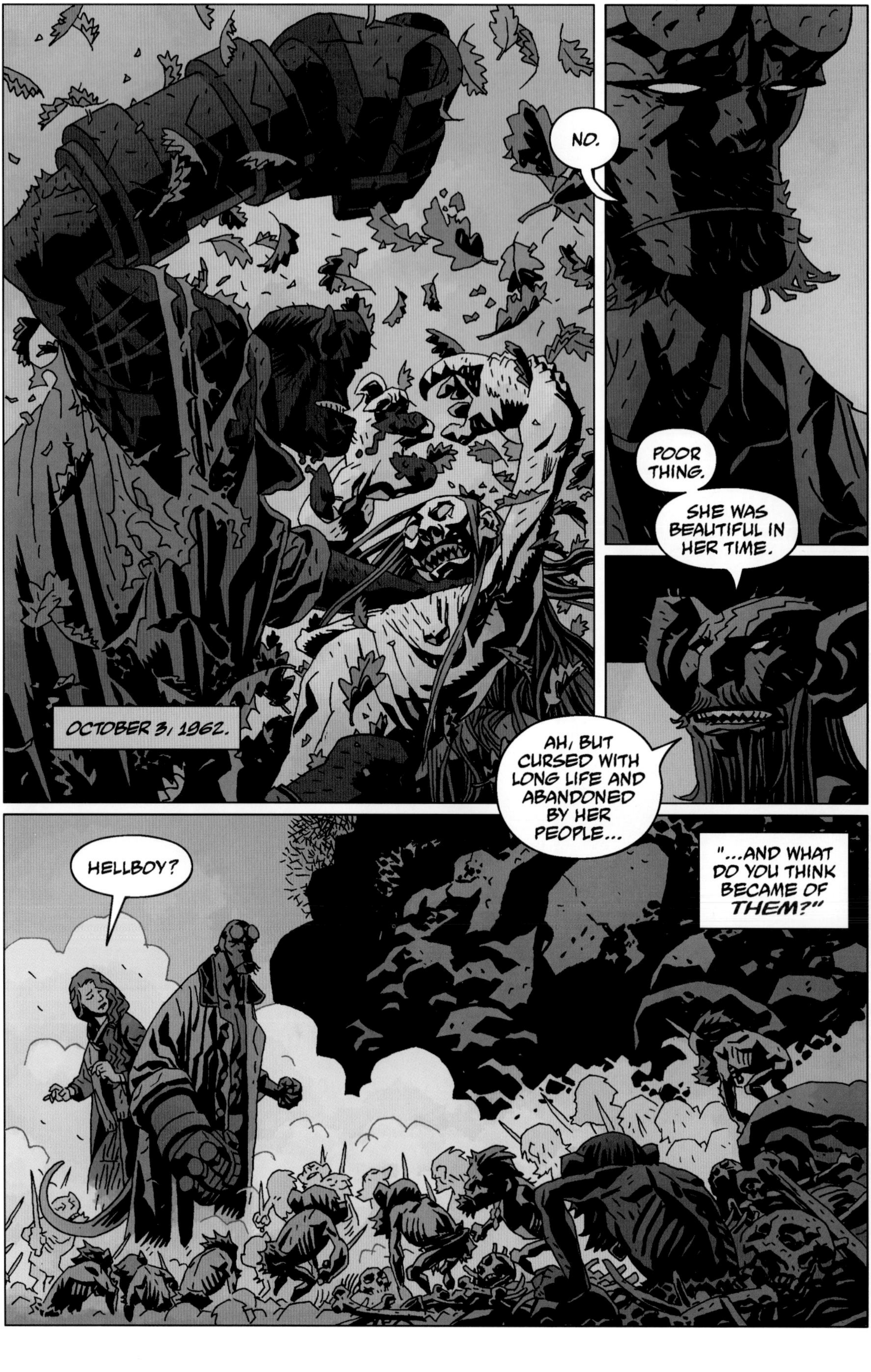
NO.
OCTOBER 3, 1962.
POOR THING.
SHE WAS BEAUTIFUL IN HER TIME.
AH, BUT CURSED WITH LONG LIFE AND ABANDONED BY HER PEOPLE...
HELLBOY?
"...AND WHAT DO YOU THINK BECAME OF *THEM?*"

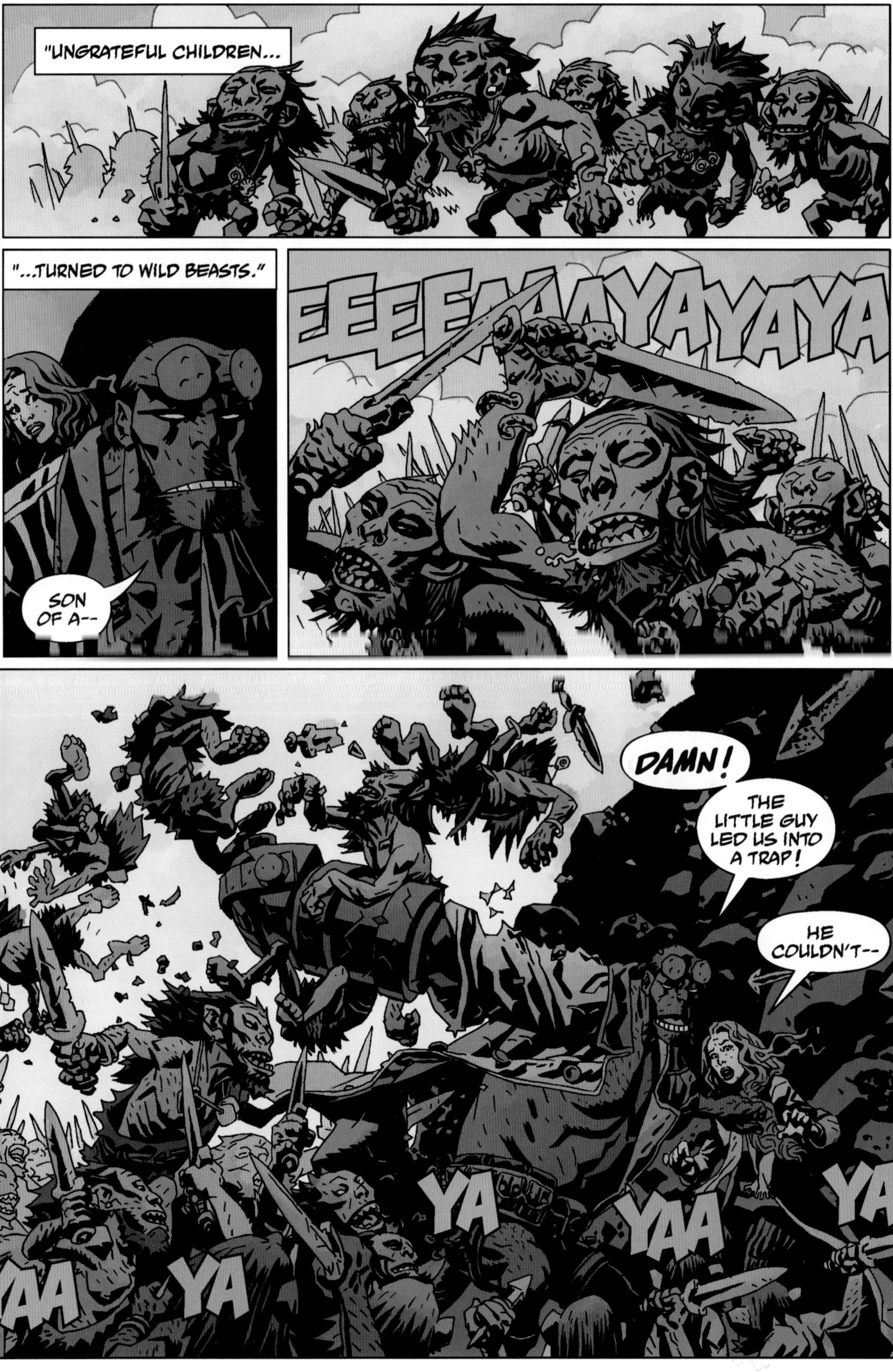
"UNGRATEFUL CHILDREN...
"...TURNED TO WILD BEASTS."
SON OF A--
EEEEAAAYAYAYAYA
DAMN!
THE LITTLE GUY LED US INTO A TRAP!
HE COULDN'T--
YA
YAA
YA
AA
YA

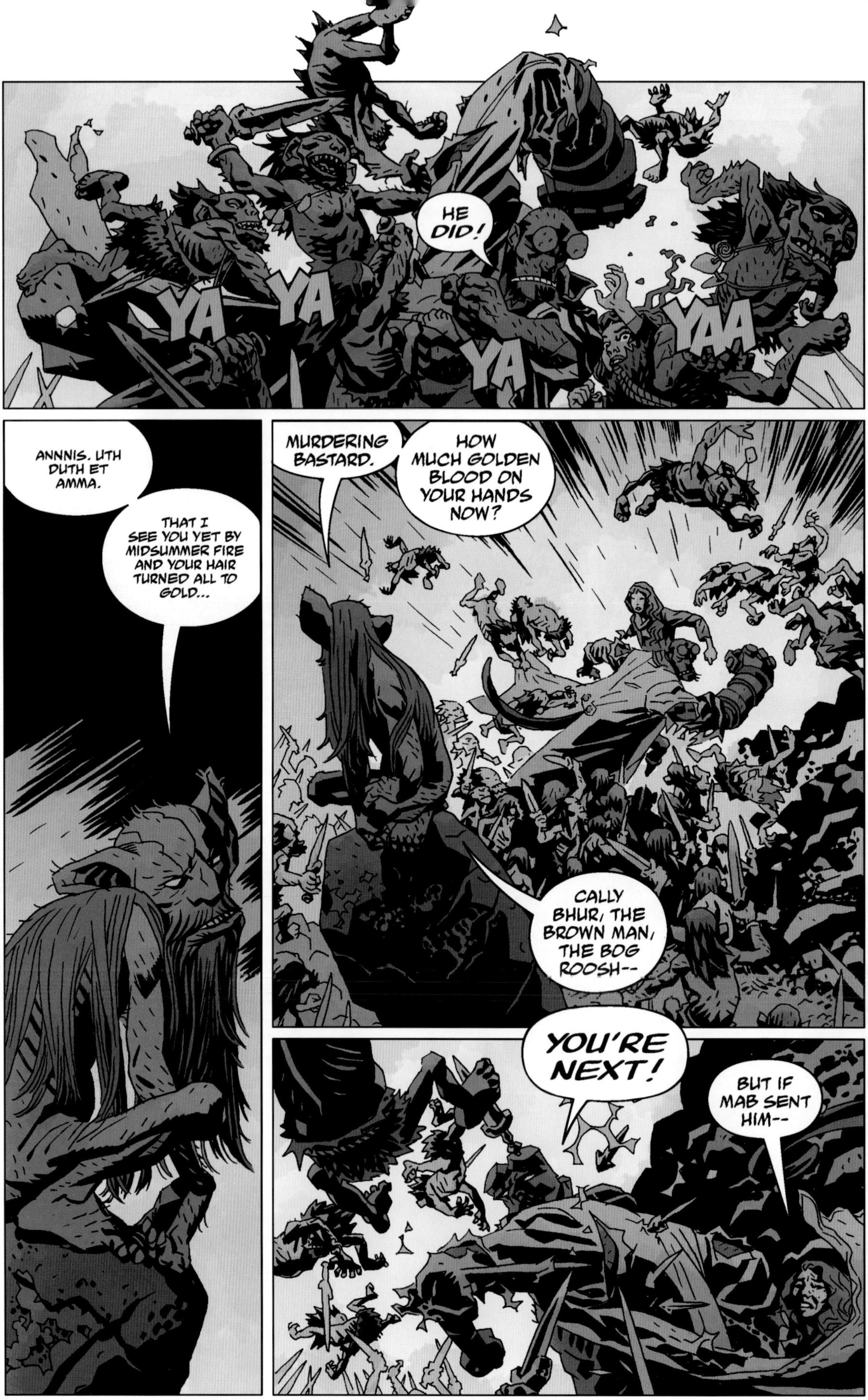
HE DID!
YA
YA
YA
YAA
ANNIS. UTH DUTH ET AMMA.
THAT I SEE YOU YET BY MIDSUMMER FIRE AND YOUR HAIR TURNED ALL TO GOLD...
MURDERING BASTARD.
HOW MUCH GOLDEN BLOOD ON YOUR HANDS NOW?
CALLY BHUR, THE BROWN MAN, THE BOG ROOSH--
YOU'RE NEXT!
BUT IF MAB SENT HIM--

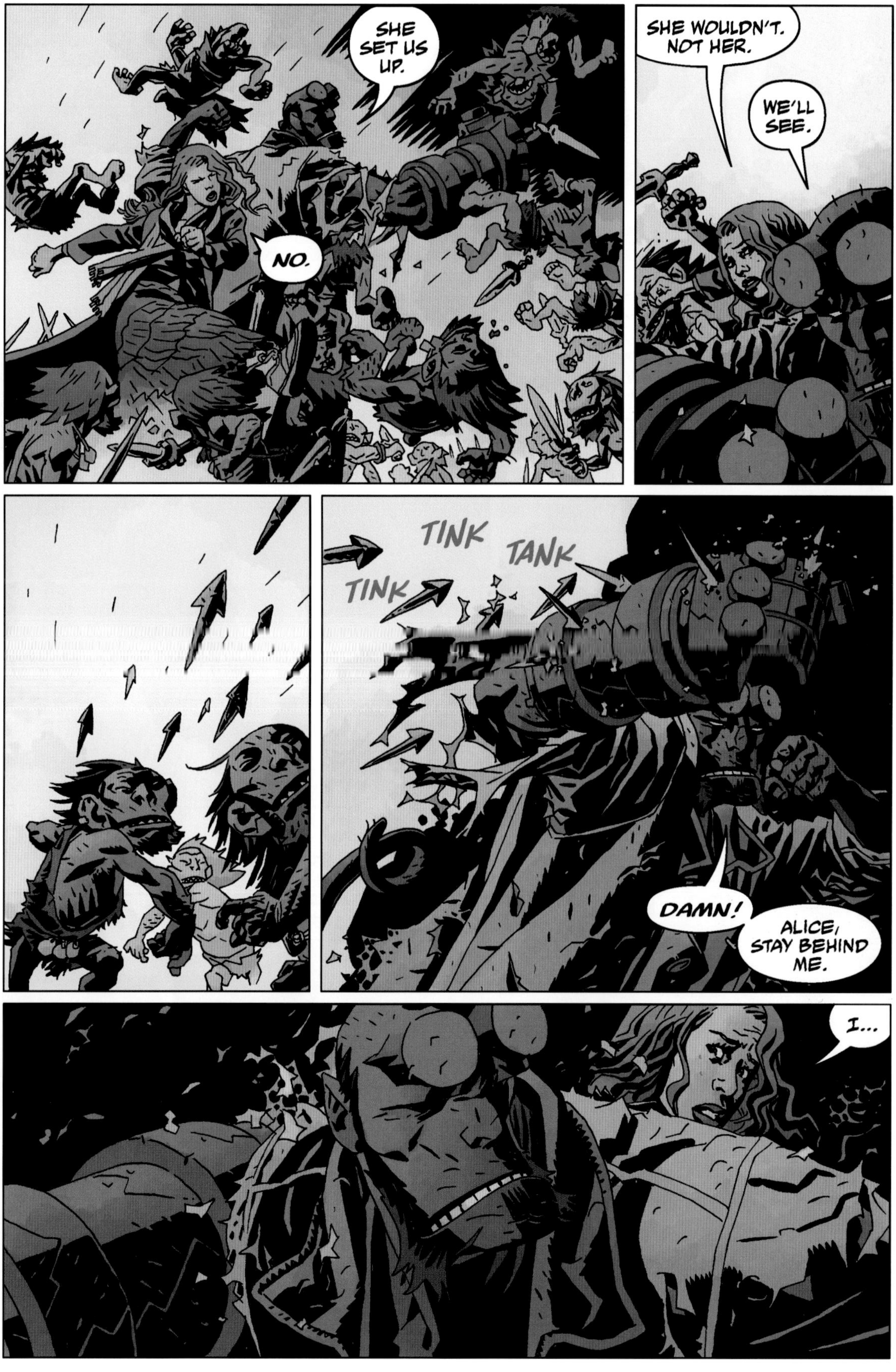
SHE SET US UP.
NO.
SHE WOULDN'T. NOT HER.
WE'LL SEE.
TINK
TANK
TINK
DAMN!
ALICE, STAY BEHIND ME.
I...

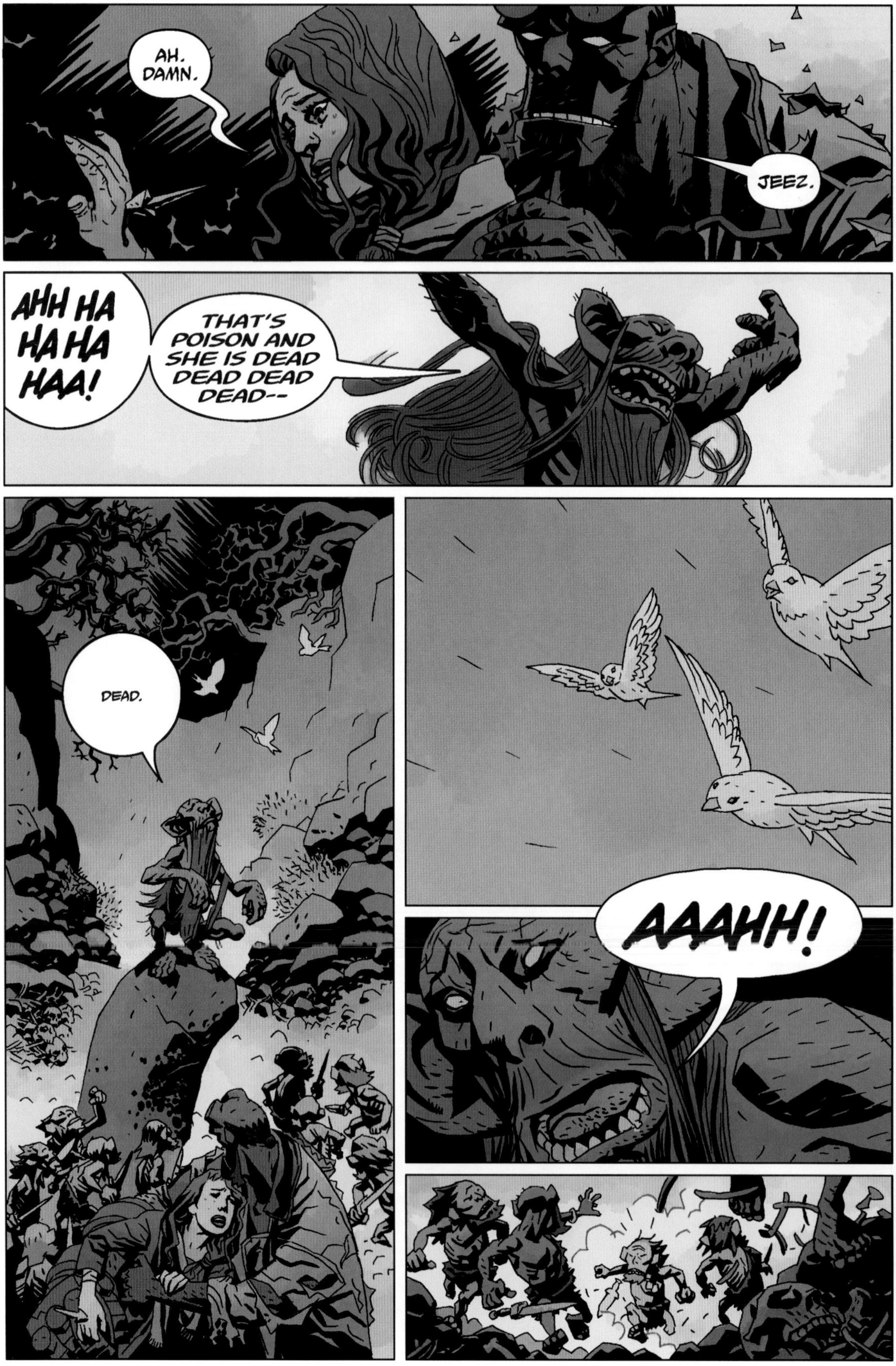
AH. DAMN.
JEEZ.
AHH HA HA HA HAA!
THAT'S POISON AND SHE IS DEAD DEAD DEAD DEAD--
DEAD.
AAAHH!

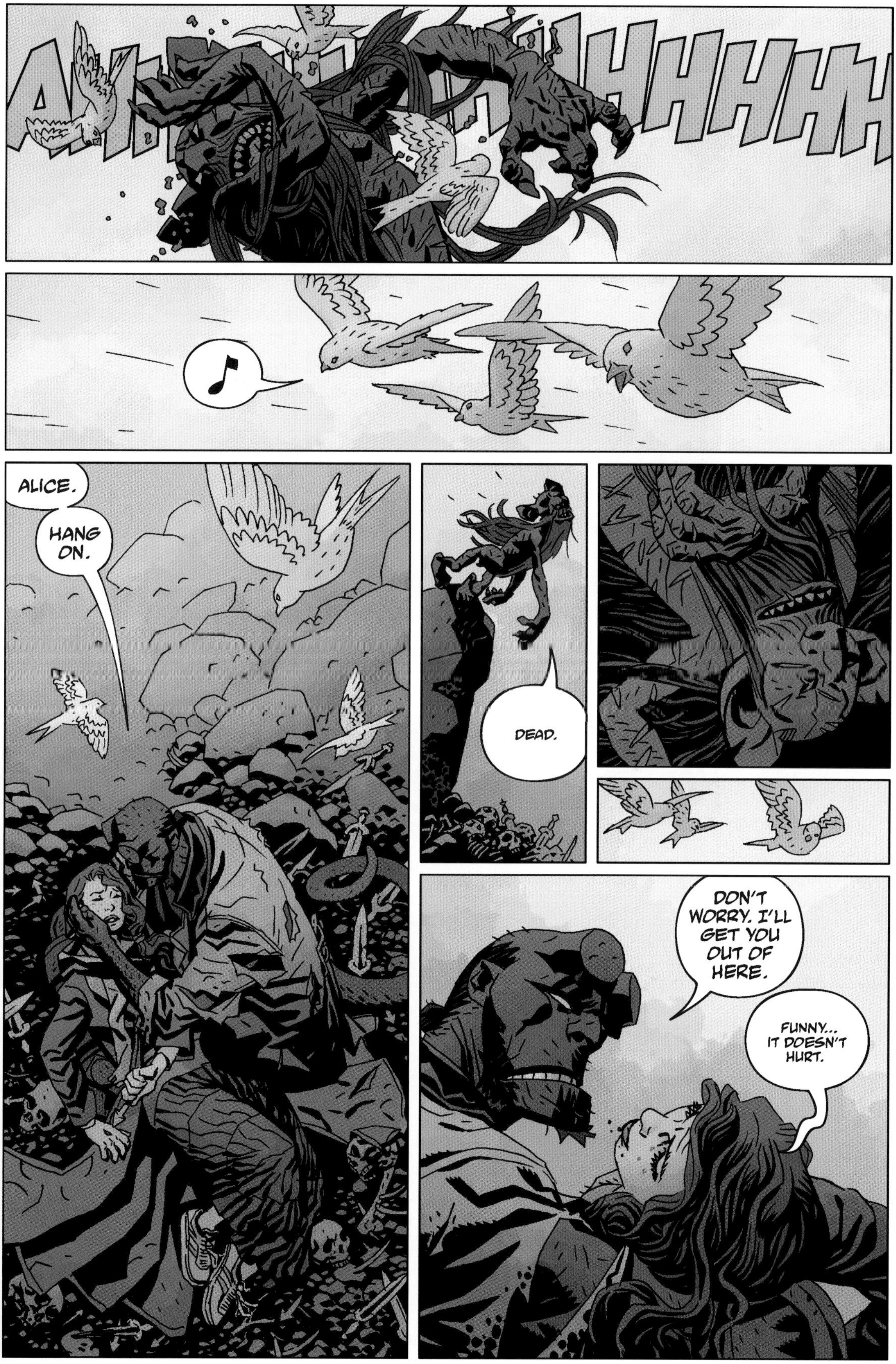
AAAAAAAAHHHHHHHH
♪
ALICE.
HANG ON.
DEAD.
DON'T WORRY. I'LL GET YOU OUT OF HERE.
FUNNY... IT DOESN'T HURT.

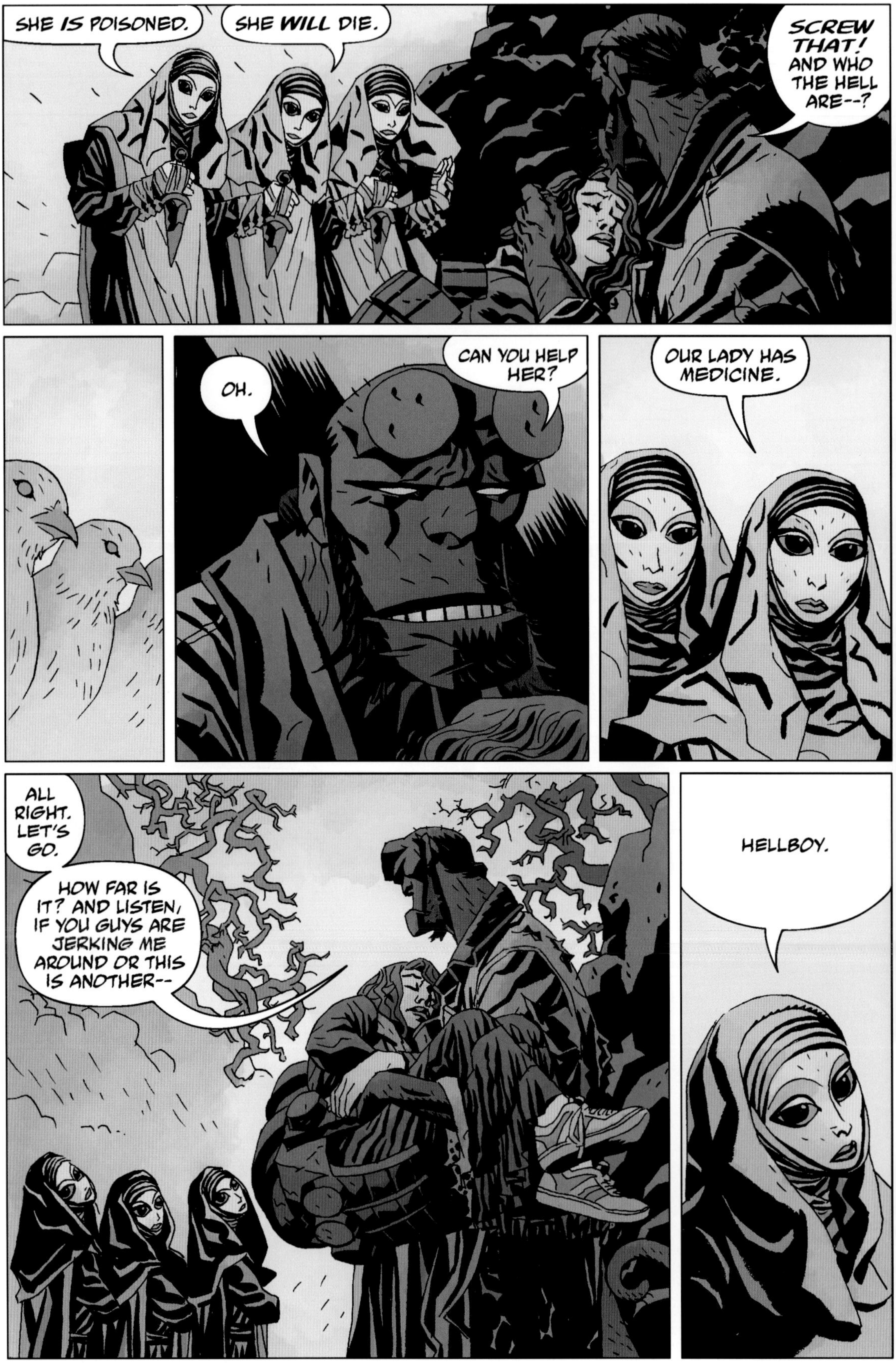
SHE IS POISONED.
SHE WILL DIE.
SCREW THAT! AND WHO THE HELL ARE--?
OH.
CAN YOU HELP HER?
OUR LADY HAS MEDICINE.
ALL RIGHT. LET'S GO.
HOW FAR IS IT? AND LISTEN, IF YOU GUYS ARE JERKING ME AROUND OR THIS IS ANOTHER--
HELLBOY.

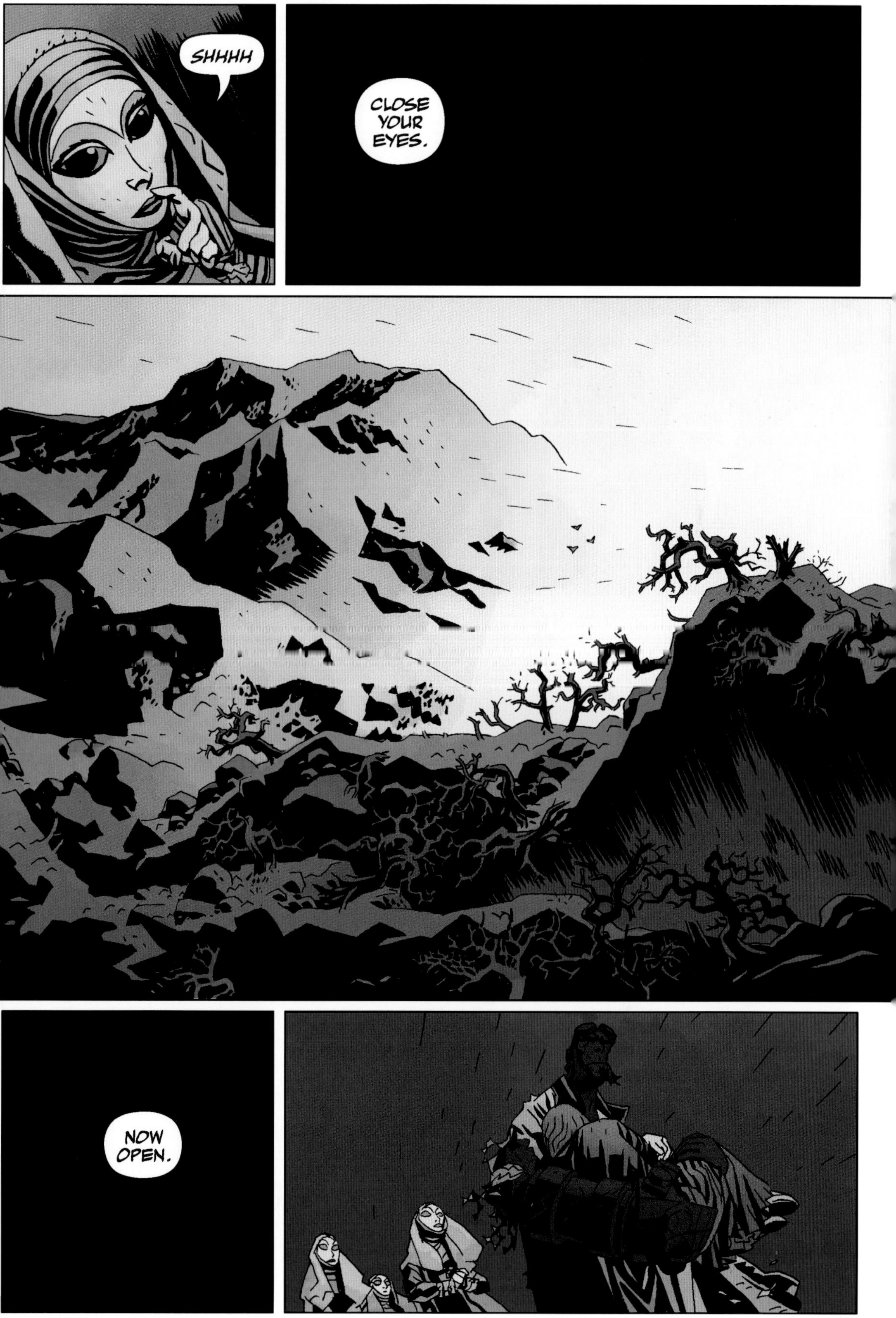
SHHHH
CLOSE YOUR EYES.
NOW OPEN.

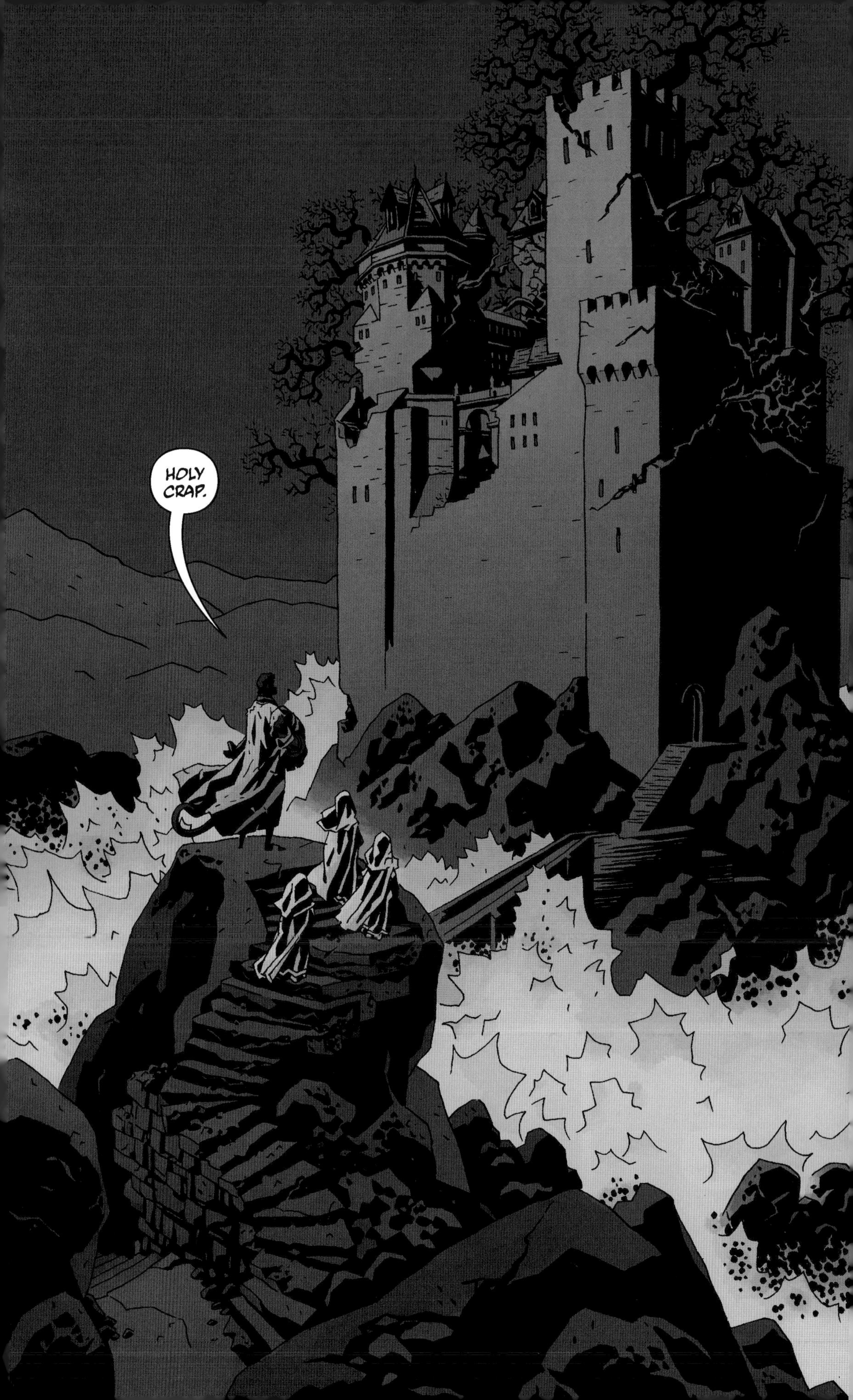
HOLY CRAP.

CHAPTER FIVE

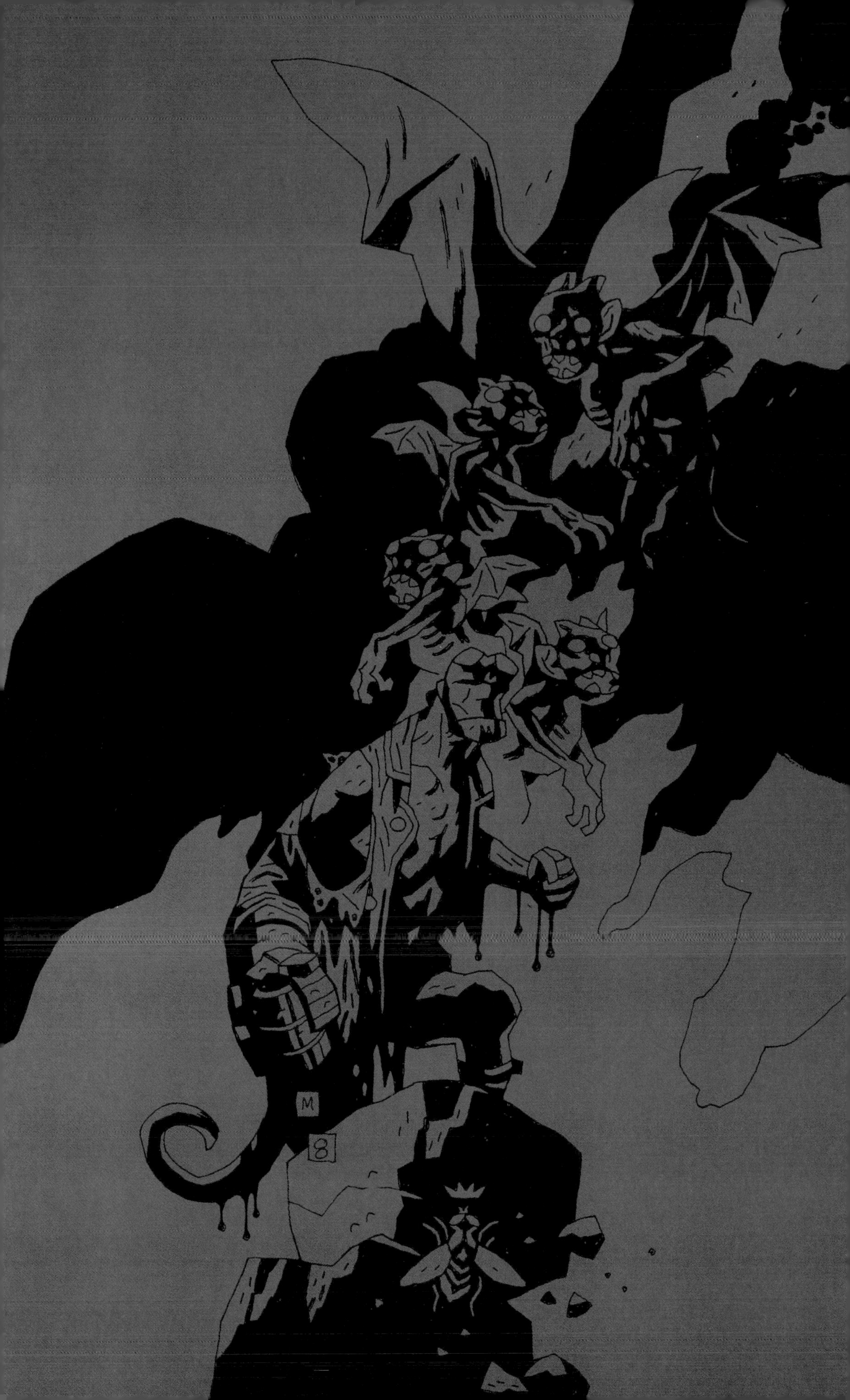

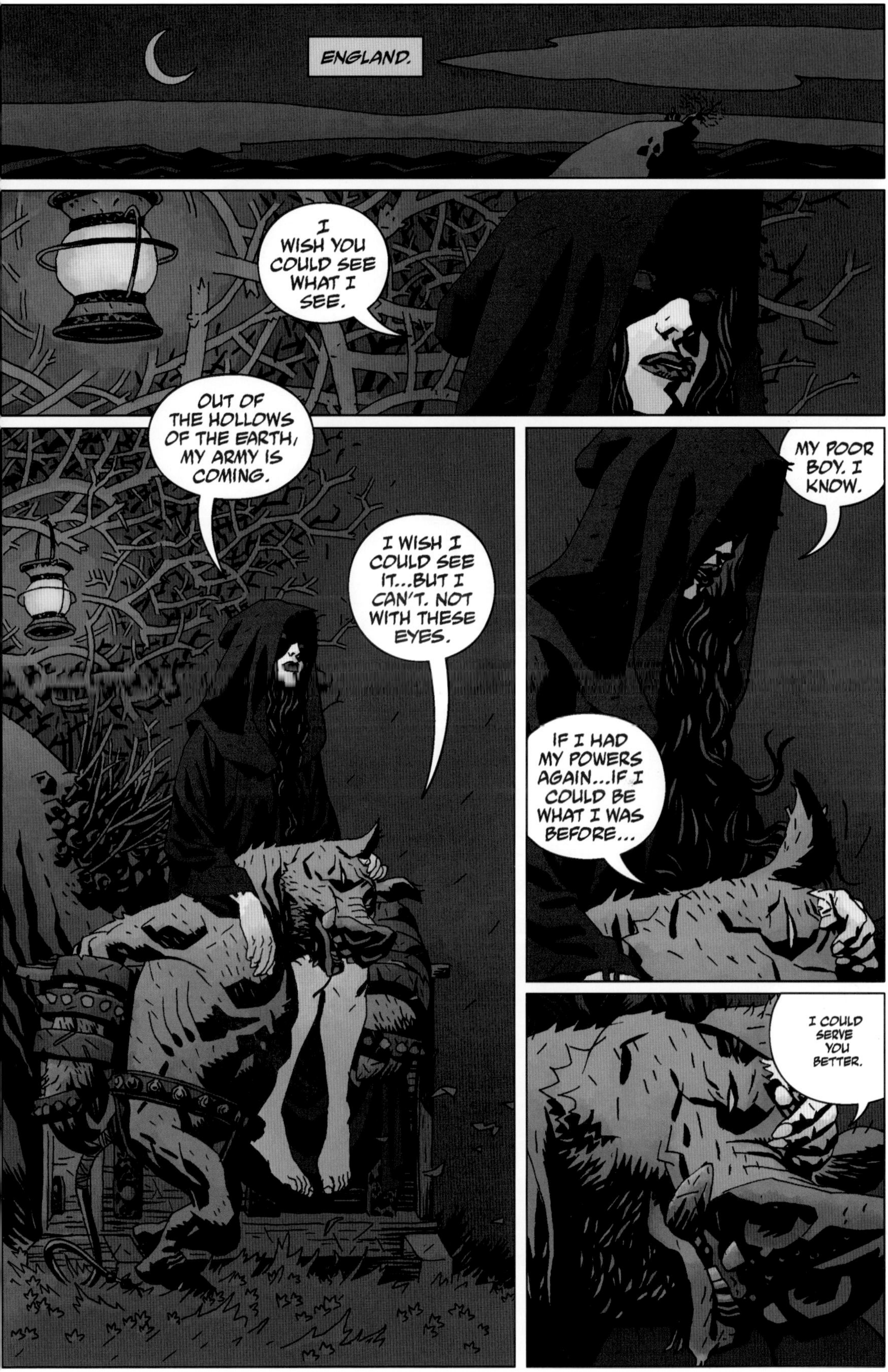
ENGLAND.
I WISH YOU COULD SEE WHAT I SEE.
OUT OF THE HOLLOWS OF THE EARTH, MY ARMY IS COMING.
I WISH I COULD SEE IT...BUT I CAN'T. NOT WITH THESE EYES.
MY POOR BOY. I KNOW.
IF I HAD MY POWERS AGAIN...IF I COULD BE WHAT I WAS BEFORE...
I COULD SERVE YOU BETTER.

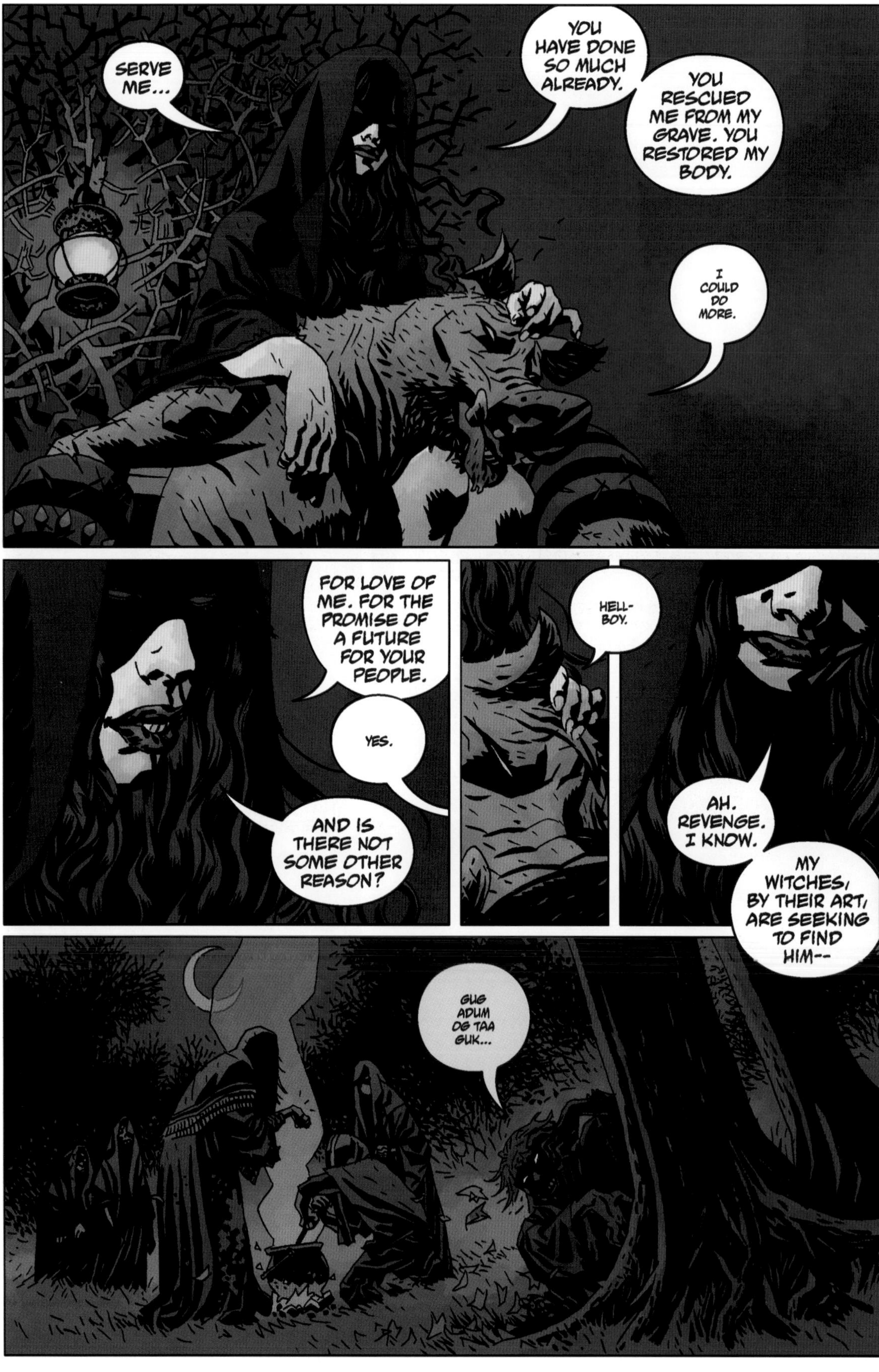
SERVE ME...
YOU HAVE DONE SO MUCH ALREADY.
YOU RESCUED ME FROM MY GRAVE. YOU RESTORED MY BODY.
I COULD DO MORE.
FOR LOVE OF ME. FOR THE PROMISE OF A FUTURE FOR YOUR PEOPLE.
YES.
AND IS THERE NOT SOME OTHER REASON?
HELL-BOY.
AH. REVENGE. I KNOW.
MY WITCHES, BY THEIR ART, ARE SEEKING TO FIND HIM--
GUG ADUM OG TAA GUK...

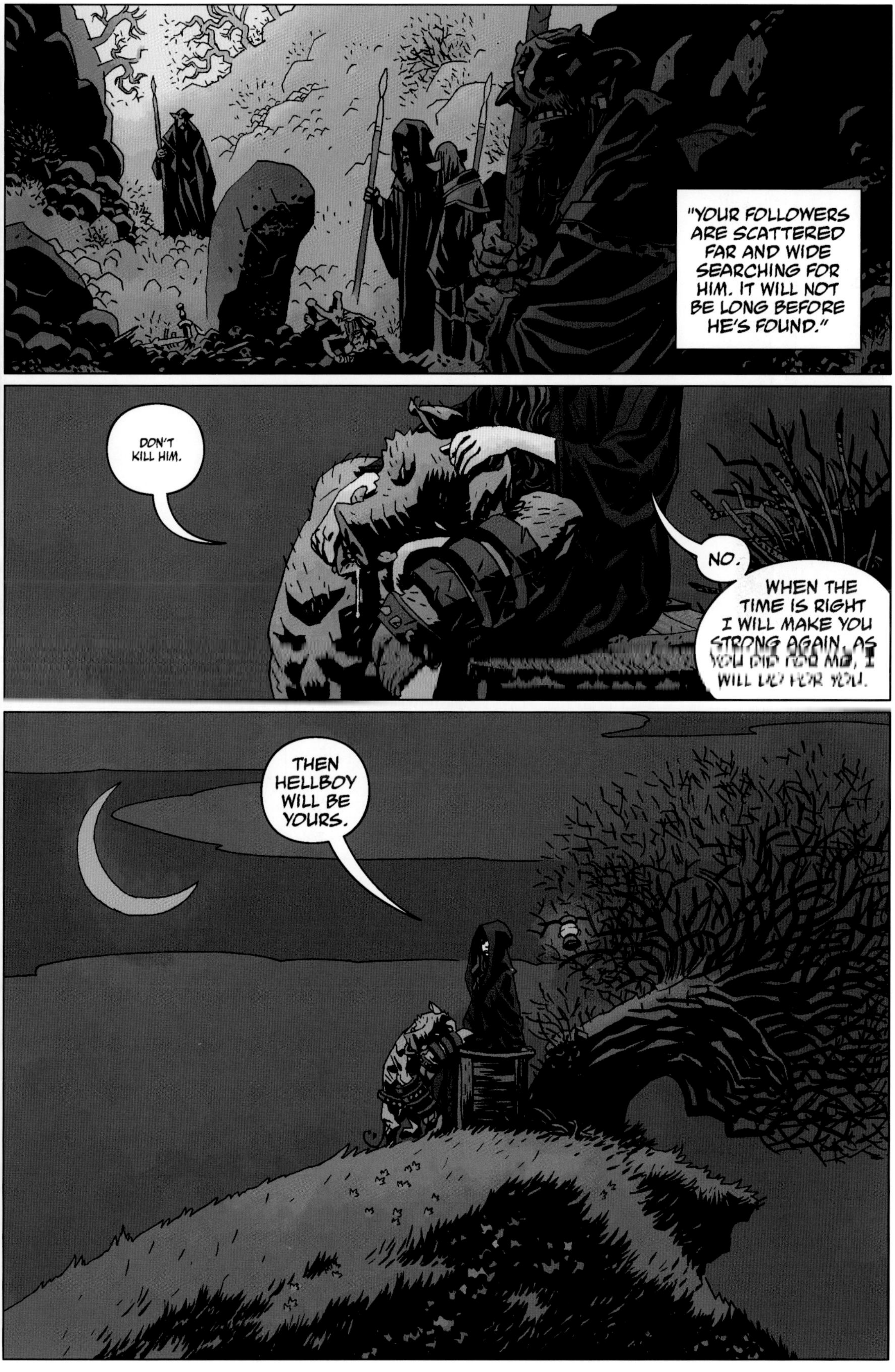

"YOUR FOLLOWERS ARE SCATTERED FAR AND WIDE SEARCHING FOR HIM. IT WILL NOT BE LONG BEFORE HE'S FOUND."
DON'T KILL HIM.
NO.
WHEN THE TIME IS RIGHT I WILL MAKE YOU STRONG AGAIN. AS YOU DID FOR ME, I WILL DO FOR YOU.
THEN HELLBOY WILL BE YOURS.

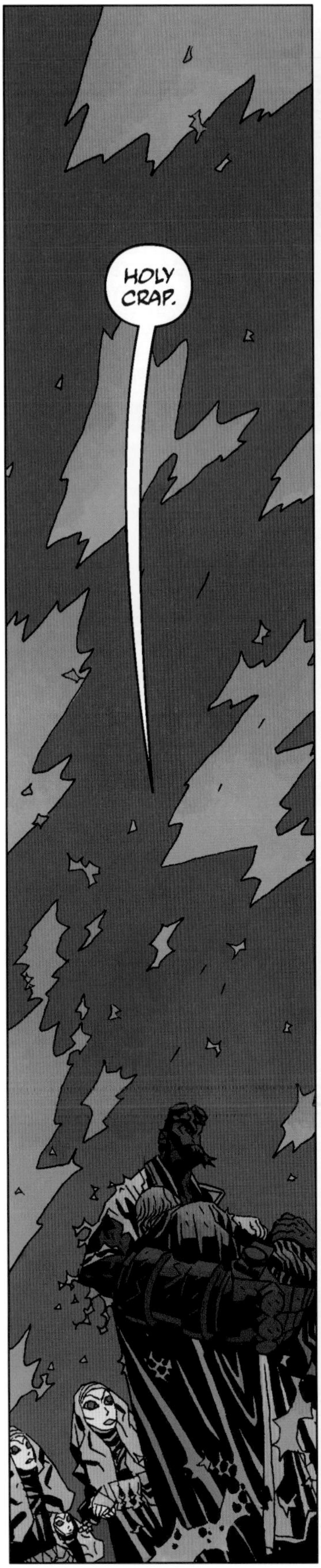
HOLY CRAP.

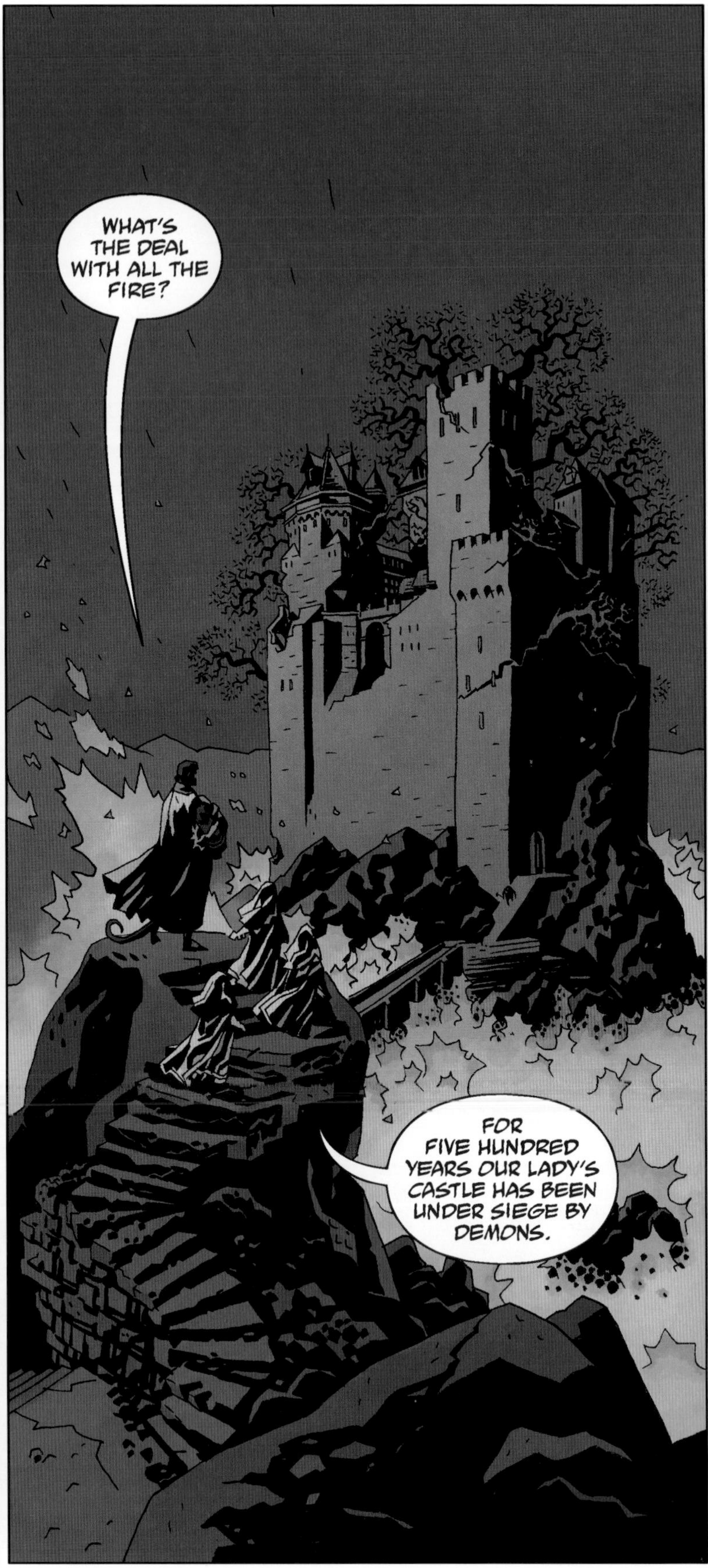
WHAT'S THE DEAL WITH ALL THE FIRE?
FOR FIVE HUNDRED YEARS OUR LADY'S CASTLE HAS BEEN UNDER SIEGE BY DEMONS.

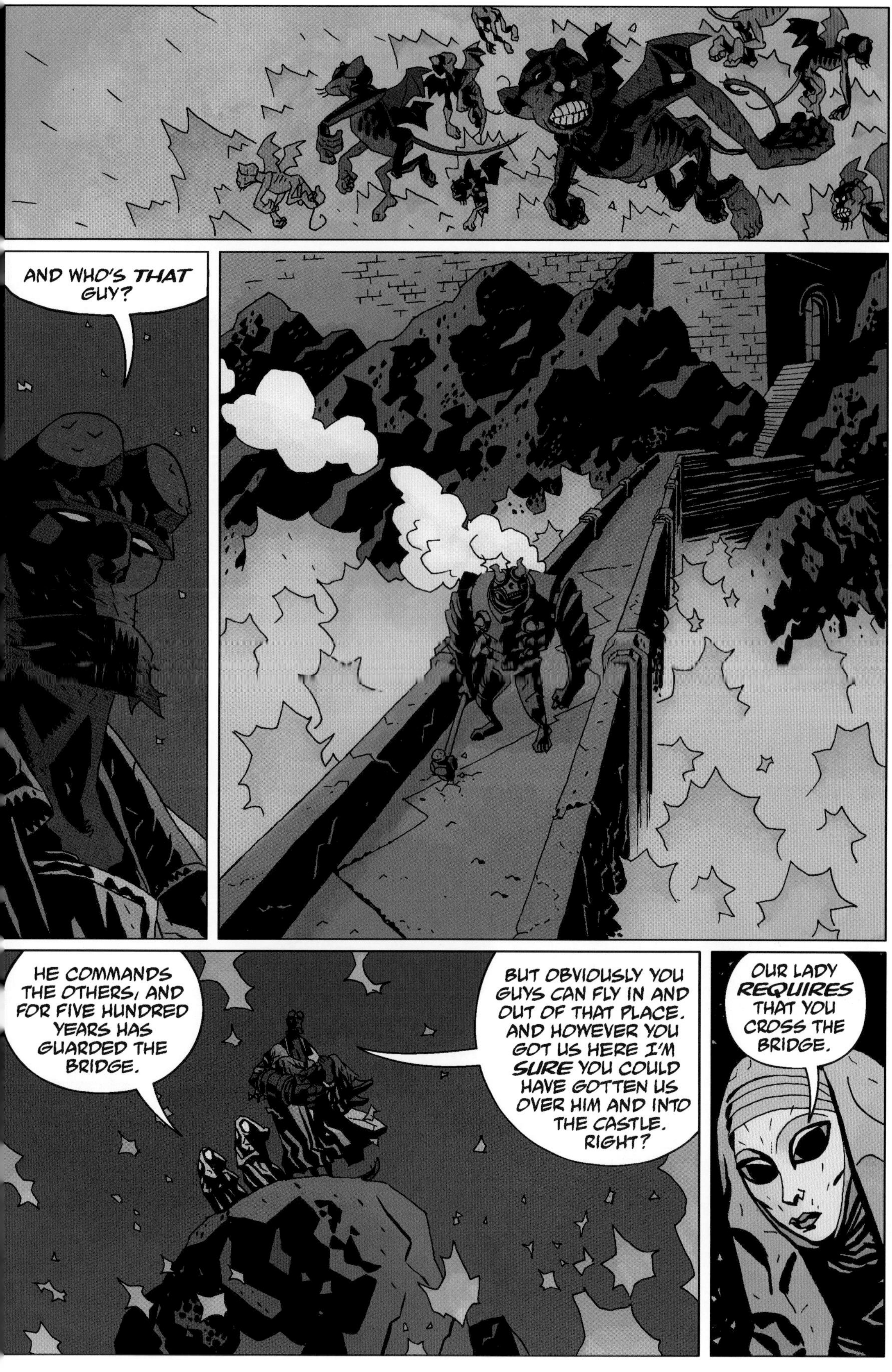
AND WHO'S THAT GUY?
HE COMMANDS THE OTHERS, AND FOR FIVE HUNDRED YEARS HAS GUARDED THE BRIDGE.
BUT OBVIOUSLY YOU GUYS CAN FLY IN AND OUT OF THAT PLACE. AND HOWEVER YOU GOT US HERE I'M SURE YOU COULD HAVE GOTTEN US OVER HIM AND INTO THE CASTLE. RIGHT?
OUR LADY REQUIRES THAT YOU CROSS THE BRIDGE.

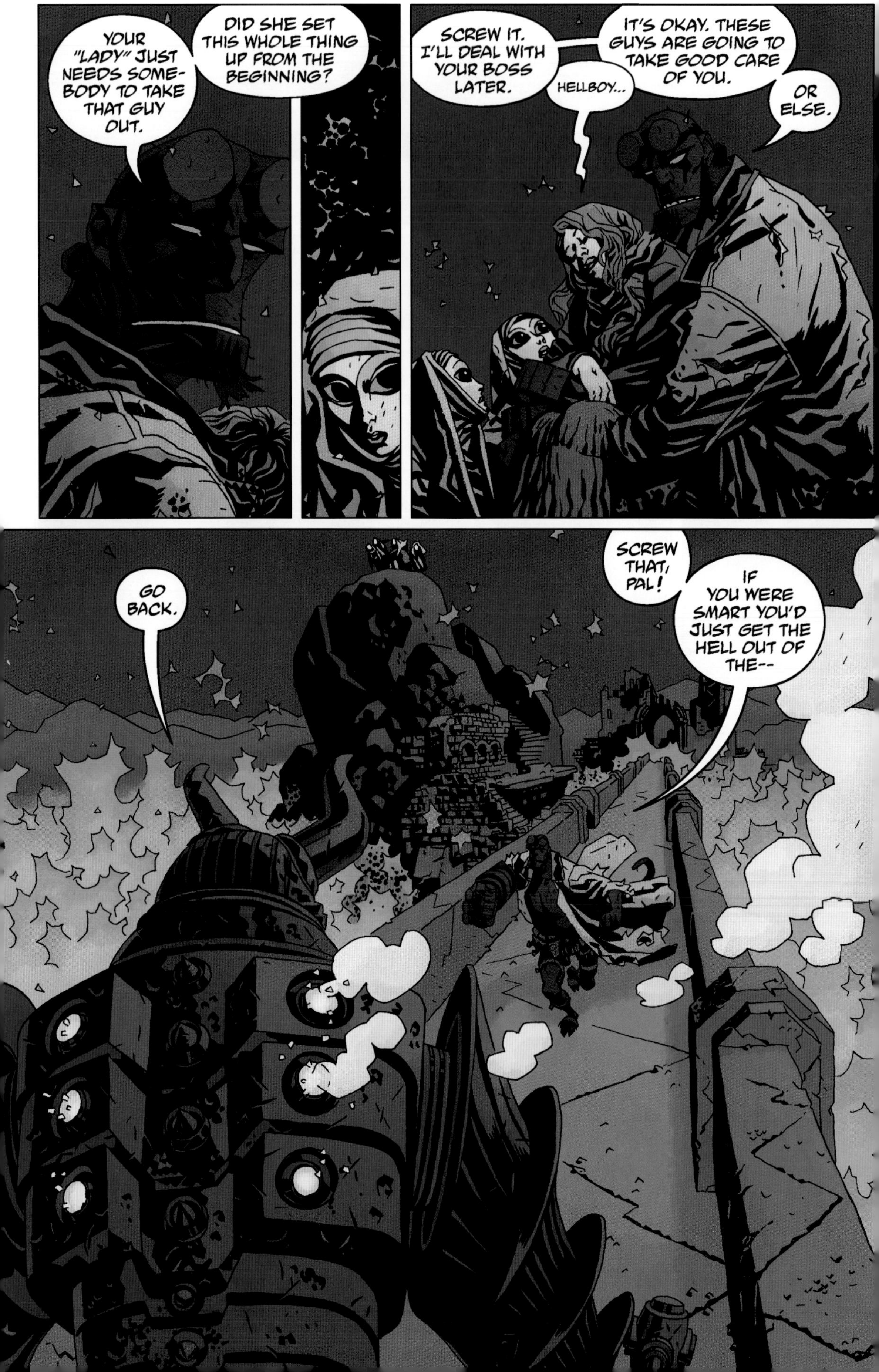
YOUR "LADY" JUST NEEDS SOME-BODY TO TAKE THAT GUY OUT.
DID SHE SET THIS WHOLE THING UP FROM THE BEGINNING?
SCREW IT. I'LL DEAL WITH YOUR BOSS LATER.
IT'S OKAY. THESE GUYS ARE GOING TO TAKE GOOD CARE OF YOU.
HELLBOY...
OR ELSE.
GO BACK.
SCREW THAT, PAL!
IF YOU WERE SMART YOU'D JUST GET THE HELL OUT OF THE--

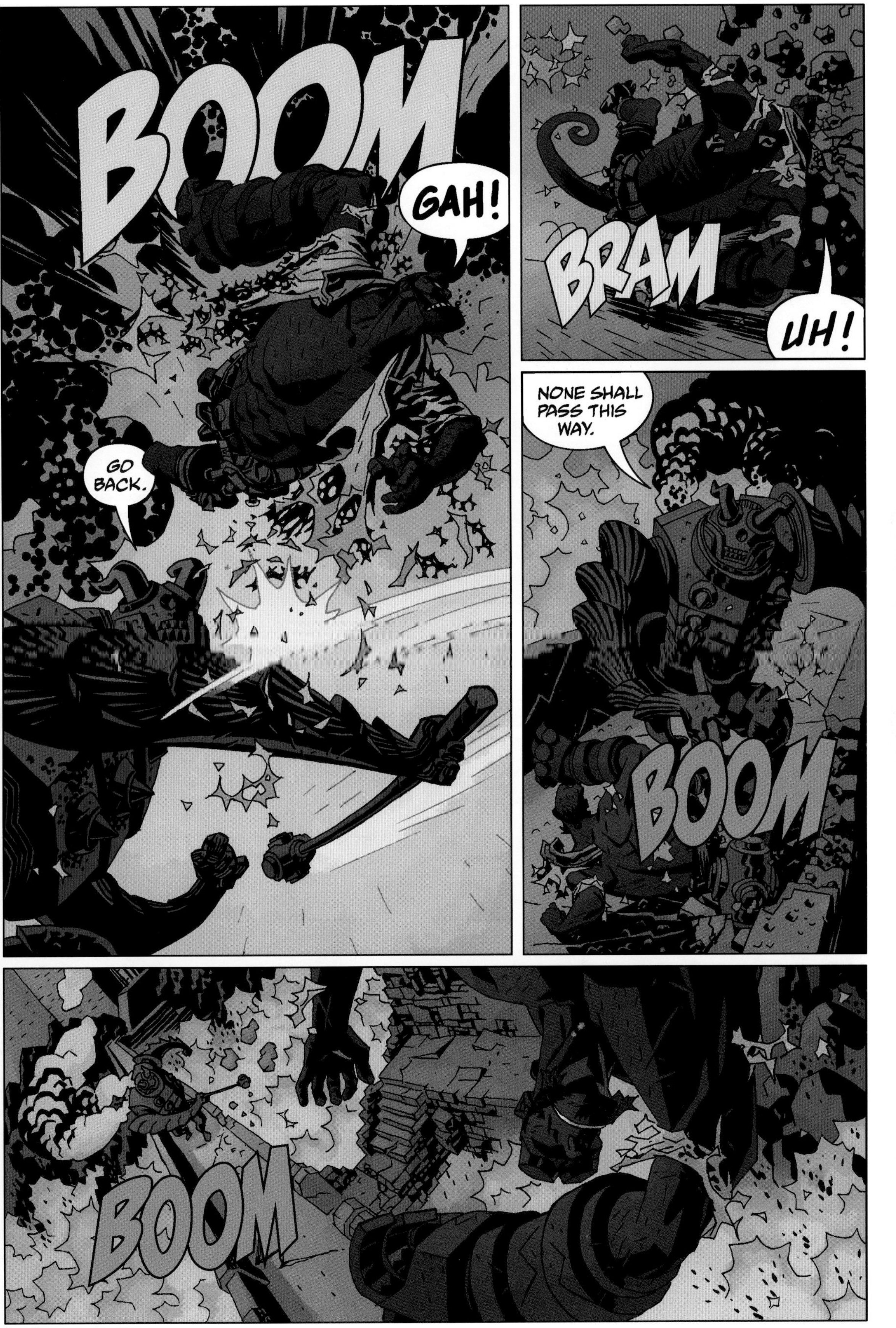
BOOM
GAH!
GO BACK.
BRAM
UH!
NONE SHALL PASS THIS WAY.
BOOM
BOOM

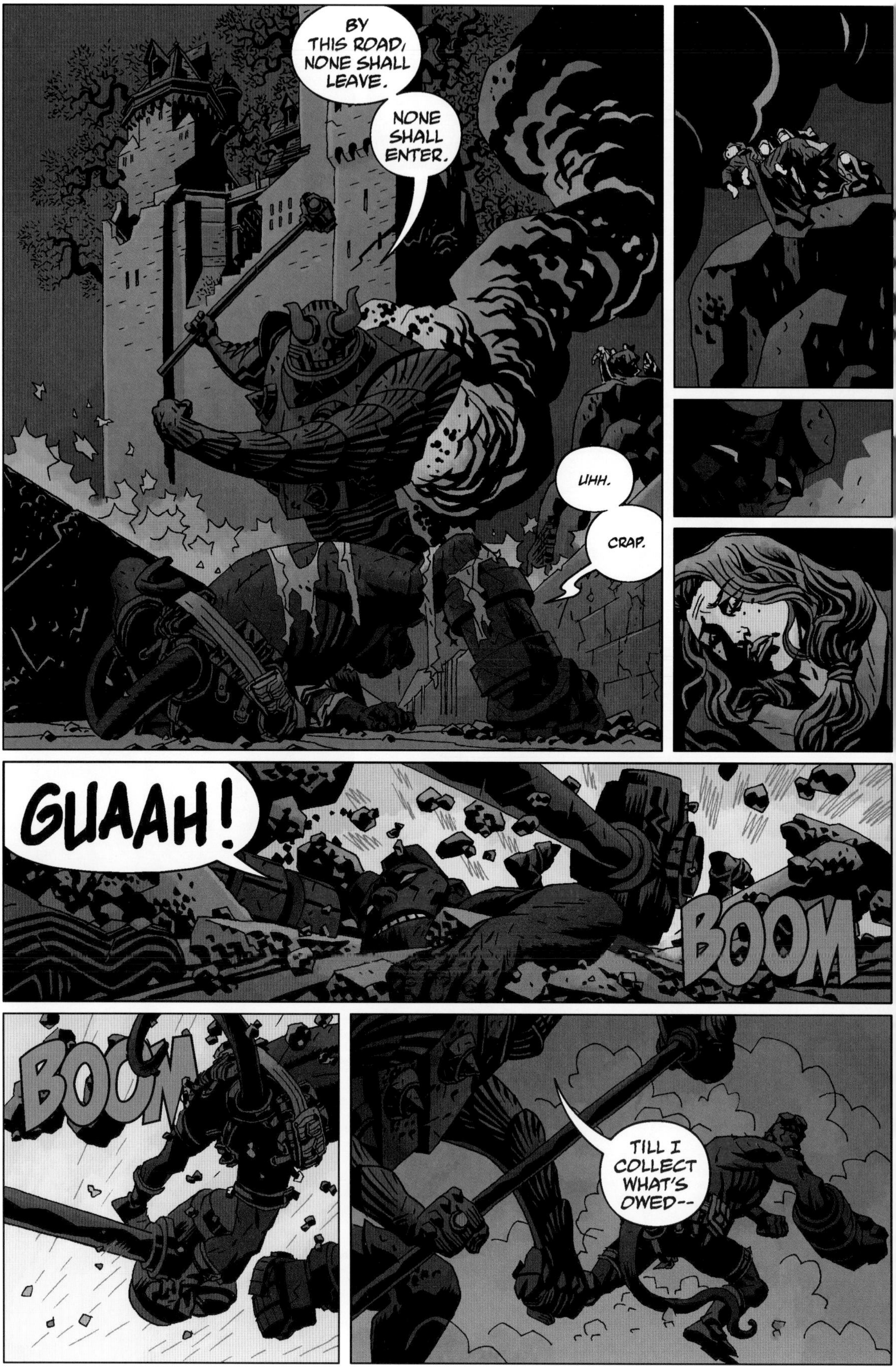
BY THIS ROAD, NONE SHALL LEAVE.
NONE SHALL ENTER.
UHH.
CRAP.
GUAAH!
BOOM
BOOM
TILL I COLLECT WHAT'S OWED--

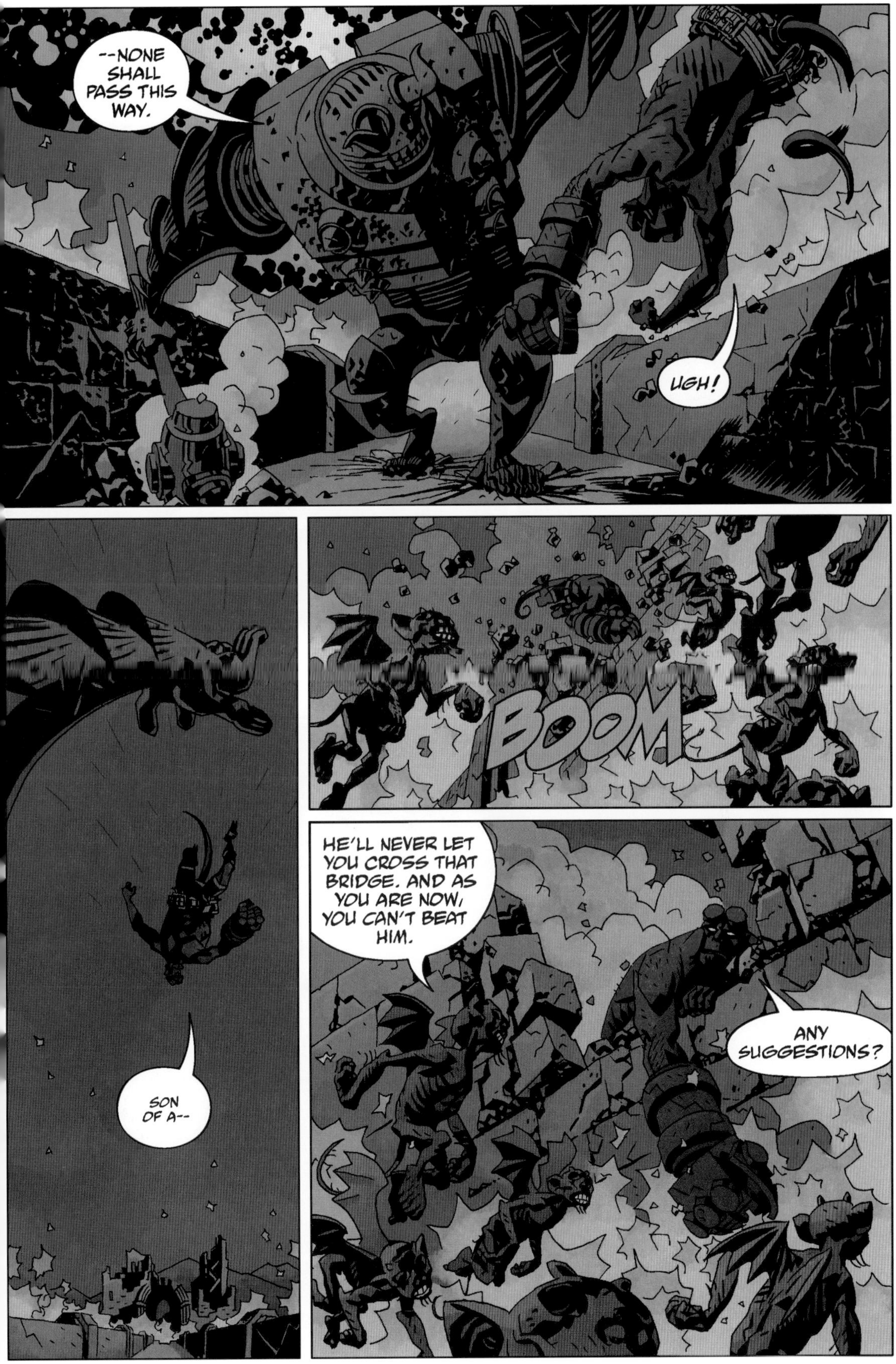
--NONE SHALL PASS THIS WAY.
UGH!
SON OF A--
BOOM
HE'LL NEVER LET YOU CROSS THAT BRIDGE. AND AS YOU ARE NOW, YOU CAN'T BEAT HIM.
ANY SUGGESTIONS?

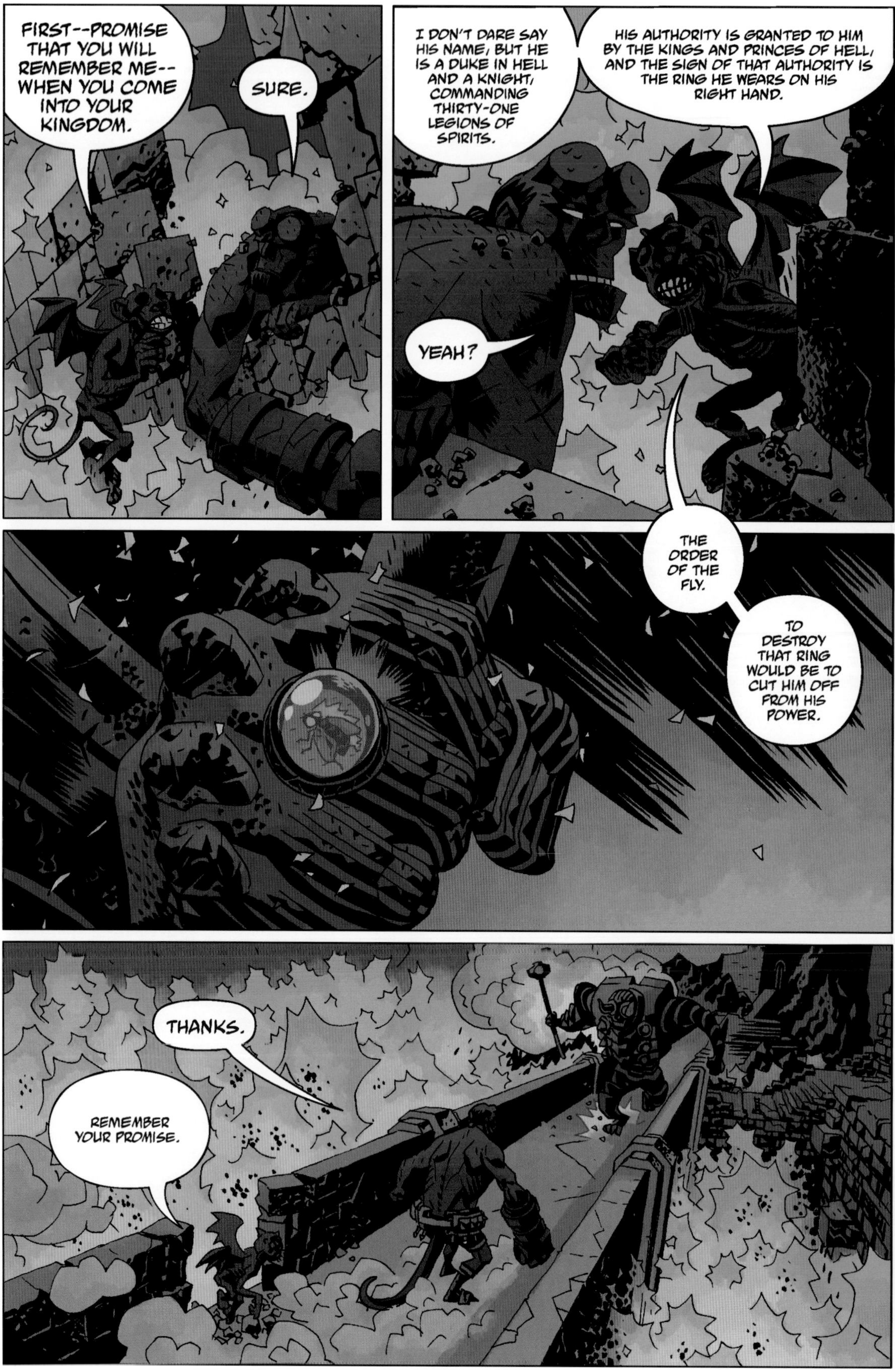
FIRST--PROMISE THAT YOU WILL REMEMBER ME--WHEN YOU COME INTO YOUR KINGDOM.
SURE.
I DON'T DARE SAY HIS NAME, BUT HE IS A DUKE IN HELL AND A KNIGHT, COMMANDING THIRTY-ONE LEGIONS OF SPIRITS.
HIS AUTHORITY IS GRANTED TO HIM BY THE KINGS AND PRINCES OF HELL, AND THE SIGN OF THAT AUTHORITY IS THE RING HE WEARS ON HIS RIGHT HAND.
YEAH?
THE ORDER OF THE FLY.
TO DESTROY THAT RING WOULD BE TO CUT HIM OFF FROM HIS POWER.
THANKS.
REMEMBER YOUR PROMISE.

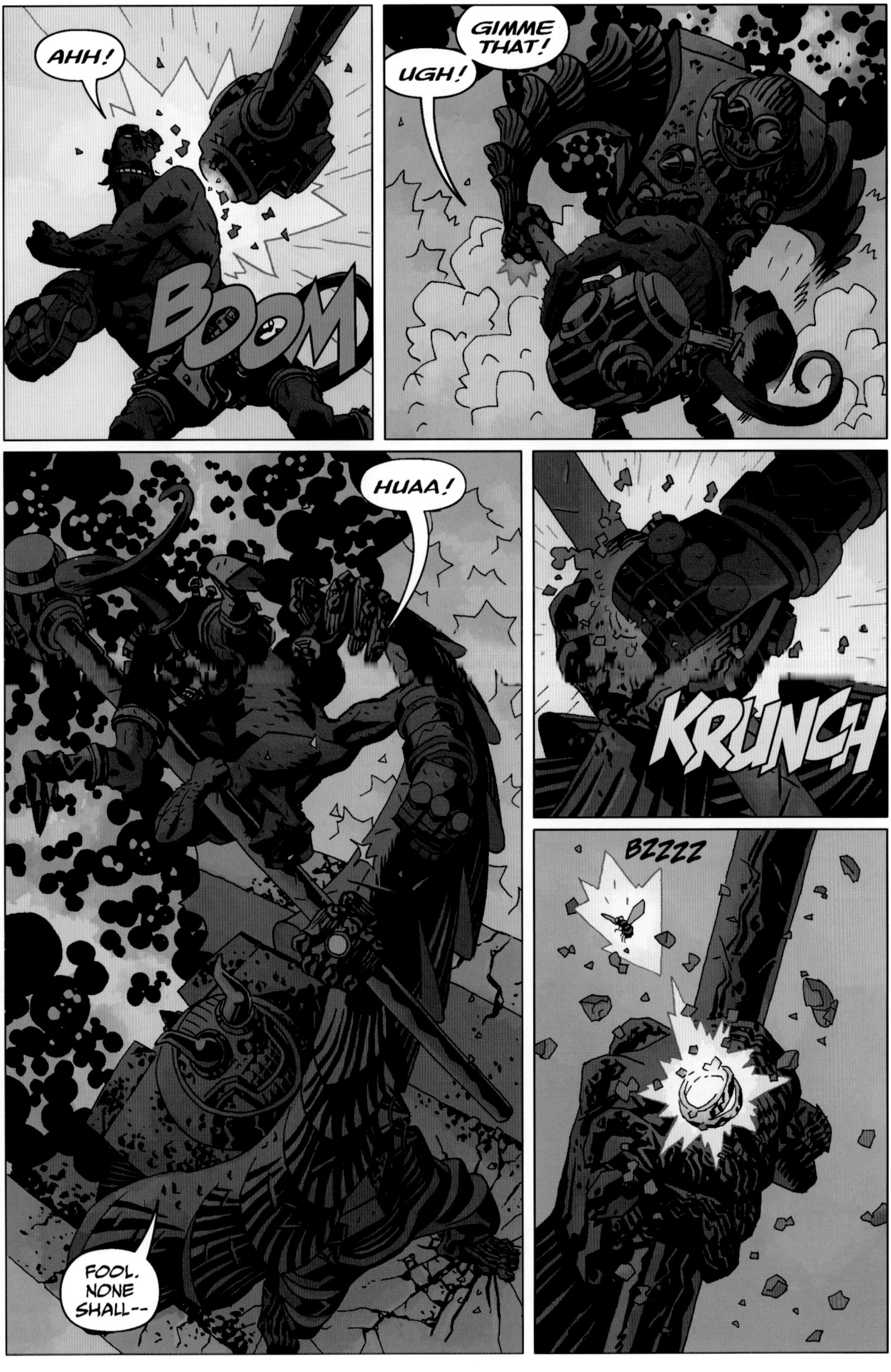
AHH!
BOOM
GIMME THAT!
UGH!
HUAA!
FOOL. NONE SHALL--
KRUNCH
BZZZZ

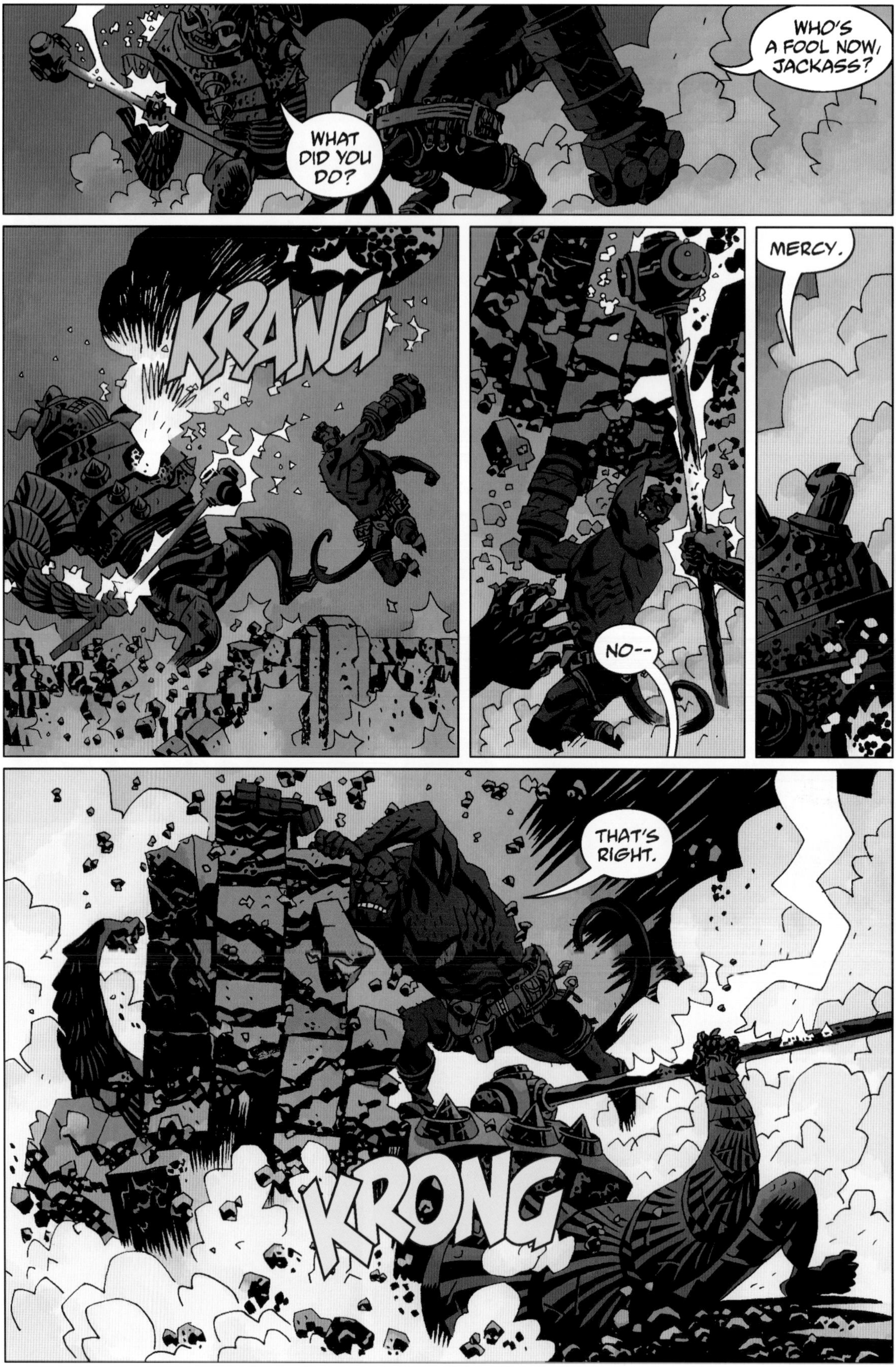
WHAT DID YOU DO?
WHO'S A FOOL NOW, JACKASS?
KRANG
NO--
MERCY.
THAT'S RIGHT.
KRONG

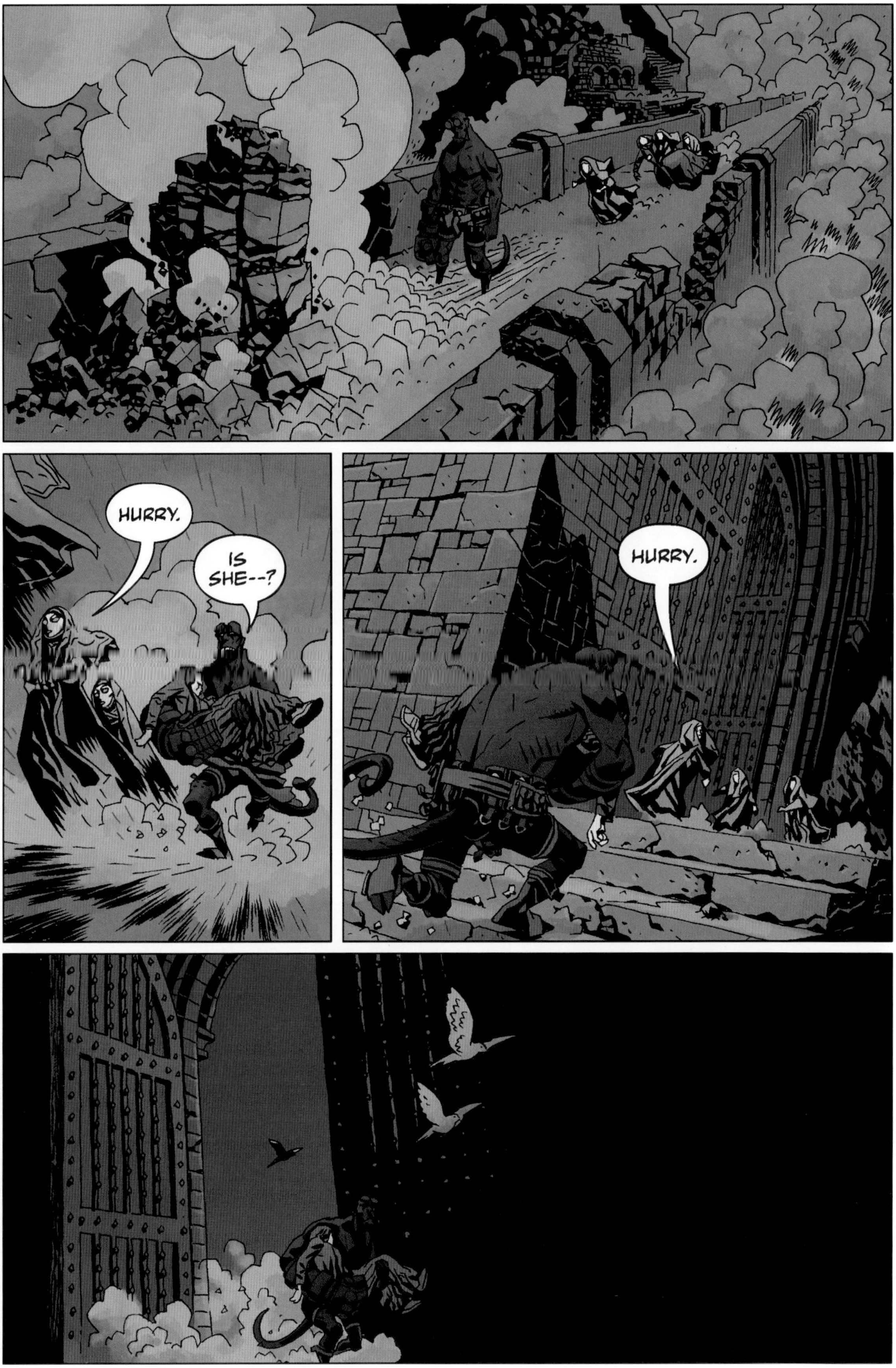
HURRY.
IS SHE--?
HURRY.

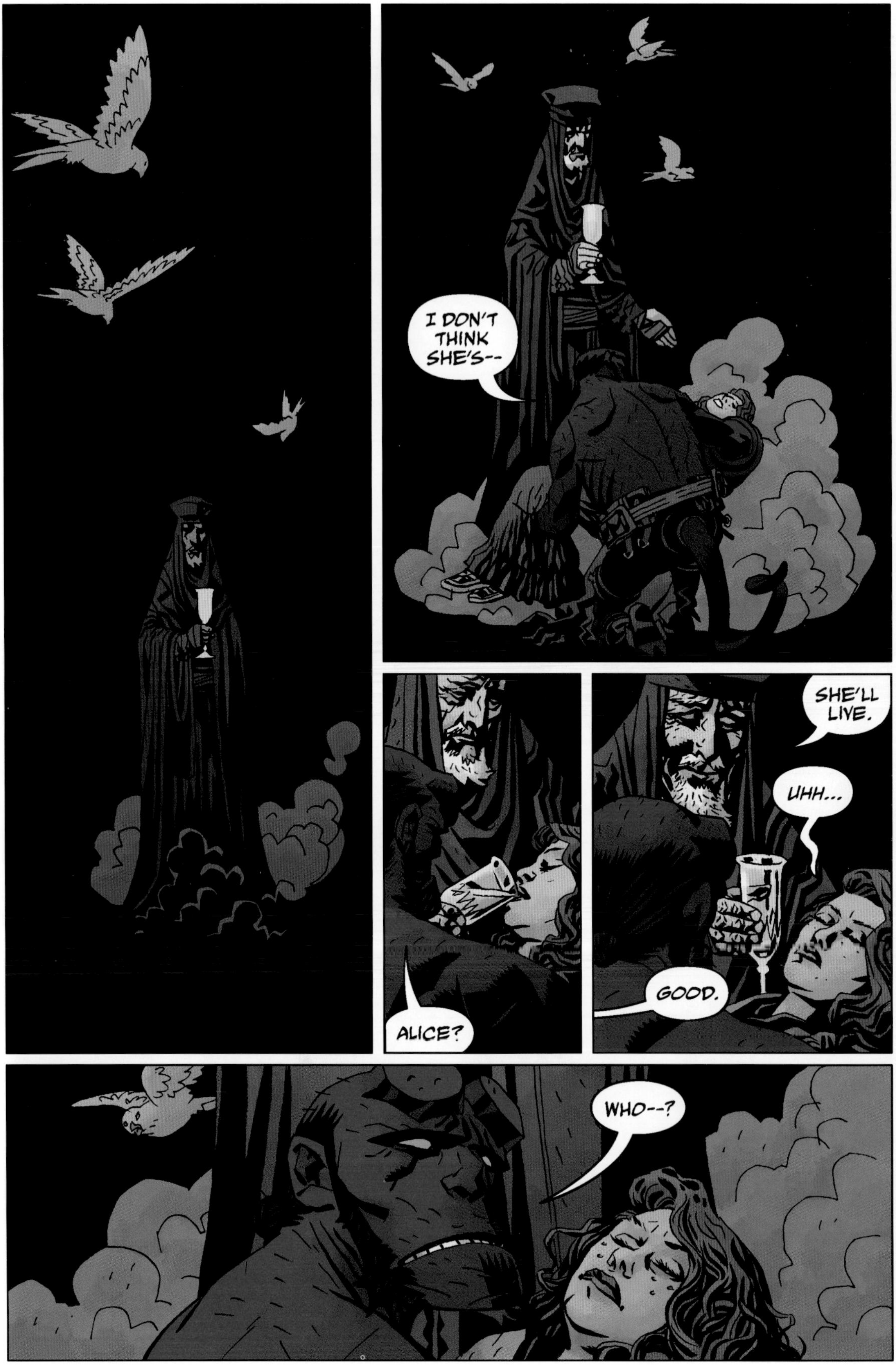
I DON'T THINK SHE'S--
ALICE?
SHE'LL LIVE.
UHH...
GOOD.
WHO--?

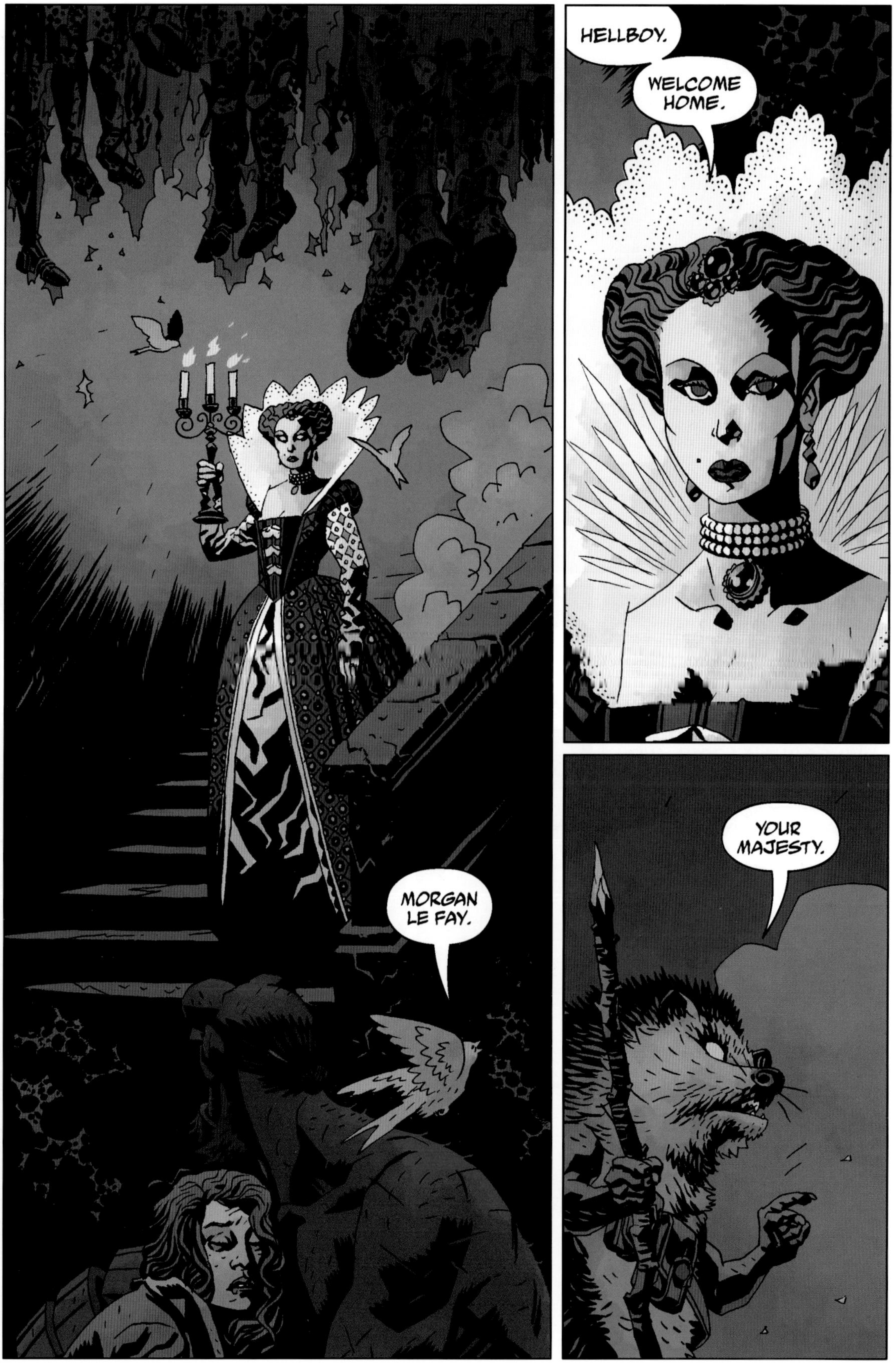
MORGAN LE FAY.
HELLBOY.
WELCOME HOME.
YOUR MAJESTY.

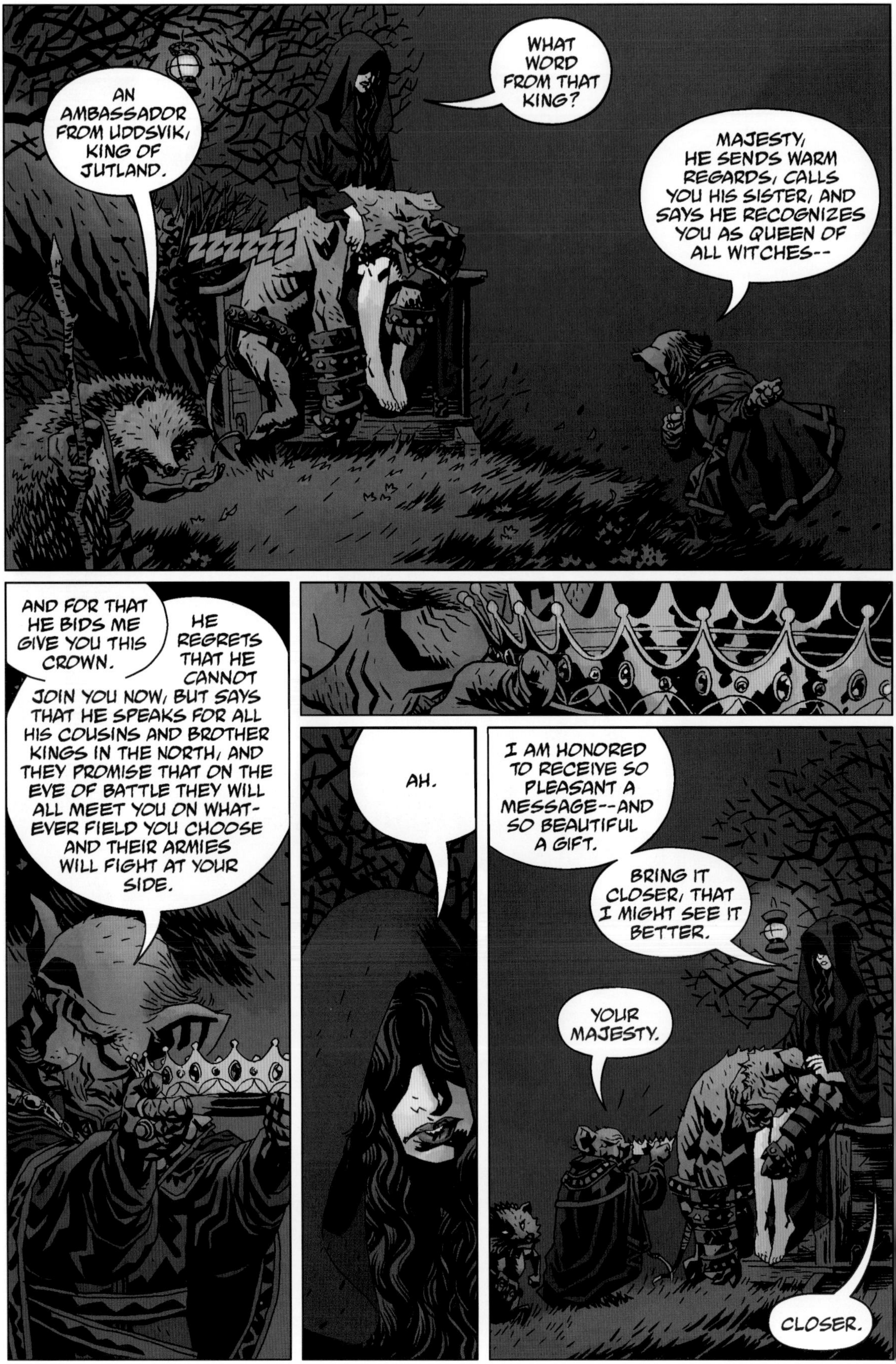
AN AMBASSADOR FROM UDDSVIK, KING OF JUTLAND.
WHAT WORD FROM THAT KING?
MAJESTY, HE SENDS WARM REGARDS, CALLS YOU HIS SISTER, AND SAYS HE RECOGNIZES YOU AS QUEEN OF ALL WITCHES--
ZZZZZZ
AND FOR THAT HE BIDS ME GIVE YOU THIS CROWN.
HE REGRETS THAT HE CANNOT JOIN YOU NOW, BUT SAYS THAT HE SPEAKS FOR ALL HIS COUSINS AND BROTHER KINGS IN THE NORTH, AND THEY PROMISE THAT ON THE EVE OF BATTLE THEY WILL ALL MEET YOU ON WHAT-EVER FIELD YOU CHOOSE AND THEIR ARMIES WILL FIGHT AT YOUR SIDE.
AH.
I AM HONORED TO RECEIVE SO PLEASANT A MESSAGE--AND SO BEAUTIFUL A GIFT.
BRING IT CLOSER, THAT I MIGHT SEE IT BETTER.
YOUR MAJESTY.
CLOSER.

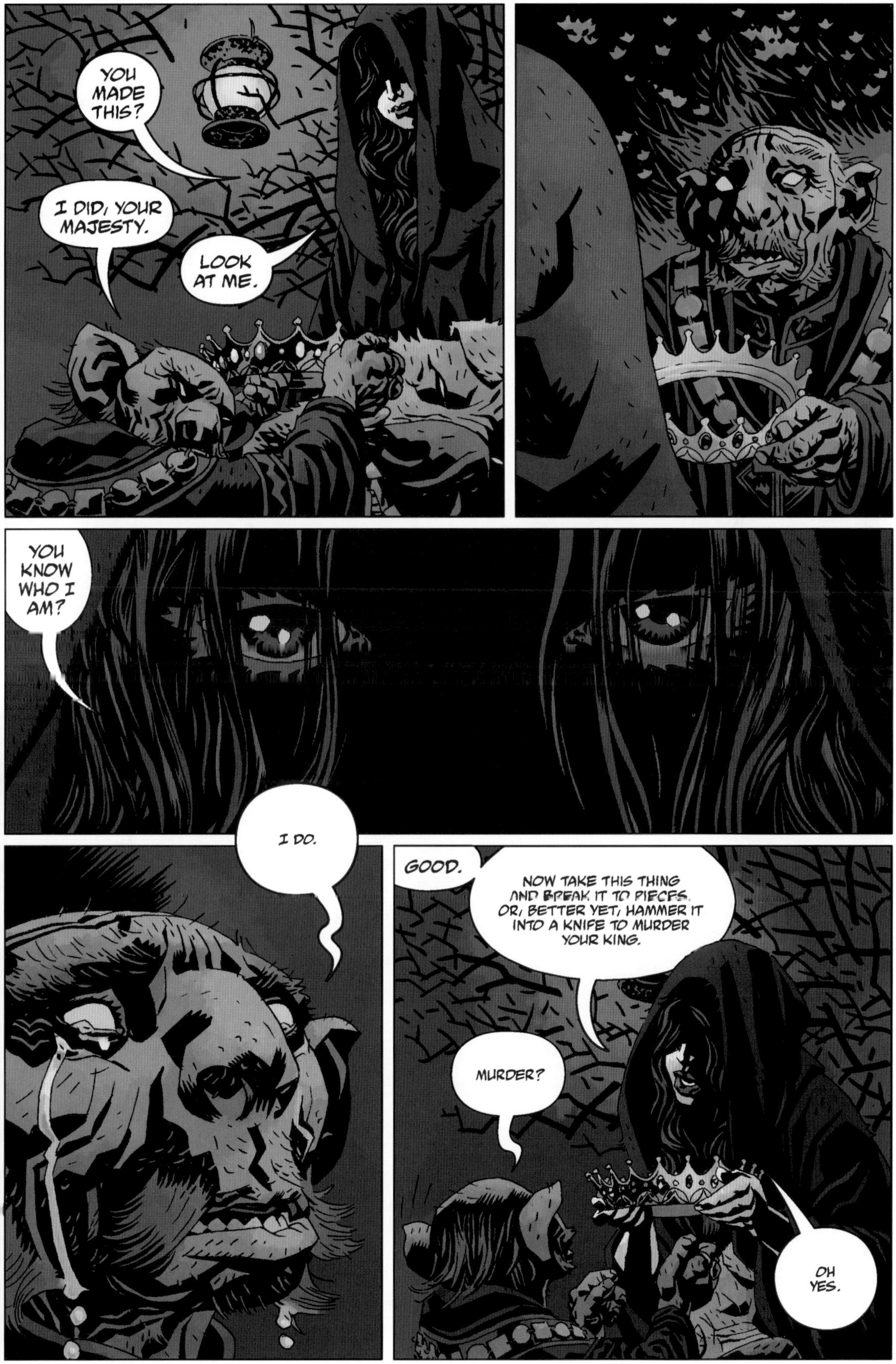
YOU MADE THIS?
I DID, YOUR MAJESTY.
LOOK AT ME.
YOU KNOW WHO I AM?
I DO.
GOOD.
NOW TAKE THIS THING AND BREAK IT TO PIECES. OR, BETTER YET, HAMMER IT INTO A KNIFE TO MURDER YOUR KING.
MURDER?
OH YES.

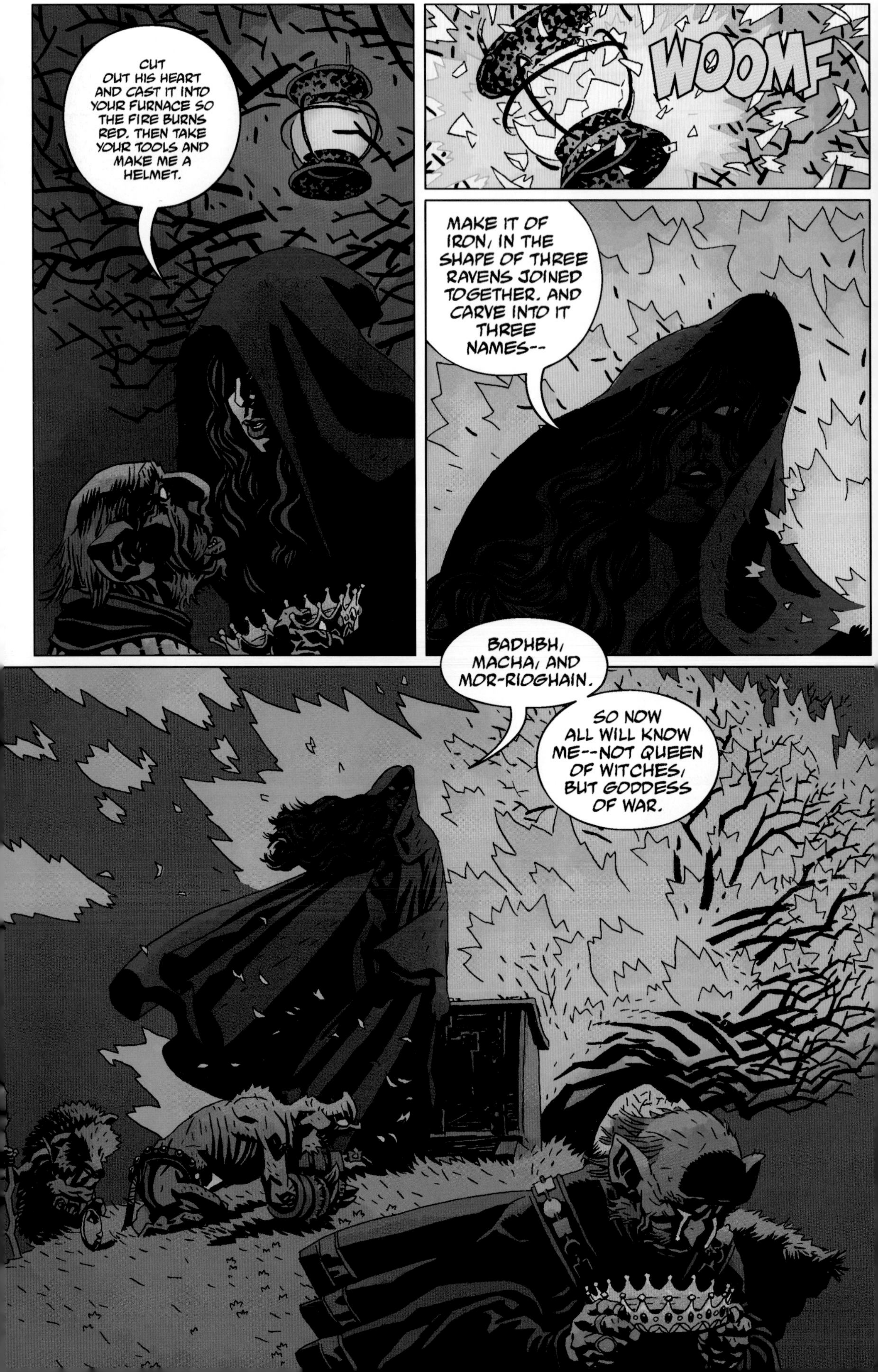
CUT OUT HIS HEART AND CAST IT INTO YOUR FURNACE SO THE FIRE BURNS RED. THEN TAKE YOUR TOOLS AND MAKE ME A HELMET.
WOOMF
MAKE IT OF IRON, IN THE SHAPE OF THREE RAVENS JOINED TOGETHER. AND CARVE INTO IT THREE NAMES--
BADHBH, MACHA, AND MOR-RIOGHAIN.
SO NOW ALL WILL KNOW ME--NOT QUEEN OF WITCHES, BUT GODDESS OF WAR.

CHAPTER SIX

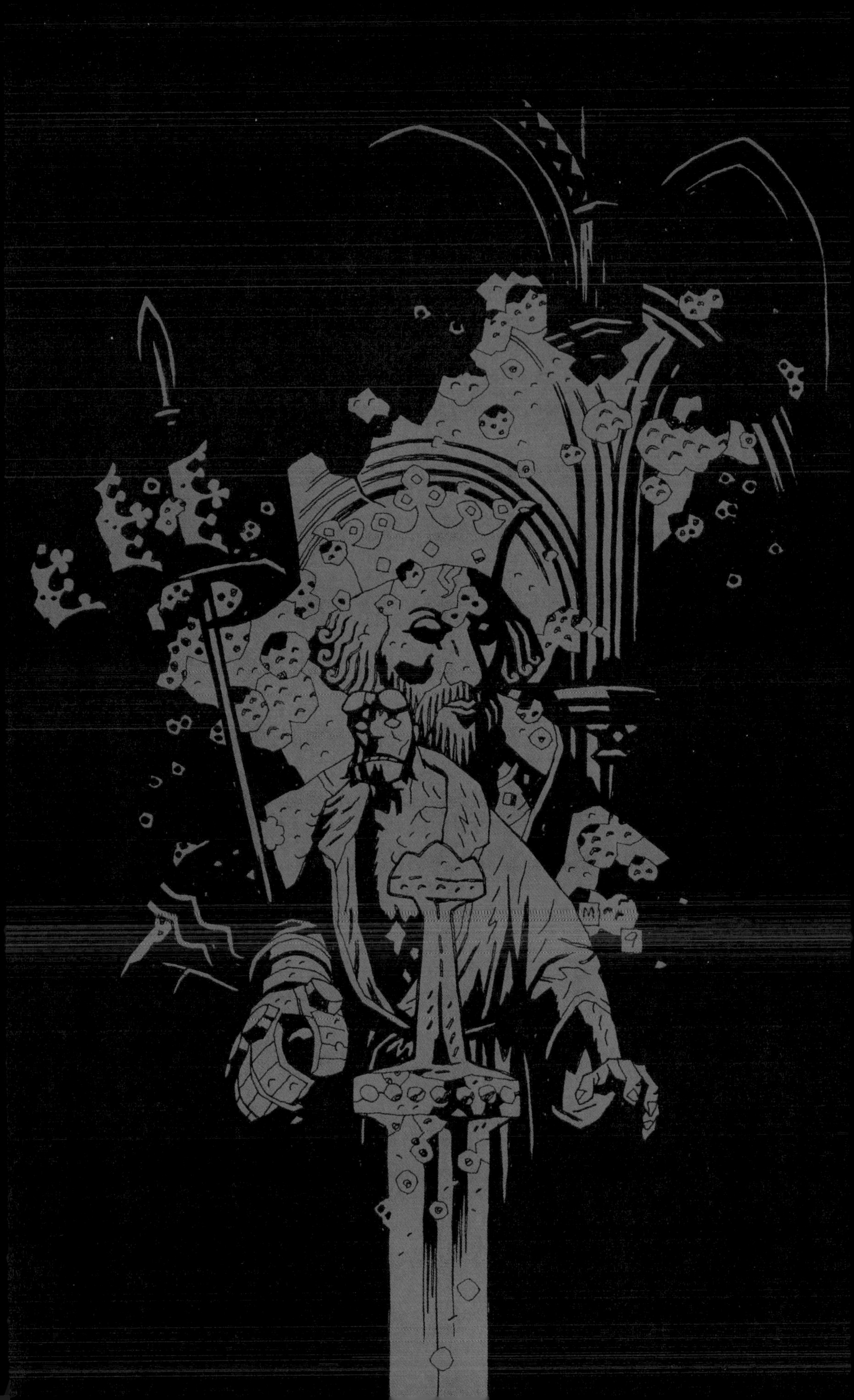

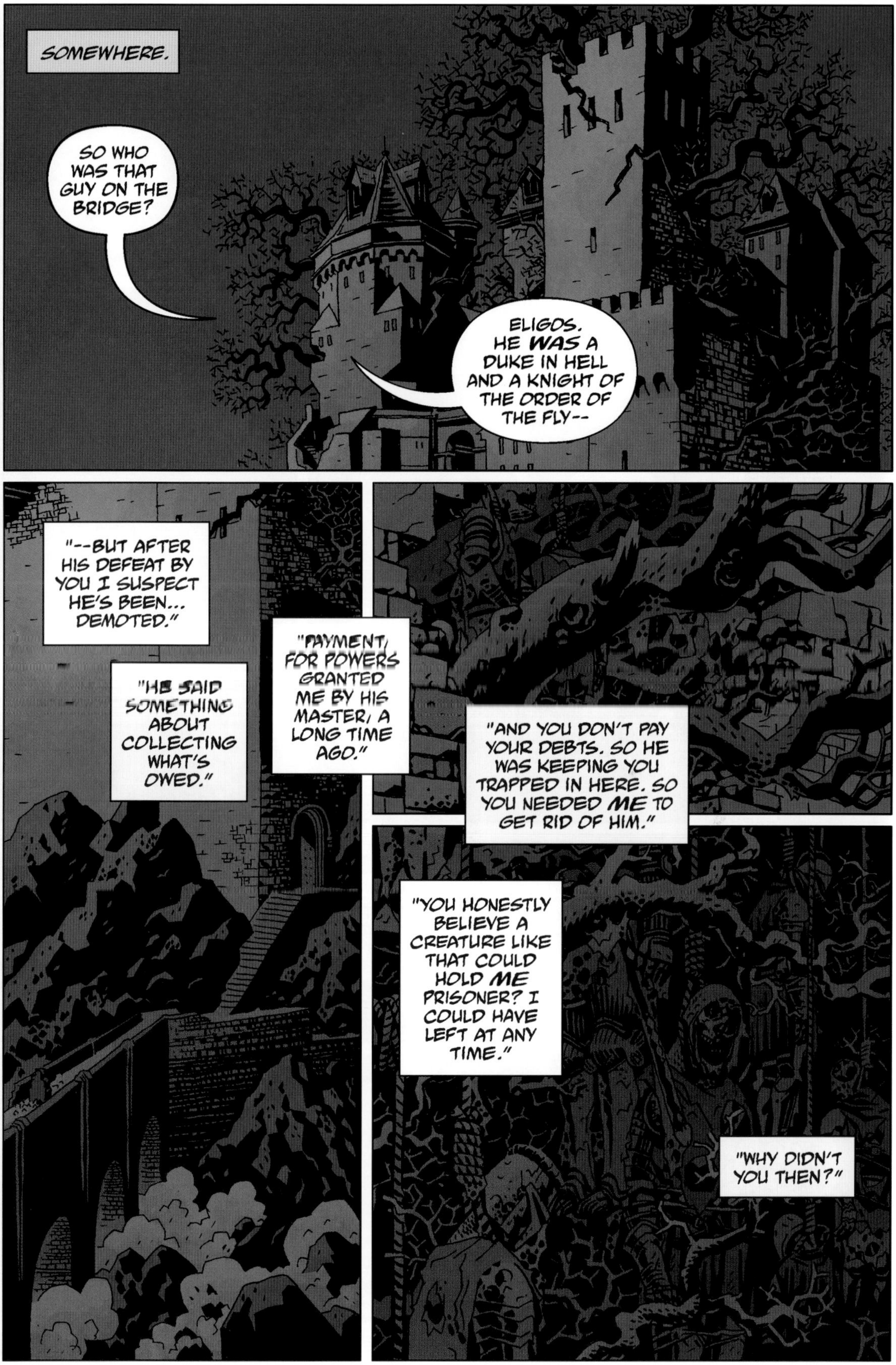
SOMEWHERE.
SO WHO WAS THAT GUY ON THE BRIDGE?
ELIGOS. HE WAS A DUKE IN HELL AND A KNIGHT OF THE ORDER OF THE FLY--
"--BUT AFTER HIS DEFEAT BY YOU I SUSPECT HE'S BEEN... DEMOTED."
"HE SAID SOMETHING ABOUT COLLECTING WHAT'S OWED."
"PAYMENT, FOR POWERS GRANTED ME BY HIS MASTER, A LONG TIME AGO."
"AND YOU DON'T PAY YOUR DEBTS. SO HE WAS KEEPING YOU TRAPPED IN HERE. SO YOU NEEDED ME TO GET RID OF HIM."
"YOU HONESTLY BELIEVE A CREATURE LIKE THAT COULD HOLD ME PRISONER? I COULD HAVE LEFT AT ANY TIME."
"WHY DIDN'T YOU THEN?"

"BECAUSE, HELLBOY, I'VE BEEN WAITING FOR YOU."

DEAR, THIS MUST BE TERRIBLY BORING.

AND YOU'VE BEEN THROUGH SO MUCH. YOU'RE NOT WELL YET. YOU SHOULD GO REST.

I'M FINE.

YOU'RE SURE?

SHE'S FINE.

WHEN I FIRST GOT HERE-- WHY DID YOU SAY WELCOME HOME?

PERHAPS YOU PREFER THE HOUSE WHERE YOU WERE BORN?

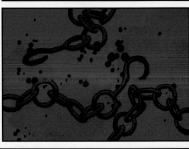

NO? I THOUGHT NOT.

WINE?

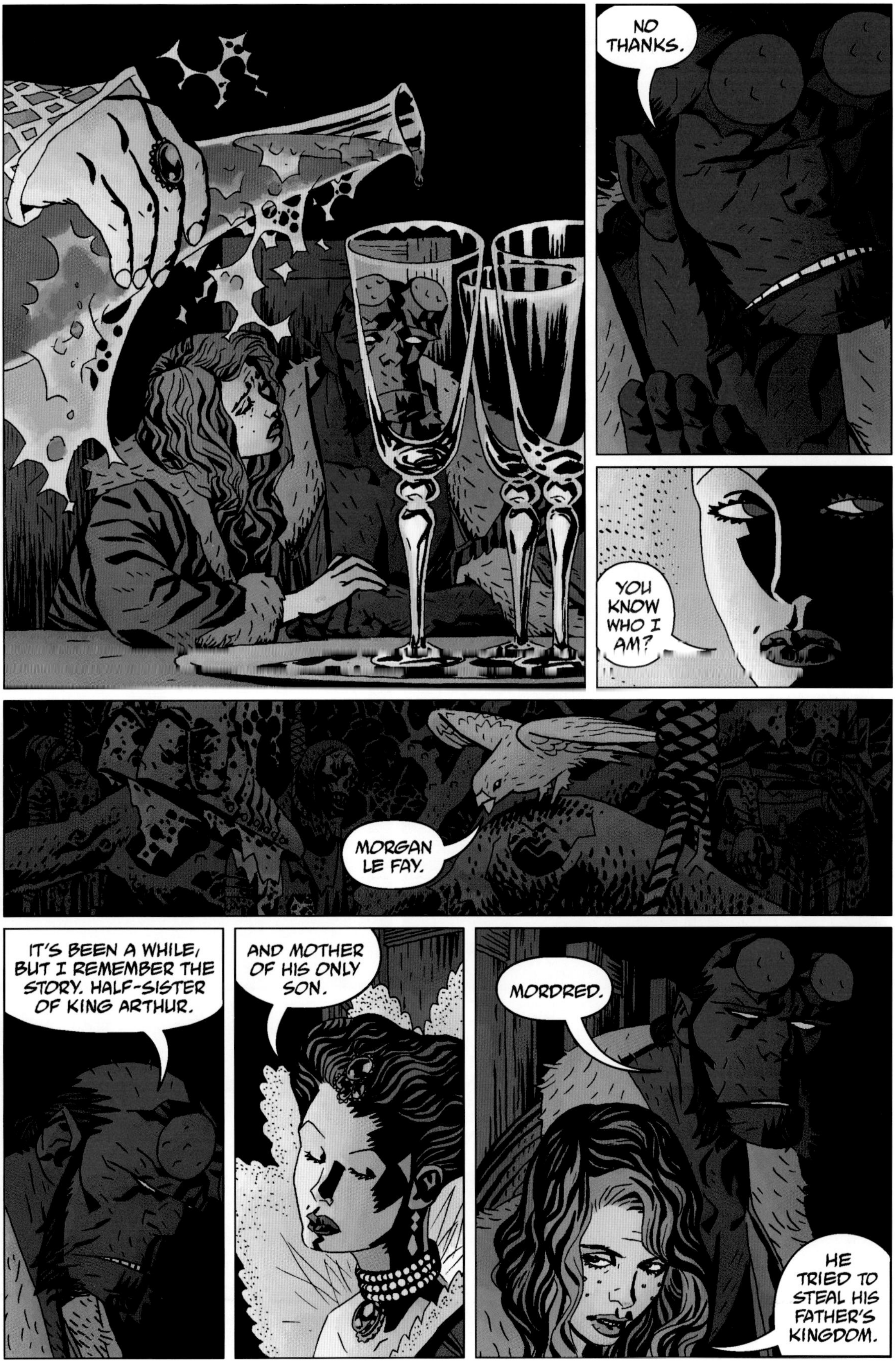

NO THANKS.
YOU KNOW WHO I AM?
MORGAN LE FAY.
IT'S BEEN A WHILE, BUT I REMEMBER THE STORY. HALF-SISTER OF KING ARTHUR.
AND MOTHER OF HIS ONLY SON.
MORDRED.
HE TRIED TO STEAL HIS FATHER'S KINGDOM.

THE TWO MET AT THE BATTLE OF CAMLAN, WHERE THEY KILLED EACH OTHER. IT'S COMMONLY BELIEVED THAT THE PENDRAGON LINE ENDED THERE.

BUT IT'S NOT TRUE.

MORDRED HAD THREE BASTARD SONS BY A WITCH NAMED KATHERYN OF GILFACH. A FEW OF ARTHUR'S KNIGHTS WHO SURVIVED CAMLAN KNEW THIS, TRACKED THE BOYS DOWN, AND PUT THEM TO DEATH.

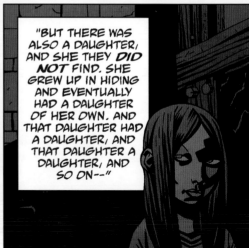

AAH!

"BUT THERE WAS ALSO A DAUGHTER, AND SHE THEY *DID NOT* FIND. SHE GREW UP IN HIDING AND EVENTUALLY HAD A DAUGHTER OF HER OWN. AND THAT DAUGHTER HAD A DAUGHTER, AND THAT DAUGHTER A DAUGHTER, AND SO ON--"

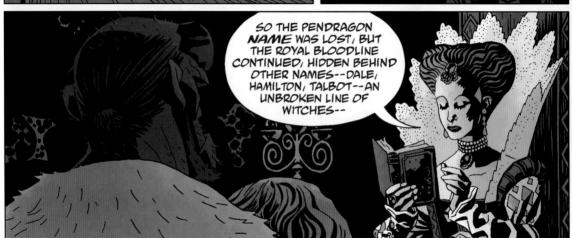

SO THE PENDRAGON *NAME* WAS LOST, BUT THE ROYAL BLOODLINE CONTINUED, HIDDEN BEHIND OTHER NAMES--DALE, HAMILTON, TALBOT--AN UNBROKEN LINE OF WITCHES--

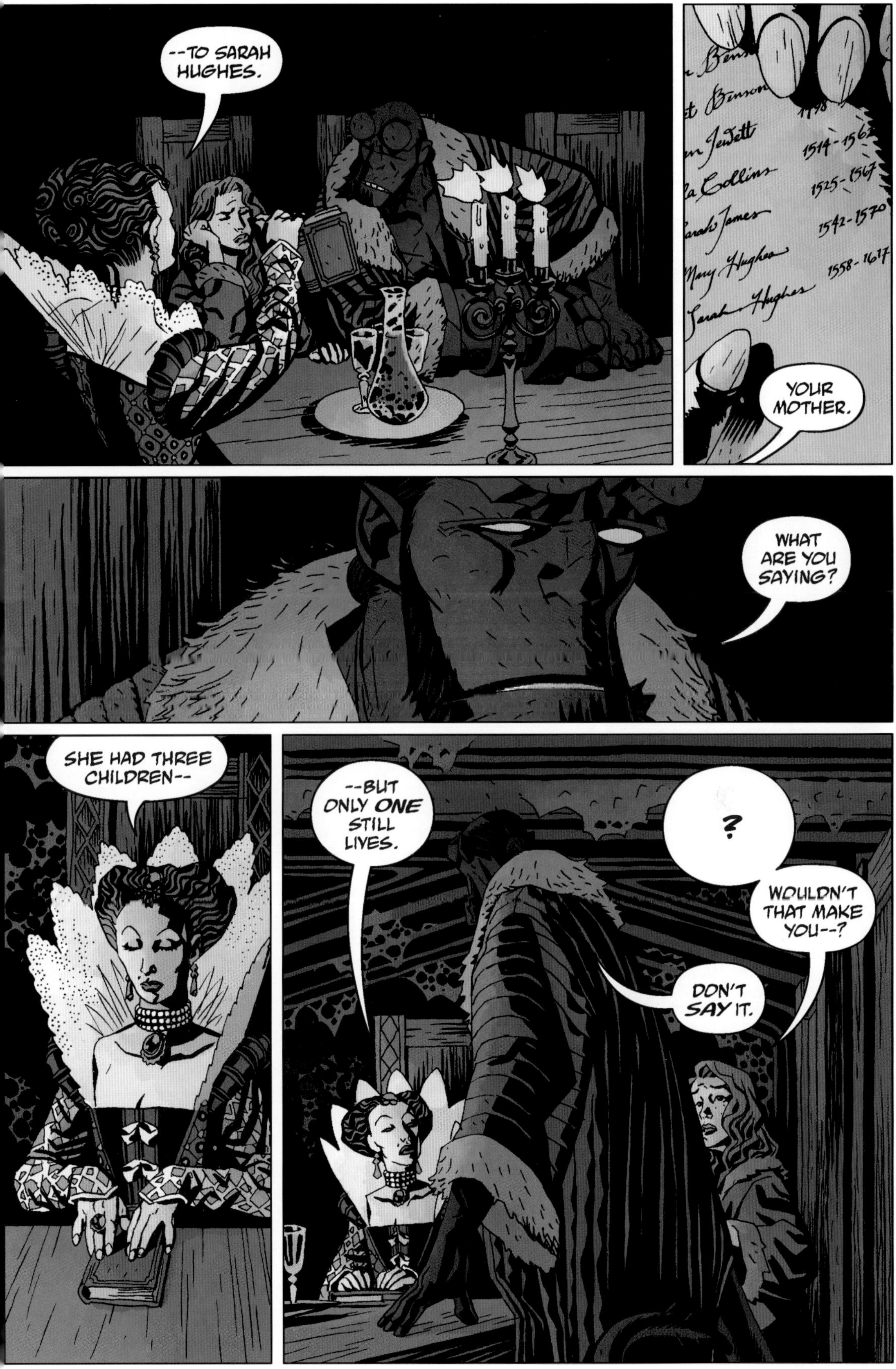

--TO SARAH HUGHES.
YOUR MOTHER.
WHAT ARE YOU SAYING?
SHE HAD THREE CHILDREN--
--BUT ONLY ONE STILL LIVES.
?
WOULDN'T THAT MAKE YOU--?
DON'T SAY IT.

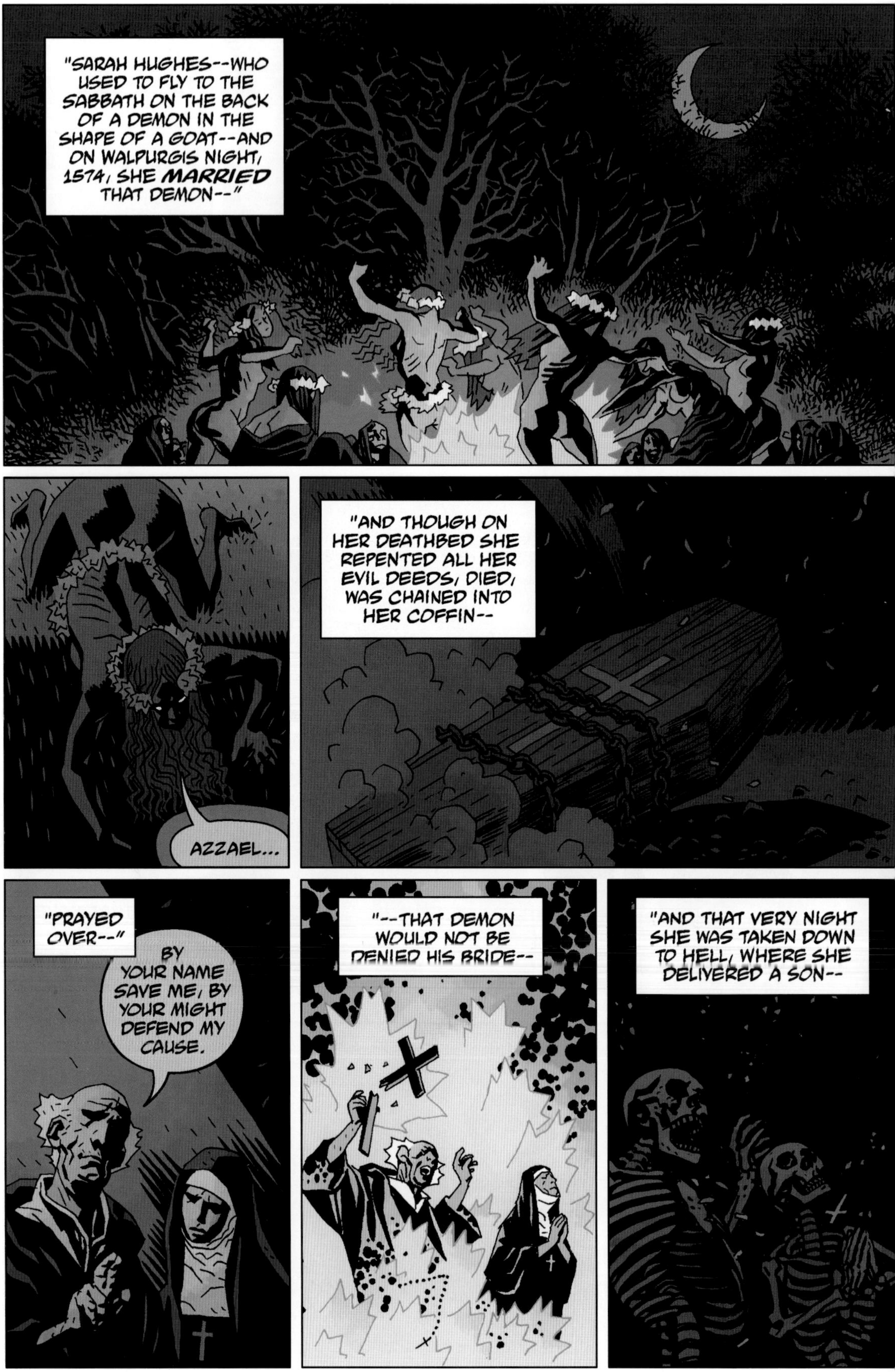
"SARAH HUGHES--WHO USED TO FLY TO THE SABBATH ON THE BACK OF A DEMON IN THE SHAPE OF A GOAT--AND ON WALPURGIS NIGHT, 1574, SHE MARRIED THAT DEMON--"
AZZAEL...
"AND THOUGH ON HER DEATHBED SHE REPENTED ALL HER EVIL DEEDS, DIED, WAS CHAINED INTO HER COFFIN--
"PRAYED OVER--"
BY YOUR NAME SAVE ME, BY YOUR MIGHT DEFEND MY CAUSE.
"--THAT DEMON WOULD NOT BE DENIED HIS BRIDE--
"AND THAT VERY NIGHT SHE WAS TAKEN DOWN TO HELL, WHERE SHE DELIVERED A SON--

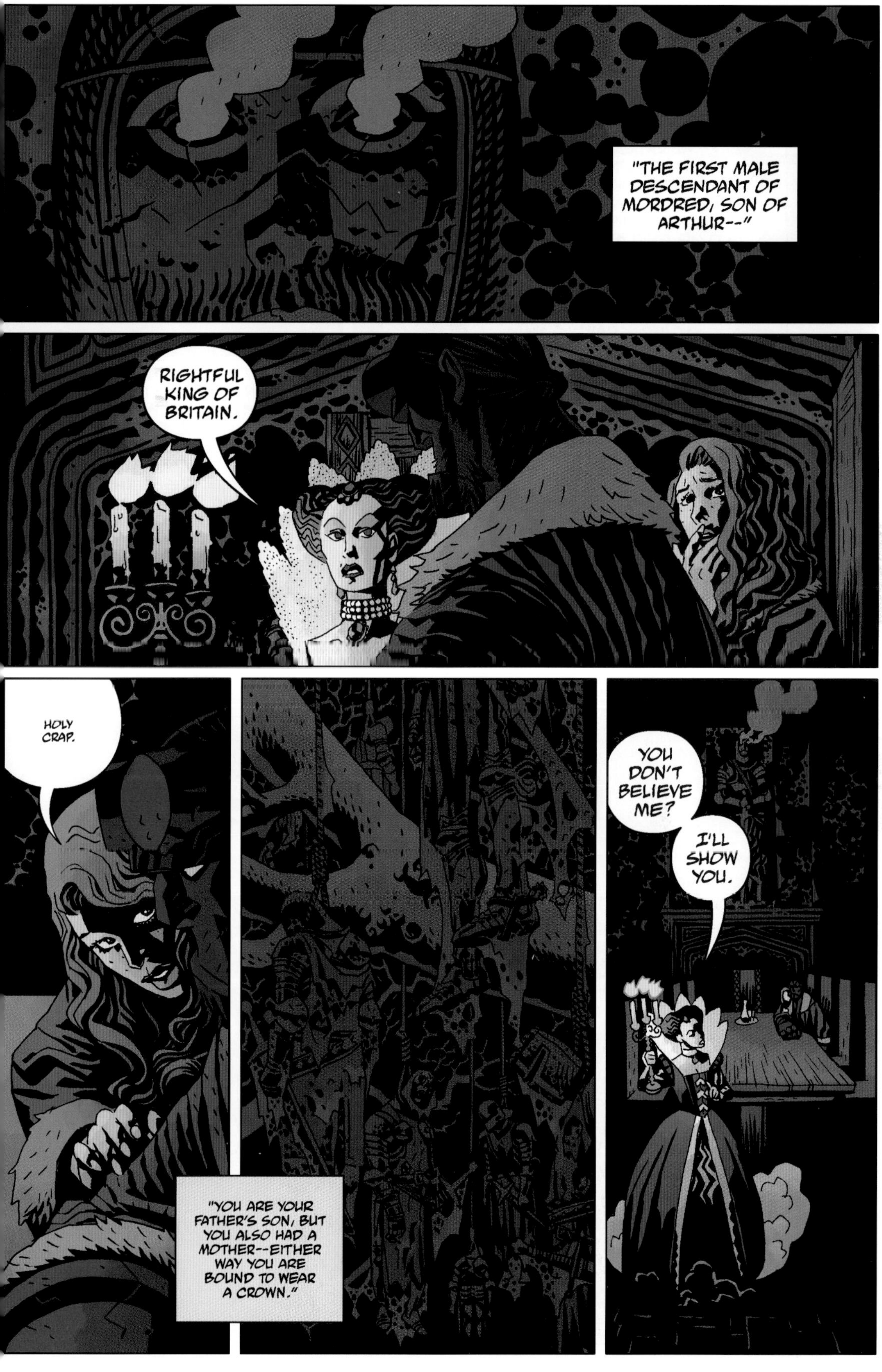
"THE FIRST MALE DESCENDANT OF MORDRED, SON OF ARTHUR--"
RIGHTFUL KING OF BRITAIN.
HOLY CRAP.
"YOU ARE YOUR FATHER'S SON, BUT YOU ALSO HAD A MOTHER--EITHER WAY YOU ARE BOUND TO WEAR A CROWN."
YOU DON'T BELIEVE ME?
I'LL SHOW YOU.

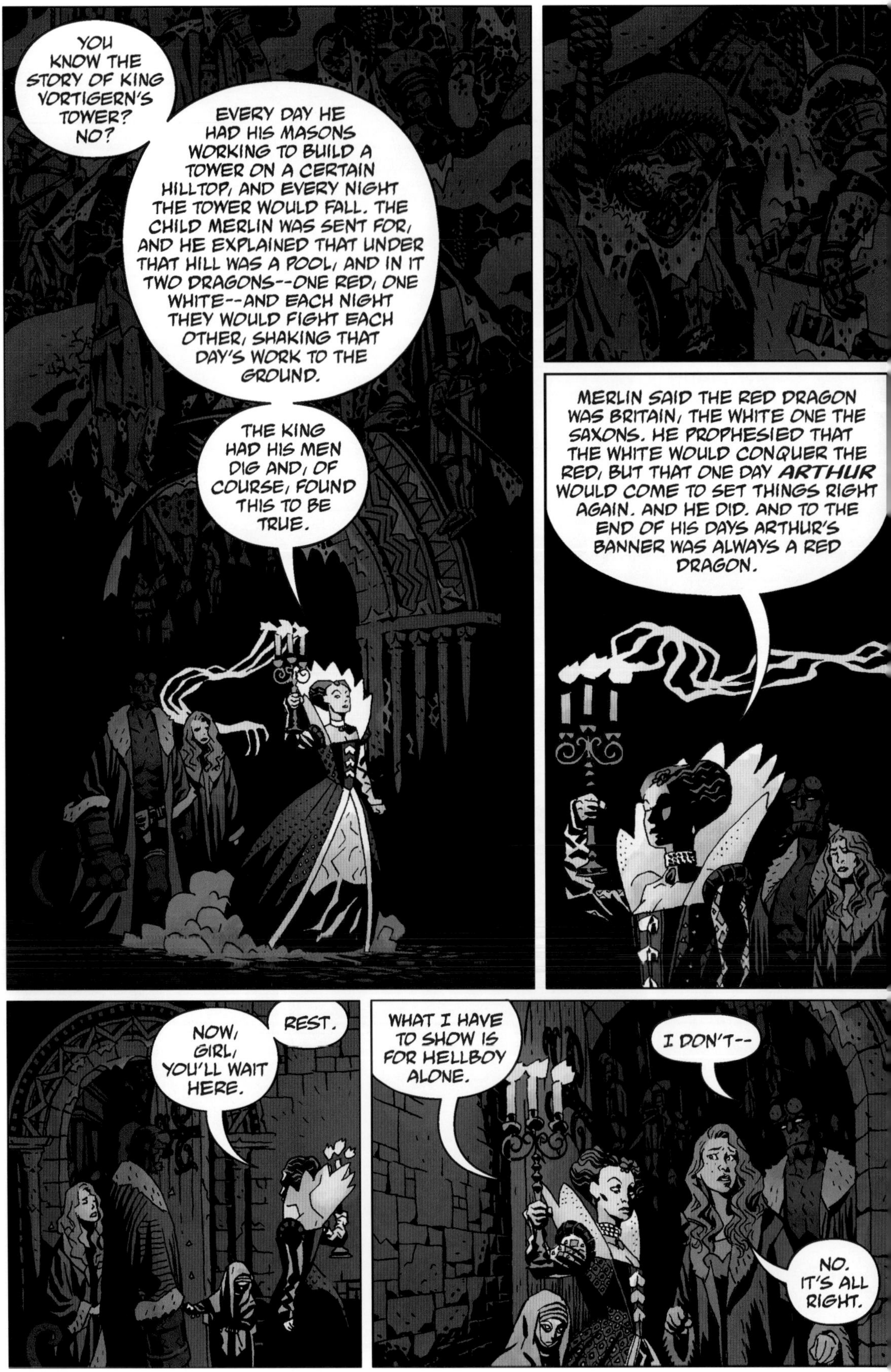
YOU KNOW THE STORY OF KING VORTIGERN'S TOWER? NO?
EVERY DAY HE HAD HIS MASONS WORKING TO BUILD A TOWER ON A CERTAIN HILLTOP, AND EVERY NIGHT THE TOWER WOULD FALL. THE CHILD MERLIN WAS SENT FOR, AND HE EXPLAINED THAT UNDER THAT HILL WAS A POOL, AND IN IT TWO DRAGONS--ONE RED, ONE WHITE--AND EACH NIGHT THEY WOULD FIGHT EACH OTHER, SHAKING THAT DAY'S WORK TO THE GROUND.
THE KING HAD HIS MEN DIG AND, OF COURSE, FOUND THIS TO BE TRUE.
MERLIN SAID THE RED DRAGON WAS BRITAIN, THE WHITE ONE THE SAXONS. HE PROPHESIED THAT THE WHITE WOULD CONQUER THE RED, BUT THAT ONE DAY ARTHUR WOULD COME TO SET THINGS RIGHT AGAIN. AND HE DID. AND TO THE END OF HIS DAYS ARTHUR'S BANNER WAS ALWAYS A RED DRAGON.
NOW, GIRL, YOU'LL WAIT HERE.
REST.
WHAT I HAVE TO SHOW IS FOR HELLBOY ALONE.
I DON'T--
NO. IT'S ALL RIGHT.

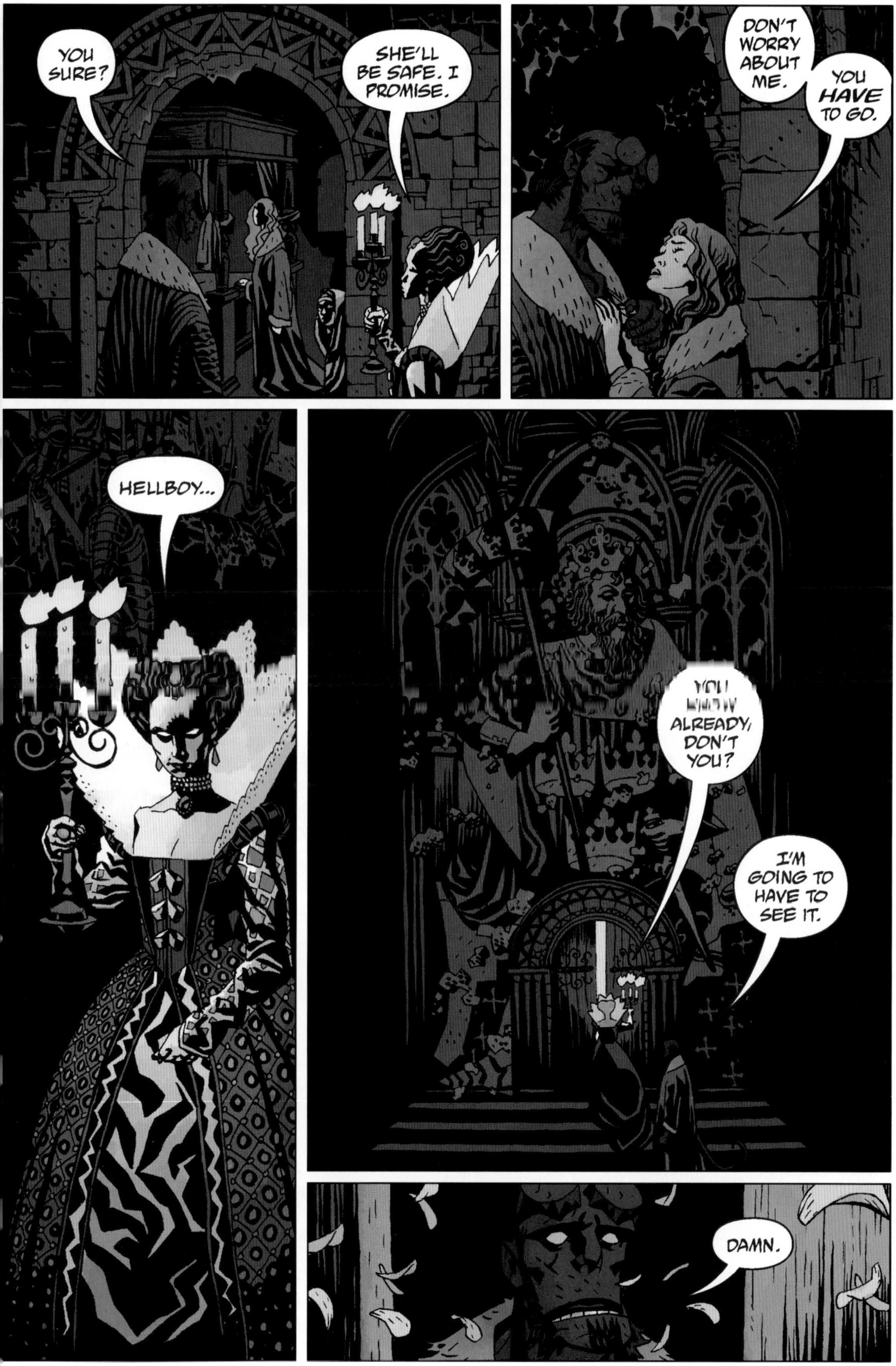
YOU SURE?
SHE'LL BE SAFE. I PROMISE.
DON'T WORRY ABOUT ME.
YOU *HAVE* TO GO.
HELLBOY...
YOU ALREADY, DON'T YOU?
I'M GOING TO HAVE TO SEE IT.
DAMN.

YOU'VE CARRIED A GUN...

...BUT YOU'VE **ALWAYS** FELT MORE NATURAL HOLDING A SWORD.

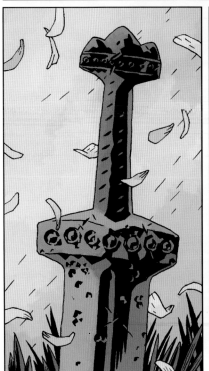

YOU FEEL IT? DRAW OUT THAT SWORD AND YOUR ARMY WILL COME.

WHAT ARMY?

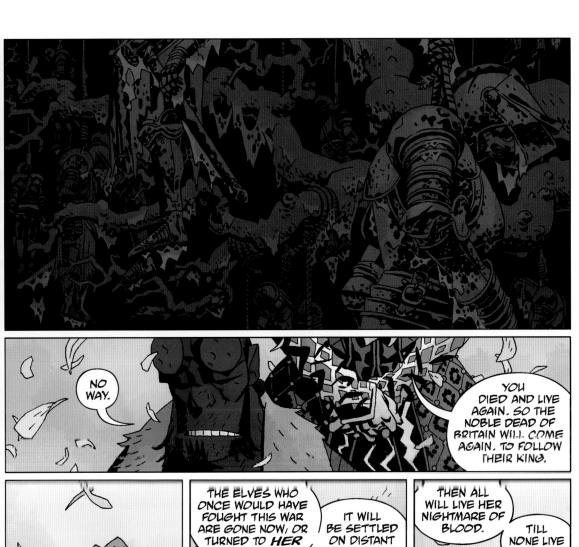

NO WAY.

YOU DIED AND LIVE AGAIN. SO THE NOBLE DEAD OF BRITAIN WILL COME AGAIN, TO FOLLOW THEIR KING.

THE ELVES WHO ONCE WOULD HAVE FOUGHT THIS WAR ARE GONE NOW, OR TURNED TO *HER* SIDE.

IT WILL BE SETTLED ON DISTANT FIELDS AND MEN WILL NEVER KNOW OF IT... UNLESS YOU FAIL.

THEN ALL WILL LIVE HER NIGHTMARE OF BLOOD.

TILL NONE LIVE AT ALL.

WHO IS SHE?

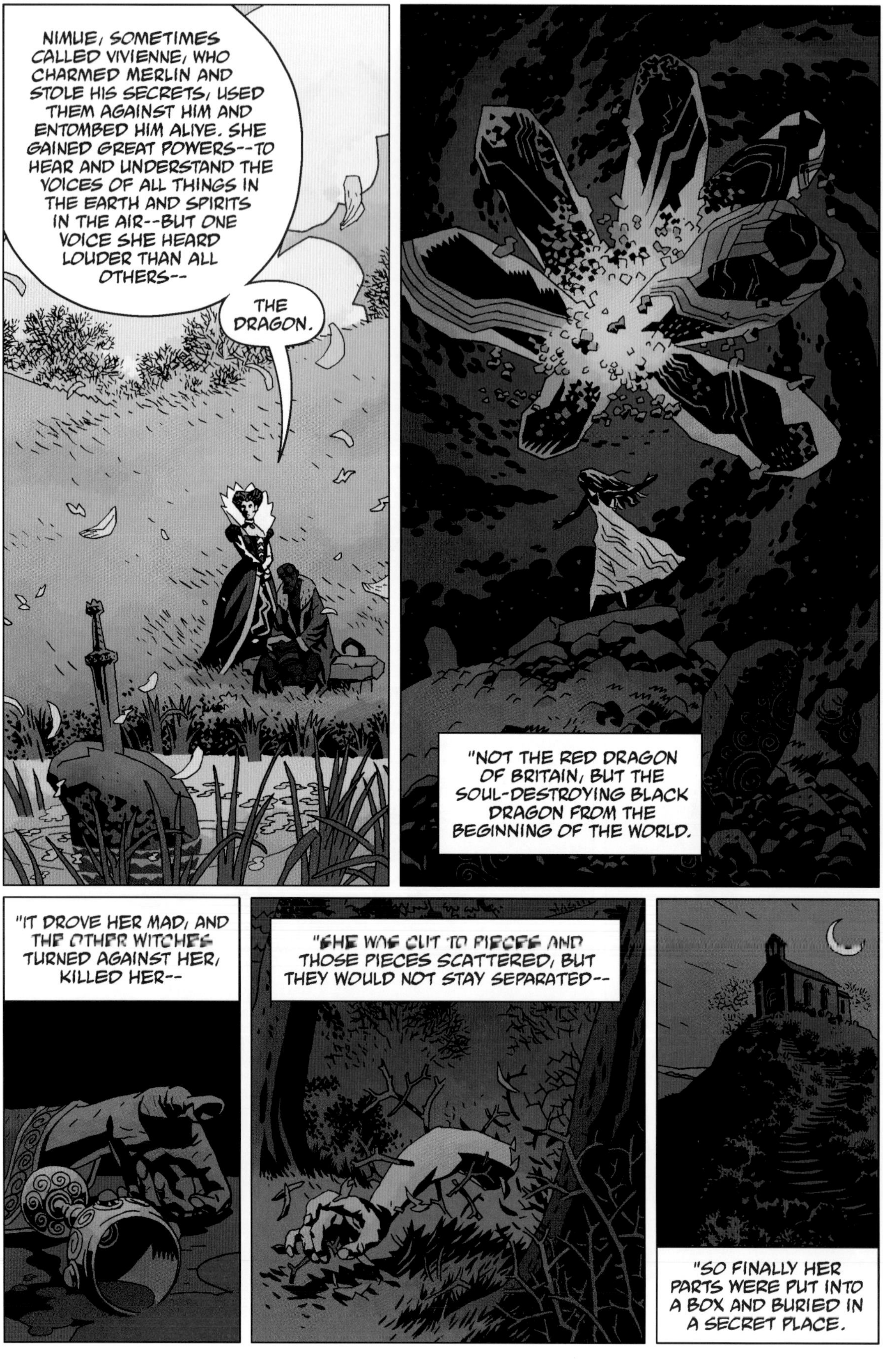
NIMUE, SOMETIMES CALLED VIVIENNE, WHO CHARMED MERLIN AND STOLE HIS SECRETS, USED THEM AGAINST HIM AND ENTOMBED HIM ALIVE. SHE GAINED GREAT POWERS--TO HEAR AND UNDERSTAND THE VOICES OF ALL THINGS IN THE EARTH AND SPIRITS IN THE AIR--BUT ONE VOICE SHE HEARD LOUDER THAN ALL OTHERS--
THE DRAGON.
"NOT THE RED DRAGON OF BRITAIN, BUT THE SOUL-DESTROYING BLACK DRAGON FROM THE BEGINNING OF THE WORLD.
"IT DROVE HER MAD, AND THE OTHER WITCHES TURNED AGAINST HER, KILLED HER--
"SHE WAS CUT TO PIECES AND THOSE PIECES SCATTERED, BUT THEY WOULD NOT STAY SEPARATED--
"SO FINALLY HER PARTS WERE PUT INTO A BOX AND BURIED IN A SECRET PLACE.

"BUT NOW SHE'S FREE AND WHOLE AGAIN. AND STILL MAD."

"AND SHE'S PULLING TOGETHER AN ARMY OF BAD GUYS. YEAH, I HEARD THIS PART."

NOW SHE CALLS HERSELF A GODDESS OF WAR, BUT HER WAR HAS NO OBJECT OTHER THAN THE SPILLING OF BLOOD.

ALL BLOOD.

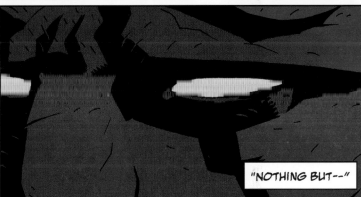

"NOTHING BUT--"

BLOOD

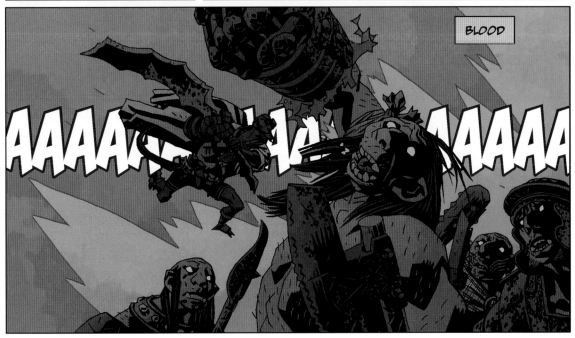

AAAA AAAA AAAA

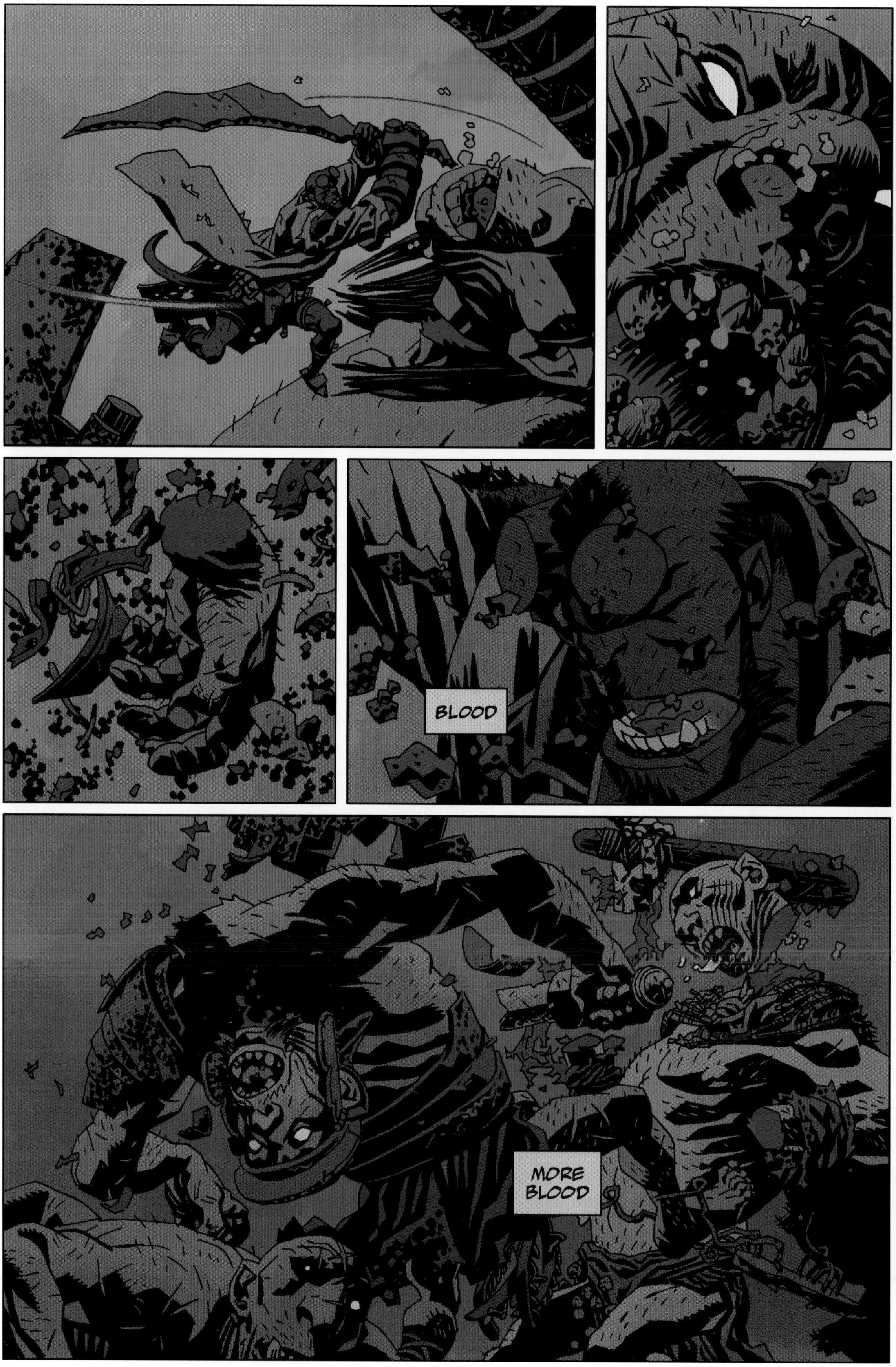
BLOOD
MORE BLOOD

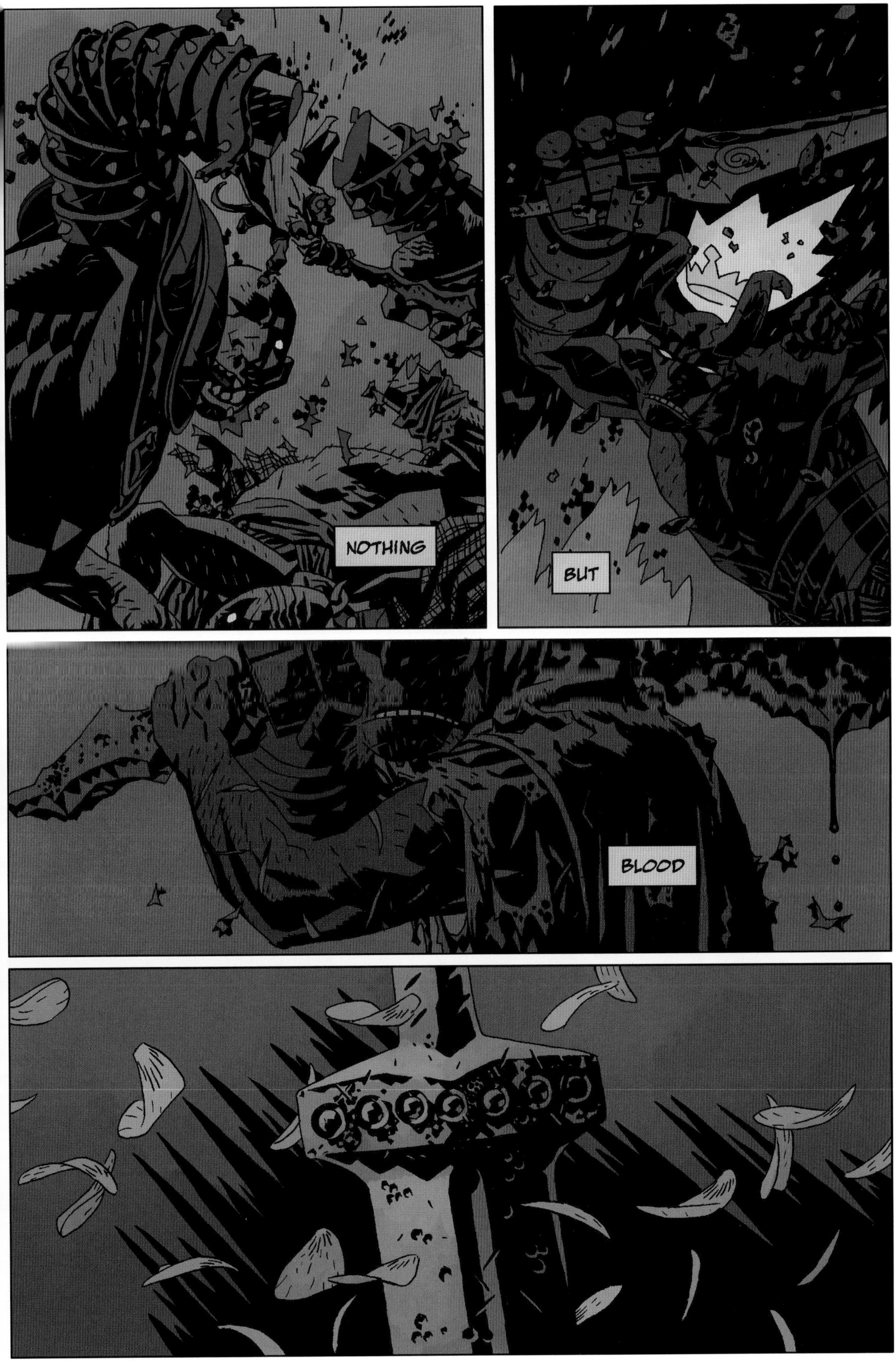
NOTHING
BUT
BLOOD

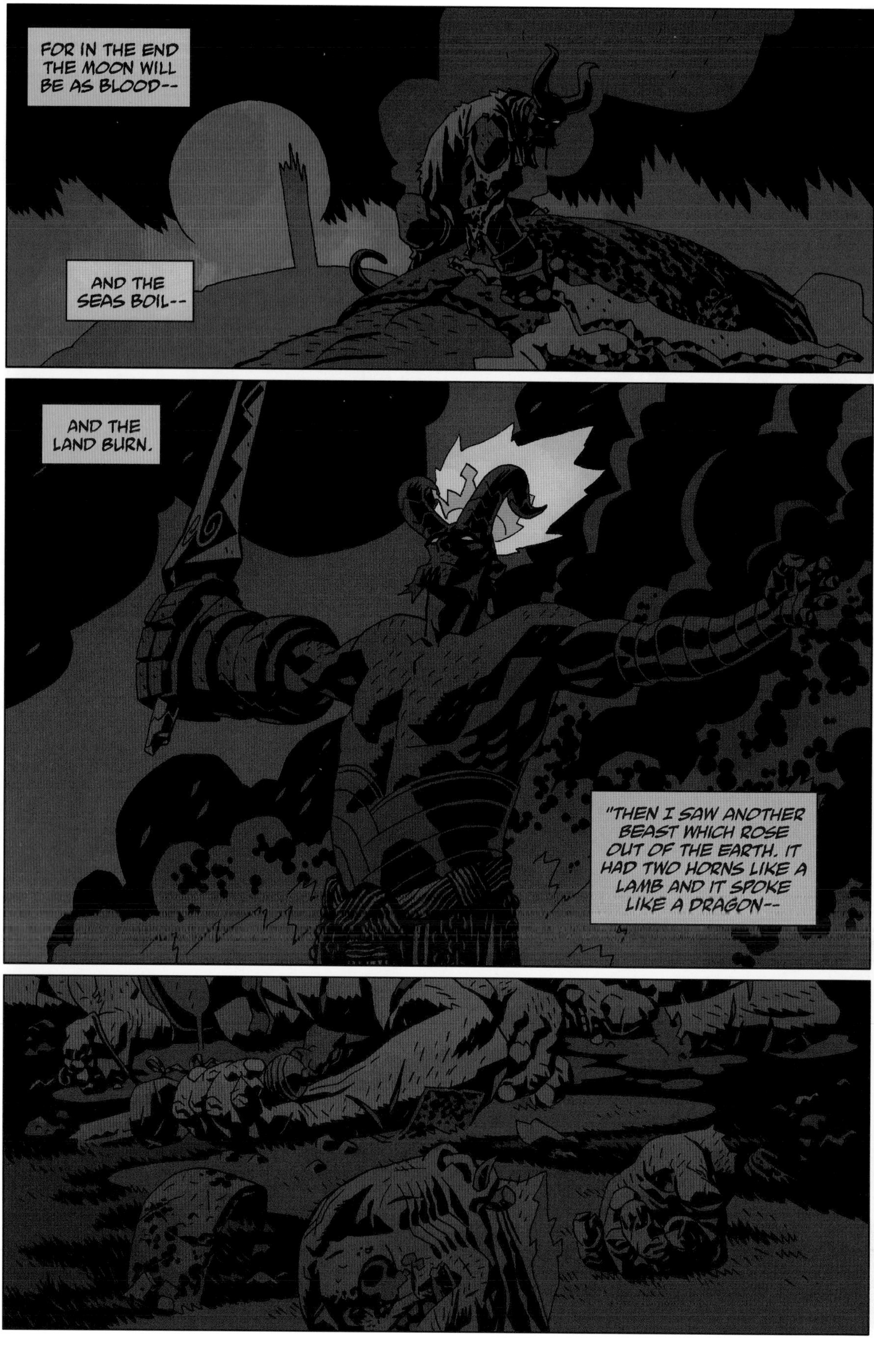
FOR IN THE END THE MOON WILL BE AS BLOOD--
AND THE SEAS BOIL--
AND THE LAND BURN.
"THEN I SAW ANOTHER BEAST WHICH ROSE OUT OF THE EARTH. IT HAD TWO HORNS LIKE A LAMB AND IT SPOKE LIKE A DRAGON--

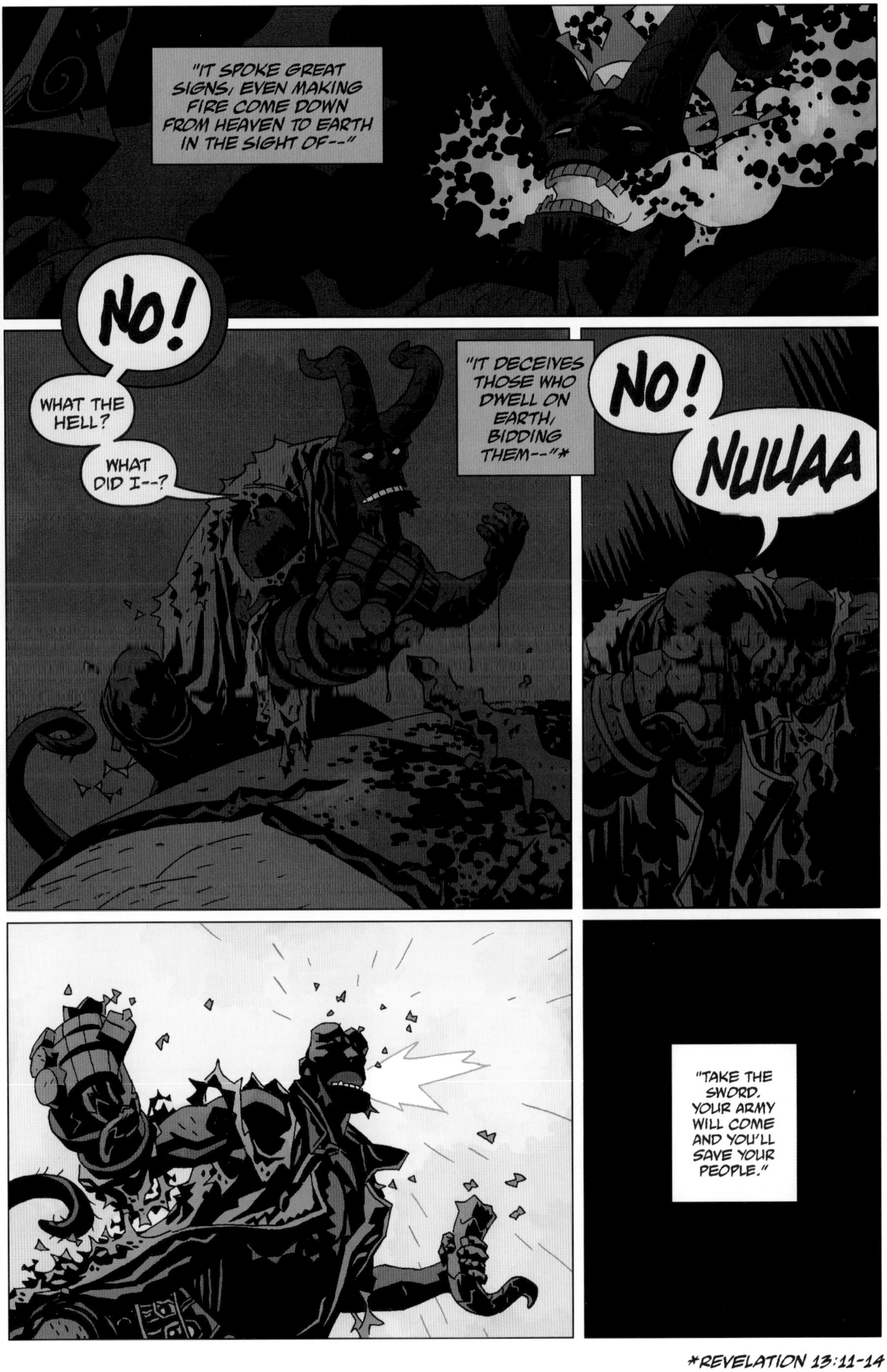
"IT SPOKE GREAT SIGNS, EVEN MAKING FIRE COME DOWN FROM HEAVEN TO EARTH IN THE SIGHT OF--"
NO!
WHAT THE HELL?
WHAT DID I--?
"IT DECEIVES THOSE WHO DWELL ON EARTH, BIDDING THEM--"*
NO! NUUAA
"TAKE THE SWORD. YOUR ARMY WILL COME AND YOU'LL SAVE YOUR PEOPLE."

*REVELATION 13:11-14

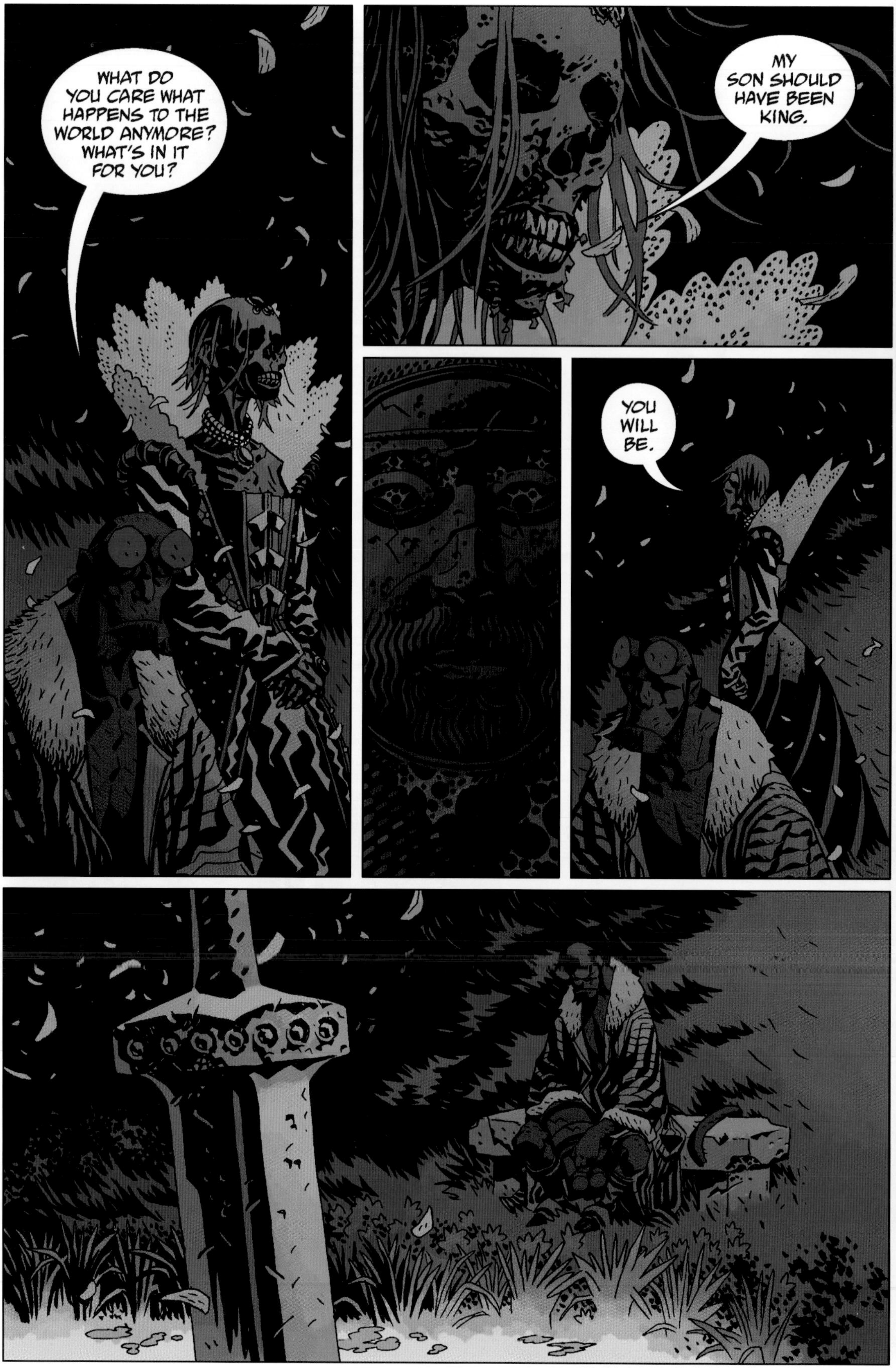
WHAT DO YOU CARE WHAT HAPPENS TO THE WORLD ANYMORE? WHAT'S IN IT FOR YOU?
MY SON SHOULD HAVE BEEN KING.
YOU WILL BE.

CHAPTER SEVEN

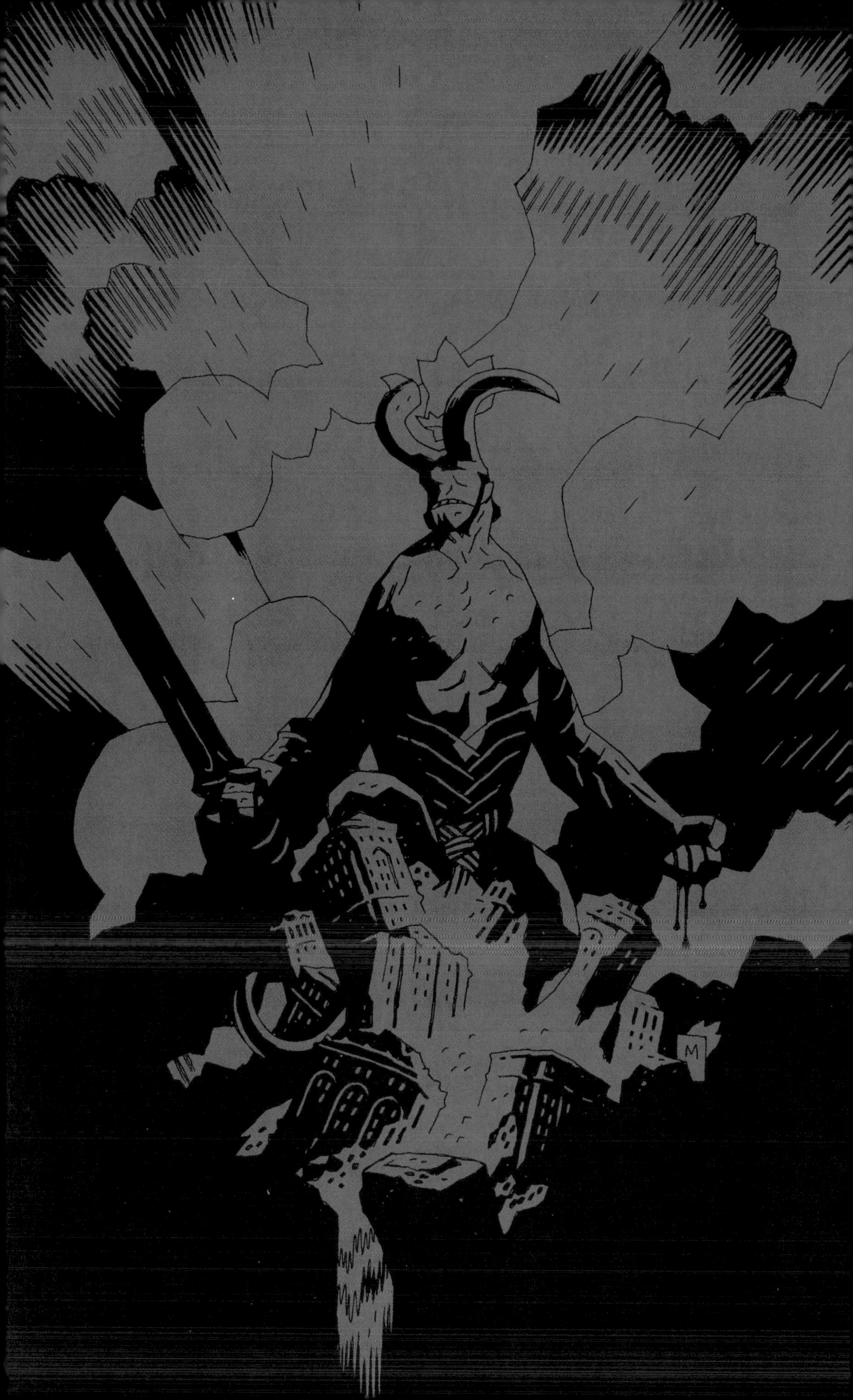

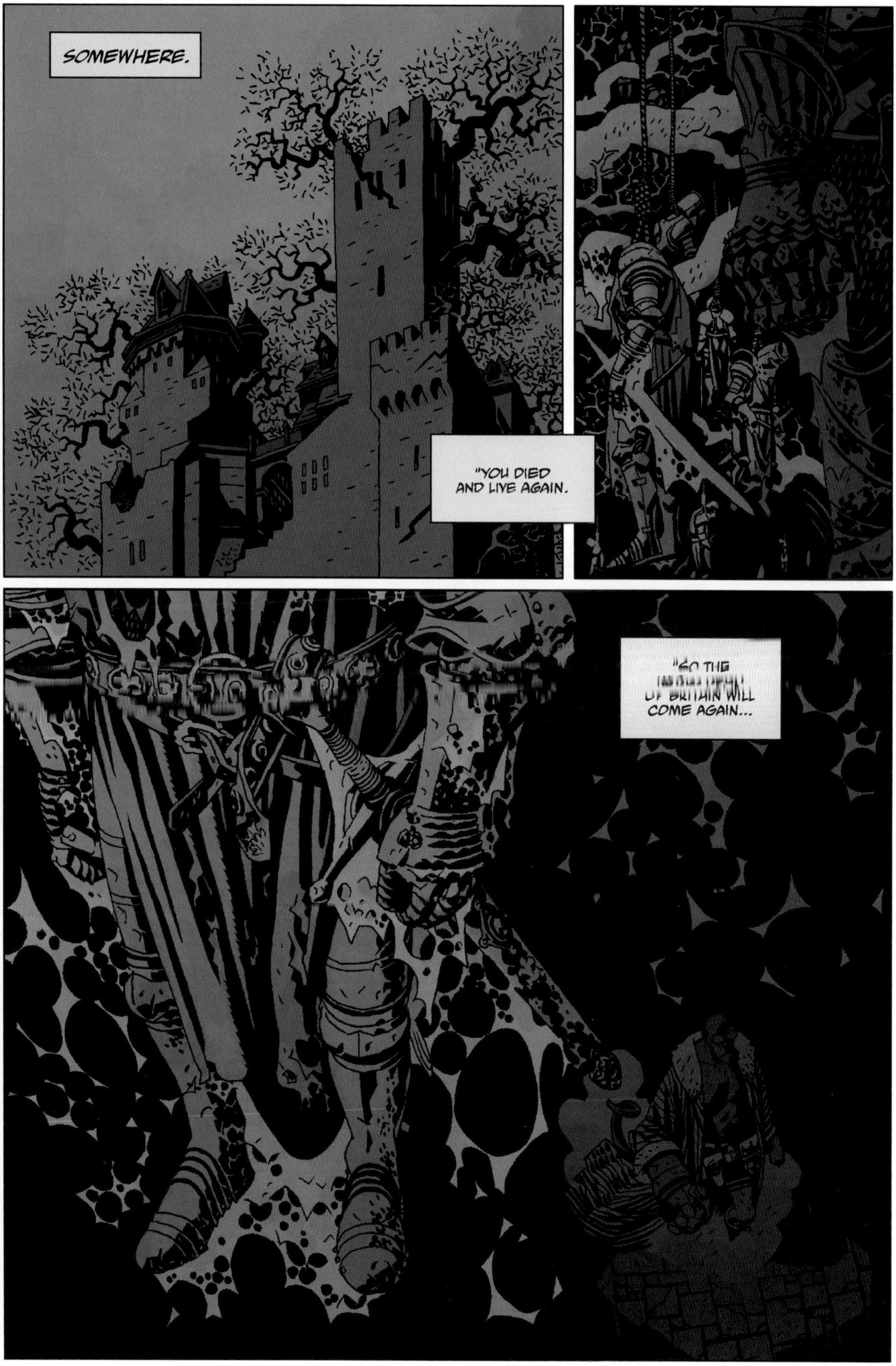
SOMEWHERE.
"YOU DIED AND LIVE AGAIN.
"SO THE
OF BRITAIN WILL
COME AGAIN...

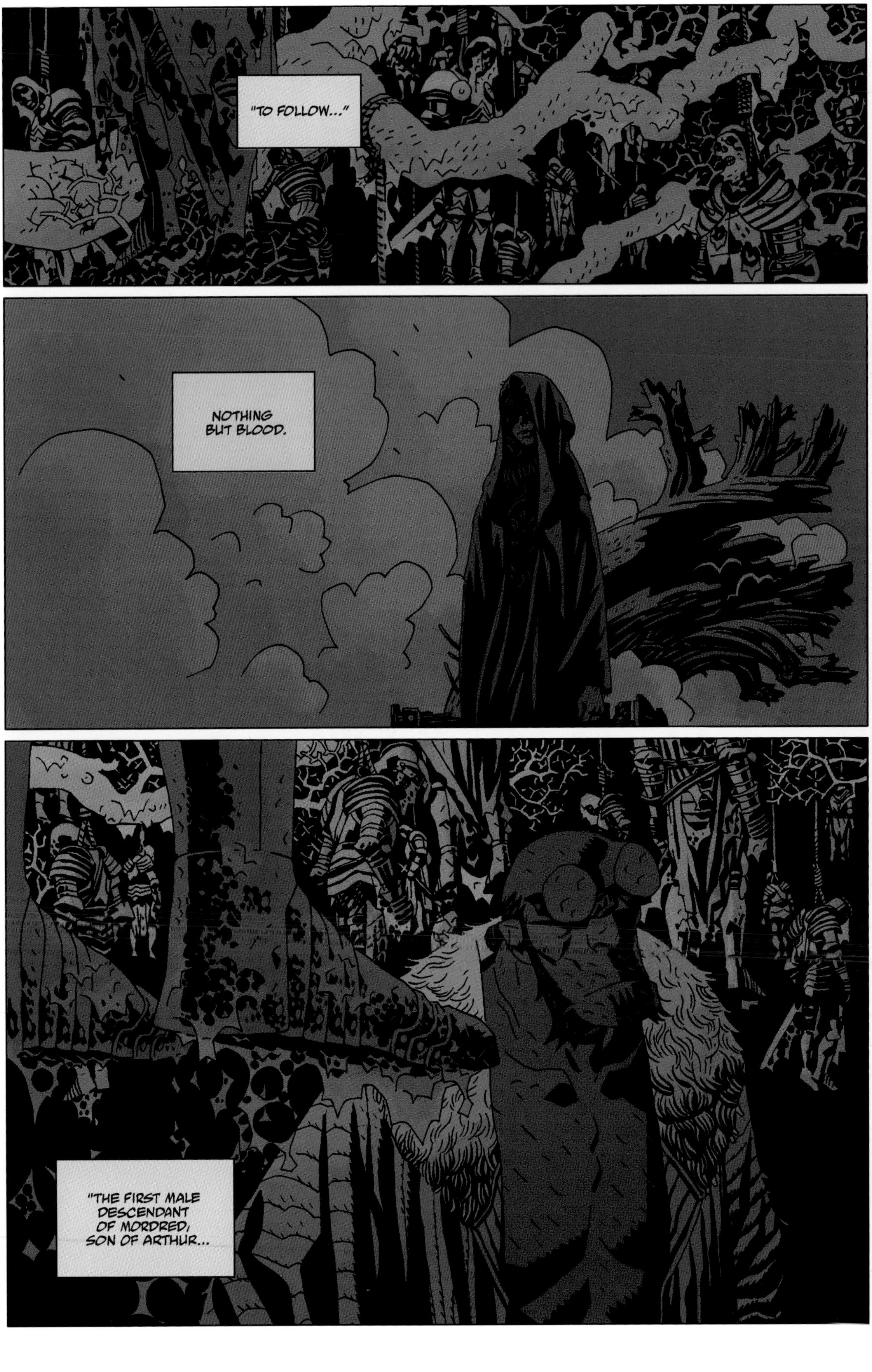
"TO FOLLOW..."
NOTHING BUT BLOOD.
"THE FIRST MALE DESCENDANT OF MORDRED, SON OF ARTHUR...

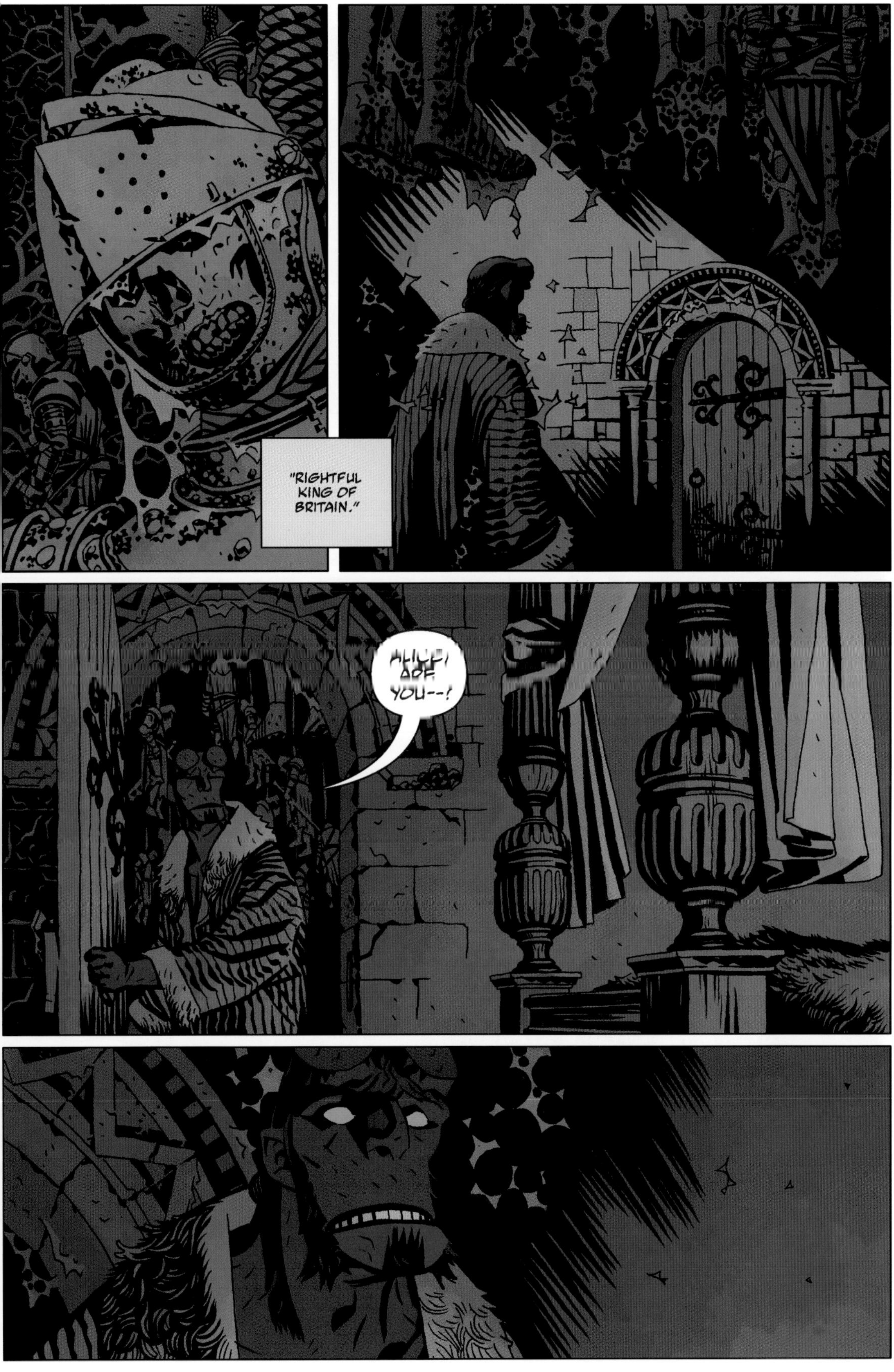
"RIGHTFUL
KING OF
BRITAIN."
YOU--!

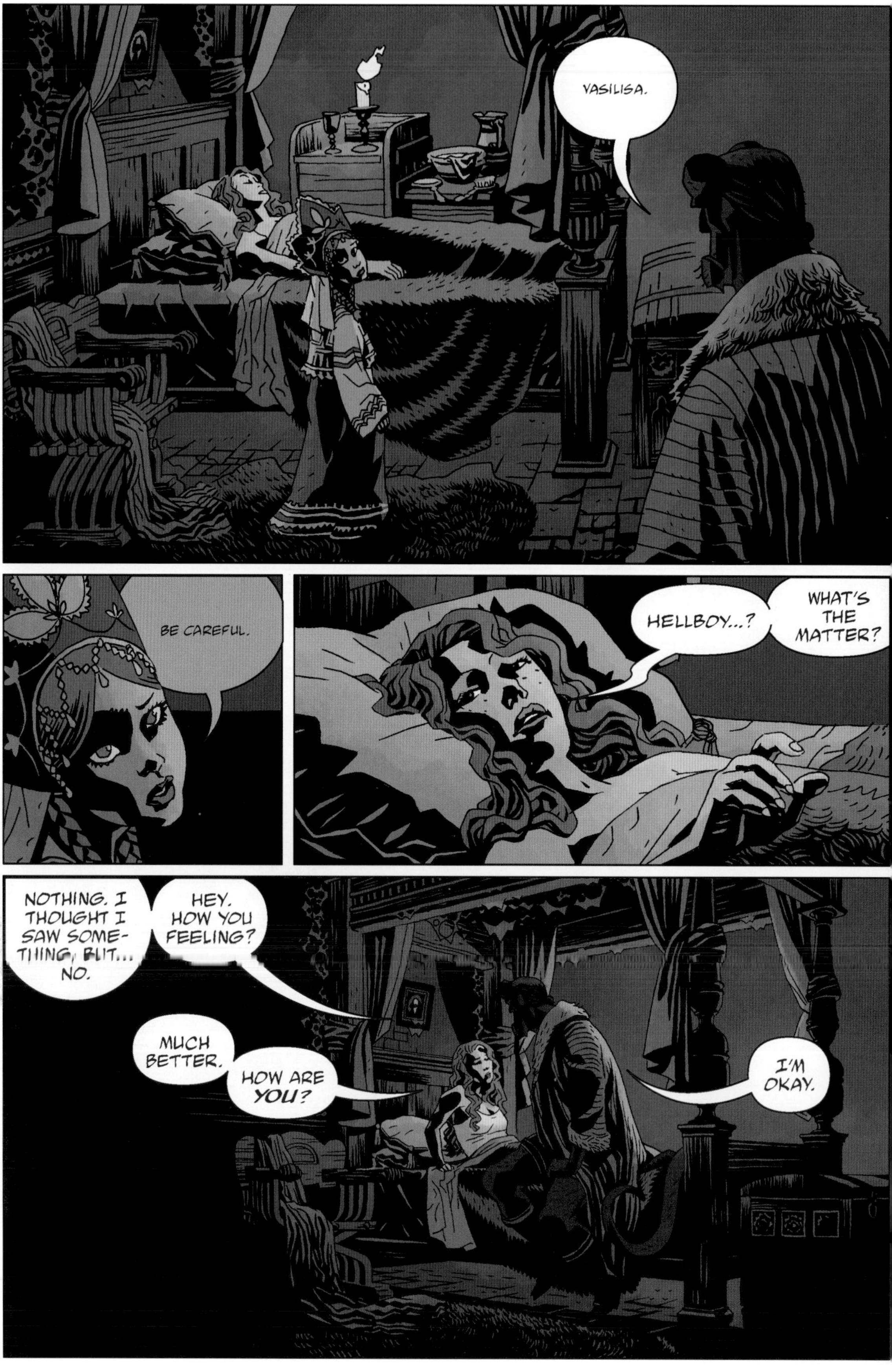
VASILISA.
BE CAREFUL.
HELLBOY...?
WHAT'S THE MATTER?
NOTHING. I THOUGHT I SAW SOMETHING, BUT... NO.
HEY. HOW YOU FEELING?
MUCH BETTER.
HOW ARE YOU?
I'M OKAY.

IT WAS THE SWORD, WASN'T IT? EXCALIBUR.

THAT'S WHAT SHE SHOWED YOU.

YEAH.

"WHY DIDN'T YOU TAKE IT?"

"I DON'T KNOW. FOR ONE THING, IT WAS STUCK IN A BIG FLOATING ROCK."

YOU COULD HAVE PULLED IT OUT. YOU *KNOW* THAT. THERE'S SOMETHING ELSE-- SOMETHING YOU'VE BEEN THINKING ABOUT SINCE YOU CAME TO MY HOUSE.

SOME- THING BAD HAPPENED TO YOU BEFORE YOU GOT THERE. WHAT WAS IT?

YOU CAN TELL ME.

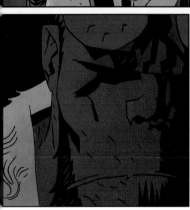

NOTHING HAPPENED.

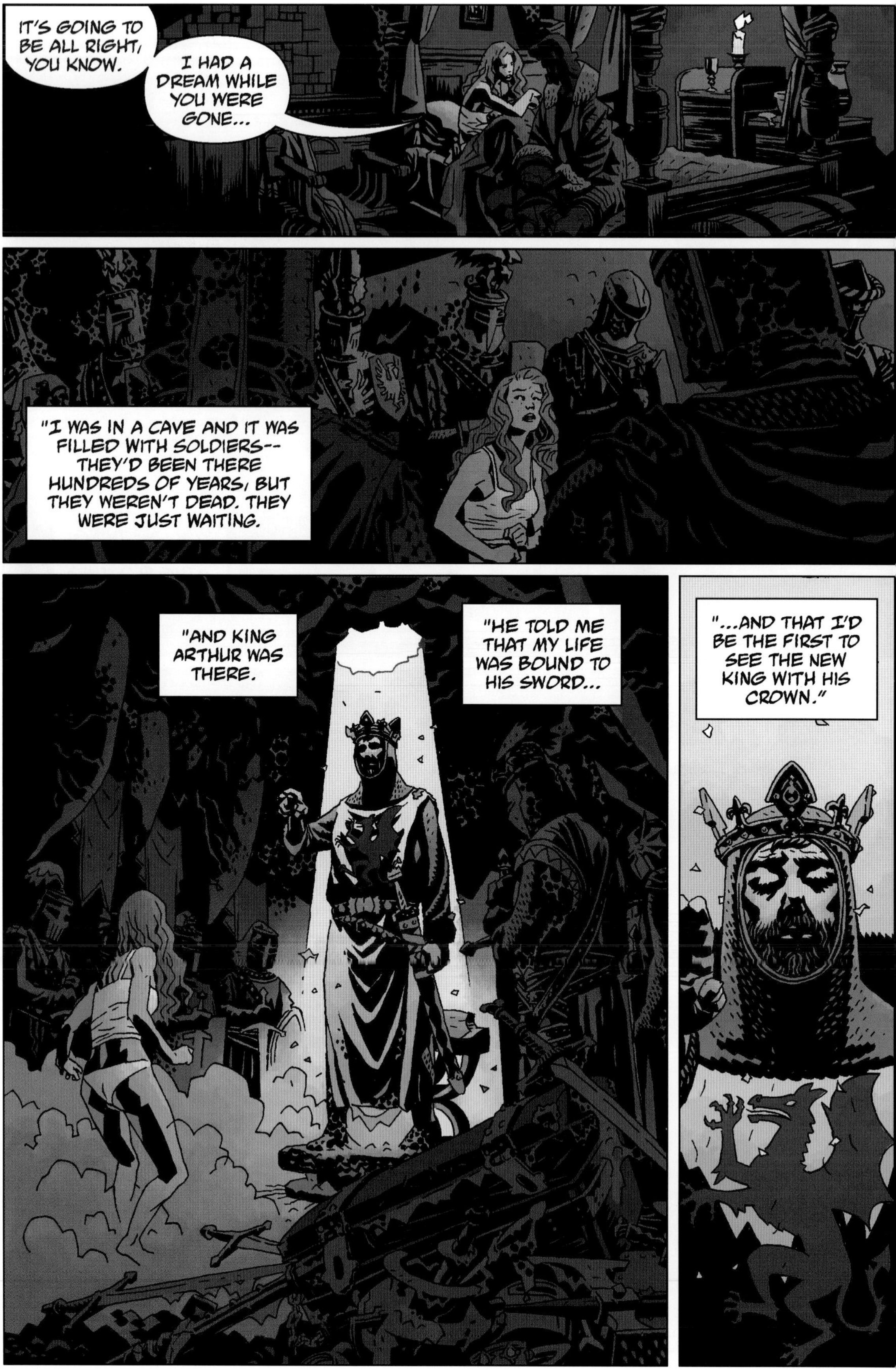
IT'S GOING TO BE ALL RIGHT, YOU KNOW.
I HAD A DREAM WHILE YOU WERE GONE...
"I WAS IN A CAVE AND IT WAS FILLED WITH SOLDIERS-- THEY'D BEEN THERE HUNDREDS OF YEARS, BUT THEY WEREN'T DEAD. THEY WERE JUST WAITING.
"AND KING ARTHUR WAS THERE.
"HE TOLD ME THAT MY LIFE WAS BOUND TO HIS SWORD...
"...AND THAT I'D BE THE FIRST TO SEE THE NEW KING WITH HIS CROWN."

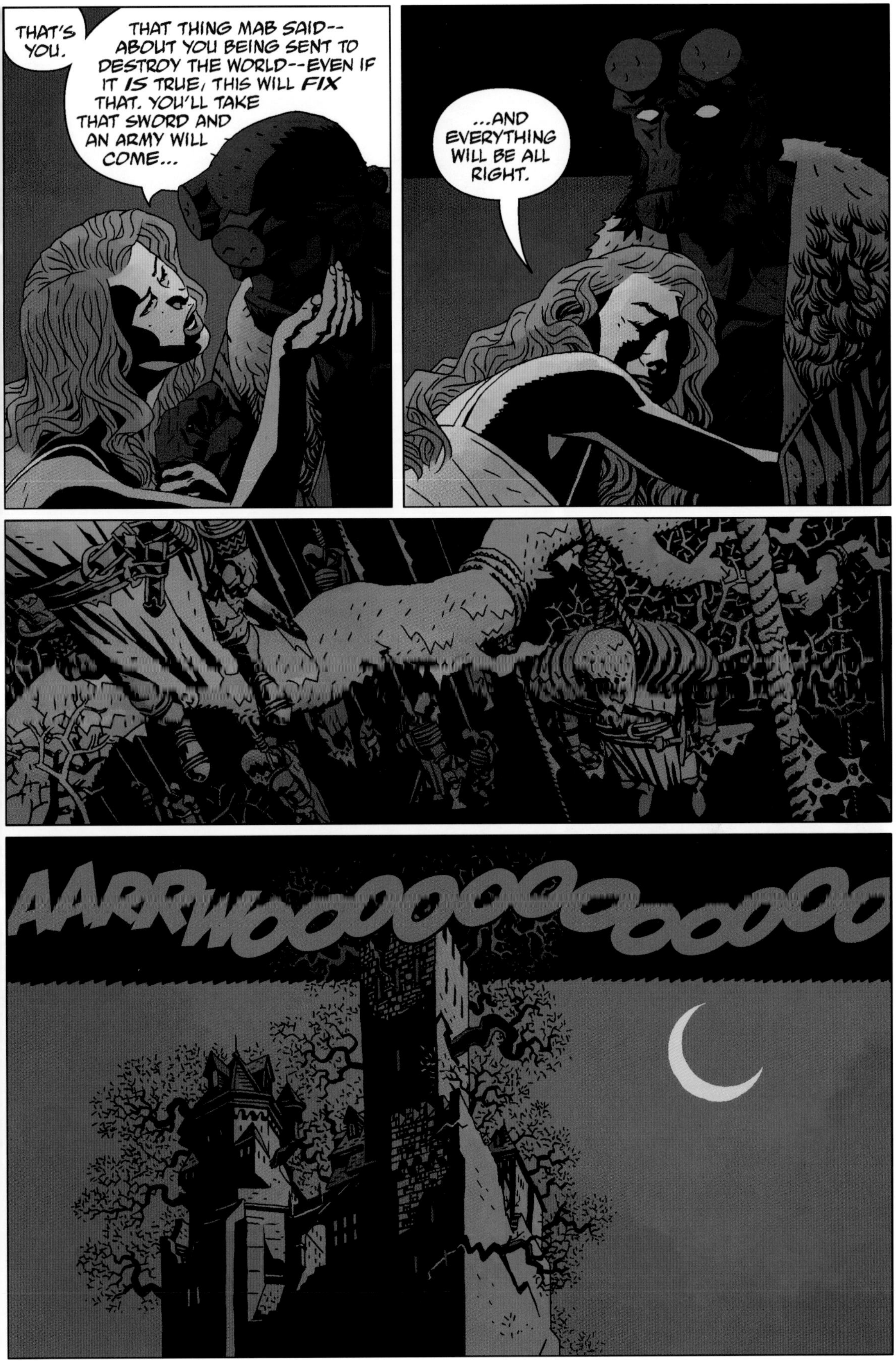
THAT'S YOU.
THAT THING MAB SAID-- ABOUT YOU BEING SENT TO DESTROY THE WORLD--EVEN IF IT IS TRUE, THIS WILL FIX THAT. YOU'LL TAKE THAT SWORD AND AN ARMY WILL COME...
...AND EVERYTHING WILL BE ALL RIGHT.
AARRWOOOOOOOOOOOO

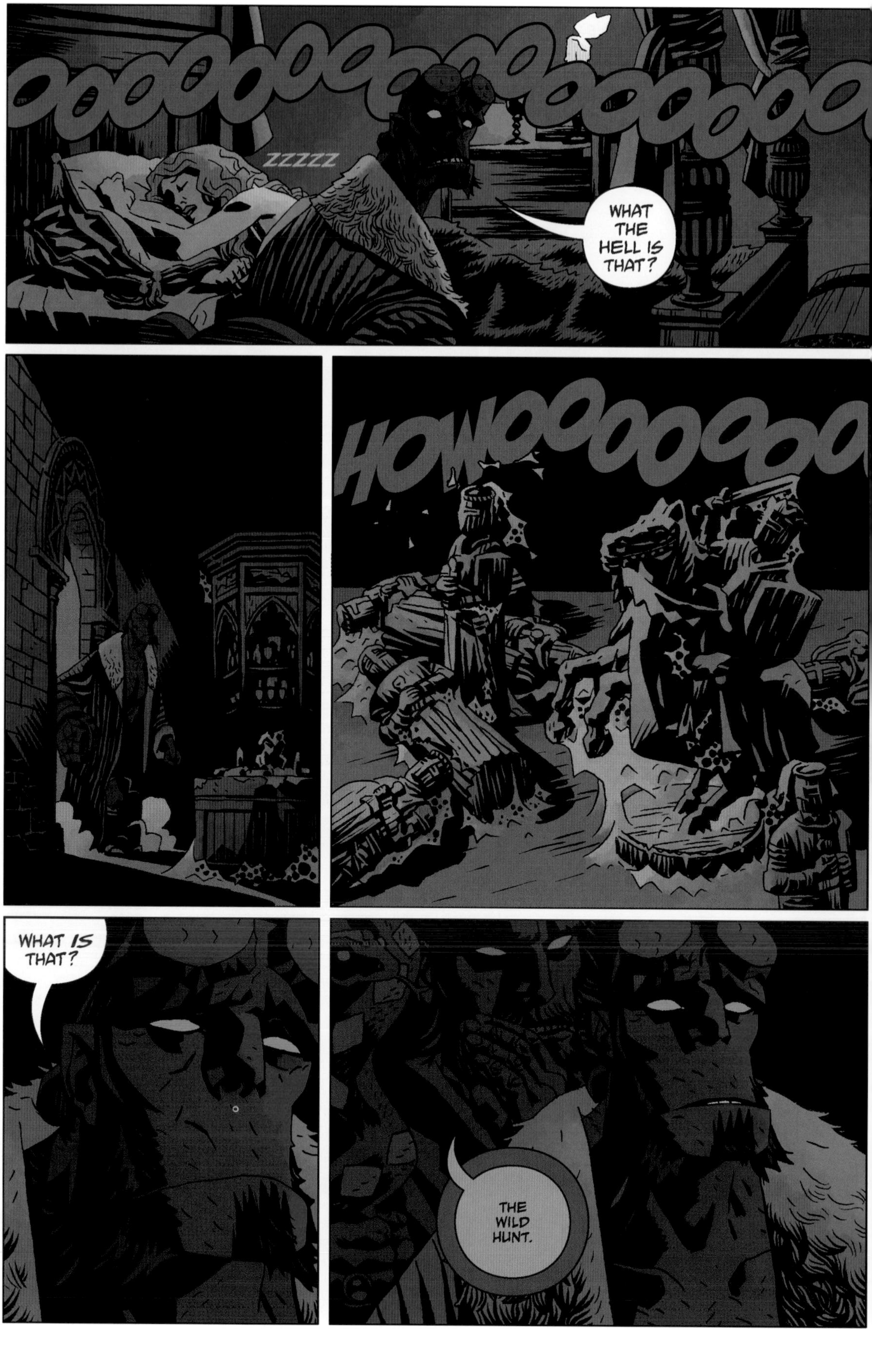
OOOOOOOOOOOOOOOOOOO
ZZZZZ
WHAT THE HELL IS THAT?
HOWOOOOOOOO
WHAT IS THAT?
THE WILD HUNT.

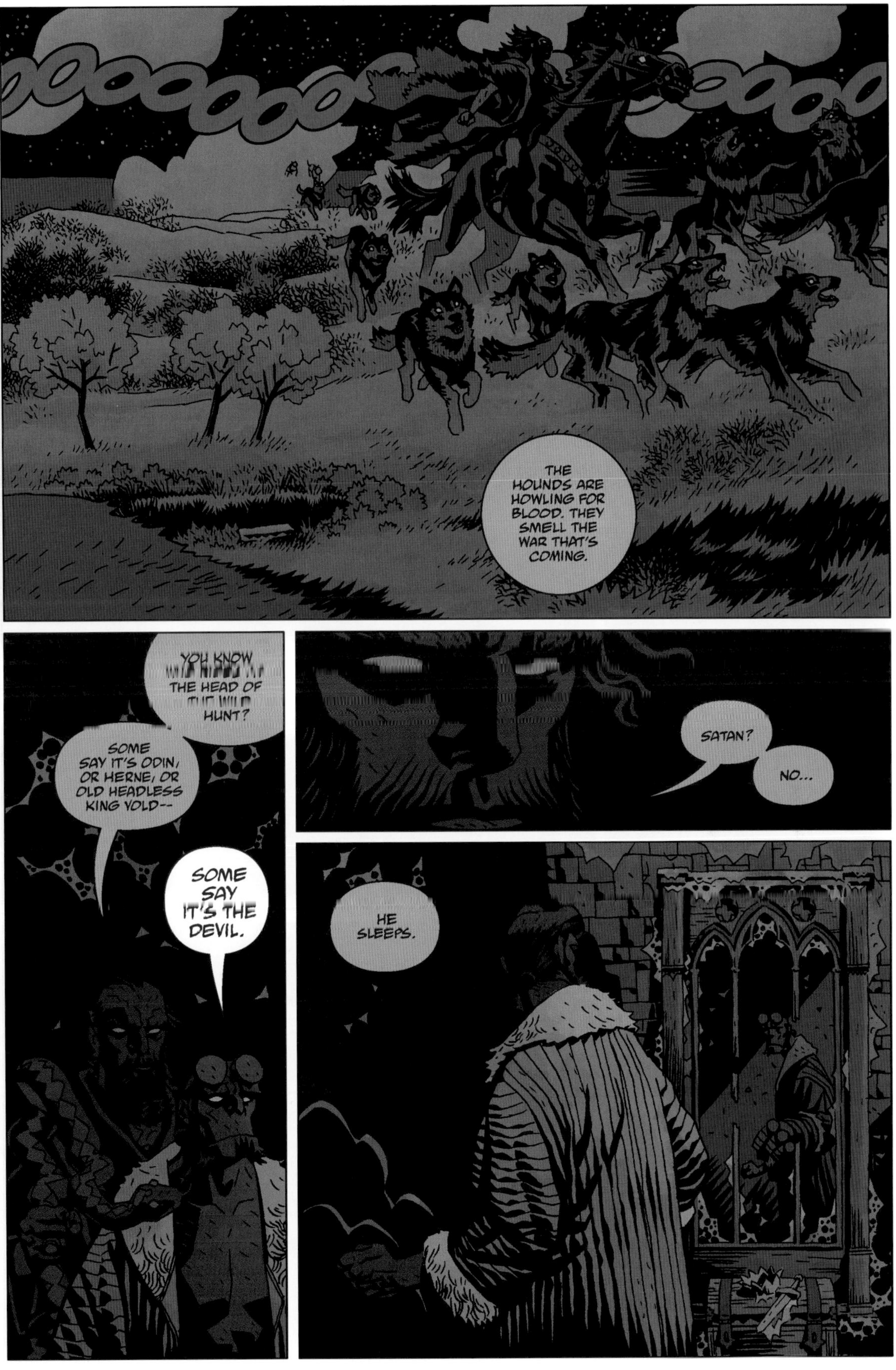

OOOOOOOO
OOOOOO
THE HOUNDS ARE HOWLING FOR BLOOD. THEY SMELL THE WAR THAT'S COMING.
YOU KNOW
THE HEAD OF
HUNT?
SOME SAY IT'S ODIN, OR HERNE, OR OLD HEADLESS KING YOLD--
SOME SAY IT'S THE DEVIL.
SATAN?
NO...
HE SLEEPS.

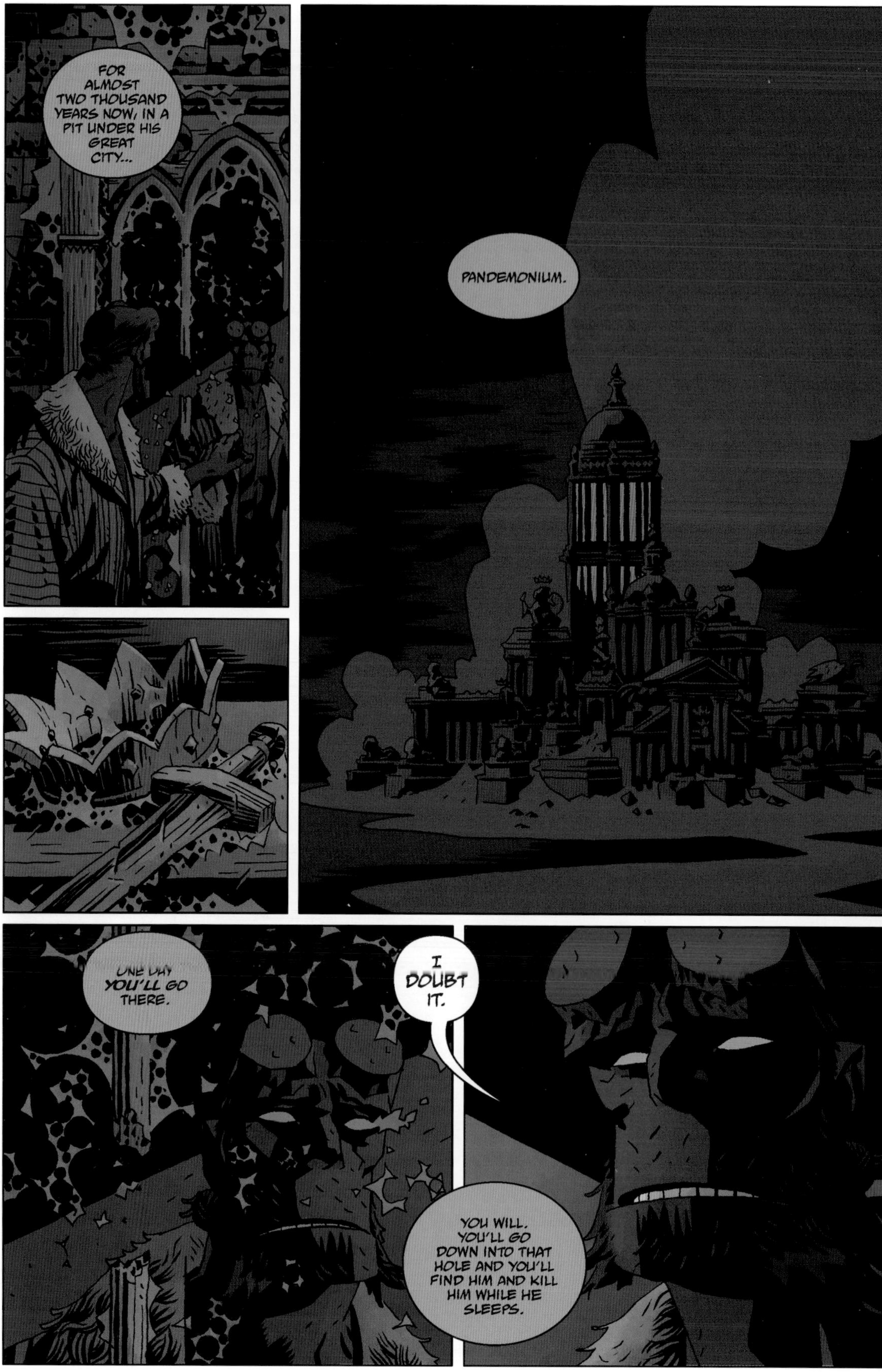
FOR ALMOST TWO THOUSAND YEARS NOW, IN A PIT UNDER HIS GREAT CITY...
PANDEMONIUM.
ONE DAY YOU'LL GO THERE.
I DOUBT IT.
YOU WILL. YOU'LL GO DOWN INTO THAT HOLE AND YOU'LL FIND HIM AND KILL HIM WHILE HE SLEEPS.

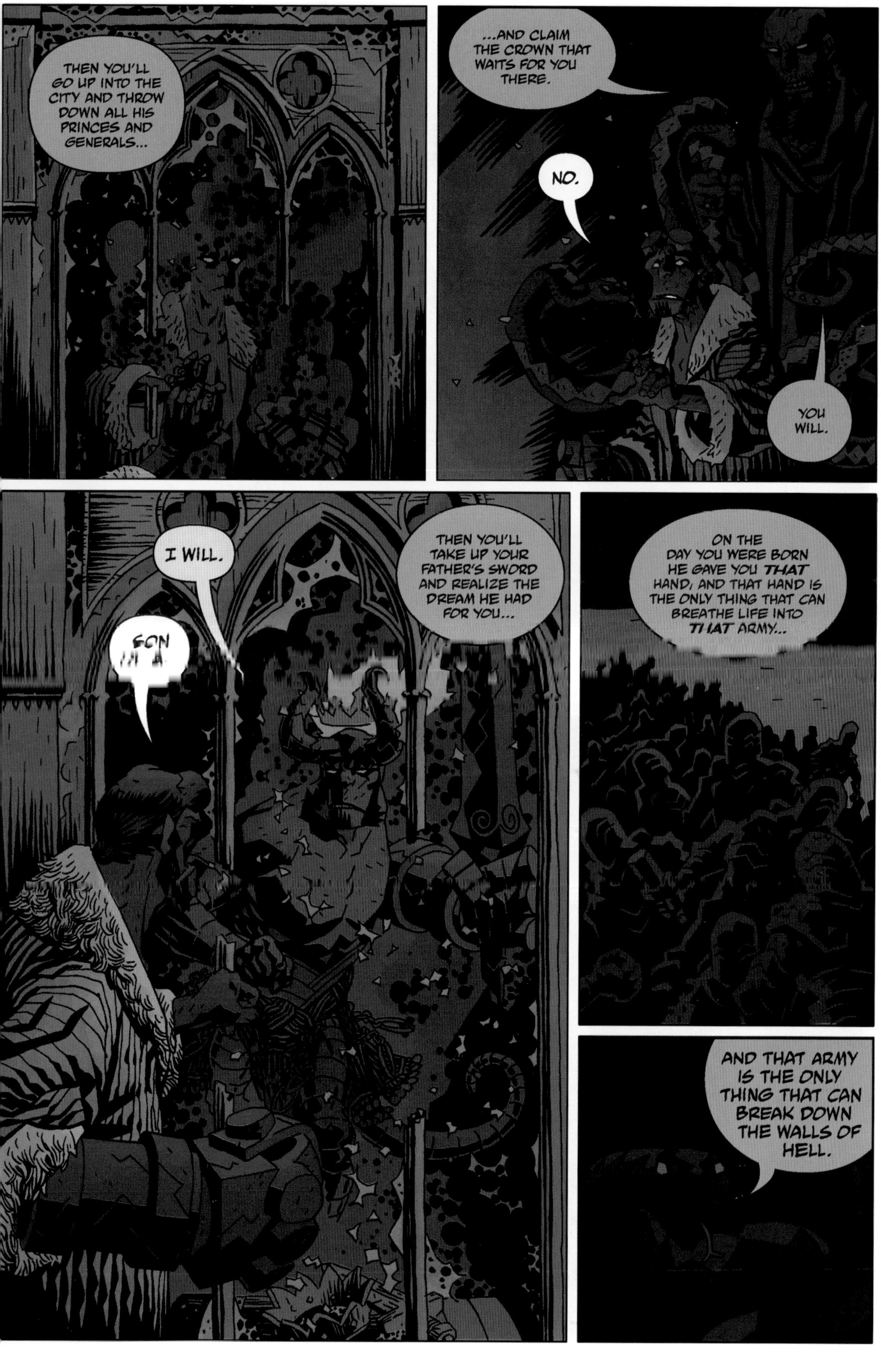
THEN YOU'LL GO UP INTO THE CITY AND THROW DOWN ALL HIS PRINCES AND GENERALS...
...AND CLAIM THE CROWN THAT WAITS FOR YOU THERE.
NO.
YOU WILL.
SON
I WILL.
THEN YOU'LL TAKE UP YOUR FATHER'S SWORD AND REALIZE THE DREAM HE HAD FOR YOU...
ON THE DAY YOU WERE BORN HE GAVE YOU THAT HAND, AND THAT HAND IS THE ONLY THING THAT CAN BREATHE LIFE INTO THAT ARMY...
AND THAT ARMY IS THE ONLY THING THAT CAN BREAK DOWN THE WALLS OF HELL.

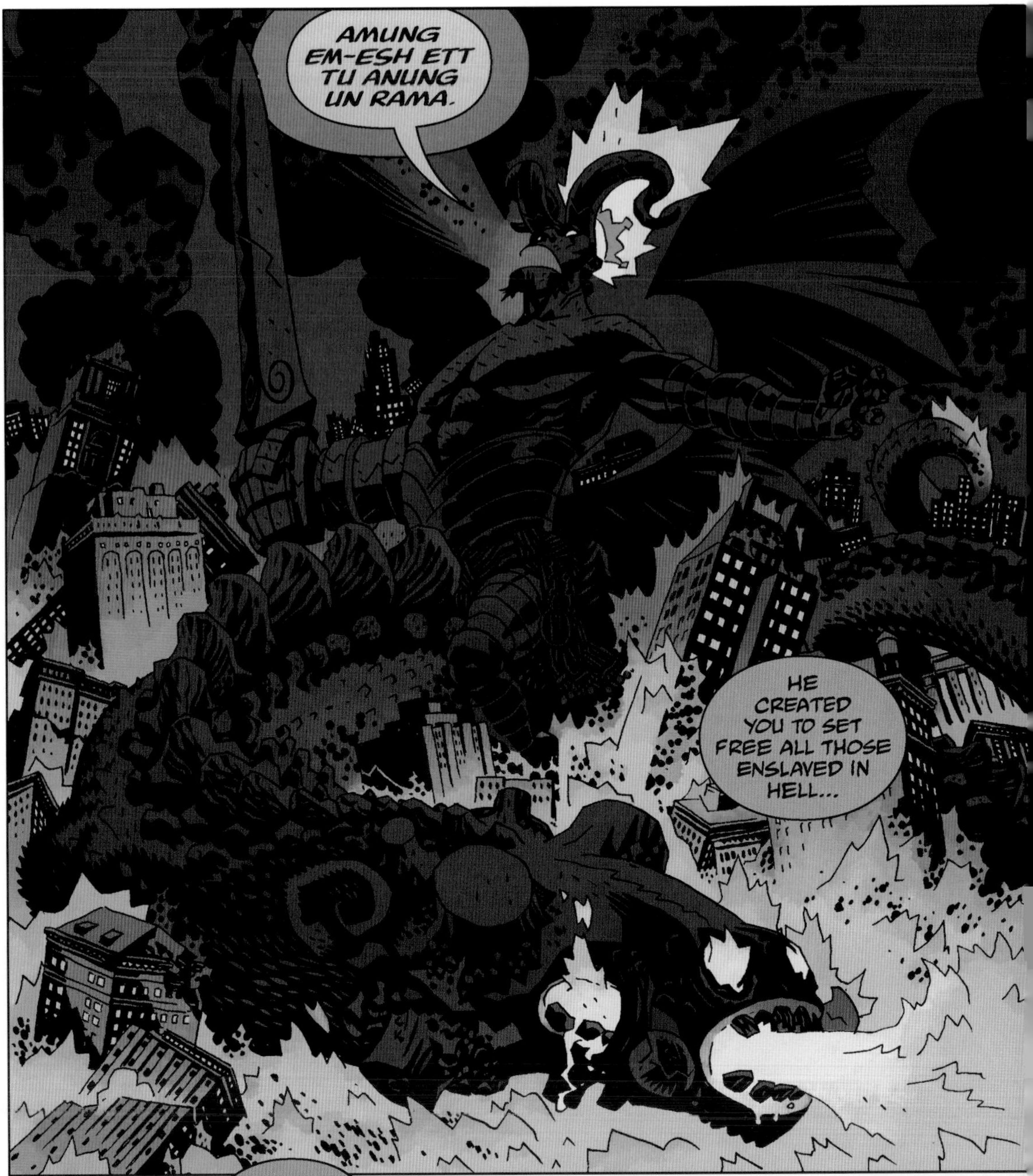
AMUNG EM-ESH ETT TU ANUNG UN RAMA.
HE CREATED YOU TO SET FREE ALL THOSE ENSLAVED IN HELL...

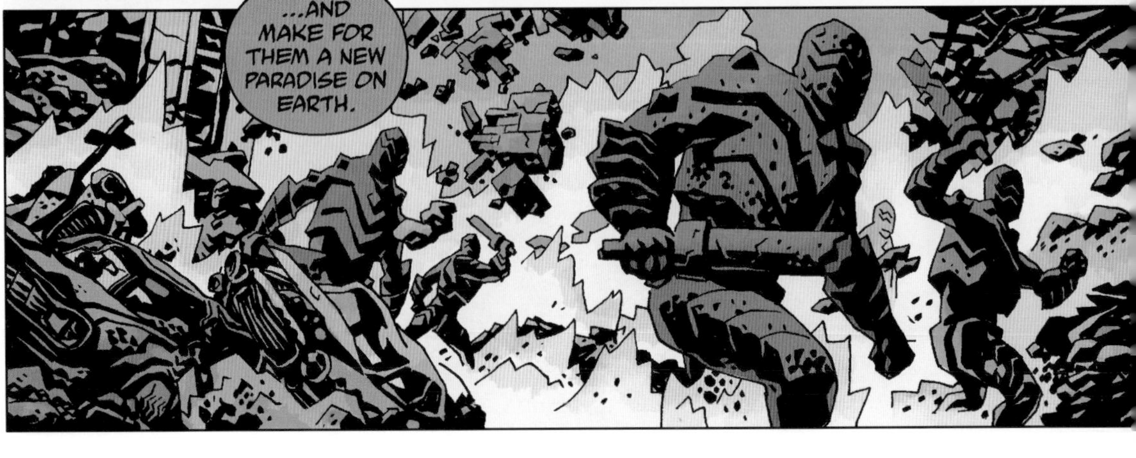
...AND MAKE FOR THEM A NEW PARADISE ON EARTH.

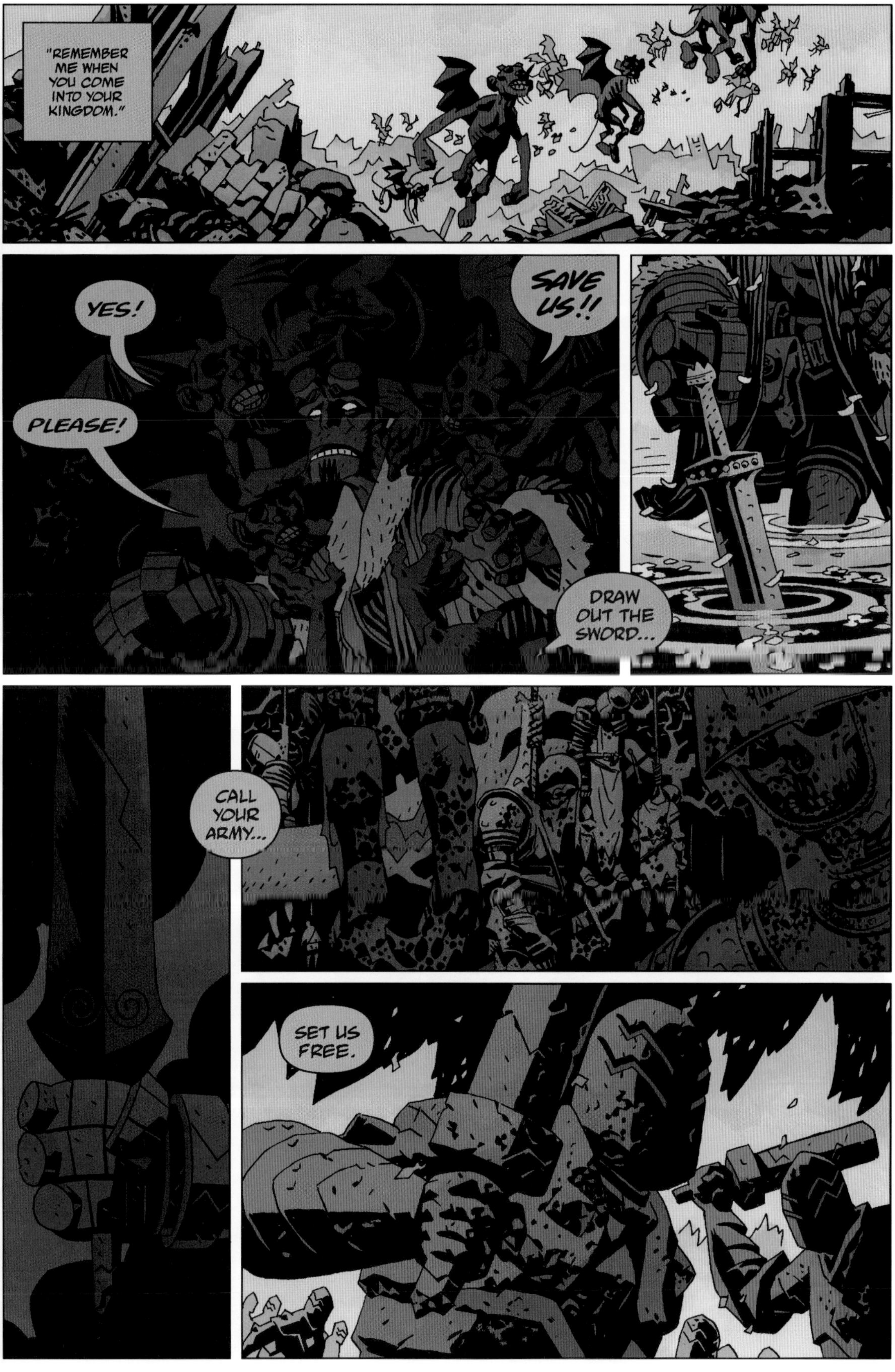
"REMEMBER ME WHEN YOU COME INTO YOUR KINGDOM."
YES!
PLEASE!
SAVE US!!
DRAW OUT THE SWORD...
CALL YOUR ARMY...
SET US FREE.

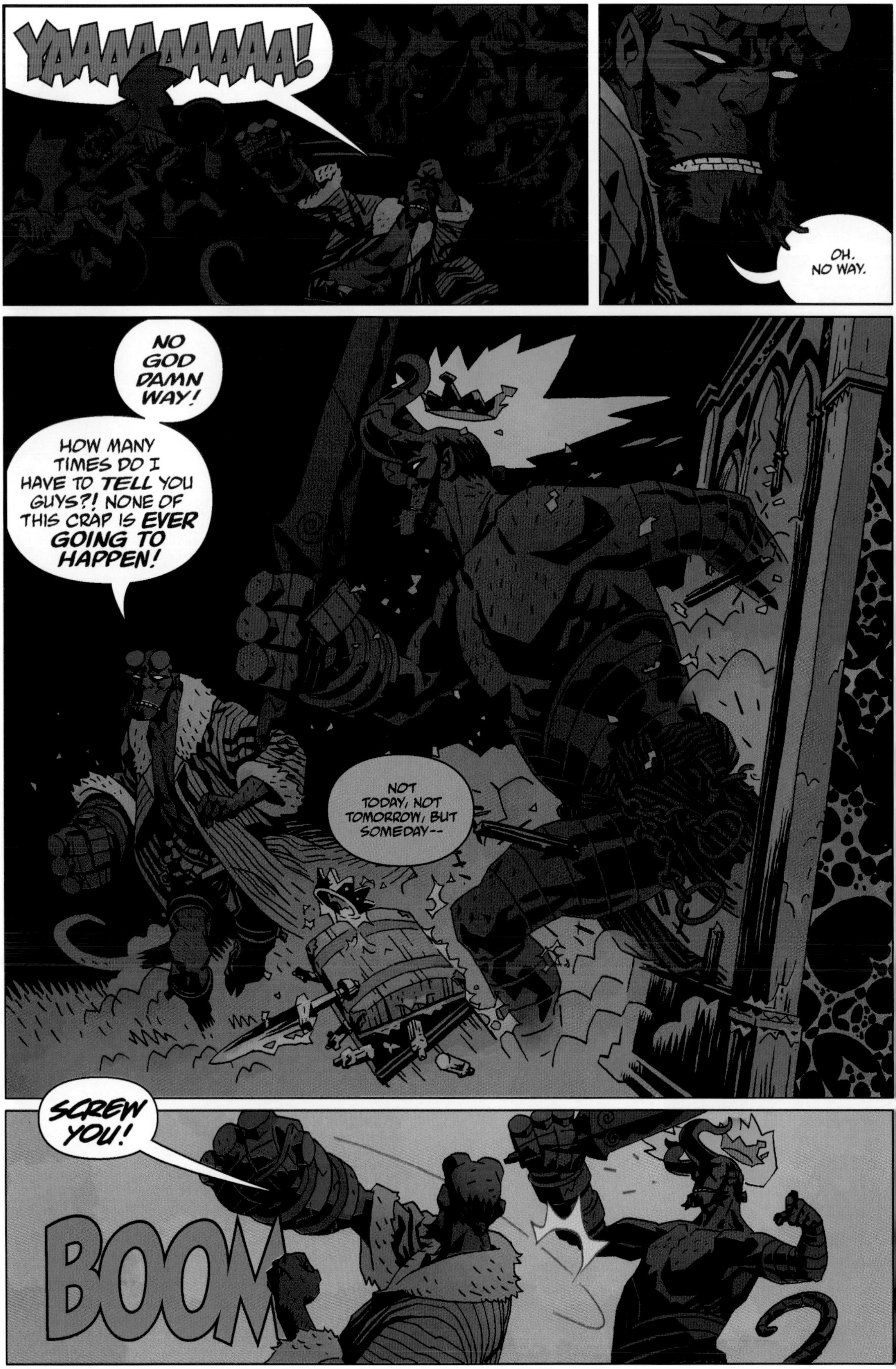
YAAAAAAAAA!
OH. NO WAY.
NO GOD DAMN WAY!
HOW MANY TIMES DO I HAVE TO TELL YOU GUYS?! NONE OF THIS CRAP IS EVER GOING TO HAPPEN!
NOT TODAY, NOT TOMORROW, BUT SOMEDAY--
SCREW YOU!
BOOM

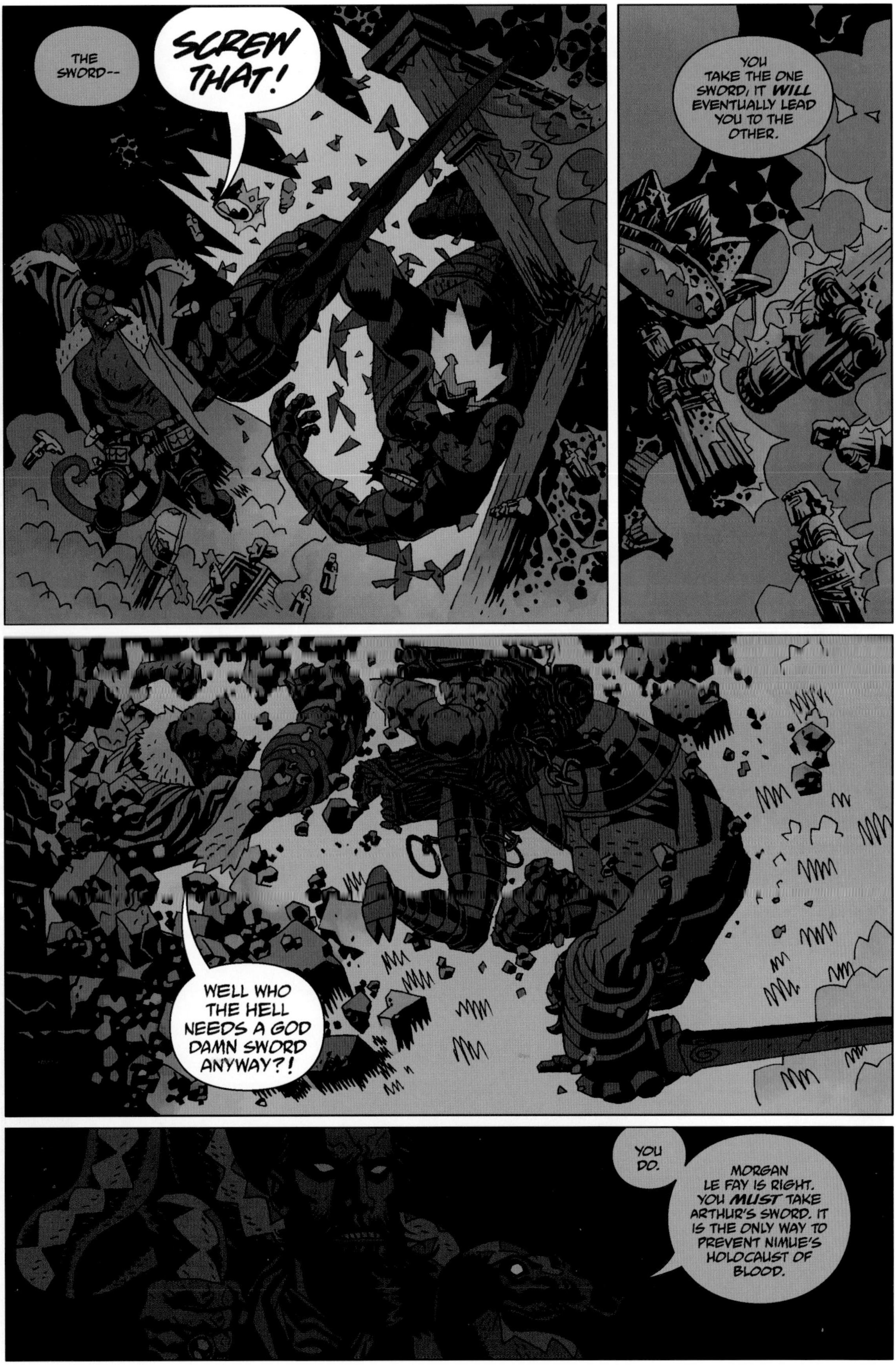
THE SWORD--
SCREW THAT!
YOU TAKE THE ONE SWORD, IT WILL EVENTUALLY LEAD YOU TO THE OTHER.
WELL WHO THE HELL NEEDS A GOD DAMN SWORD ANYWAY?!
YOU DO.
MORGAN LE FAY IS RIGHT. YOU MUST TAKE ARTHUR'S SWORD. IT IS THE ONLY WAY TO PREVENT NIMUE'S HOLOCAUST OF BLOOD.

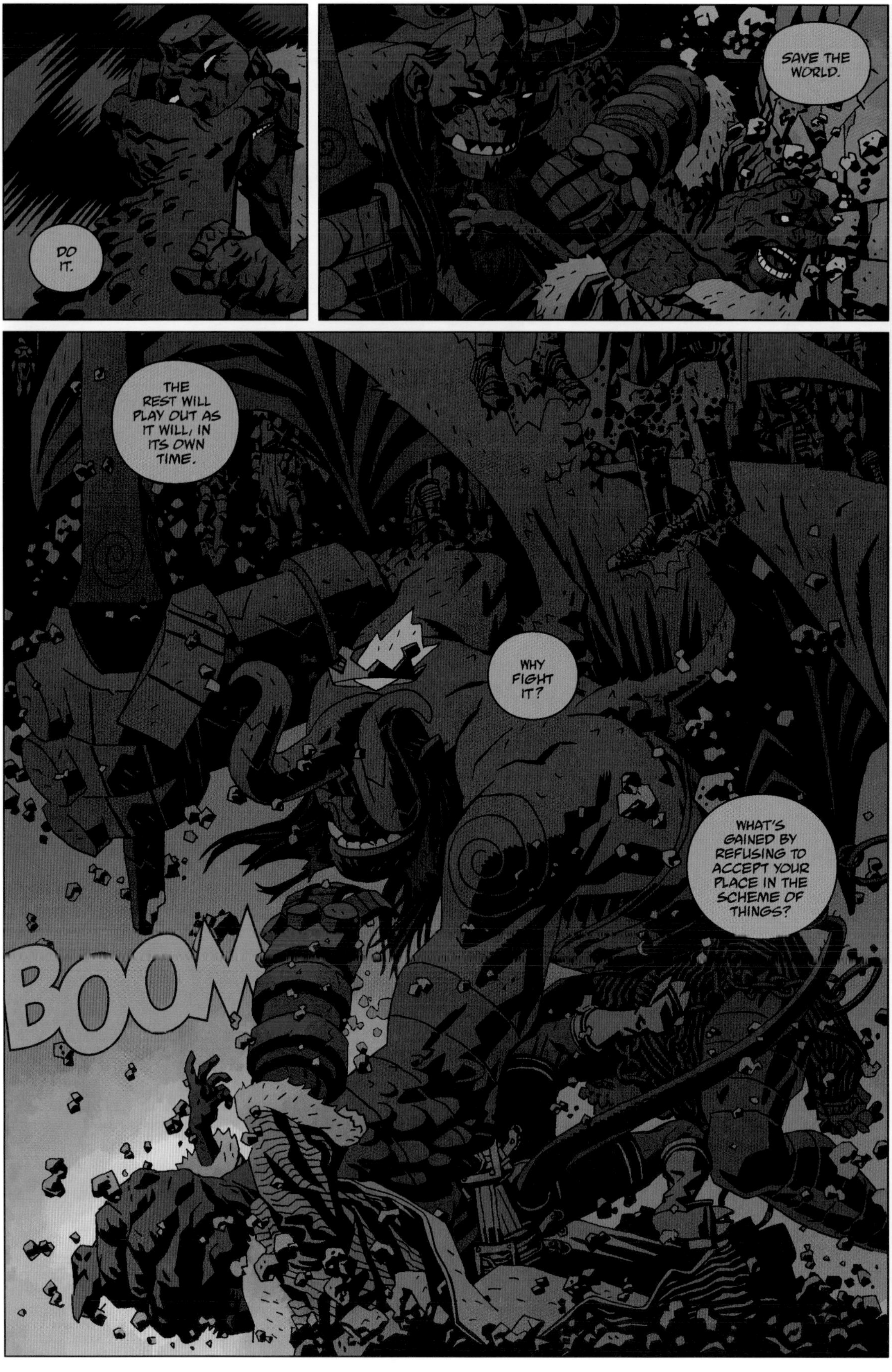

DO IT.
SAVE THE WORLD.
THE REST WILL PLAY OUT AS IT WILL, IN ITS OWN TIME.
WHY FIGHT IT?
WHAT'S GAINED BY REFUSING TO ACCEPT YOUR PLACE IN THE SCHEME OF THINGS?
BOOM

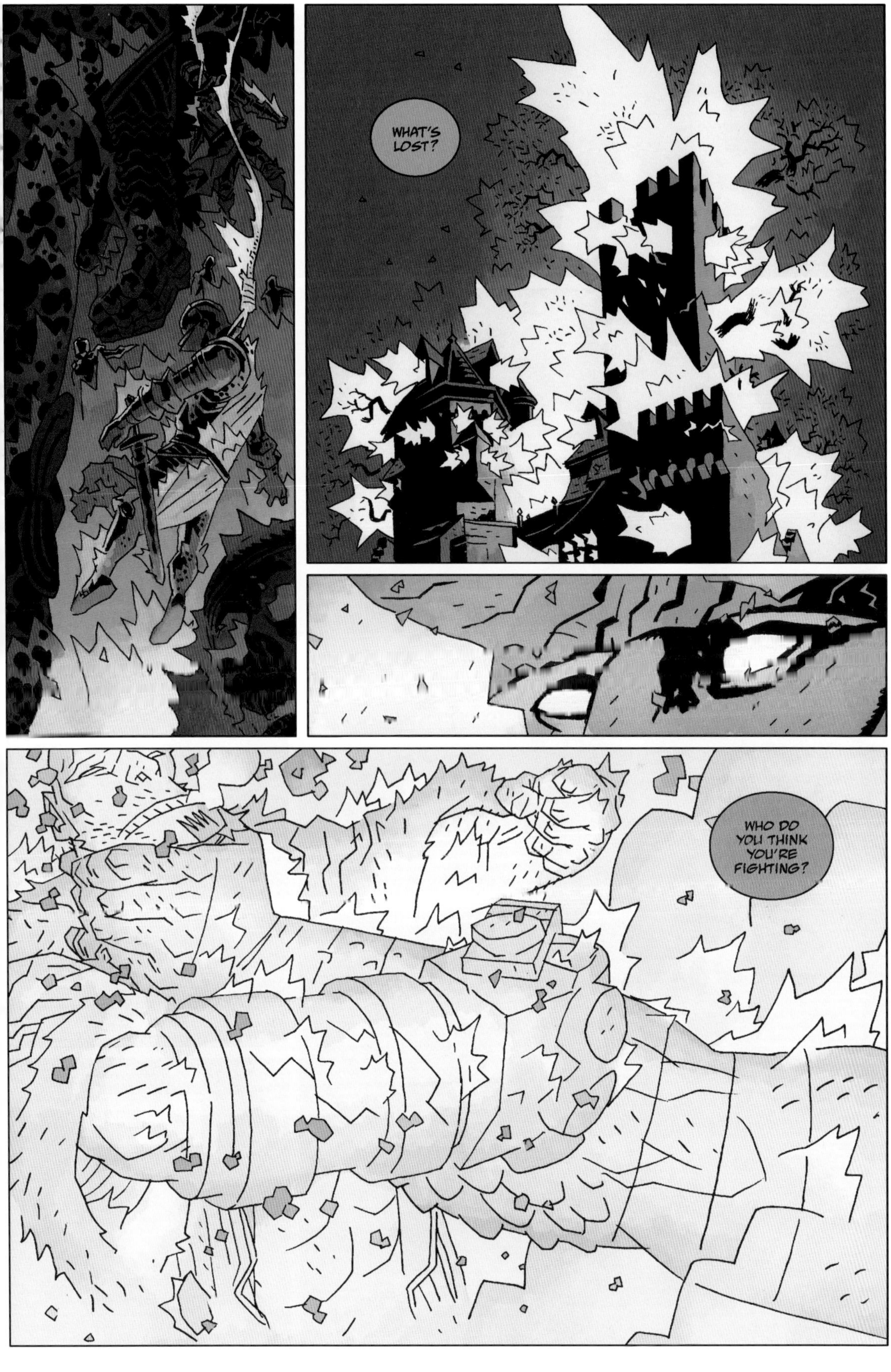
WHAT'S LOST?
WHO DO YOU THINK YOU'RE FIGHTING?

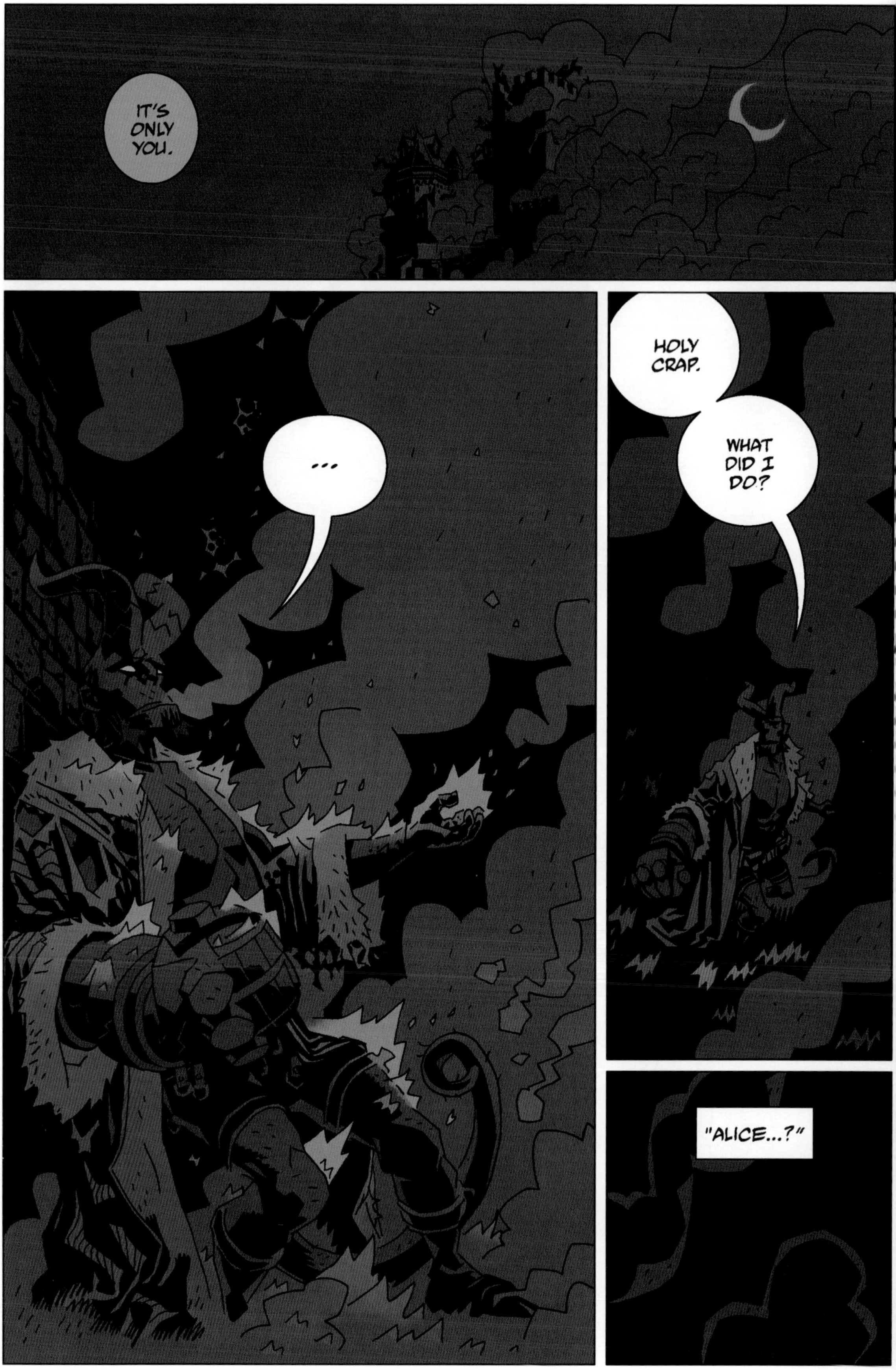
IT'S ONLY YOU.
...
HOLY CRAP.
WHAT DID I DO?
"ALICE...?"

CHAPTER EIGHT

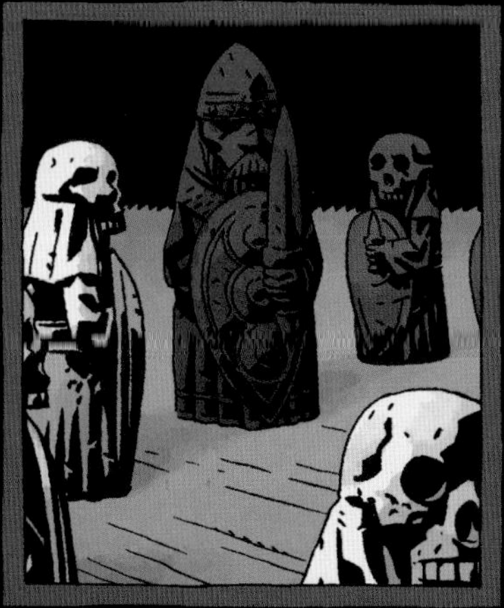

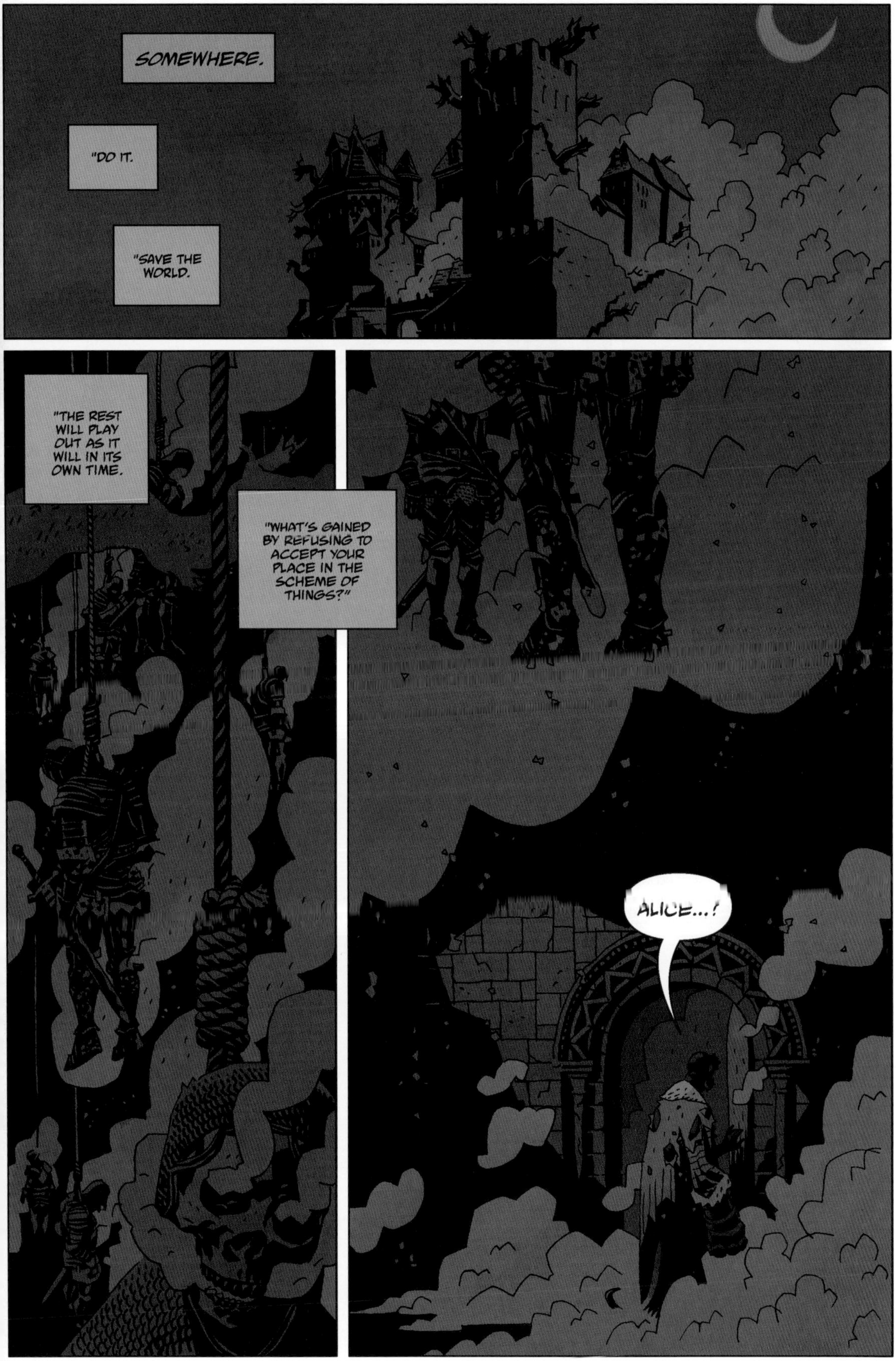
SOMEWHERE.
"DO IT.
"SAVE THE WORLD.
"THE REST WILL PLAY OUT AS IT WILL IN ITS OWN TIME.
"WHAT'S GAINED BY REFUSING TO ACCEPT YOUR PLACE IN THE SCHEME OF THINGS?"
ALICE...?

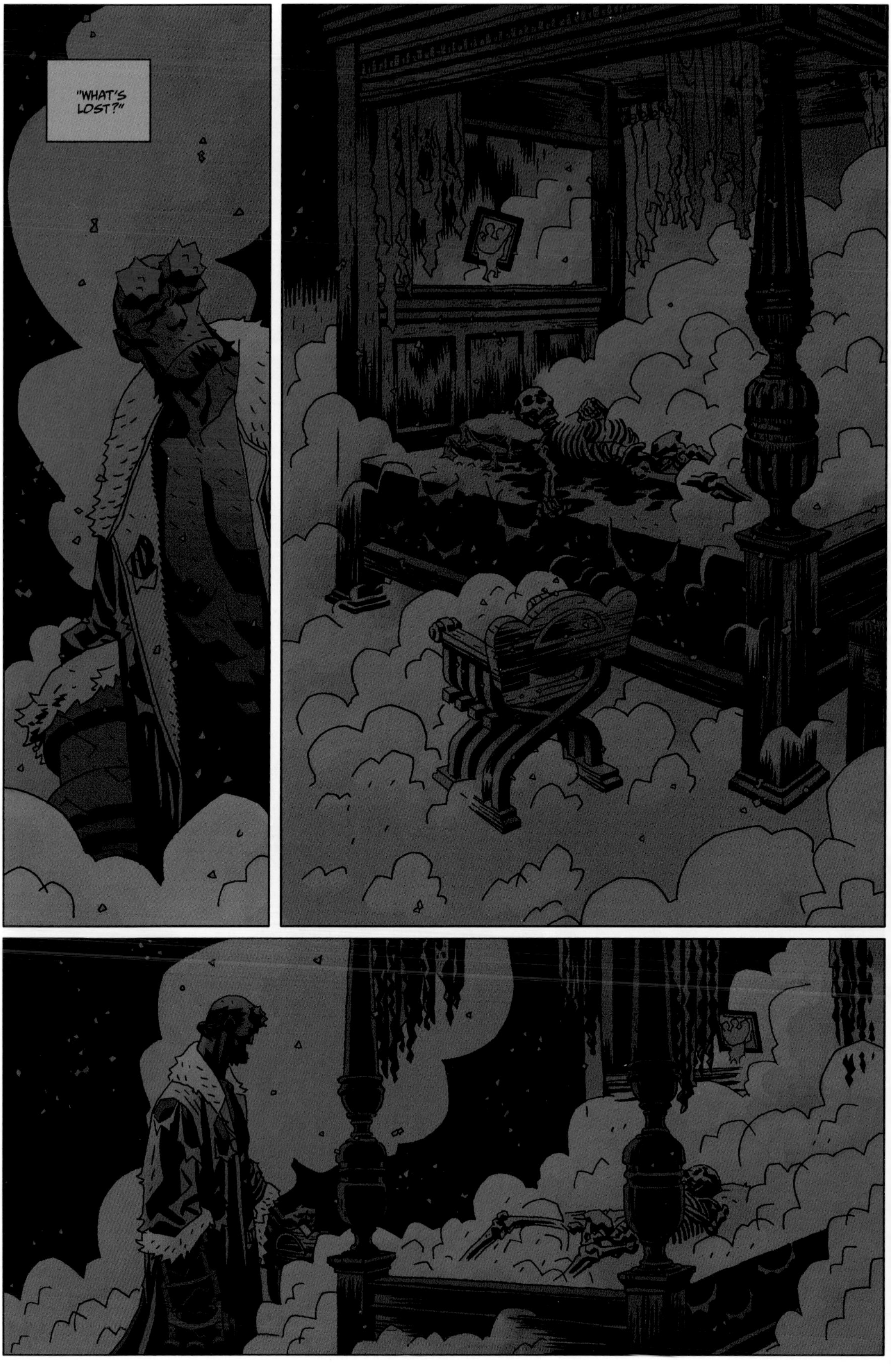
"WHAT'S LOST?"

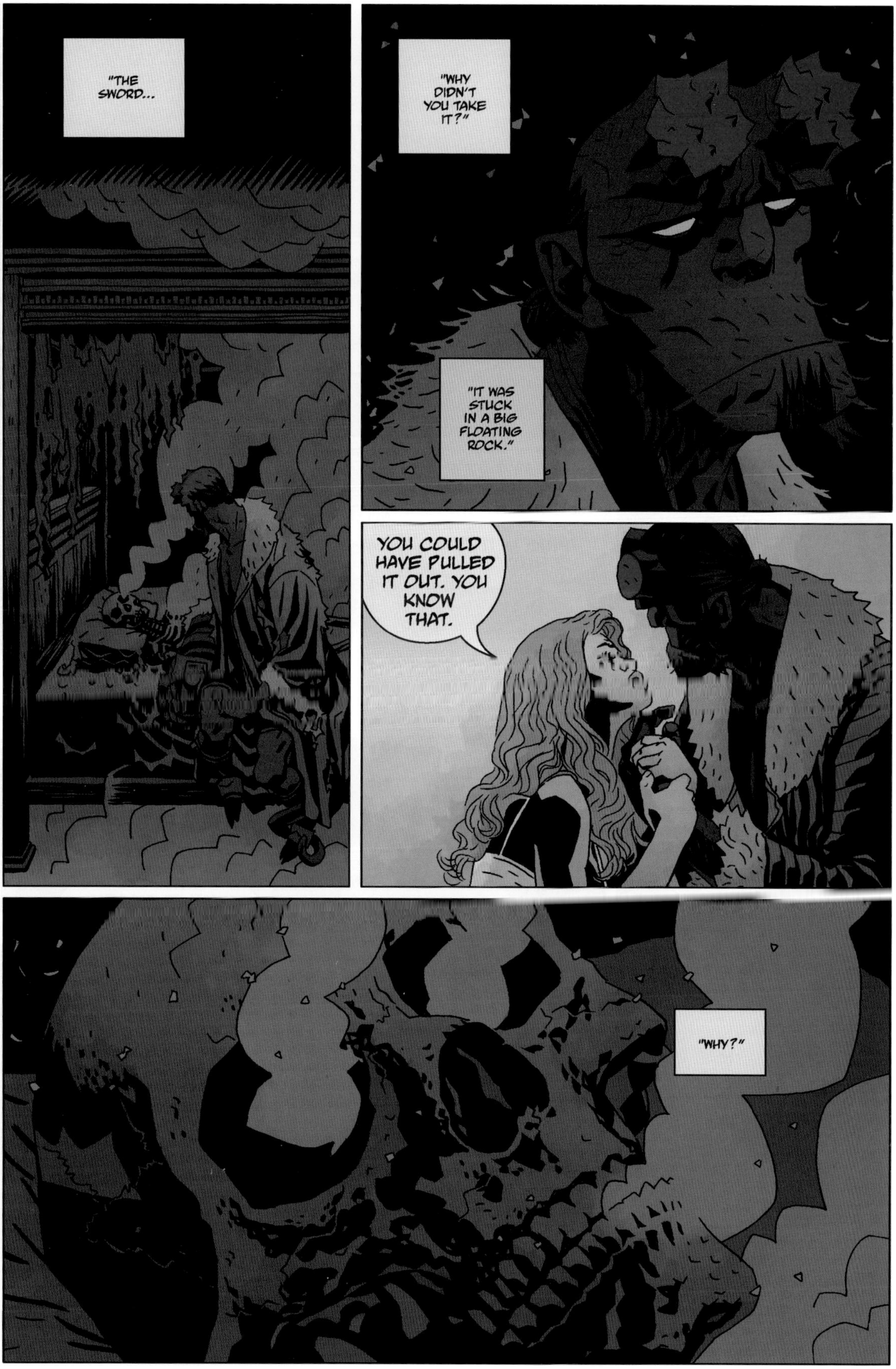
"THE SWORD...
"WHY DIDN'T YOU TAKE IT?"
"IT WAS STUCK IN A BIG FLOATING ROCK."
YOU COULD HAVE PULLED IT OUT. YOU KNOW THAT.
"WHY?"

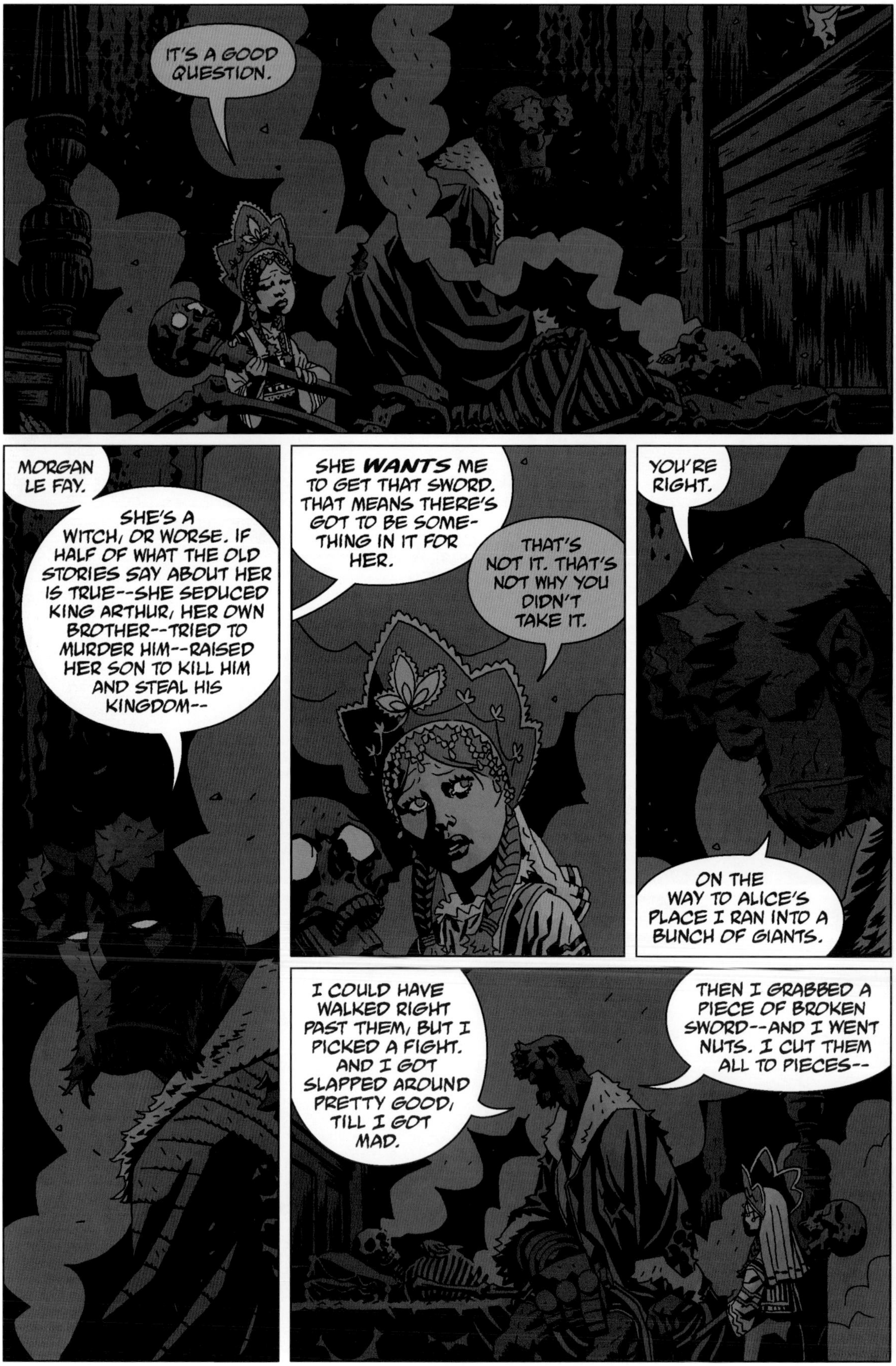
IT'S A GOOD QUESTION.
MORGAN LE FAY.
SHE'S A WITCH, OR WORSE. IF HALF OF WHAT THE OLD STORIES SAY ABOUT HER IS TRUE--SHE SEDUCED KING ARTHUR, HER OWN BROTHER--TRIED TO MURDER HIM--RAISED HER SON TO KILL HIM AND STEAL HIS KINGDOM--
SHE **WANTS** ME TO GET THAT SWORD. THAT MEANS THERE'S GOT TO BE SOME-THING IN IT FOR HER.
THAT'S NOT IT. THAT'S NOT WHY YOU DIDN'T TAKE IT.
YOU'RE RIGHT.
ON THE WAY TO ALICE'S PLACE I RAN INTO A BUNCH OF GIANTS.
I COULD HAVE WALKED RIGHT PAST THEM, BUT I PICKED A FIGHT. AND I GOT SLAPPED AROUND PRETTY GOOD, TILL I GOT MAD.
THEN I GRABBED A PIECE OF BROKEN SWORD--AND I WENT NUTS. I CUT THEM ALL TO PIECES--

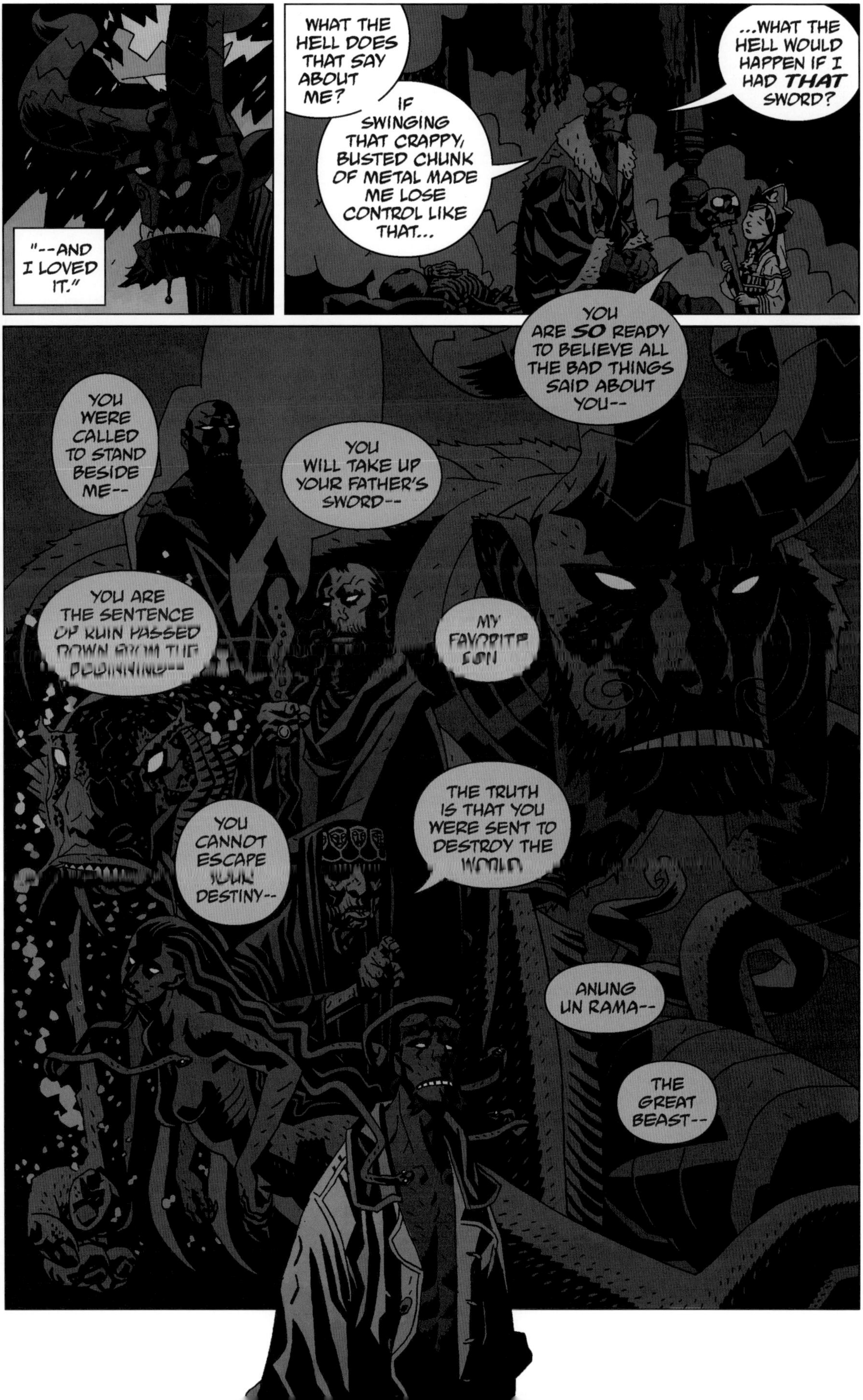
"--AND I LOVED IT."
WHAT THE HELL DOES THAT SAY ABOUT ME?
IF SWINGING THAT CRAPPY, BUSTED CHUNK OF METAL MADE ME LOSE CONTROL LIKE THAT...
...WHAT THE HELL WOULD HAPPEN IF I HAD THAT SWORD?
YOU ARE SO READY TO BELIEVE ALL THE BAD THINGS SAID ABOUT YOU--
YOU WERE CALLED TO STAND BESIDE ME--
YOU WILL TAKE UP YOUR FATHER'S SWORD--
YOU ARE THE SENTENCE OF RUIN PASSED
MY FAVORITE
YOU CANNOT ESCAPE
DESTINY--
THE TRUTH IS THAT YOU WERE SENT TO DESTROY THE
ANUNG UN RAMA--
THE GREAT BEAST--

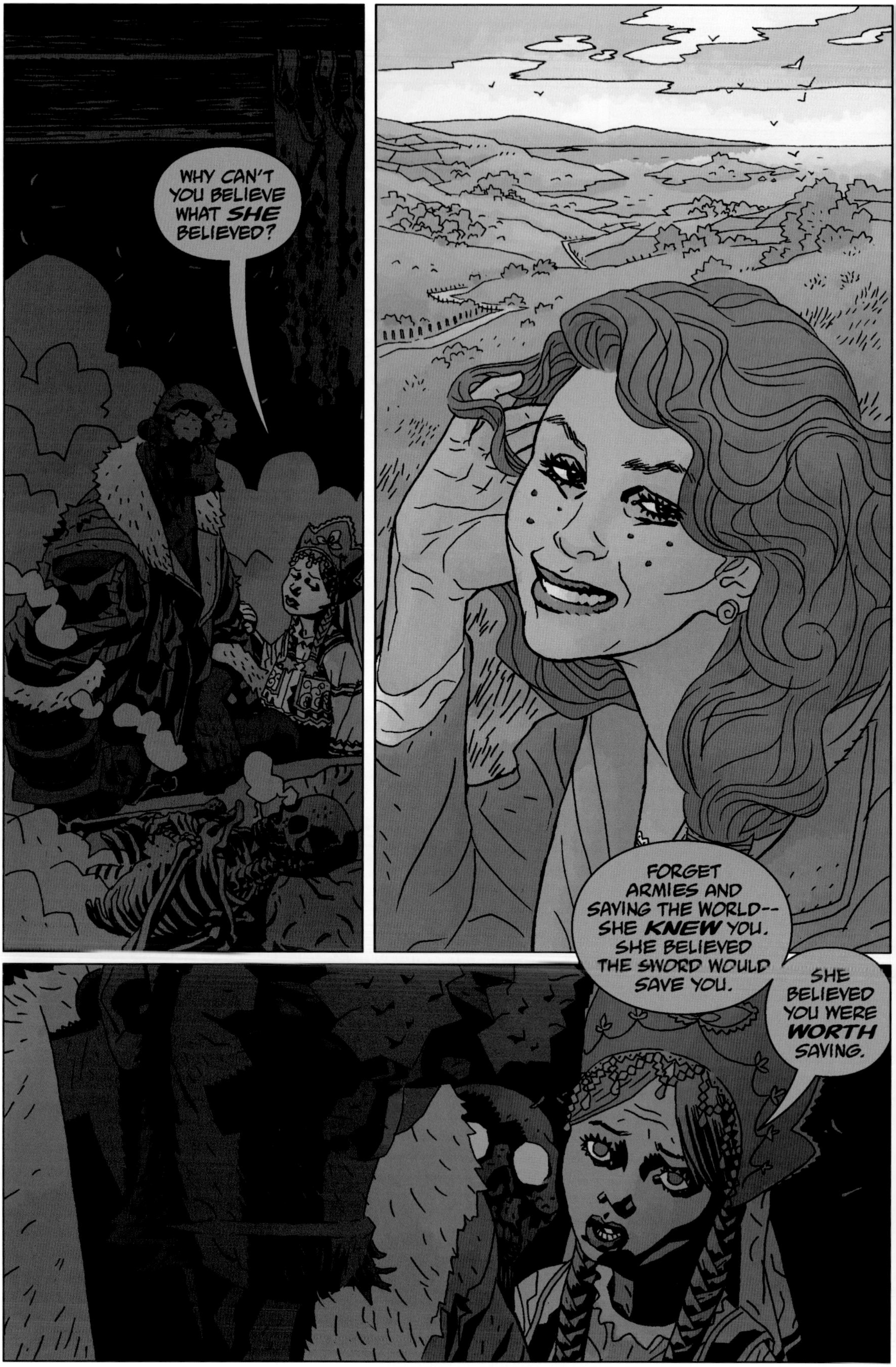
WHY CAN'T YOU BELIEVE WHAT SHE BELIEVED?
FORGET ARMIES AND SAVING THE WORLD-- SHE KNEW YOU. SHE BELIEVED THE SWORD WOULD SAVE YOU.
SHE BELIEVED YOU WERE WORTH SAVING.

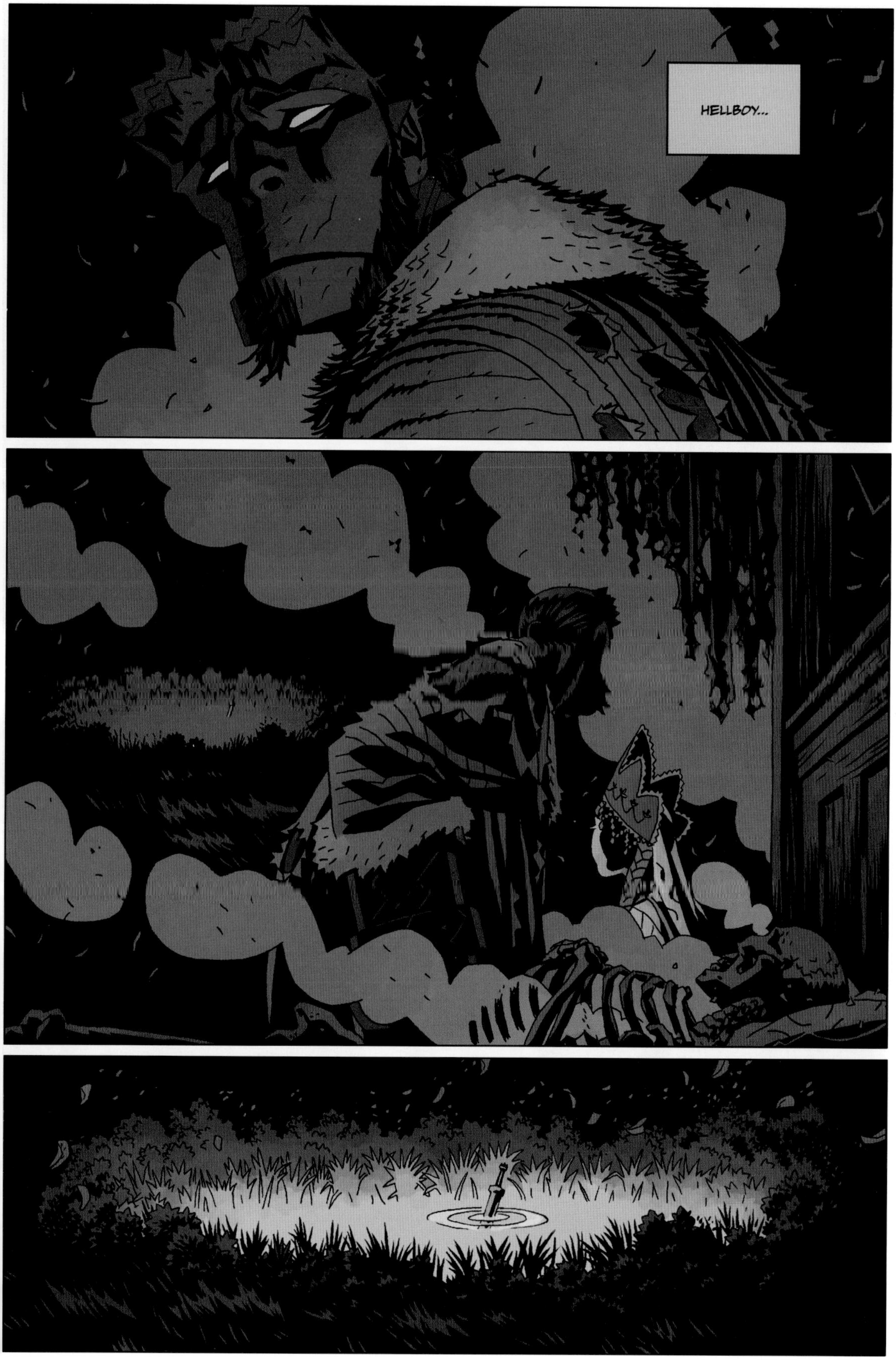
HELLBOY...

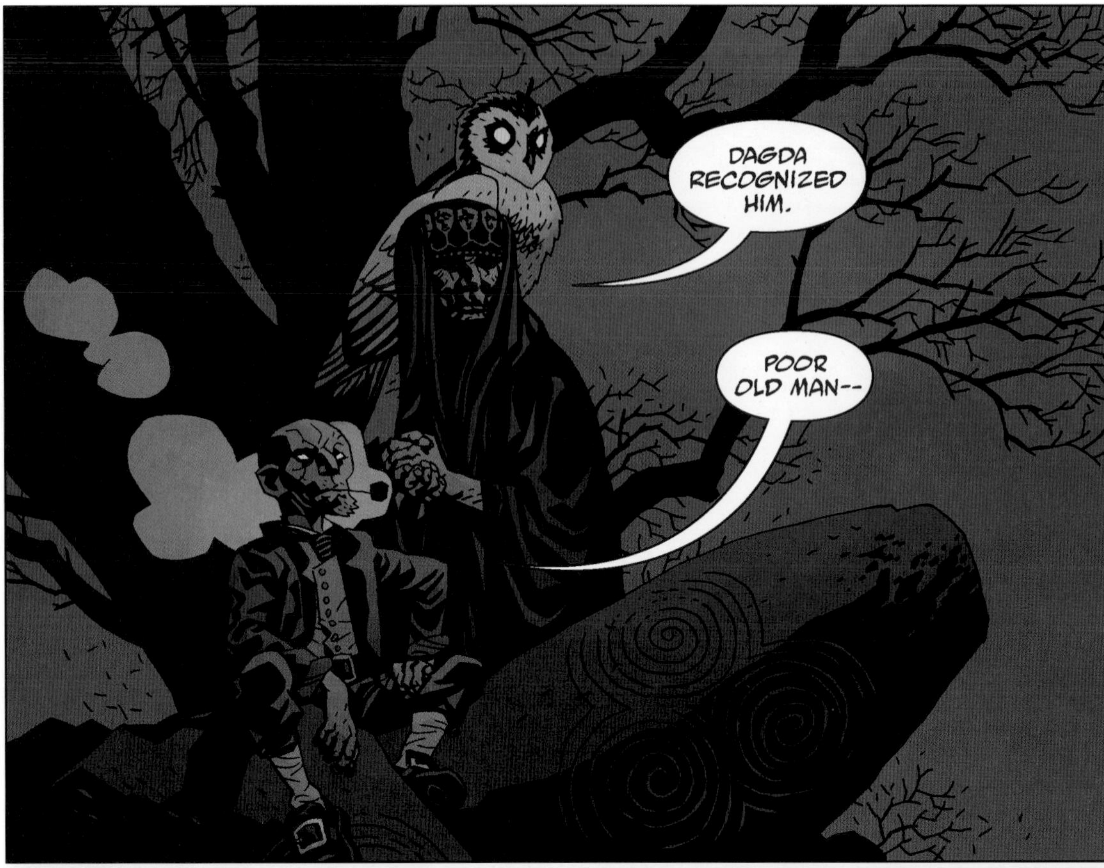
DAGDA RECOGNIZED HIM.
POOR OLD MAN--

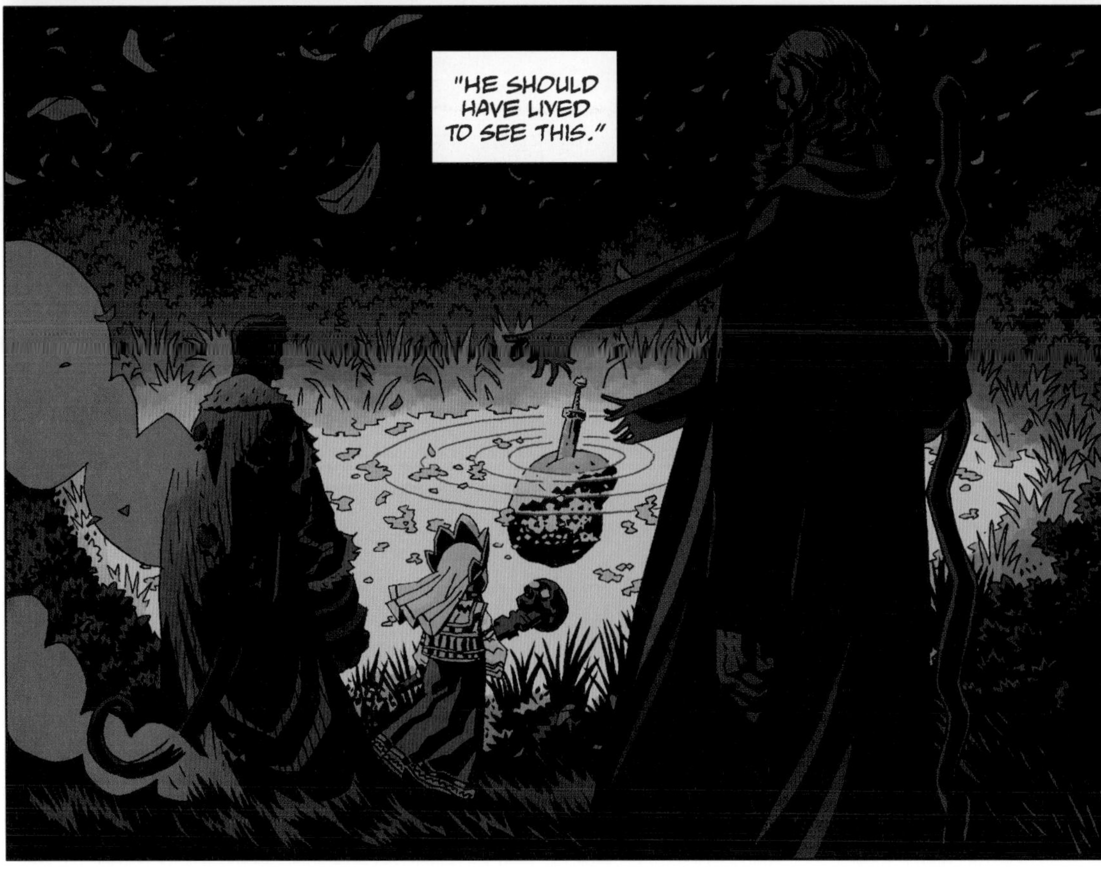
"HE SHOULD HAVE LIVED TO SEE THIS."

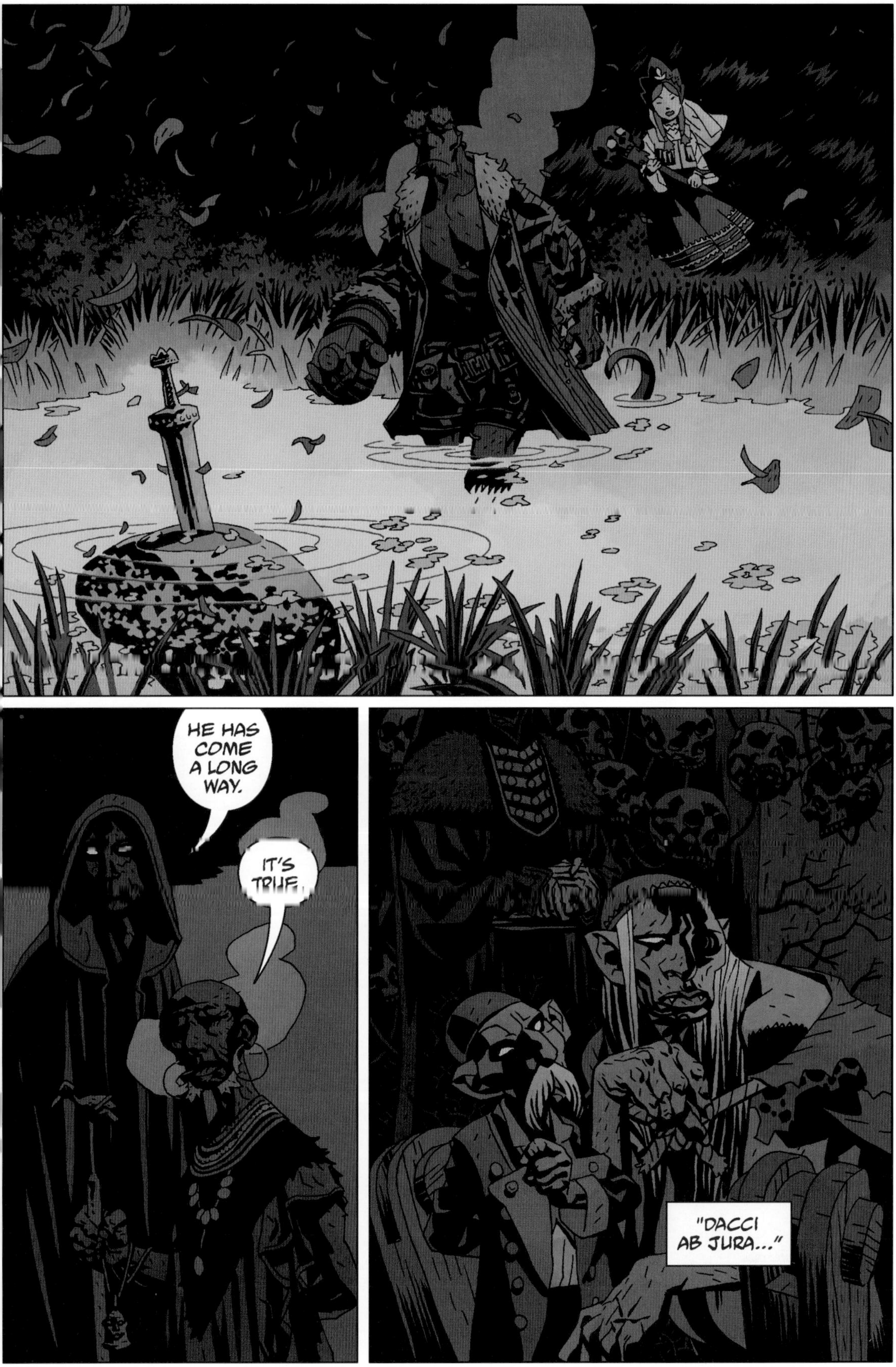
HE HAS COME A LONG WAY.
IT'S TRUE.
"DACCI AB JURA..."

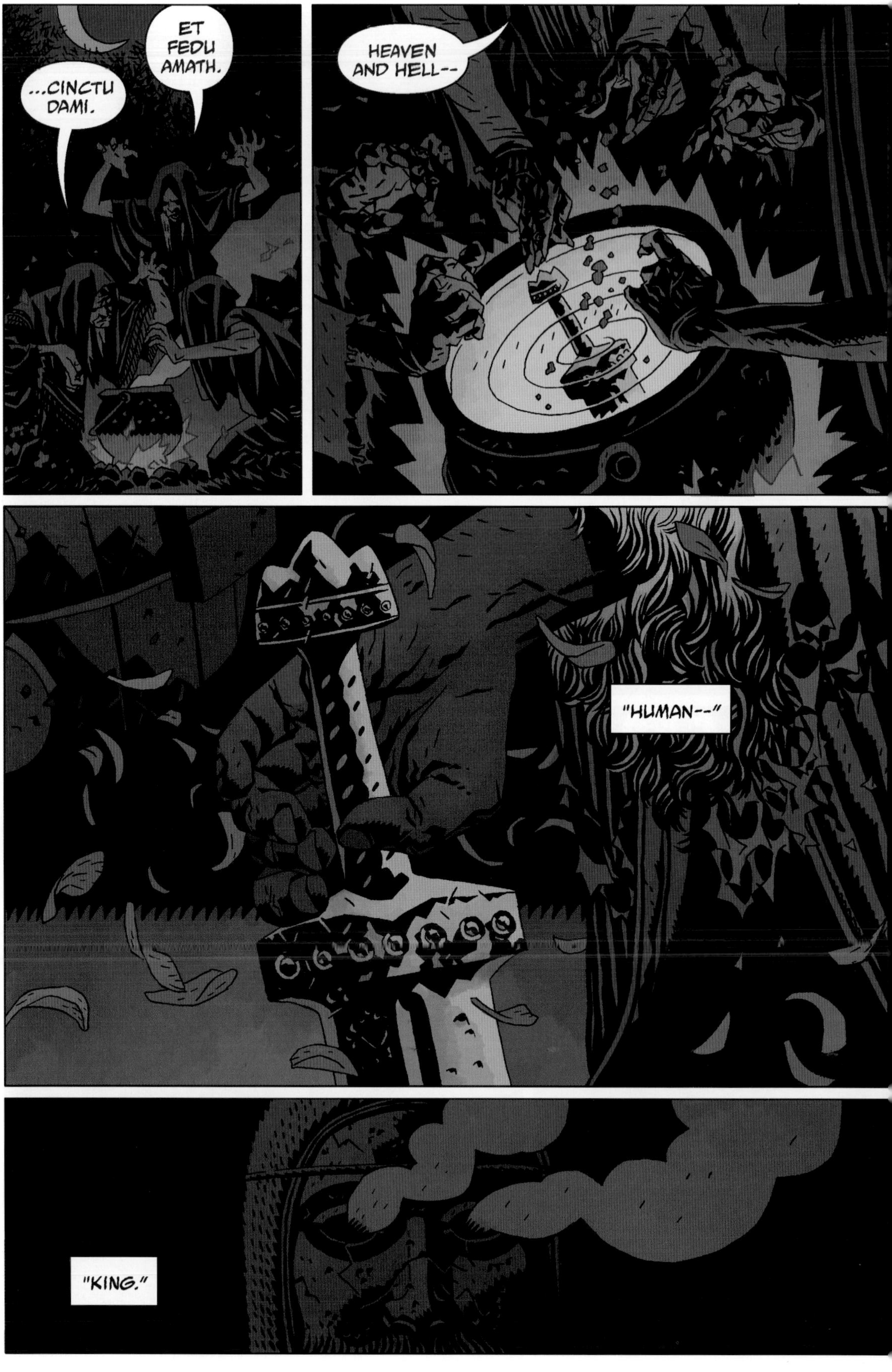
...CINCTU DAMI.
ET FEDU AMATH.
HEAVEN AND HELL--
"HUMAN--"
"KING."

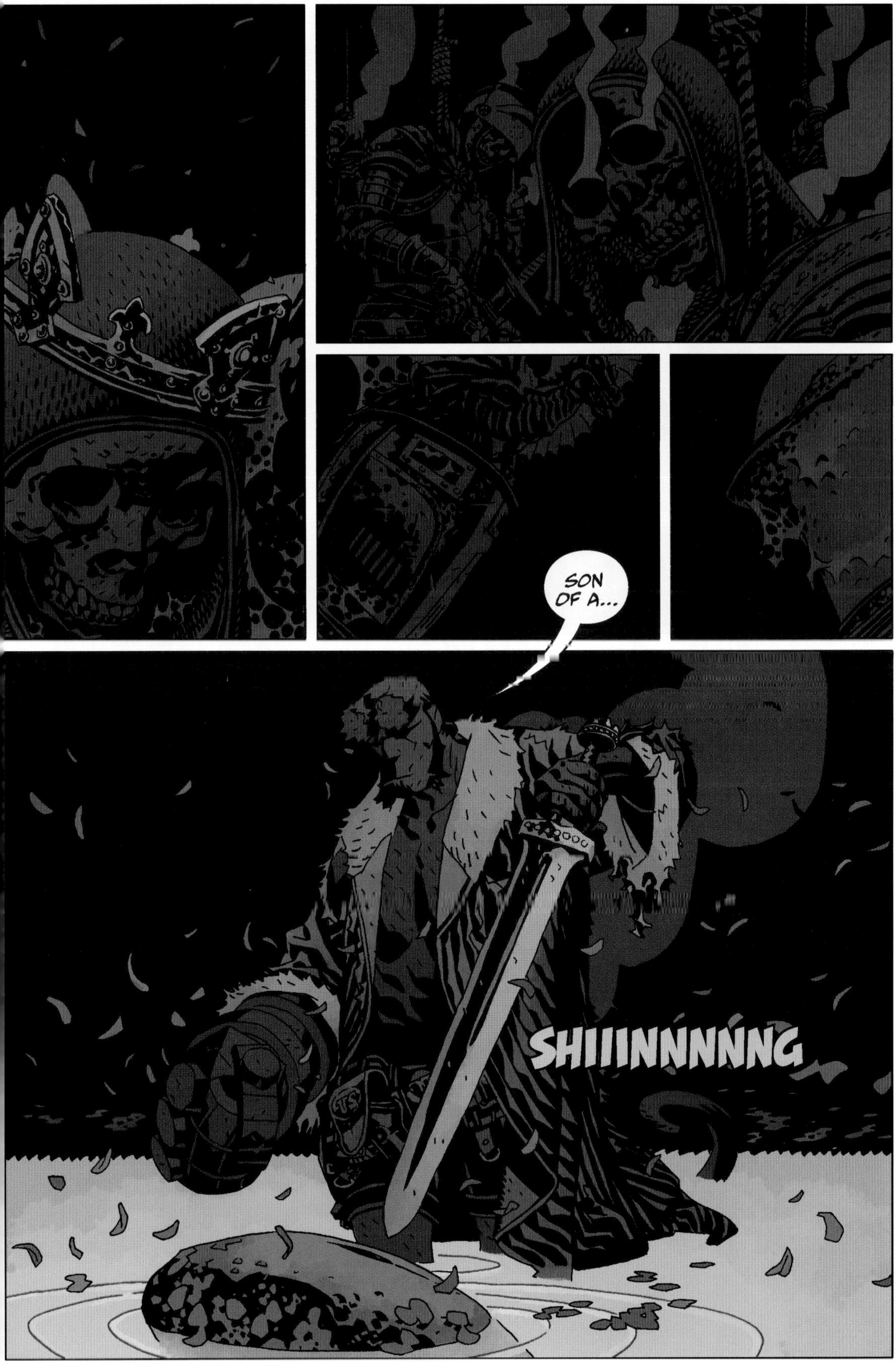
SON OF A...
SHIIINNNNNG

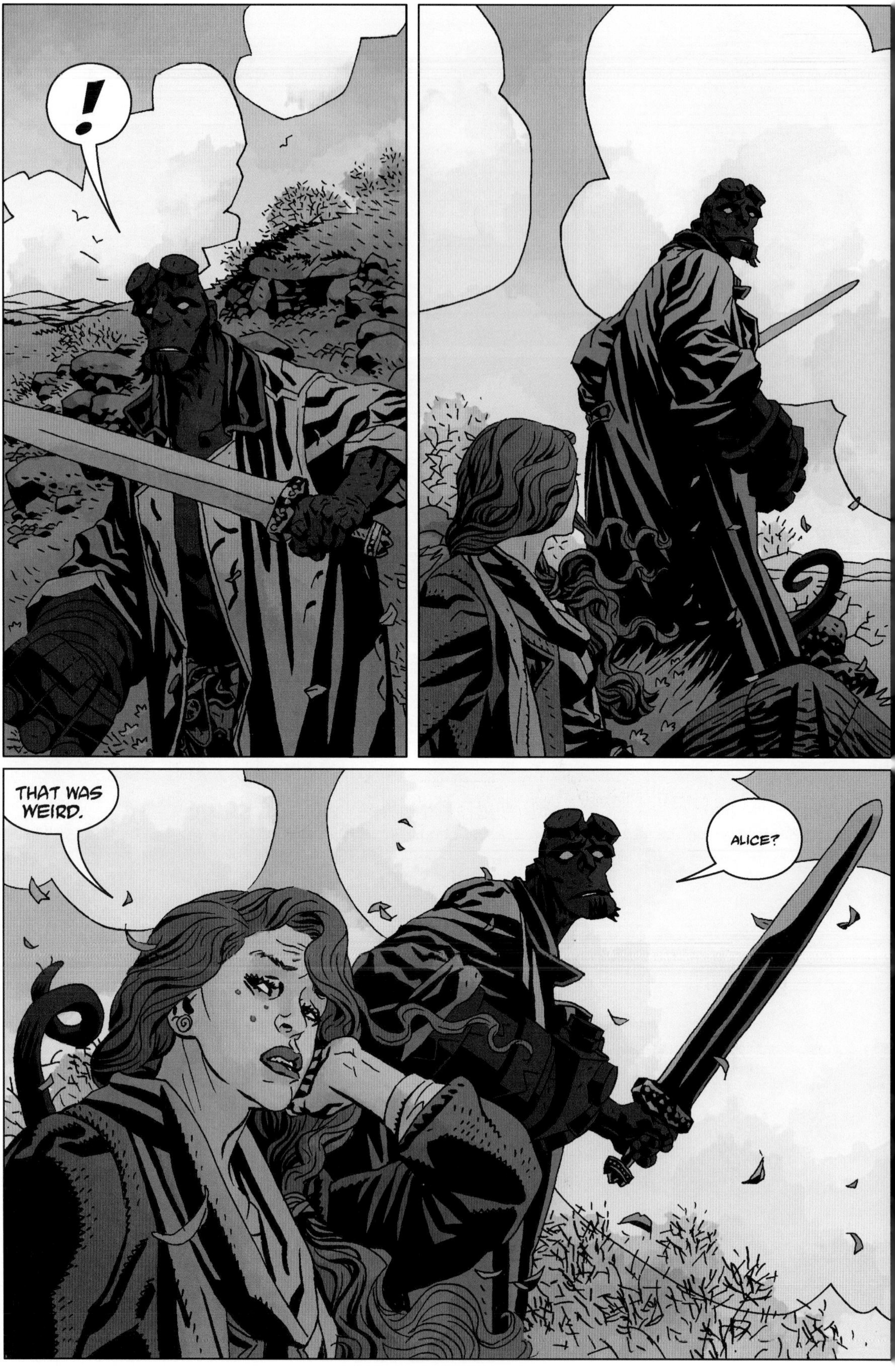
!
THAT WAS WEIRD.
ALICE?

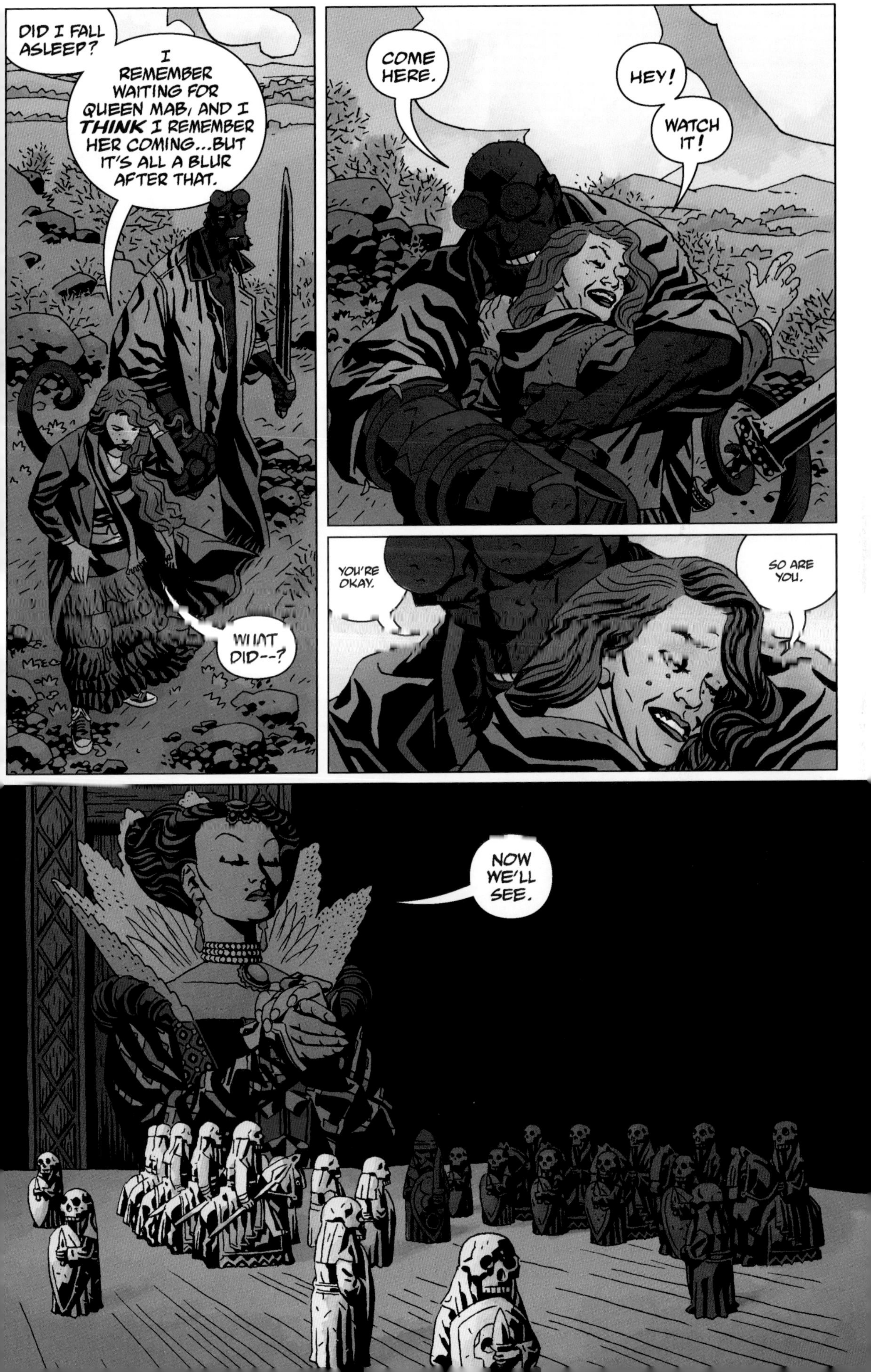
DID I FALL ASLEEP?
I REMEMBER WAITING FOR QUEEN MAB, AND I **THINK** I REMEMBER HER COMING...BUT IT'S ALL A BLUR AFTER THAT.
WHAT DID--?
COME HERE.
HEY!
WATCH IT!
YOU'RE OKAY.
SO ARE YOU.
NOW WE'LL SEE.

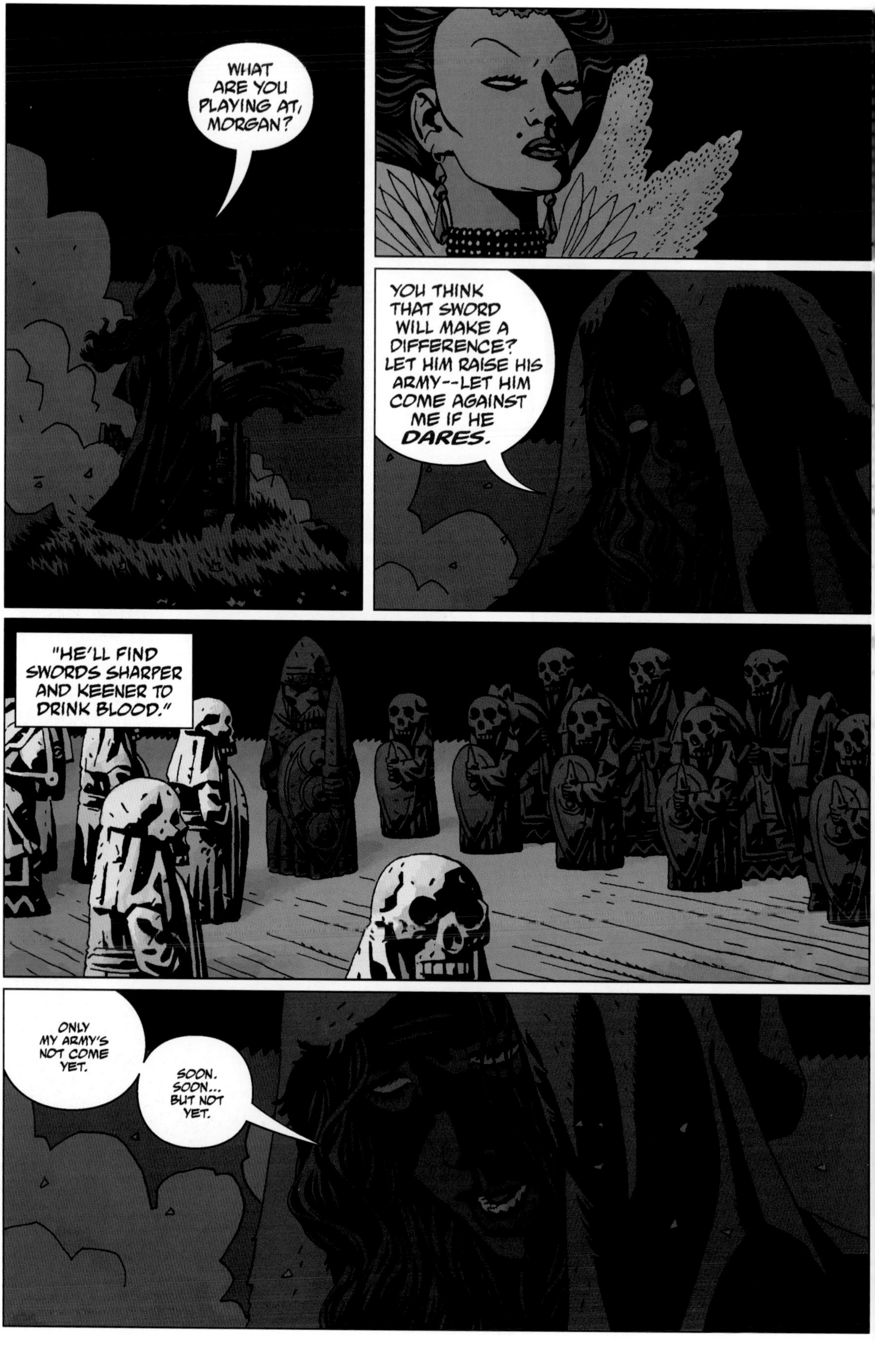
WHAT ARE YOU PLAYING AT, MORGAN?
YOU THINK THAT SWORD WILL MAKE A DIFFERENCE? LET HIM RAISE HIS ARMY--LET HIM COME AGAINST ME IF HE DARES.
"HE'LL FIND SWORDS SHARPER AND KEENER TO DRINK BLOOD."
ONLY MY ARMY'S NOT COME YET.
SOON. SOON... BUT NOT YET.

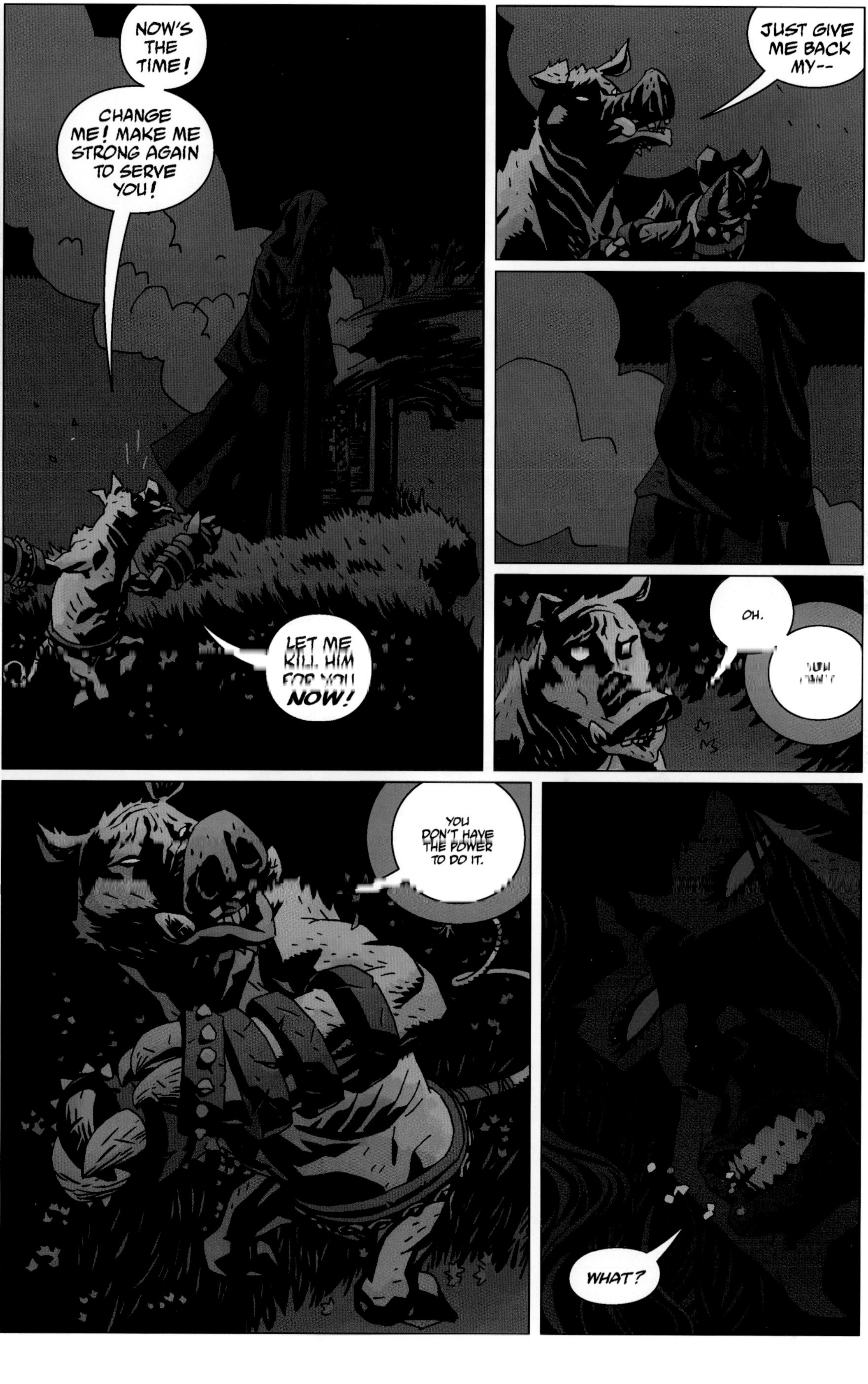
NOW'S THE TIME!
CHANGE ME! MAKE ME STRONG AGAIN TO SERVE YOU!
LET ME KILL HIM FOR YOU NOW!
JUST GIVE ME BACK MY--
OH.
YOU DON'T HAVE THE POWER TO DO IT.
WHAT?

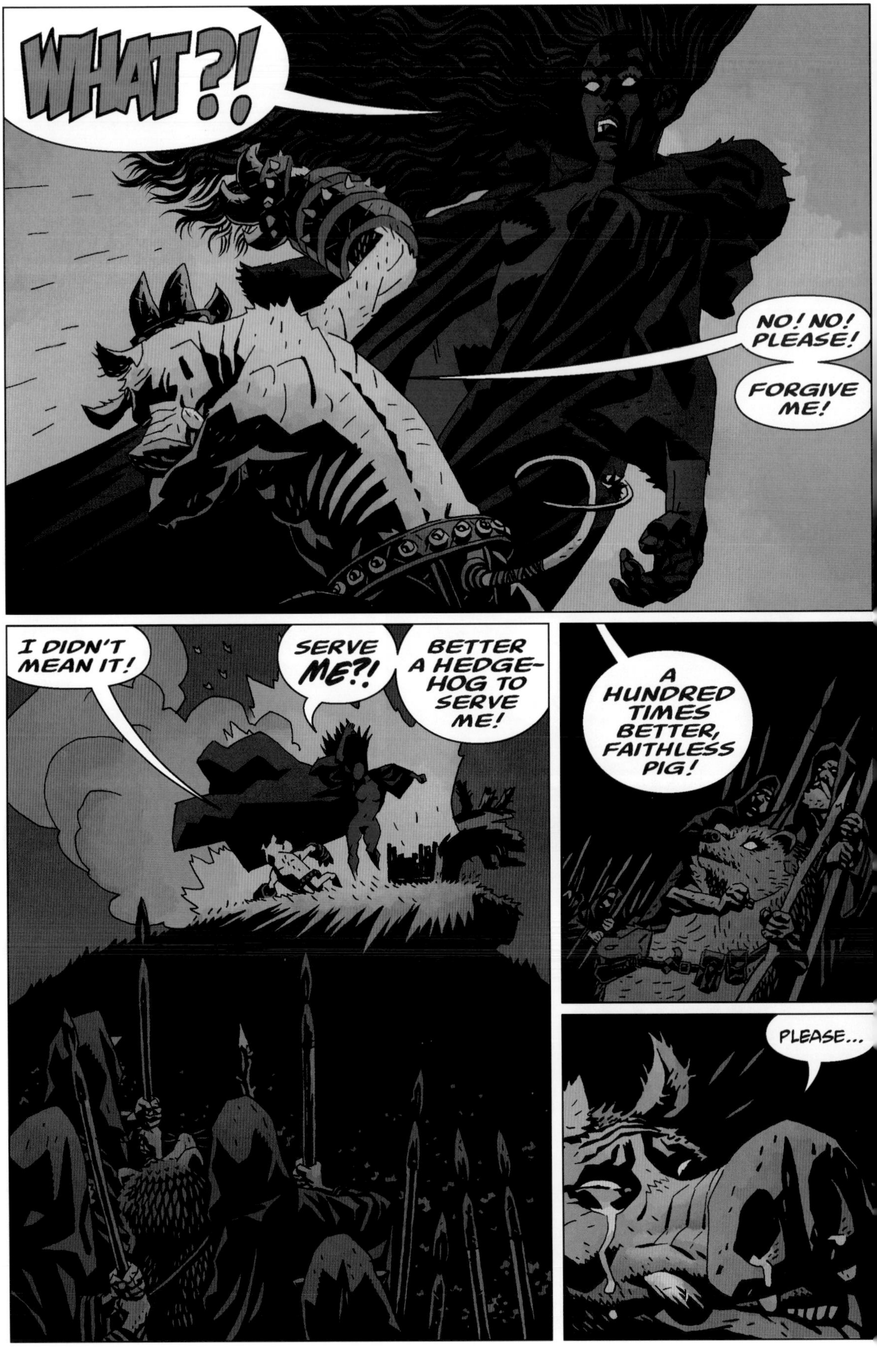
WHAT?!
NO! NO! PLEASE!
FORGIVE ME!
I DIDN'T MEAN IT!
SERVE ME?!
BETTER A HEDGE-HOG TO SERVE ME!
A HUNDRED TIMES BETTER, FAITHLESS PIG!
PLEASE...

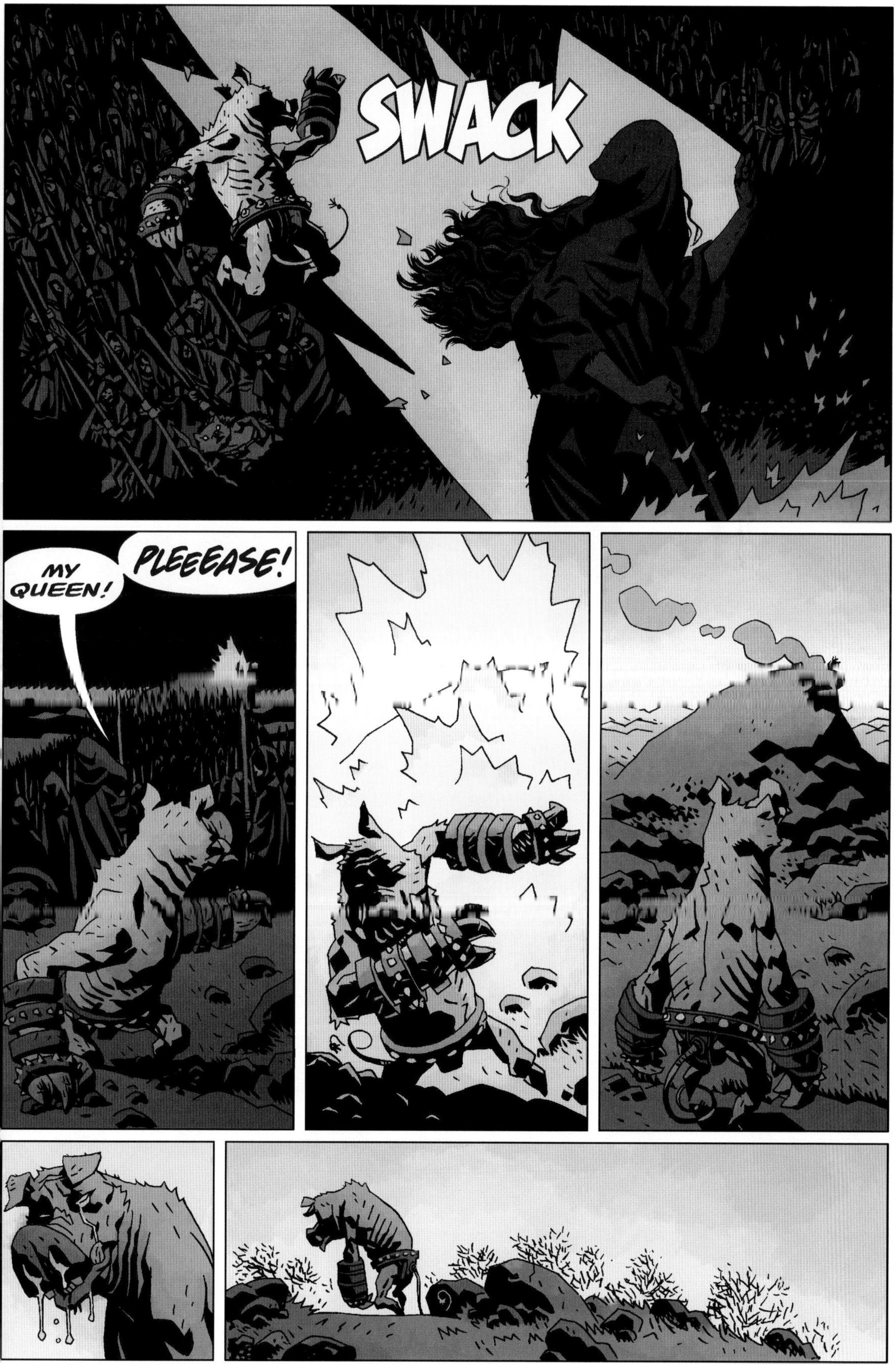
SWACK
MY QUEEN!
PLEEEASE!

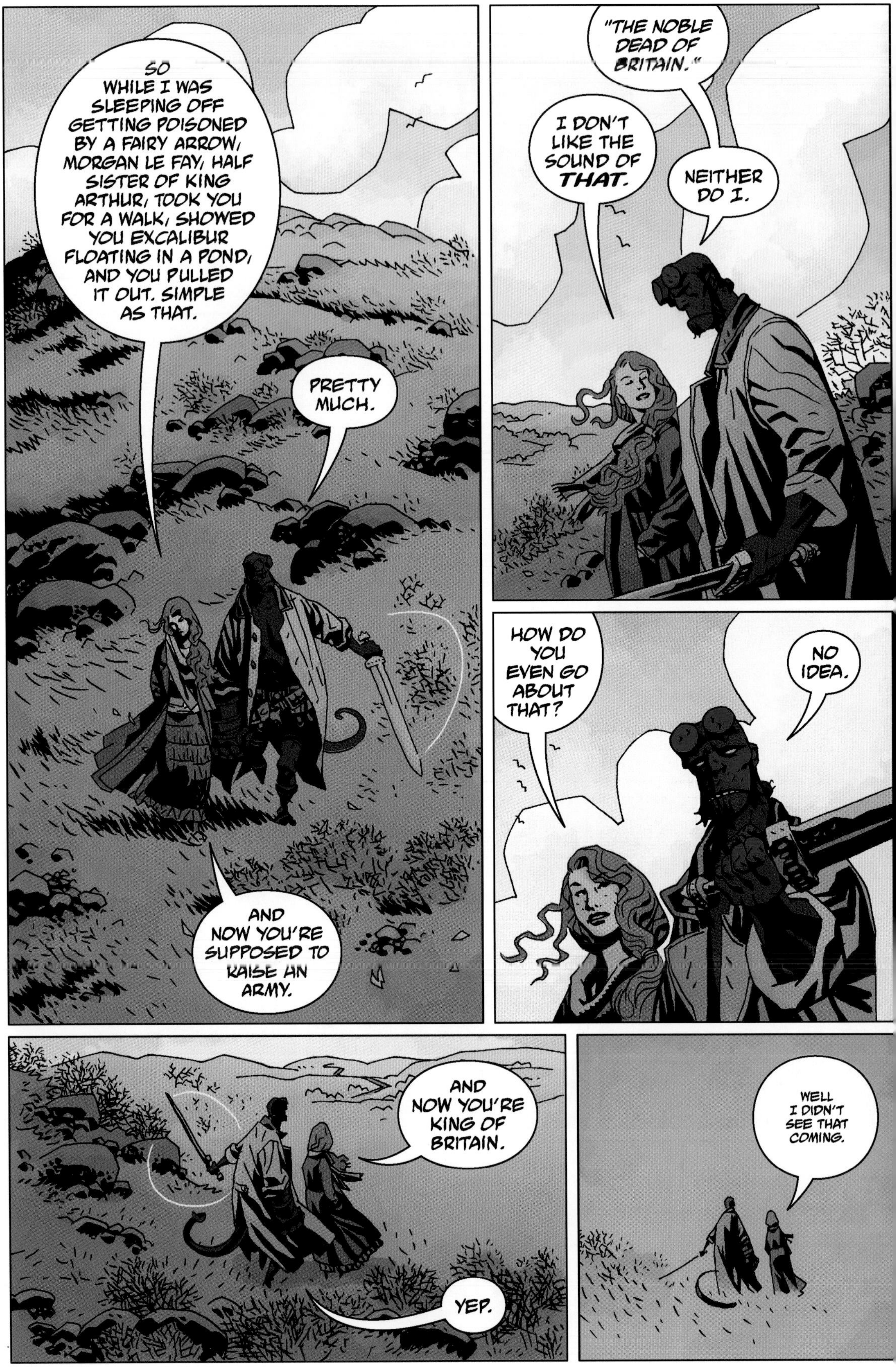
SO WHILE I WAS SLEEPING OFF GETTING POISONED BY A FAIRY ARROW, MORGAN LE FAY, HALF SISTER OF KING ARTHUR, TOOK YOU FOR A WALK, SHOWED YOU EXCALIBUR FLOATING IN A POND, AND YOU PULLED IT OUT. SIMPLE AS THAT.
PRETTY MUCH.
AND NOW YOU'RE SUPPOSED TO RAISE AN ARMY.
"THE NOBLE DEAD OF BRITAIN."
I DON'T LIKE THE SOUND OF THAT.
NEITHER DO I.
HOW DO YOU EVEN GO ABOUT THAT?
NO IDEA.
AND NOW YOU'RE KING OF BRITAIN.
YEP.
WELL I DIDN'T SEE THAT COMING.

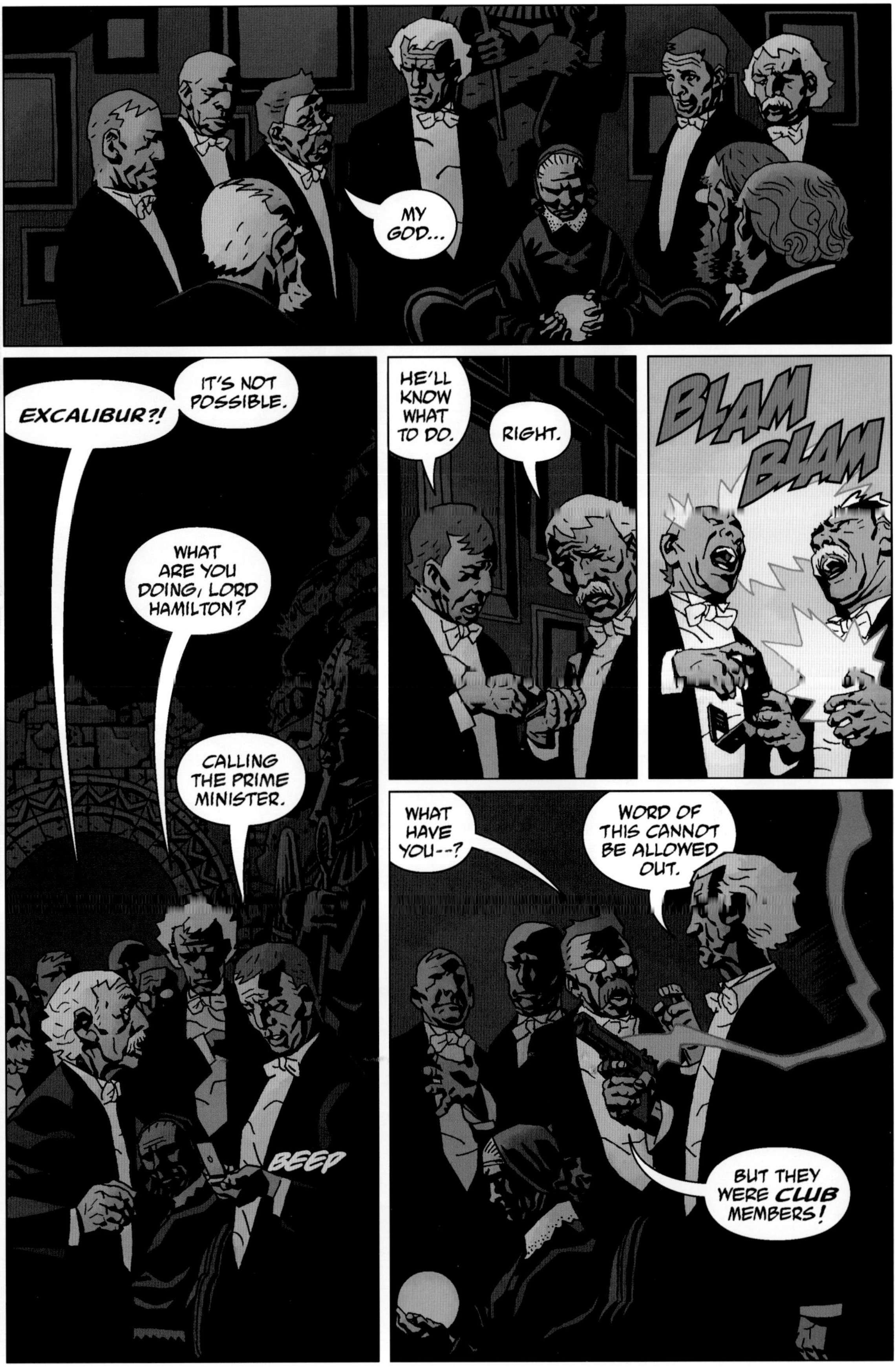
MY GOD...
EXCALIBUR?!
IT'S NOT POSSIBLE.
WHAT ARE YOU DOING, LORD HAMILTON?
CALLING THE PRIME MINISTER.
BEEP
HE'LL KNOW WHAT TO DO.
RIGHT.
BLAM
BLAM
WHAT HAVE YOU--?
WORD OF THIS CANNOT BE ALLOWED OUT.
BUT THEY WERE CLUB MEMBERS!

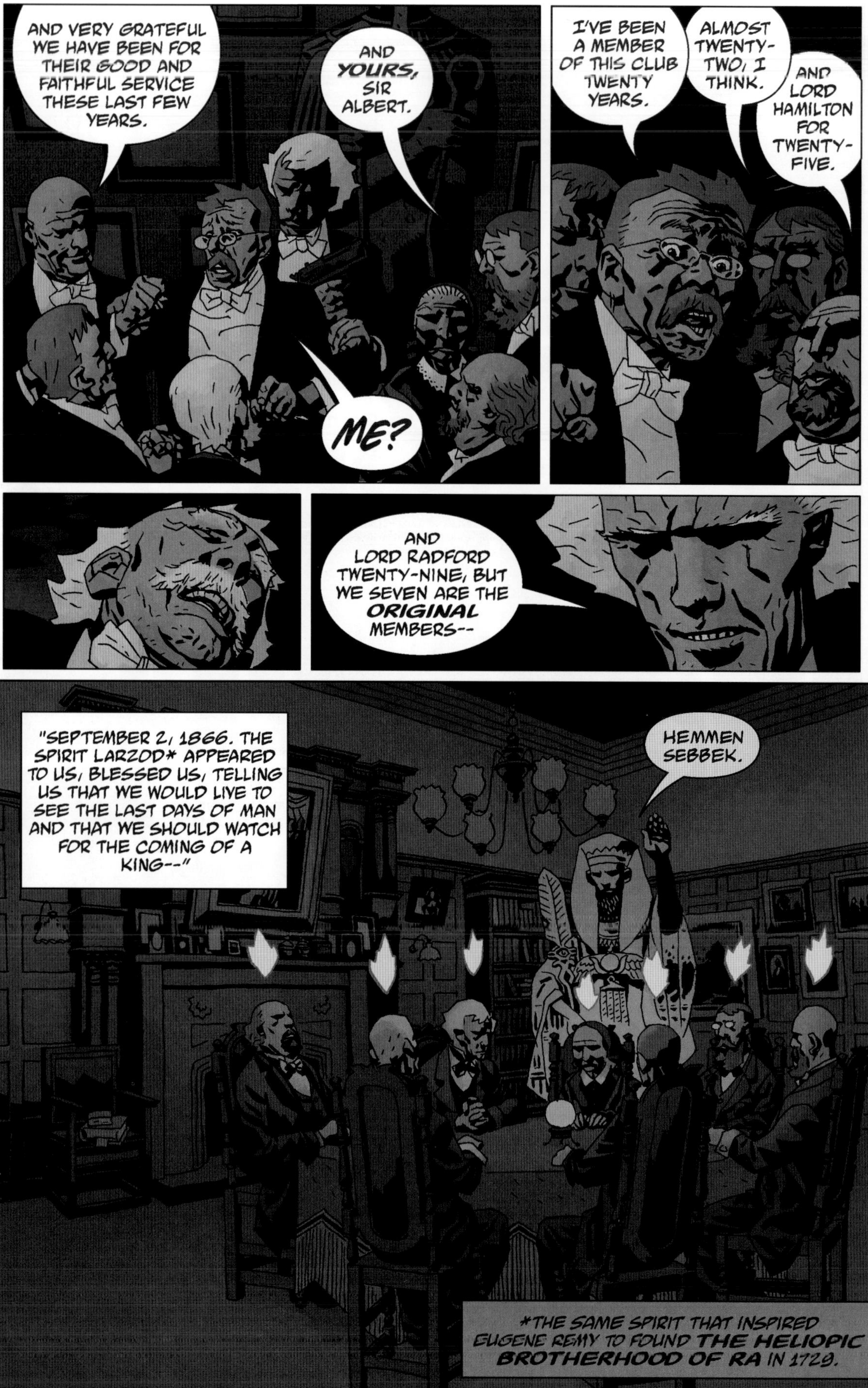
AND VERY GRATEFUL WE HAVE BEEN FOR THEIR GOOD AND FAITHFUL SERVICE THESE LAST FEW YEARS.
AND YOURS, SIR ALBERT.
ME?
I'VE BEEN A MEMBER OF THIS CLUB TWENTY YEARS.
ALMOST TWENTY-TWO, I THINK.
AND LORD HAMILTON FOR TWENTY-FIVE.
AND LORD RADFORD TWENTY-NINE, BUT WE SEVEN ARE THE ORIGINAL MEMBERS--
"SEPTEMBER 2, 1866. THE SPIRIT LARZOD* APPEARED TO US, BLESSED US, TELLING US THAT WE WOULD LIVE TO SEE THE LAST DAYS OF MAN AND THAT WE SHOULD WATCH FOR THE COMING OF A KING--"
HEMMEN SEBBEK.
*THE SAME SPIRIT THAT INSPIRED EUGENE REMY TO FOUND THE HELIOPIC BROTHERHOOD OF RA IN 1729.

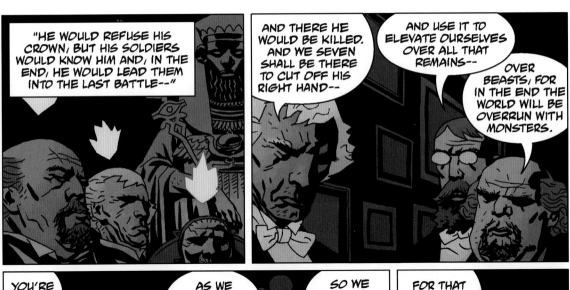

"HE WOULD REFUSE HIS CROWN, BUT HIS SOLDIERS WOULD KNOW HIM AND, IN THE END, HE WOULD LEAD THEM INTO THE LAST BATTLE--"

AND THERE HE WOULD BE KILLED. AND WE SEVEN SHALL BE THERE TO CUT OFF HIS RIGHT HAND--

AND USE IT TO ELEVATE OURSELVES OVER ALL THAT REMAINS--

OVER BEASTS, FOR IN THE END THE WORLD WILL BE OVERRUN WITH MONSTERS.

YOU'RE ALL MAD!

AS WE WERE SEVEN IN THE BEGINNING--

SO WE SHOULD BE SEVEN IN THE END--

FOR THAT BATTLE AND THAT KING ARE UPON US.

BLAM

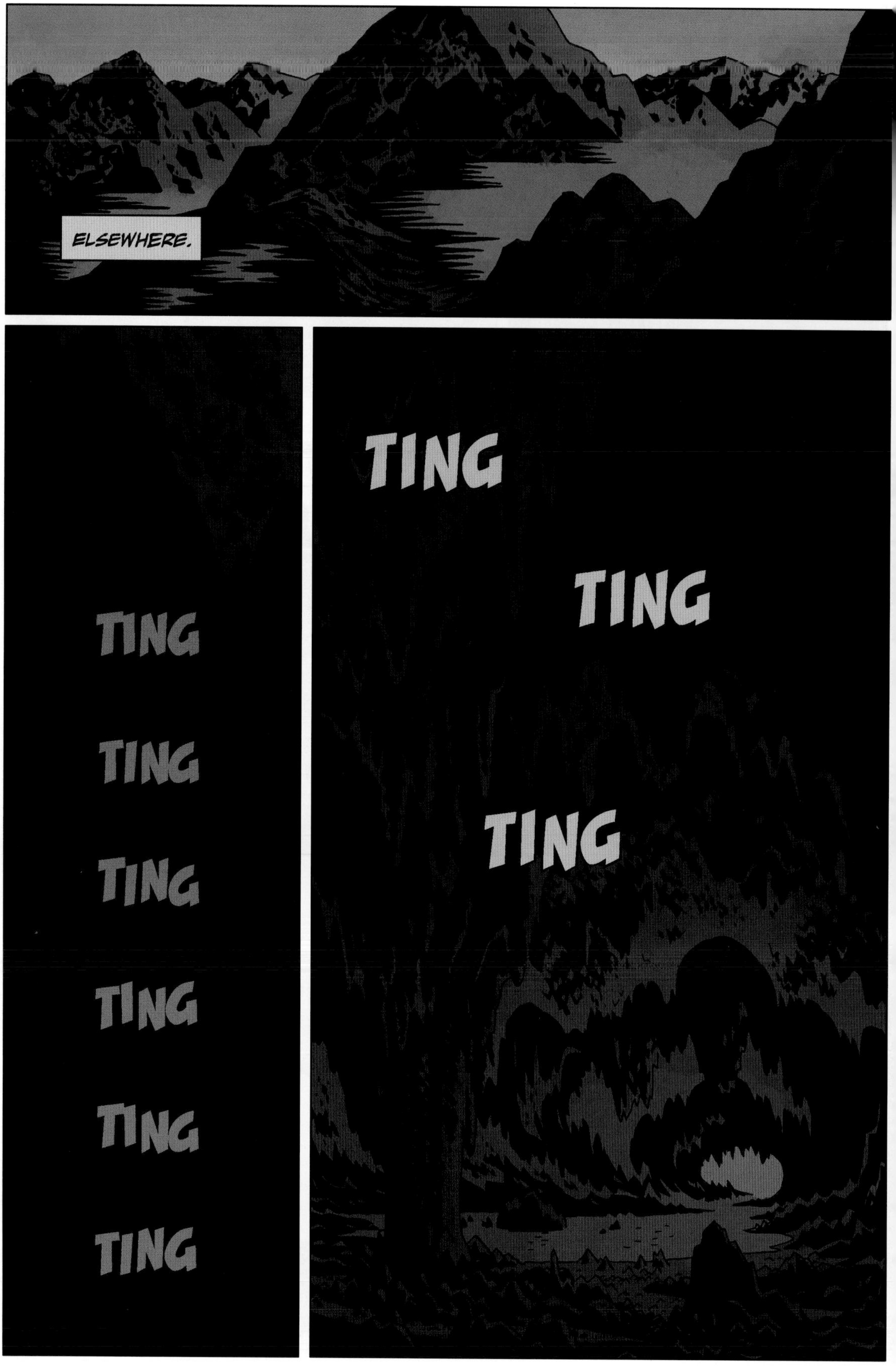
ELSEWHERE.
TING
TING
TING
TING
TING
TING
TING
TING
TING

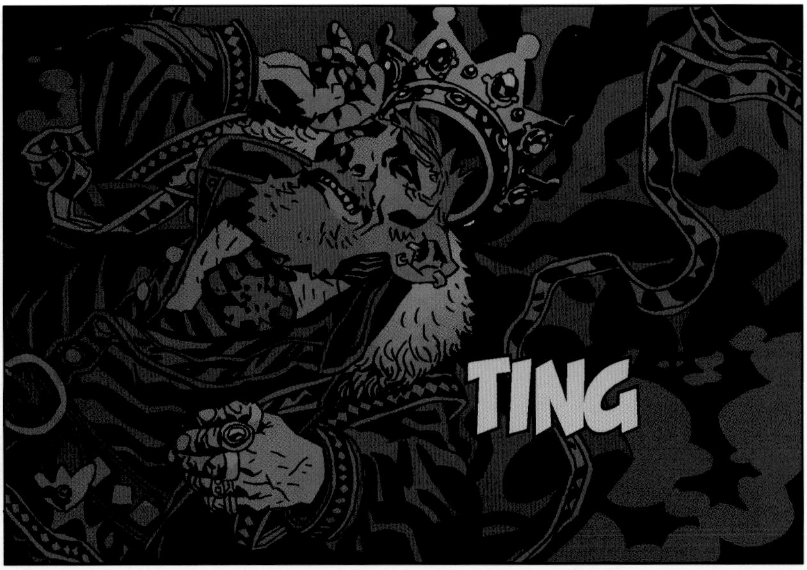
TING

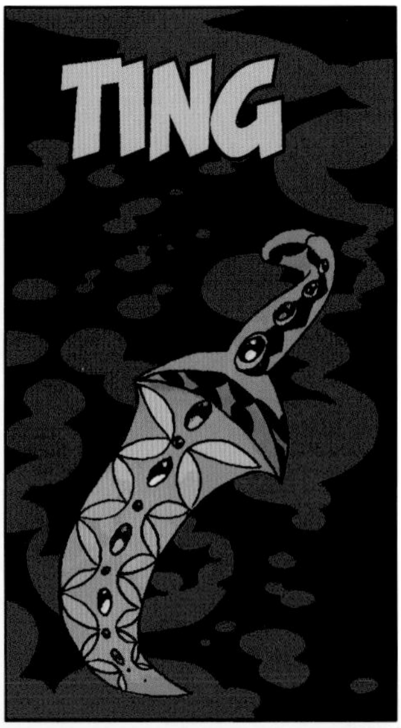
TING

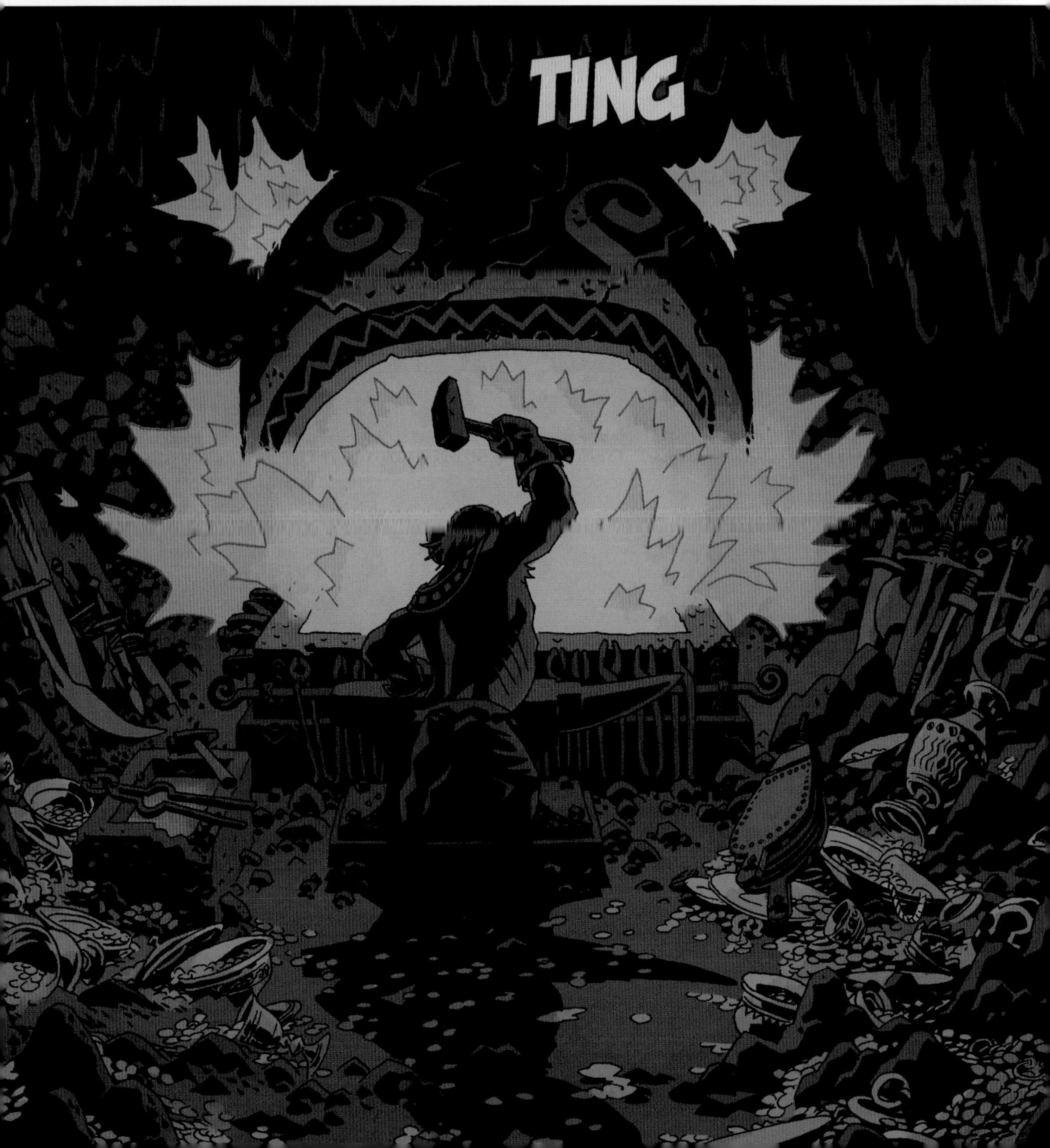
TING

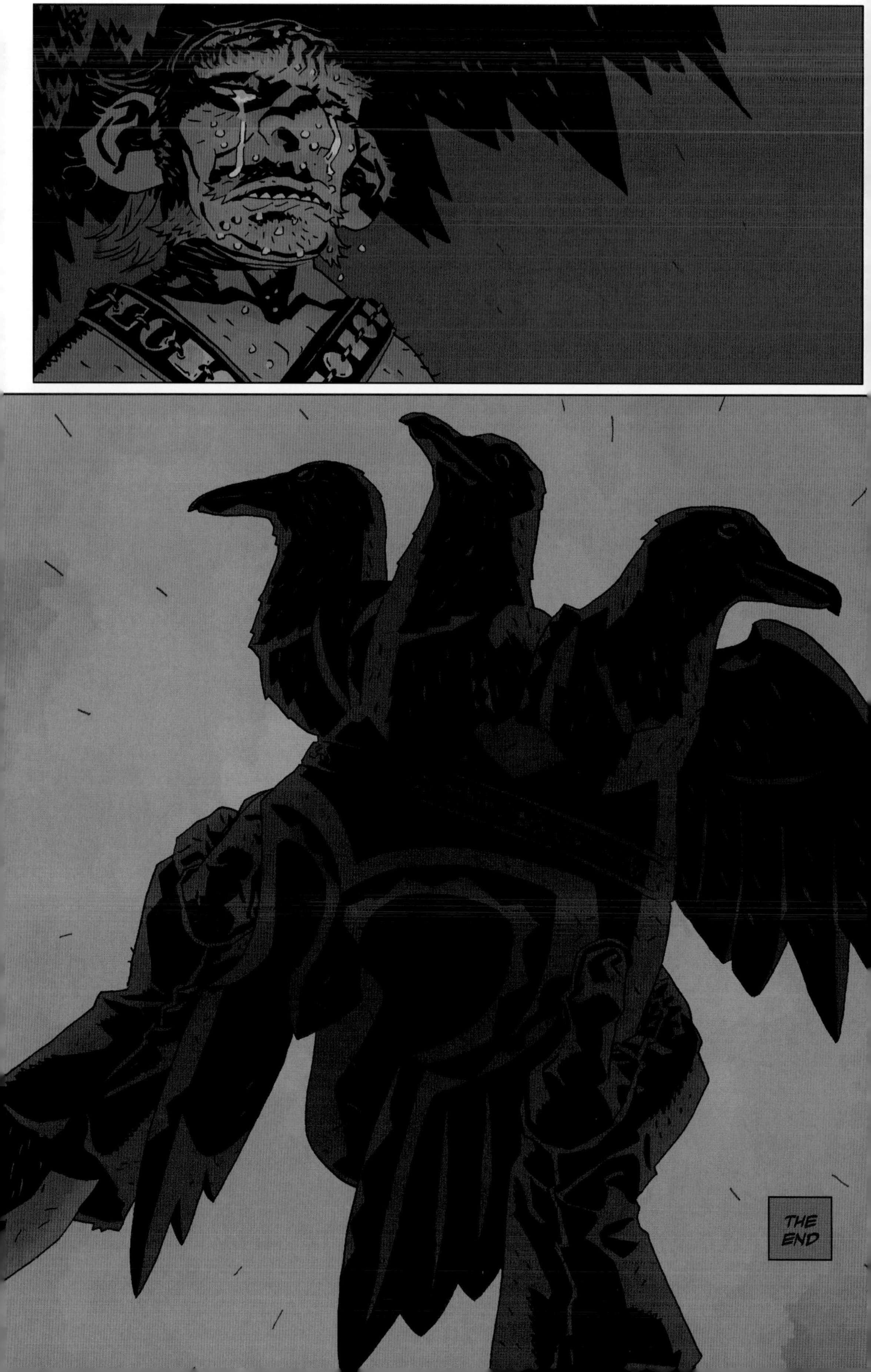
THE END

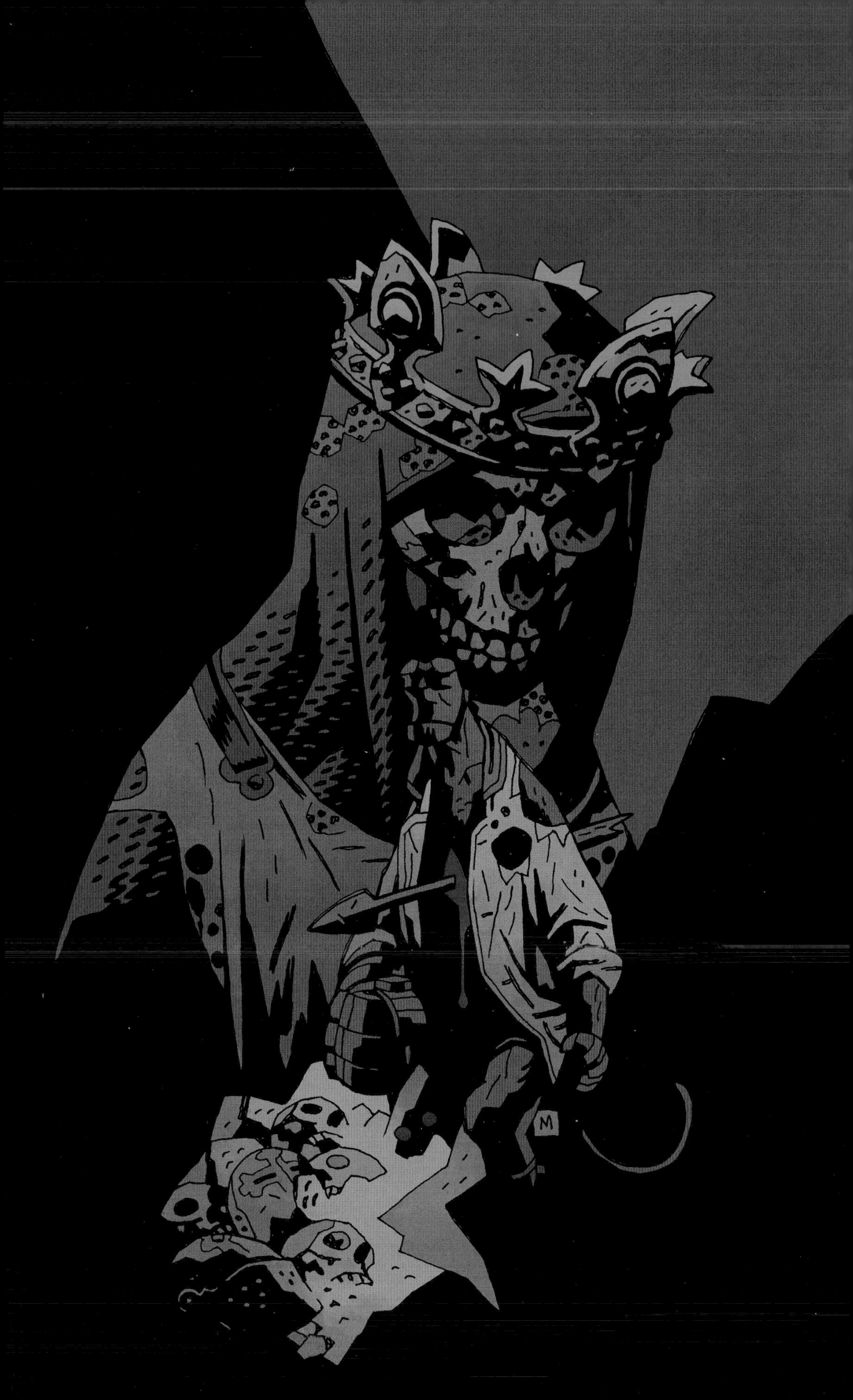

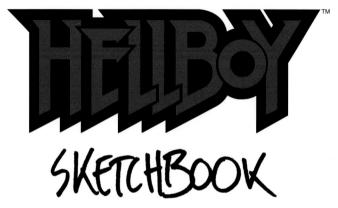

SKETCHBOOK

With notes from the artists

Duncan Fegredo: I recall asking Mike what to do with Hellboy's tail whilst on horseback. I have a tendency to want to work out How to Make Things Work . . . Mike's answer to this and many other conundrums? "Don't draw it, lose it in shadow!" Now why didn't I think of that? This sketch was drawn a little way into *The Wild Hunt*. I'd gotten used to drawing horses by this stage and remembered a friend's request for a cowboy Hellboy. This is about as close as I got. Yee-haw, or something like that.

Facing: Unused cover art for The Wild Hunt #2.

DF: As always on viewing a self-rejected Mignola cover (and there are many), my initial reaction is, "Wow, gorgeous!" immediately followed up with, "*Why?*"

Mike Mignola: I felt this cover lacked focus—I wanted to draw a stronger connection between Hellboy and the crown on the skeletal King Arthur.

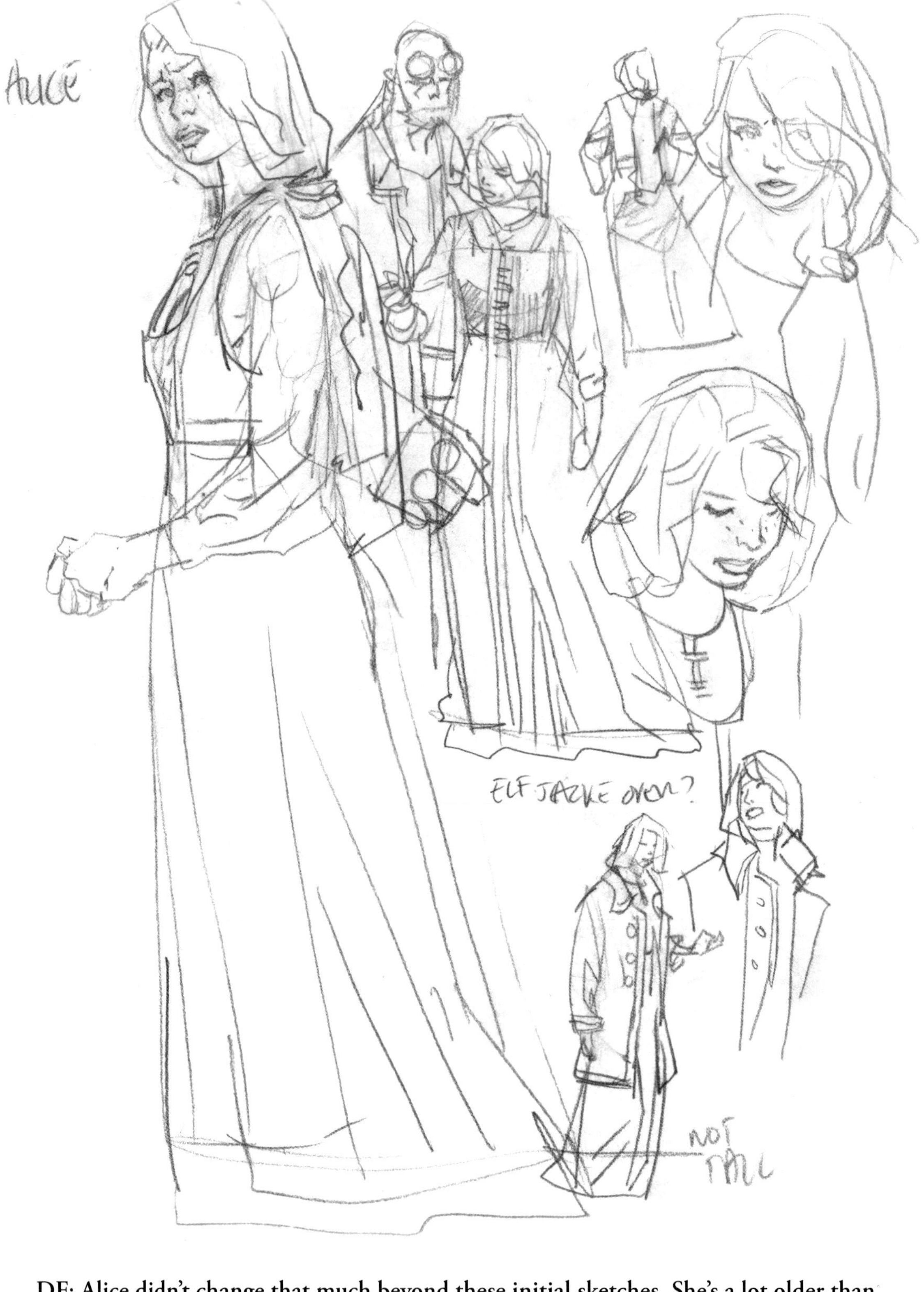
ALICE
ELF JACKE OVER?
NOT TALL

DF: Alice didn't change that much beyond these initial sketches. She's a lot older than she appears, so I wanted a timeless quality to the way she dressed, with just a hint of the modern world.

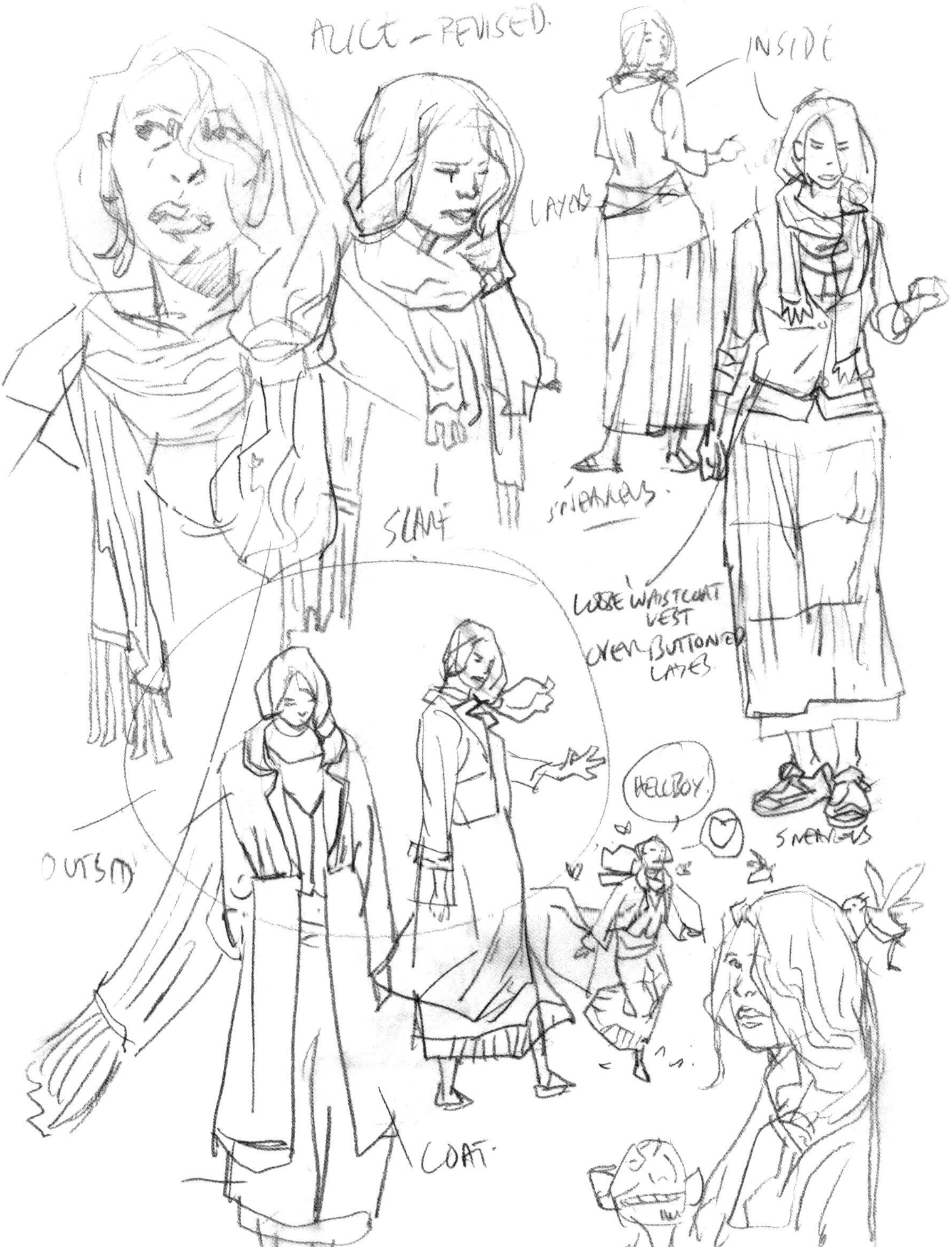
ALICE - REVISED.
INSIDE
LAYERS
SCARF
SNEAKERS.
LOOSE WAISTCOAT
VEST
OVER BUTTONED
LAYERS
HELLBOY!
SNEAKERS
COAT.

Scenes between Hellboy and Alice were initially a challenge, but so rewarding. The gentle play of body language between the two allowed for subtle shifts in mood—light to dark and back again.

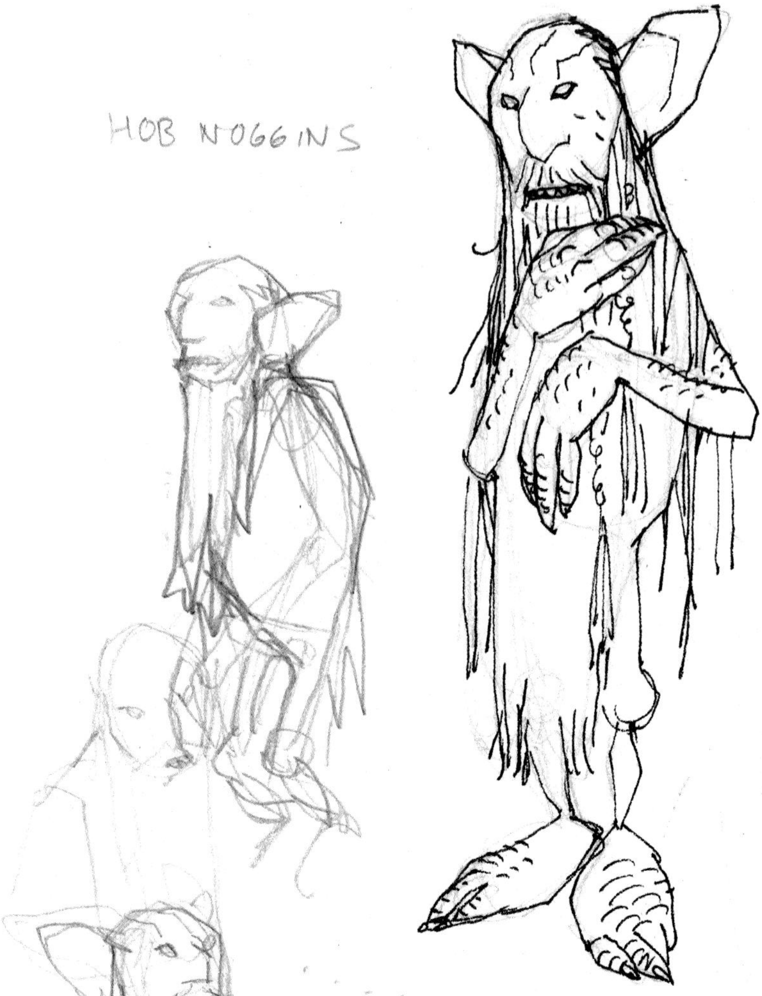
HOB NOGGINS

MM: I did these sketches years ago and now can't remember why. I was going to use this guy for something, but whatever it was never happened. I always liked him, though, and I'm glad he finally found a home—even though (for him) it turned out to be sort of a sad and tragic home. Oh well.

DF: I loved this little guy's big-mouthed grin and tried to keep him as close to Mike's designs as possible. Such fun to draw, as you could be so theatrical with his body language, that combination of comic tragedy. Plus, I liked drawing him scampering around Hellboy's ankles.

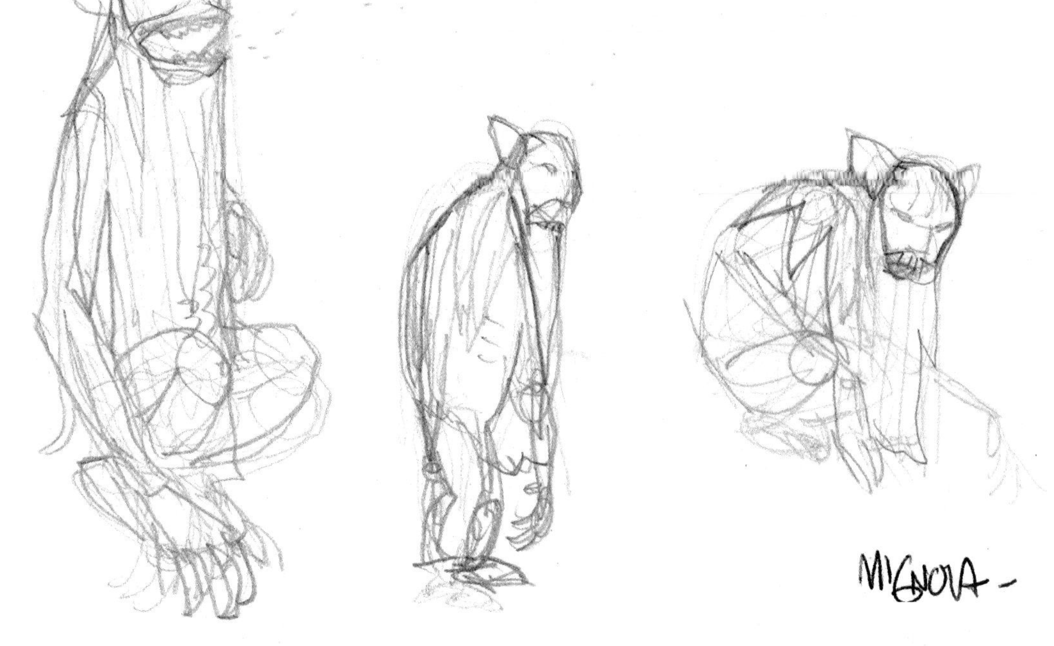
MIGNOLA

MM: These guys were just too much fun. I wanted to put them on the cover to issue #4, which meant I had to draw them long before Duncan was working on those story pages, so I went ahead and designed them. If I'd had to draw several pages of them swarming all over Hellboy, they might have gotten to be a lot less fun.

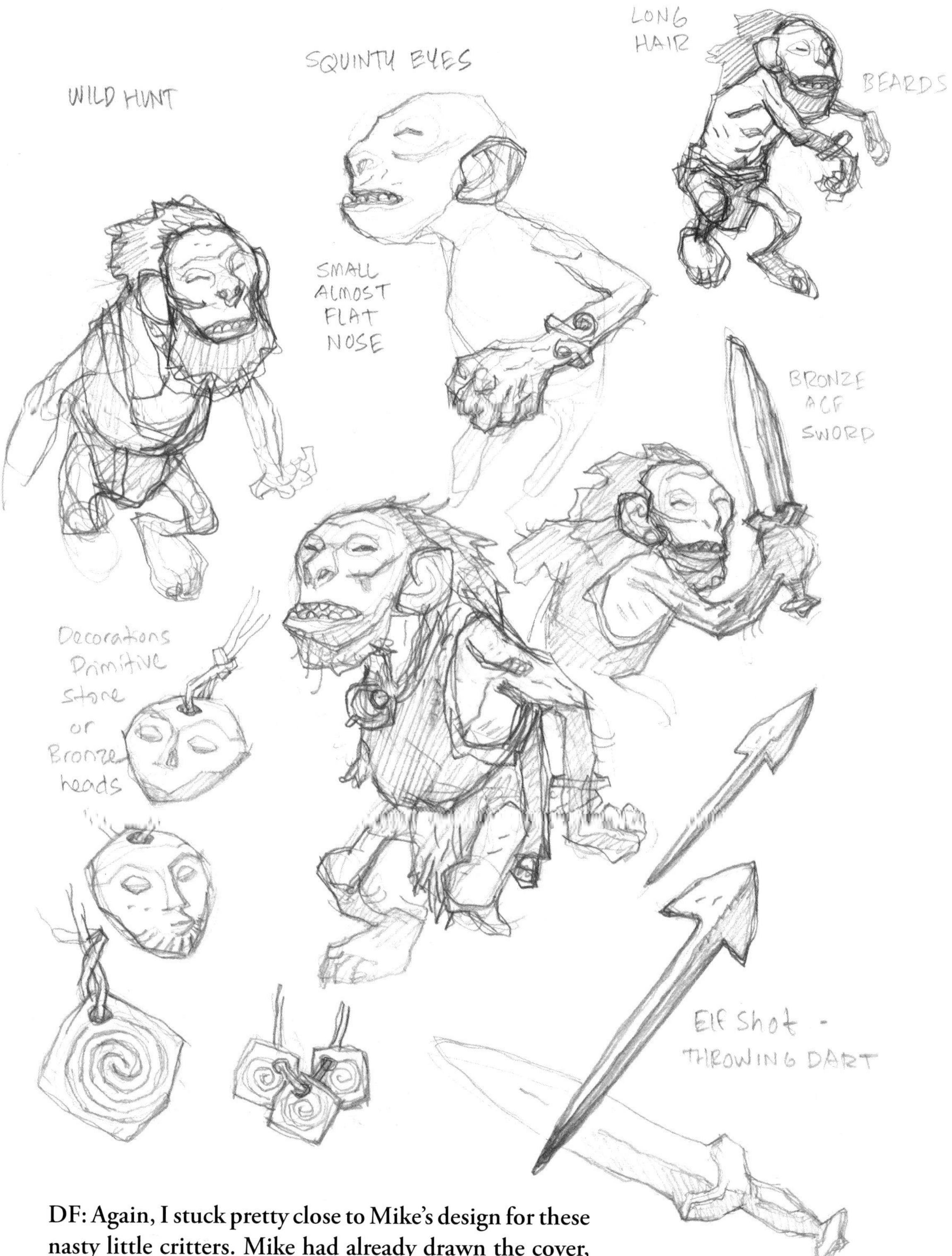

LONG HAIR
SQUINTY EYES
BEARDS
WILD HUNT
SMALL ALMOST FLAT NOSE
BRONZE AGE SWORD
Decorations Primitive stone or Bronze heads
Elf Shot - THROWING DART

DF: Again, I stuck pretty close to Mike's design for these nasty little critters. Mike had already drawn the cover, so I felt I should up the ante, and had them absolutely cover Hellboy and Alice. Time consuming, but fun.

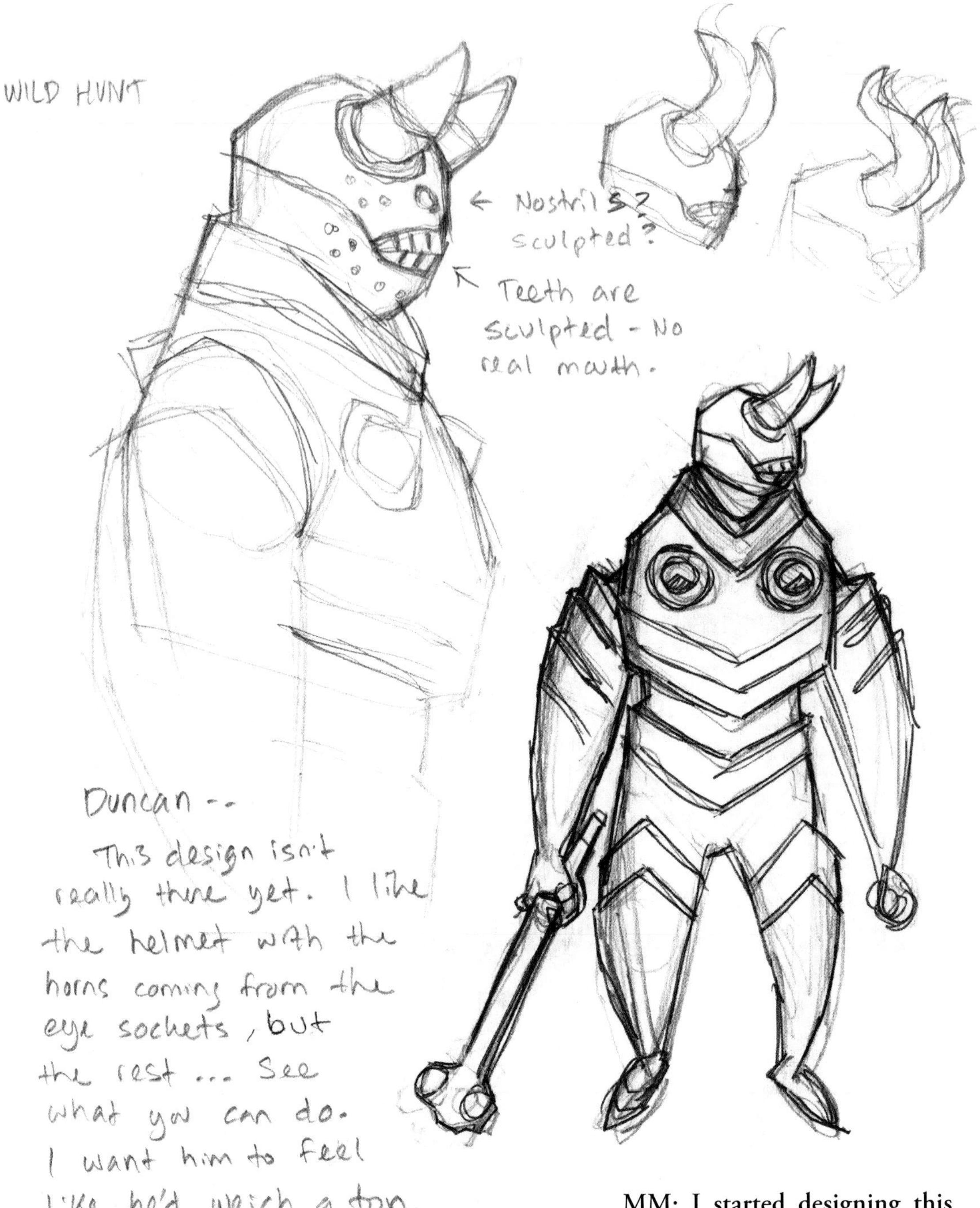
WILD HUNT
← Nostrils? sculpted?
Teeth are sculpted - No real mouth.
Duncan --
This design isn't really there yet. I like the helmet with the horns coming from the eye sockets, but the rest ... See what you can do.
I want him to feel like he'd weigh a ton.
And I don't want suit of armor joints -- It's not a suit really -- More like a sculpted (forged) iron skin.

MM: I started designing this guy long before I knew what I was going to do with him. I liked his head and the general shape of his body, but never quite knew how to finish him. I was happy to turn these sketches over to Duncan and let him turn them into something.

DF: Love the horns for eyes.

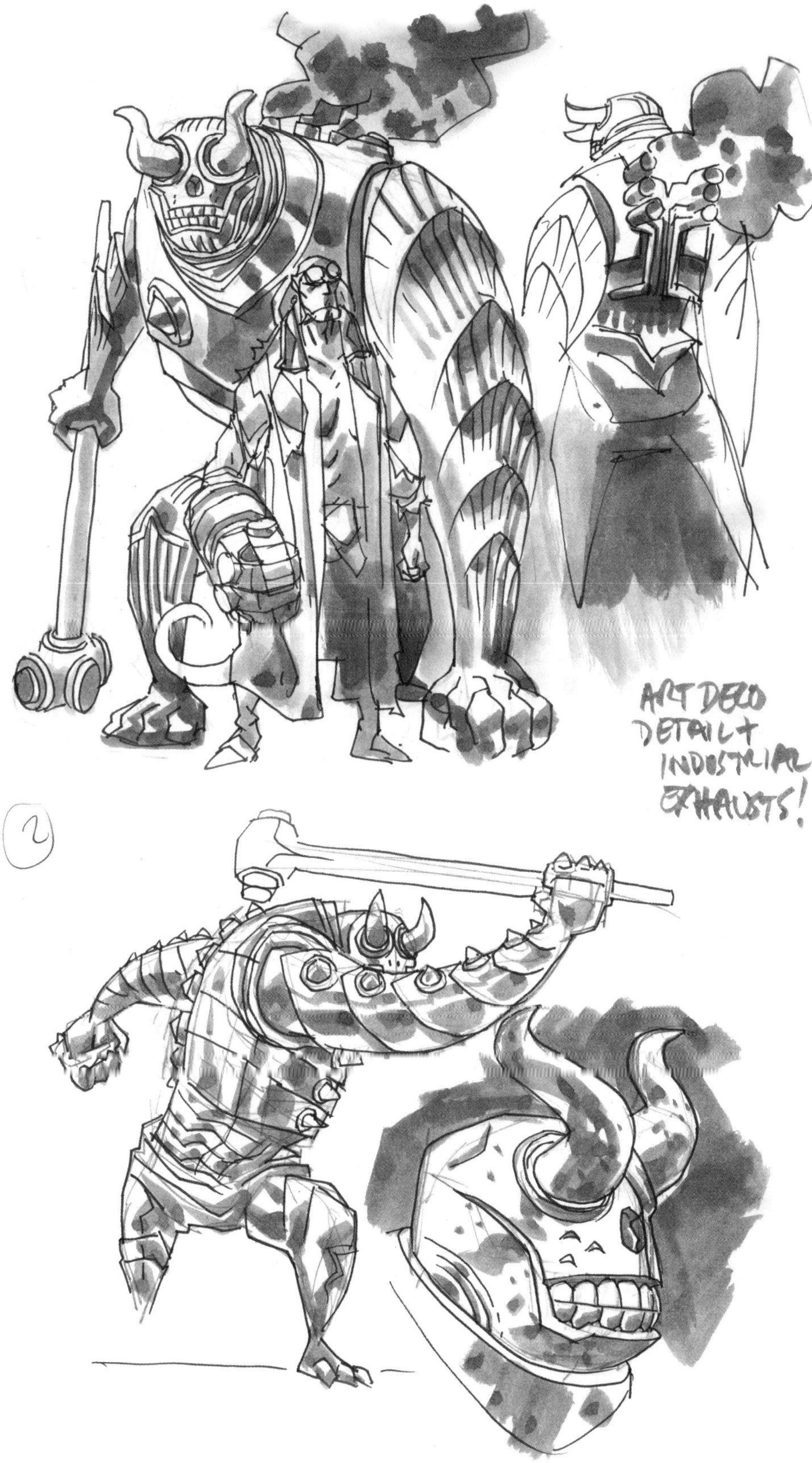
ART DECO
DETAIL +
INDUSTRIAL
EXHAUSTS!
2

DF: I think the design worked here at least; not so much in my final execution. I'm not sure where the exhausts on his back came from. I suspect it was that art-deco surface detail I was playing with; it reminded me a little of a 1950s locomotive or something. Whatever; they stuck, and he became a literal engine of war.

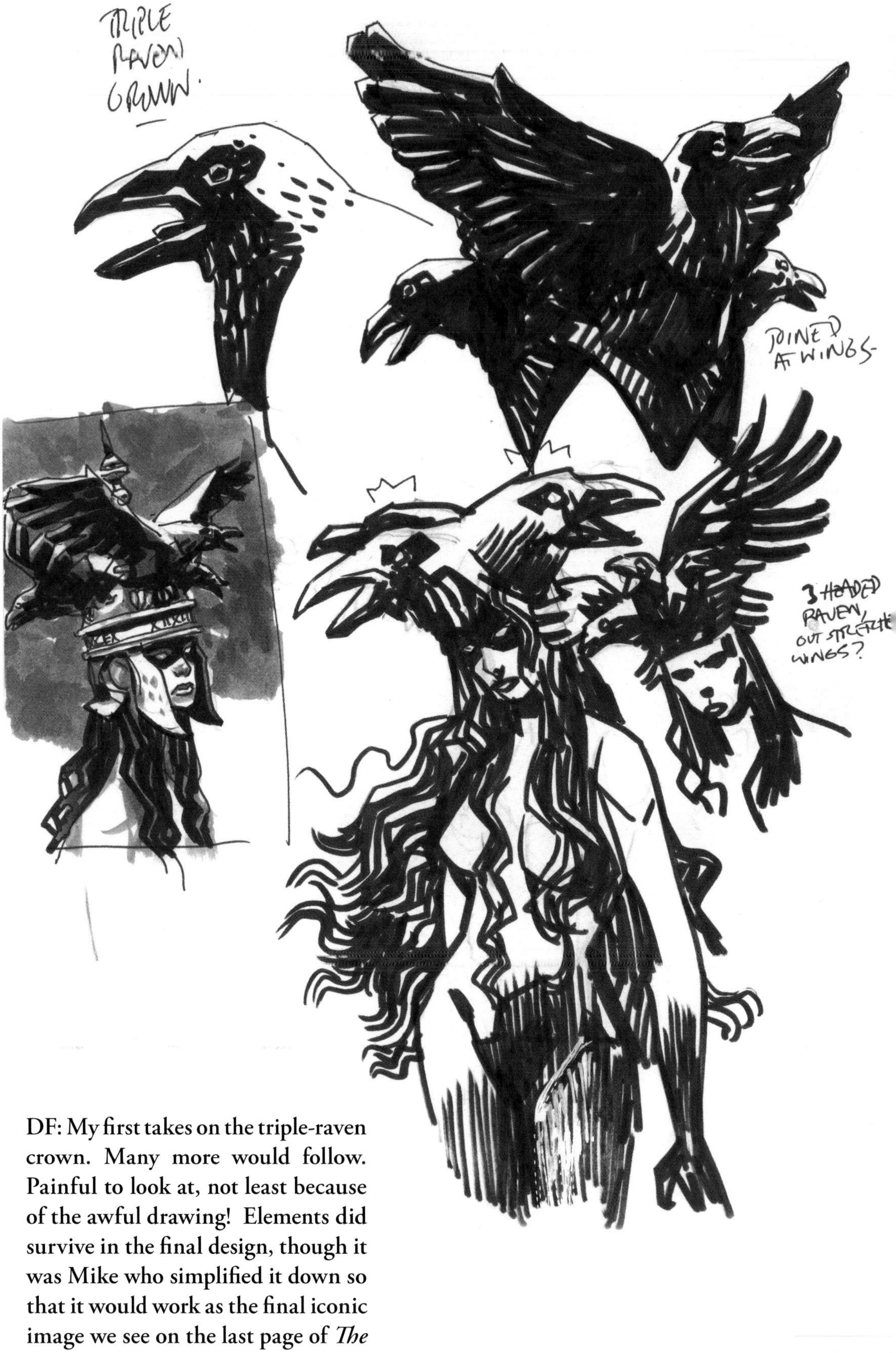

TRIPLE RAVEN CROWN.
JOINED AT WINGS-
3 HEADED RAVEN, OUT STRETCHE WINGS?

DF: My first takes on the triple-raven crown. Many more would follow. Painful to look at, not least because of the awful drawing! Elements did survive in the final design, though it was Mike who simplified it down so that it would work as the final iconic image we see on the last page of *The Wild Hunt*.

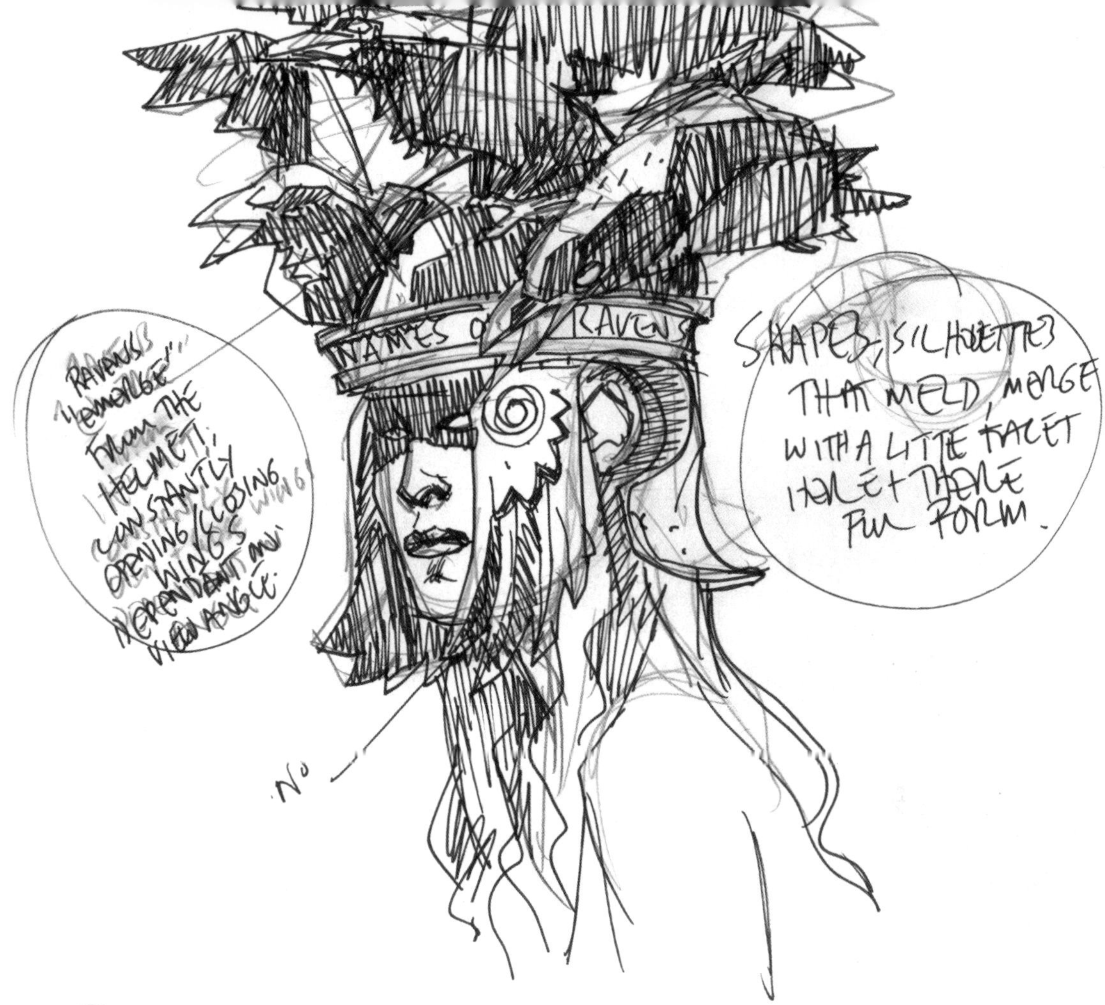
NAMES OF RAVENS
SHAPES, SILHOUETTES THAT MELD, MERGE WITH A LITTLE FACET HERE + THERE
NO

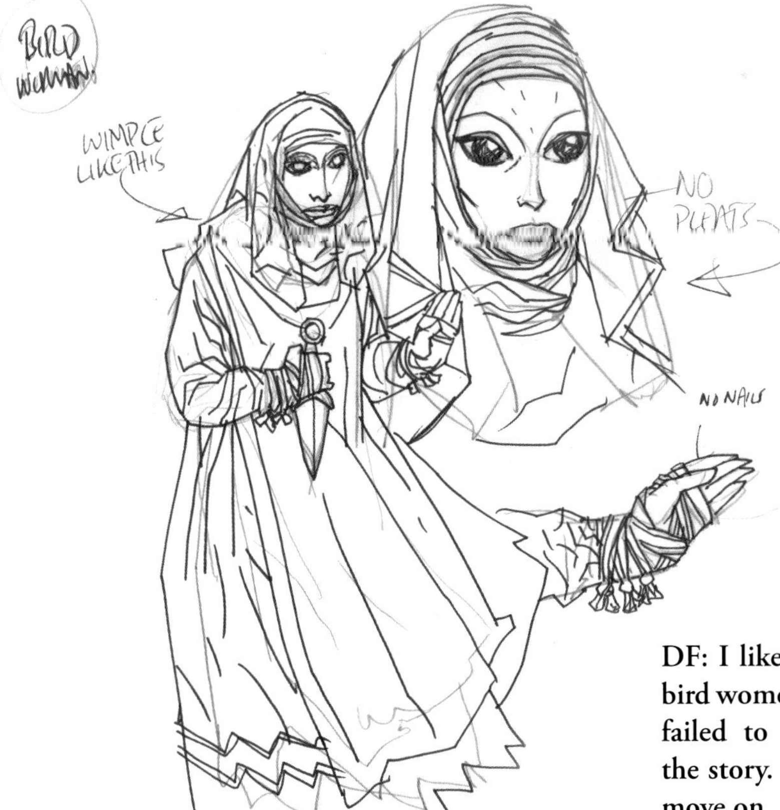
BIRD WOMAN
WIMPLE LIKE THIS
NO PLEATS
NO NAILS

DF: I like these sketches of the bird women but feel I absolutely failed to make them work in the story. Sorry about that; let's move on.

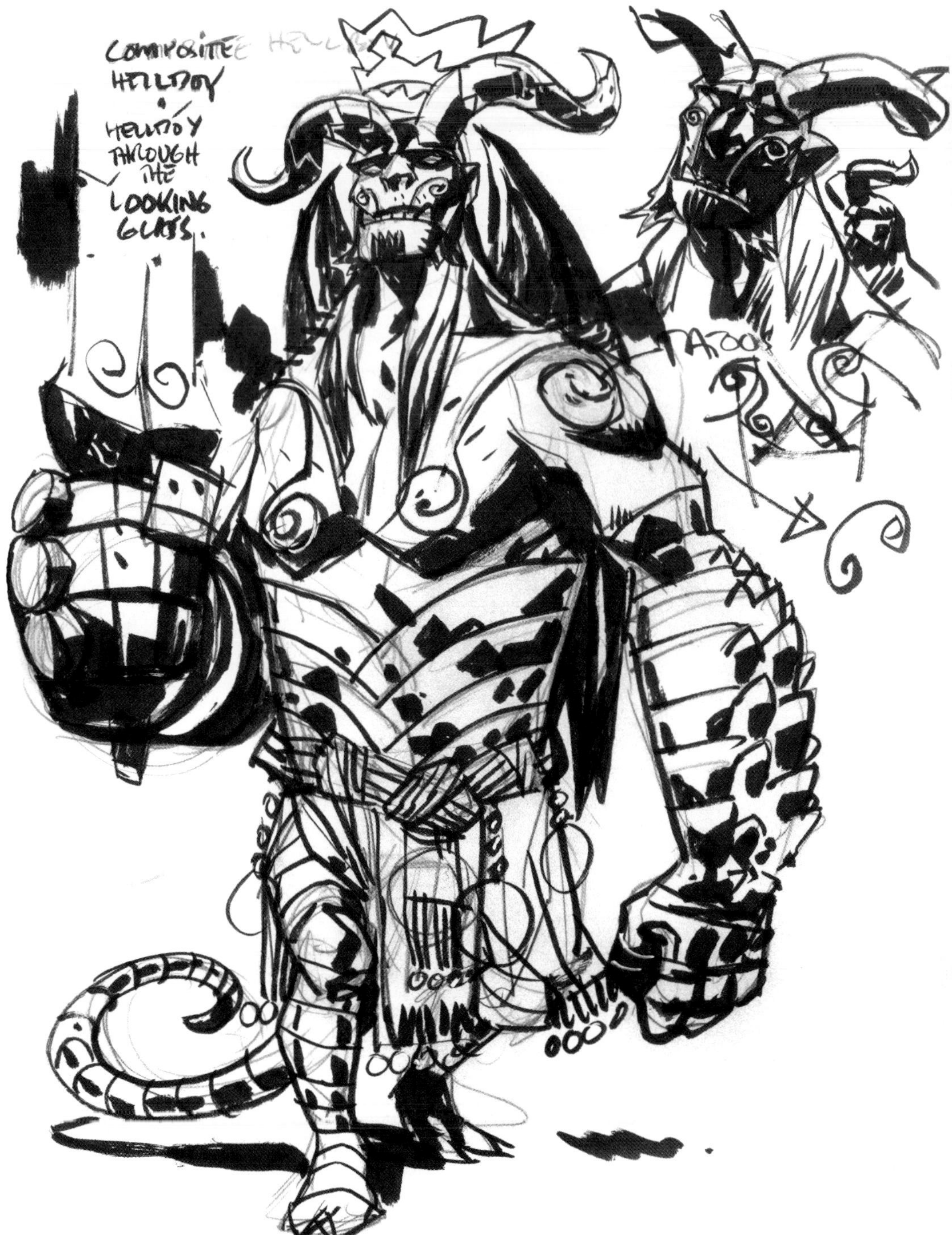
COMPOSITE HELLBOY
HELLBOY THROUGH THE LOOKING GLASS.

DF: Hellboy through the looking glass, indeed! Note the wonky horns, so they would fit on the sketchbook page . . . which might also explain those dinky legs—very dainty!

Facing: Unused cover art for The Wild Hunt *#7.*

DF: "Wow, gorgeous . . . *Why?*"

MM: Both Scott Allie (my editor) and I felt this was just too quiet for the cover of that issue.

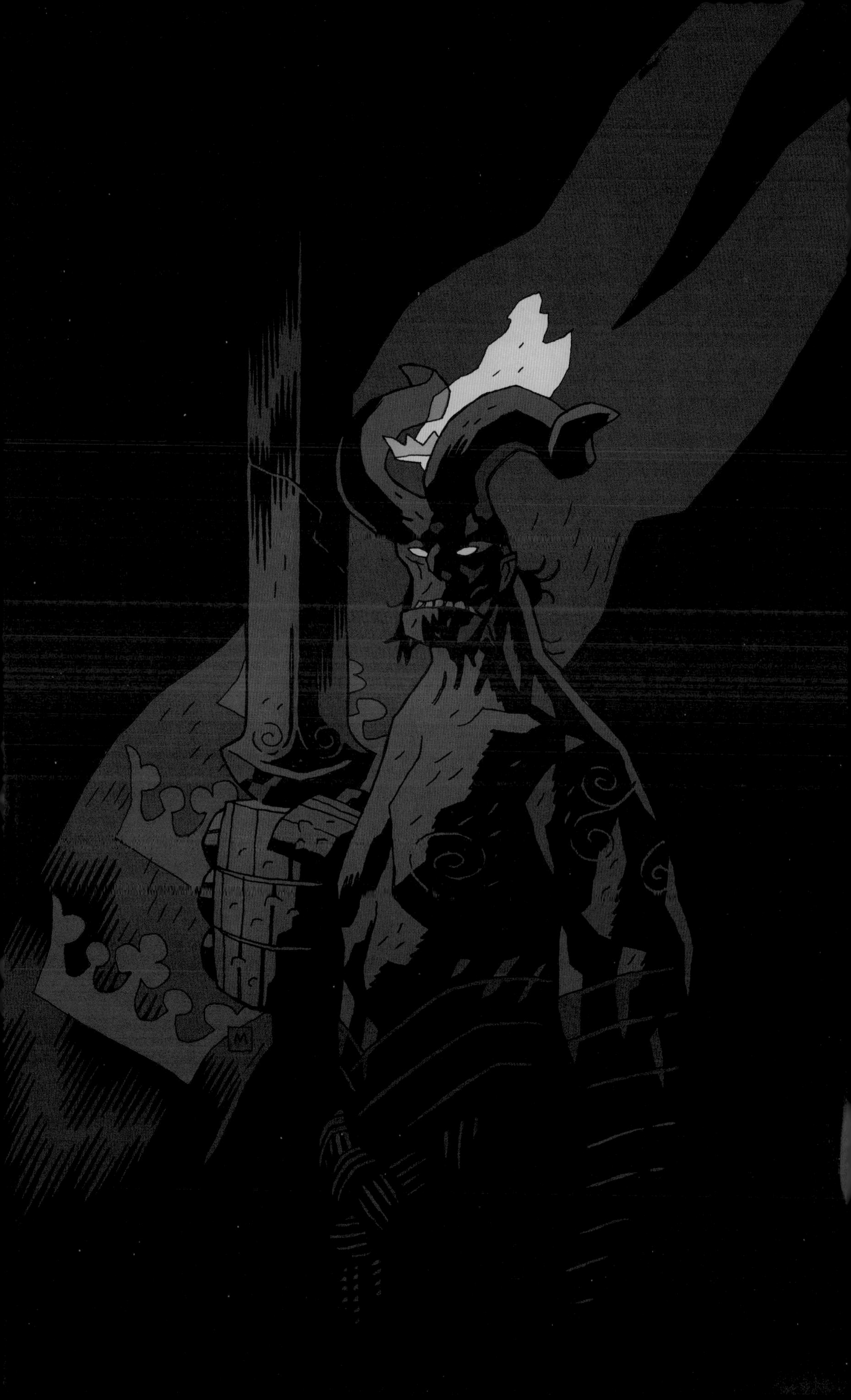

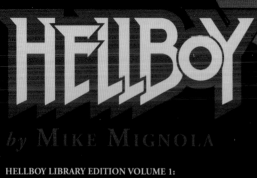

HELLBOY™

by MIKE MIGNOLA

HELLBOY LIBRARY EDITION VOLUME 1:
*SEED OF DESTRUCTION
AND WAKE THE DEVIL*
ISBN 978-1-59307-910-9 | $49.99

HELLBOY LIBRARY EDITION VOLUME 2:
*THE CHAINED COFFIN
AND THE RIGHT HAND OF DOOM*
ISBN 978-1-59307-989-5 | $49.99

HELLBOY LIBRARY EDITION VOLUME 3:
CONQUEROR WORM AND STRANGE PLACES
ISBN 978-1-59582-352-6 | $49.99

✠

SEED OF DESTRUCTION
With John Byrne
ISBN 978-1-59307-094-6 | $17.99

WAKE THE DEVIL
ISBN 978-1-59307-095-3 | $17.99

THE CHAINED COFFIN AND OTHERS
ISBN 978-1-59307-091-5 | $17.99

THE RIGHT HAND OF DOOM
ISBN 978-1-59307-093-9 | $17.99

CONQUEROR WORM
ISBN 978-1-59307-092-2 | $17.99

THE TROLL WITCH AND OTHERS
ISBN 978-1-59307-860-7 | $17.99

DARKNESS CALLS
ISBN 978-1-59307-896-6 | $19.99

THE WILD HUNT
ISBN 978-1-59582-352-6 | $19.99

THE CROOKED MAN AND OTHERS
ISBN 978-1-59582-477-6 | $17.99

THE ART OF HELLBOY
ISBN 978-1-59307-089-2 | $29.99

HELLBOY II: THE ART OF THE MOVIE
ISBN 978-1-59307-964-2 | $24.99

HELLBOY: THE COMPANION
ISBN 978-1-59307-655-9 | $14.99

To find a comics shop in your area,
call 1-888-266-4226
For more information or to order direct:
• On the web: darkhorse.com
• E-mail: mailorder@darkhorse.com
• Phone: 1-800-862-0052
Mon.–Fri. 9 AM to 5 PM Pacific Time

HELLBOY WEIRD TALES
Volume 1
ISBN 978-1-56971-622-9 | $17.99
Volume 2
ISBN 978-1-56971-953-4 | $17.99

✠

ODD JOBS
ISBN 978-1-56971-440-9 | $14.99

ODDER JOBS
ISBN 978-1-59307-226-1 | $14.99

ODDEST JOBS
ISBN 978-1-59307-944-4 | $14.99

✠

B.P.R.D.: HOLLOW EARTH
By Mignola, Chris Golden,
Ryan Sook, and others
ISBN 978-1-56971-862-9 | $17.99

B.P.R.D.: THE SOUL OF VENICE
By Mignola, Mike Oeming, Guy Davis,
Scott Kolins, Geoff Johns, and others
ISBN 978-1-59307-132-5 | $17.99

B.P.R.D.: PLAGUE OF FROGS
By Mignola and Guy Davis
ISBN 978-1-59307-288-9 | $17.99

B.P.R.D.: THE DEAD
By Mignola, Arcudi, and Guy Davis
ISBN 978-1-59307-380-0 | $17.99

B.P.R.D: THE BLACK FLAME
By Mignola, Arcudi, and Davis
ISBN 978-1-59307-550-7 | $17.99

B.P.R.D: THE UNIVERSAL MACHINE
By Mignola, Arcudi, and Davis
ISBN 978-1-59307-710-5 | $17.99

B.P.R.D: THE GARDEN OF SOULS
By Mignola, Arcudi, and Davis
ISBN 978-1-59307-882-9 | $17.99

B.P.R.D.: KILLING GROUND
By Mignola, Arcudi, and Davis
ISBN 978-1-59307-956-7 | $17.99

B.P.R.D: 1946
By Mignola, Dysart, and Azaceta
ISBN 978-1-59582-191-1 | $17.99

B.P.R.D.: THE WARNING
By Mignola, Arcudi, and Davis
ISBN 978-1-59582-304-5 | $17.99

B.P.R.D.: THE BLACK GODDESS
By Mignola, Arcudi, and Davis
ISBN 978-1-59582-411-0 | $17.99

B.P.R.D: 1947
By Mignola, Dysart, Fábio Moon, and Gabriel Bá
ISBN 978-1-59582-478-3 | $17.99

B.P.R.D.: WAR ON FROGS
By Mignola, Arcudi, and Karl Moline
ISBN 978-1-59582-480-6 | $17.99

✠

ABE SAPIEN: THE DROWNING
By Mignola, Jason Shawn Alexander,
and Dave Stewart
ISBN 978-1-59582-185-0 | $17.99

LOBSTER JOHNSON:
THE IRON PROMETHEUS
By Mignola, Jason Armstrong, and Dave Stewart
ISBN 978-1-59307-975-8 | $17.99

WITCHFINDER:
IN THE SERVICE OF ANGELS
By Mignola, Ben Stenbeck, and Dave Stewart
ISBN 978-1-59582-483-7 | $17.99

DARK HORSE COMICS®
darkhorse.com
drawing on your nightmares™